The Criminal Justice Student Writer's Manual

William A. Johnson, Jr.
Richard P. Rettig
Greg Scott
Stephen Garrison

Prentice Hall, Upper Saddle River, NJ 07458

Library of Congress Cataloging-in-Publication Data

The criminal justice student writer's manual / William A. Johnson, Jr.
  ... [et al.].
      p.   cm.
   Includes bibliographical references and index.
   ISBN (invalid) 0-13-531278-1
    1. Criminal justice, Administration of--United States--Authorship.
   2. Criminal justice, Administration of--Research--United States.
   3. Legal composition--United States. 4. Report writing--United
States.   I. Johnson, William A., 1942-
   HV9950.C74323   1999   98-40825
   808'.066364--dc21   CIP

Editorial/Production Supervision,
  Interior Design, and Electronic Paging: *Naomi Sysak*
Acquisitions Editor: *Neil Marquardt*
Cover Design: *Bruce Kenselaar*
Manufacturing Buyer: *Ed O'Dougherty*
Managing Editor: *Mary Carnis*
Marketing Manager: *Frank Mortimer, Jr.*
Director of Production: *Bruce Johnson*

10 9 8 7 6 5 4 3

ISBN 0-13-531278-7

Prentice-Hall International (UK) Limited, *London*
Prentice-Hall of Australia Pty. Limited, *Sydney*
Prentice-Hall of Canada, Inc., *Toronto*
Prentice-Hall Hispanoamericana, S. A., *Mexico*
Prentice-Hall of India Private Limited, *New Delhi*
Prentice-Hall of Japan, Inc., *Tokyo*
Pearson Education Asia Pte. Ltd., *Singapore*
Editora Prentice-Hall do Brasil, Ltda., *Rio de Janeiro*

To

Doc James—Thanks for the push!
Marie Rettig-Hood
Heather
Melissa

Contents

To the Student

Successful students, like successful social scientists and criminal justice professionals, are competent writers. As criminal justice students we observe social and legal institutions and study the behavior of people who interact within them. We write to record what we observe, to explain what we record, and to defend what we explain. As citizens we write to take part in making decisions that guide the management of our courts, police, and prisons. From the Bill of Rights to the U.S. Criminal Code, writing has defined the freedom we enjoy today.

The Criminal Justice Student Writer's Manual is designed to help you do two things: (1) improve your writing ability, and (2) begin to perfect the research skills required in the field of criminal justice. These objectives are addressed in the four major sections of this book. The introduction tells you what criminal justice is all about. Intended for both first-time and experienced criminal justice students, it offers a basic historical orientation and an overview of the various components of the criminal justice system. Part One addresses fundamental concerns of all writers, exploring the reasons why we write, describing the writing process itself, and examining those elements of grammar, style, and punctuation that most often cause confusion among writers in general. A vital concern throughout this Part One is the three-way interrelationship among writer, topic, and audience. Our discussion of this relationship aims at building your self-confidence as you clarify your goals. Writing is not a magical process beyond the control of most people. It is instead a series of complimentary skills which any writer can improve with practice, and the end result of this practice is the power to communicate your ideas effectively. Part One of this manual treats the act of writing not as an empty exercise undertaken only to produce a grade, but as a powerful learning tool, as well as the primary medium by which students and professionals in criminal justice accomplish their goals.

One crucial requirement for success in criminal justice writing is the ability to format a paper according to standards accepted universally by scholars in the field. In the last chapter in Part One we explain and demonstrate the procedures for documenting research and formatting papers in accordance with three distinct reference styles, those of the American Sociological Association's *Style Guide*, the American Psychological Association's *Publication Manual*, and the Student Citation System.

Part Two focuses on the research process. In the first chapter in this part we describe the research process in detail, explaining how you can maintain self-confidence by establishing control over your project. Also discussed is the crucial responsibility of every writer to use source material ethically. In Chapter 6 we list and describe traditional sources of information for criminal justice researchers, including libraries, government agencies, and private research organizations that may provide you with information not available in your library. Chapter 7 is an introduction to a major new source of information, the Internet. In this chapter we demonstrate how to find and utilize resources within this burgeoning new territory that are important to your topic. The final chapter in Part Two deals with conducting quantitative research in criminal justice. We examine several common research designs used to conduct quantitative research, while focusing on the scientific method and critical thinking.

In Part Three we explain six distinct types of papers that are commonly assigned in criminal justice classes. Each chapter begins by exploring the purposes and characteristics of the paper covered. Next, the steps for writing a successful paper are carefully articulated and typical formats provided. Each chapter encourages you to use your imagination and resourcefulness in working through the requirements of the assignment.

Your instructor may give you a specific paper assignment from one of these chapters. If the assignment is not specific, you may want to select an assignment and discuss your selection with your instructor before proceeding.

This manual is a reference book. It has been written to help you become a better writer. We wish you all success as you accept a primary challenge of academic and professional life: to write and write well.

William Johnson, Richard Rettig,
Greg Scott, and Steve Garrison

To the Instructor

How many times have you assigned papers in your criminal justice classes and found yourself teaching the class how to write the paper—not only content, but form and grammar as well? This book, which may accompany the primary text you assign in any criminal justice class or stand on its own, allows you to assign one of the papers explained in Part Three with the understanding that virtually everything the student needs to know, from grammar to sources of information to citing sources, is here within one book.

You can direct the students in your Introduction to Criminal Justice class, for example, to "write a reaction paper according to the directions in Chapter 9, following the instructions in Part One for formatting, grammar, and source citations and those in Part Two for organizing the research process and finding available resources." Almost every question a student could ask about the paper is answered in this book, but it also allows you to supplement your assignment with special instructions. In Part Three we have outlined six projects commonly assigned by criminal justice instructors:

1. Reaction papers (to help sharpen critical thinking and writing skills)
2. Article critiques
3. Book reviews
4. Case studies (including different types of case studies)
5. Policy analysis papers (how to critique an existing policy or recommend a new one)
6. Legal briefs (how to read and write legal briefs)

While some of the assignments are appropriate to beginning classes—especially Chapters 9 and 10—others are tailored for more advanced students. Writing a reaction paper according to the directions in Chapter 9, for example, is an excellent exercise for beginning students.

Using the guidelines from this manual to complete any of the assignments included will help your students to become more competent problem solvers and to develop skills that are important in every profession.

The four of us bring to the writing of this book a total of over 85 years of experience teaching courses in criminal justice, sociology, political science, and English. By combining the latest social science research and writing techniques with a broad spectrum of writing activities, we have designed a book to assist you in leading students toward success in both their schoolwork and their professional careers.

William Johnson, Richard Rettig,
Greg Scott, and Steve Garrison

Acknowledgment

We would like to thank Mary Carnis, Neil Marquardt, Naomi Sysak, and all those that assisted in compiling and editing this book. We would also like to thank the following reviewers for their helpful comments:

Elaine F. Cohen, Broward Community College, Davie, Florida
James E. Newman, Rio Hondo College, Whitter, California

A special thanks to Shelby Johnson, a film and dance major at Middlebury College in Vermont, for carefully reading and editing the manuscript. Her excellent suggestions significantly improved this book.

Introduction: The Discipline of Criminal Justice

WHY READ THIS INTRODUCTION?

If you are about to write your first paper in criminal justice, this introduction should be very helpful. It will help you understand what criminal justice is all about and what professionals in criminal justice are trying to achieve when they write. It provides a brief overview of the discipline which will help you understand basic concepts and apply them in your writing. The knowledge it offers can save you time and energy.

Criminal justice is taught under different conditions at different colleges and universities by instructors who have varying amounts and types of resources at their disposal. If you have already studied criminal justice in some detail, you may choose to skip this introduction and read Chapters 1 through 8 before selecting the chapters in Part Three that provide directions for the specific type of paper you have been assigned. However, you may find that reading this introduction will help to refresh your memory and establish your writing efforts more firmly within the broader framework of the discipline. Wherever you are in your progress toward mastering the methods and contributing to the discipline of criminal justice, we encourage you to read this section.

THE CRIMINAL JUSTICE PROCESS

Loosely Coupled Agencies

The principal characteristics of the criminal justice process should be clearly understood by every student of the discipline. The process is an arrangement of *loosely coupled agencies* with constitutional powers of investigation, arrest, prosecution, and punishment of criminal offenders. Ideally, the concept of justice embodies a society's highest cultural beliefs and values. Reality, however, seldom approaches the ideal in social life and is complicated by the fact that justice wears many hats when viewed and interpreted from different social vantage points. Each of the many agencies involved in criminal justice affects all the others. In the United States this systematic effort is marked by a significant degree of fragmentation and decentralization. Each agency practices a great deal of discretion in decision making, within the bounds of legal rules, policies, and procedures. For a brief discussion of these ideas, see Jacob (1987).

Competing Values

In American society there is little consensus on how to deal with the problems of crime. Policy choices always involve balancing competing values, and criminal justice can never be fully understood without examining the concept of *social justice*, which embraces all aspects of civilized life. On one hand, the public demands order and security, while on the other hand, the public wishes to uphold the rule of law and democratic government. So in American society, where democracy and social justice are valued, the creation of criminal laws and procedures must be closely associated with *democratic ideals*. Allocating massive resources to the police and removing limitations on their investigative and arrest powers would reduce crime, but it would also create a police state and result in a loss of freedom and justice. Concern for the crime victim and for the public harm must be balanced with the social duty to protect the accused and set limits on the kinds of punishment imposed.

Education

In the past, criminal justice was often seen as a technical/vocational subject in post-secondary education. However, in recent years it has been expanded and linked with criminology, sociology, and political science to provide a full agenda of interdisciplinary studies in crime, criminal behavior, and the administration of criminal justice systems, at both the undergraduate and graduate levels.

Today's college graduates who desire a career in criminal justice need more than just technical training. They need to feel a strong sense of identification with the values of our culture, and they should find satisfaction in helping to strengthen those values. It is vital for people who are beginning their careers in the justice system to develop a sense of professionalism in their respective fields: policing, courts, corrections, the juvenile system, and the private criminal justice sector. After all, criminal justice is an extremely important field. Its purpose is to establish effective ways to redress wrongs and assist victims, thereby working to build an environment characterized by fairness and feelings of trust.

BRIEF HISTORY OF CRIMINAL LAW

Four Stages in Response to Crime

Allen and Simonsen (1998) discuss four stages in the development of law as a response to crime: (1) personal revenge, (2) fines, (3) courts, and (4) assumption by the state of the obligation to punish and prevent wrongdoing.

From at least the time of the second millennium before the birth of Christ, society practiced the principle of *lex talionis* ("law of equivalent retaliation"), in other words, a system of law that takes into account the concept of *vengeance*. Talion law was developed to limit the extent to which crime victims or their family members could claim retaliation in kind—to exact from the criminal, in the words of an ancient expression, "an eye for an eye, a tooth for a tooth." This principle continues today in the concept of making penalties appropriate to the severity of the offense.

In the second stage of the development of law, physical retaliation against the wrongdoer was replaced by fines. The necessity for deliberations over the claims of the victim and the amount of the fine led to the establishment of *courts*, the third stage in the development of law. In the fourth stage, *the state* took over the responsibility for protecting citizens and punishing wrongdoing. Crimes came to be regarded not merely as offenses against persons but as offenses against the community and state.

U.S. Criminal Law

Criminal law in the United States is a combination of two strains or traditions: (1) common law, which developed in Saxon England and was based on customs and precedents; and (2) civil law, which is derived from Roman antecedents guided by earlier attempts to regulate human conduct by written and legislated codes that defined offenses and prescribed penalties for their commission.

U.S. law is tied historically to English common law. *Common law* is judge-made law, molded, refined, examined, and changed in a collection of actual decisions handed down from generation to generation in the form of reported cases. Judges based their decisions on existing principles of law, which reflected the living values, attitudes, and ethical ideals of the English people.

Today, *statutory laws* are enacted by state legislatures and the U.S. Congress and are compiled in codes, which can be modified by legislative action. *Administrative laws* are rulings by government agencies at the local, state, and federal level, which can be enforced by the criminal justice system.

The courts interpret *criminal statutes*, and these decisions are known as *case law*. These judicial interpretations are influenced by the principle of *stare decisis* ("let the decision stand")—the rule that requires judges to follow *precedent* on making their decisions.

Under the U.S. Constitution, criminal laws are written and enforced generally by agencies of the states. About 85 percent of all criminal cases are heard in state courts. The federal government monitors the states but has few police powers. Agencies such as the Federal Bureau of Investigation, the Drug Enforcement Agency, and the Secret Service have limited authority to enforce certain laws pertaining to specific powers authorized by Congress. This jurisdictional division has been modified in recent times as people and goods have moved increasingly across state lines. For example, federal courts and policing agencies are increasingly involved in actions against organized crime, drugs, pornography, and gambling.

THE U.S. CRIMINAL JUSTICE SYSTEM

Macro and Micro Systems

From a social science perspective, the concept of *system* implies some unity of purpose, but it does not assume that organizations will act as rationally ordered machines. At the *macro level*, the criminal justice system is made up of a number of parts or subsystems—*police, prosecution, defense, courts, corrections*—each with its own goals and needs. These subsystems are interdependent; that is, changes in the operation of one unit will bring about changes in other units. For example, an increase in the number of felony cases processed will affect the work not only of the clerks and judges of the criminal court, but also of the police, prosecution, probation, and correctional subsystems. Each subsystem makes its own distinctive contribution in achieving the goals of the criminal justice system.

Micro level analysis—how individual actors play their roles—is concerned with interaction between individuals and groups that are a part of the larger order. For example, *exchange relationships* such as plea bargaining in a criminal case can result in an exchange that benefits all parties involved; the defendant achieves a lower sentence, attorneys move a case in an expeditious manner, and the court docket is cleared to process other cases. The concept of exchange makes us aware that decisions are the products of interactions among individuals and that the major subsystems—police, prosecutor, court, and corrections—are tied together by the actions of individual decision makers.

Principal Components

In the United States, the principal subsystems of criminal justice consist of the *police*, *courts* (prosecution and defense), and *corrections*, with the court and correction systems having a counterpart referred to as the *juvenile justice system*. There is also a large *private criminal justice sector*. Altogether, over 60,000 public and private agencies utilize an annual budget of over $74 billion and a staff of about 1.7 million people (Gilliard and Beck 1996).

As the following overview of its components shows, almost all employees of this vast enterprise need good writing and comprehension skills.

THE POLICE

Complexity and fragmentation characterize the number and jurisdiction of the approximately 17,000 public organizations in the United States engaged in law enforcement activities. Only 50 of these law enforcement agencies are federal; the rest are state and local (Gilliard and Beck 1996).

The responsibilities of police organizations to keep the peace fall into four categories, discussed briefly below. Police do their best to ensure the protection of rights and persons in a wide variety of situations, ranging from street-corner brawls to domestic quarrels. They are charged with *apprehending law violators* and *fighting crime*. But this responsibility actually accounts for only a small proportion of law enforcement agencies' time and resources. Much of their time is spent in *crime prevention* activities, helping educate the public about the threat of crime and thus helping to reduce the number of situations in which crimes are most likely to be committed. Police also provide a variety of *social services*: They recover stolen property, direct traffic, provide emergency medical aid, get cats out of trees, and help people who have locked themselves out of their apartments. It is easy to see why police officers must be good communicators.

THE COURTS

The United States has a dual court system with a separate judicial structure for each state in addition to a national structure. Each system has its own series of courts. The U.S. Supreme Court is the judicial body in which the two systems are brought together. The Supreme Court does not have the power to review all decisions of state courts in criminal cases. They only accept cases involving a federal law or rights guaranteed by the U.S. Constitution.

Interpretation of the law can vary from state to state. Judges can apply the law as they feel it should be applied until they are overruled by a higher court. Each state's adjudicatory procedures have evolved through a blend of legislative enactments and judicial interpretation of both state and federal laws. Thus, how a law is expressed and argued, in both the courtroom and on paper, can have a major effect on the lives of U.S. citizens.

CORRECTIONS

On any given day, approximately 4 million Americans are under the supervision of the adult corrections system. Only about a third of convicted offenders are actually incarcerated. The remainder are under supervision in the community through probation, parole, community-based halfway houses, work-release programs, and supervised activities (Gilliard and Beck 1996).

The federal government, all the states, most counties, and all but the smallest cities are engaged in the corrections enterprise. Increasingly, nonprofit private organizations such as the YMCA have contracted with governments to perform correctional services. For-profit businesses have undertaken the construction and administration of institutions through contracts with governments.

A breakdown of the numbers of citizens monitored by the country's various penal systems indicates the complexity and scope of the corrections arm of the criminal justice system. According to Gilliard and Beck (1996), an estimated 1,585,400 persons were incarcerated in the United States in 1995. U.S. prisons and jails held 600 persons per 100,000 residents. Prisoners in the custody of the 50 states, the District of Columbia, and the federal government accounted for two-thirds of the incarcerated inmates (1,078,357). The other third were held in local jails (507,044 inmates).

On December 31, 1995, a total of 1,127,132 prisoners were under federal or state jurisdiction, a measure that, unlike custody, includes persons under the legal authority of a prison system held elsewhere or outside its facilities, such as the parole or probation systems. The total increased 6.8 percent from the end of 1994. The states and the District of Columbia added 66,843 prisoners; the federal system, 5216 (Gilliard and Beck 1996).

On June 30, 1995, local jail authorities held or supervised an estimated 541,913 offenders. Six percent of these offenders (34,869) were supervised outside a jail facility in an alternative program such as electronic monitoring, house detention (without electronic monitoring), or day reporting. In 1995 local jail authorities held an estimated 507,044 offenders in their facilities, an increase of 4.2 percent during the 12 previous months (Gilliard and Beck 1996).

Relative to the number of U.S. residents, the rate of incarceration in 1995 was 600 inmates per 100,000 U.S. residents—up from 461 per 100,000 in 1990. As of December 31, 1995, one in every 167 U.S. residents was incarcerated (Gilliard and Beck 1996).

Since 1985 the total number of inmates in the custody of state and federal prisons and local jails has more than doubled, to nearly 1.6 million, an increase of 113 percent. The incarcerated population has grown an average of 7.9 percent annually since 1985. The state and federal prison population has grown 8.3 percent annually, while the local jail population has grown 7.0 percent. Over the 10-year period from 1985 to 1995, correctional authorities have found beds for nearly 841,200 additional inmates, the equivalent of almost 1618 inmates per week (Gilliard and Beck 1996).

At year-end 1985, one in every 320 U.S. residents was incarcerated. By year-end 1995 that ratio had increased to 1 in every 167. Since 1985 the U.S. prison and jail population has nearly doubled on a per capita basis. In 1995 the number of inmates per 100,000 U.S. residents was 600, up from 313 in 1985 (Gilliard and Beck 1996).

THE JUVENILE JUSTICE SYSTEM

On another level, the *juvenile justice system* functions to assist adolescents who have been identified as youth in trouble, and their families, with the rules, regulations, and laws of U.S. society. There are many employment opportunities in the juvenile court and corrections fields for students with good writing and other communications skills.

JUVENILE COURTS   In the United States, juvenile courts processed more than 1.5 million delinquency cases in 1994. This number represented a 5 percent increase over the 1993 caseload and a 41 percent increase over the number of cases handled in 1985. More than half (55 percent) of the delinquency cases disposed by U.S. courts with juvenile jurisdiction in 1994 were processed formally; that is, a petition was filed charging the youth with delinquency. Of the cases that were formally petitioned and scheduled for an adjudicatory or waiver hearing in juvenile court, 58 percent were adjudicated delinquent, and slightly more than 1 percent were transferred to adult criminal court. Transfers to criminal court were more common in cases involving person offenses and drug offenses. Of all delinquency cases adjudicated in juvenile court in 1994, 29 percent resulted in out-of-home placement, and 53 percent were placed on probation (Butts 1995).

These statistics, summarized by Butts (1995) in the *Juvenile Justice and Delinquency Prevention Bulletin*, are among the findings published in *Juvenile Court Statistics 1994* (Butts et al. 1996), the latest in a series of annual reports on cases handled by U.S. courts with juvenile jurisdiction. This report series started in 1929 and continues to be the nation's primary source of information on juvenile court activities. Although courts with juvenile jurisdiction handle a variety of cases, including abuse, neglect, adoption, and traffic violations, *Juvenile Court Statistics* reports focus on the disposition of delinquency cases and formally handled status offense cases. Each report includes national estimates of the number of cases handled by juvenile courts, with an appendix that lists caseload statistics for individual states and jurisdictions within each state.

Some important descriptive statistics from *Juvenile Court Statistics 1994* include:

- The number of homicide cases handled in U.S. juvenile courts increased 144 percent between 1985 and 1994. The homicide caseload was 19 percent higher in 1994 than in 1990.

- In 22 percent of delinquency cases processed in 1994, the most serious charge was a person offense. Person offenses accounted for 16 percent of all cases in 1985.

- The number of cases involving drug offenses increased 35 percent between 1993 and 1994.

- The number of delinquency cases involving female juveniles increased 54 percent between 1985 and 1994, while cases involving males increased 38 percent.

- Juveniles were held in secure detention facilities at some point between referral and disposition in 21 percent of all delinquency cases disposed in 1994, compared with 20 percent in 1985.

- Delinquency cases were more likely to be processed formally with the filing of a petition in 1994 than in 1985—55 percent compared with 46 percent.

- The number of delinquency cases judicially transferred to criminal court grew 71 percent between 1985 and 1994, although the chances of a case being transferred in 1994 were the same as in 1985—1.4 percent of formally processed cases.

These national estimates of juvenile court cases are based on data from more than 1800 courts that had jurisdiction over 67 percent of the U.S. juvenile population in 1994 (Butts 1995). A case disposed during the calendar year by a court with juvenile jurisdiction represents the unit of count in this study and in each *Juvenile Court Statistics* report. It is possible for a juvenile to have been involved in more than one case during the calendar year. Each case represents a youth processed by a juvenile court on a new referral, regardless of the number of individual offenses contained in that referral. Cases involving multiple offenses are categorized according to the most serious offense. For example, a case involving both a charge of vandalism and a charge of robbery would be characterized as a robbery case. Similarly, cases involving multiple dispositions are categorized according to the most restrictive disposition. A case that resulted in both probation and placement in a residential facility would be coded as residential placement.

DELINQUENCY CASES   Delinquency offenses are acts committed by a juvenile that if committed by an adult could result in criminal prosecution. Juvenile courts handled an estimated 1,555,200 delinquency cases in 1994. A property offense was the most serious charge involved in 52 percent of these cases. The most serious charge was a person offense in 22 percent of the cases, a drug offense in 8 percent, and a public order offense in 19 percent. Larceny–theft, simple assault, burglary, vandalism, and obstruction of justice were the most common delinquency offenses seen by juvenile courts in 1994. Together, these five offenses made up nearly 60 percent of the delinquency cases processed during 1994 (Butts 1995).

Between 1985 and 1994, the total number of delinquency cases handled by U.S. juvenile courts increased 41 percent. The largest relative percentage increases occurred in cases involving weapons offenses (156 percent), homicide (144 percent), and aggravated assault (134 percent). Offense categories showing the smallest increases or even decreases included liquor law violations (-34 percent), nonviolent sex offenses (-24 percent), and burglary (5 percent) (Butts 1995).

In the United States, citizens' expectations of criminal justice agencies have become critically important. Past offender-based control strategies of getting tough on criminals have not worked to reduce crime significantly. Since the early 1980s, criminal justice has been both underfunded and underconceptualized. More and more citizens are reaffirming both punitive and treatment approaches and are calling for the justice system to articulate a vision for success. As taxpayers continue to feel the pain of criminal behavior, they appear to be more willing to support programs that include public safety, accountability of offenders, and compensating development of those convicted of criminal behavior. This means that thousands of new jobs are being created in the criminal justice arena and many related fields. All of these jobs require good writing and oral communication skills. A partial list of potential jobs in criminal justice is provided at the end of this introduction.

PROFESSIONAL POSITIONS IN CRIMINAL JUSTICE

Administrative and Management Jobs

As college students complete their undergraduate degrees and move on to the master's level they become more eligible to apply for administrative and management jobs across the criminal justice field. We will use law enforcement and corrections as the primary examples in our discussion of required professional skills. However, much of the material on management and administration is generalizable to all areas of criminal justice.

Any profession is characterized by a specialized body of knowledge and a set of internal guidelines that hold members accountable for their actions. A well-focused code of ethics, equitable recruitment and selection practices, and informed promotional strategies among many agencies, contribute to the growing level of professionalism among American law enforcement and corrections agencies today. However, in the United States the public perception is that while management in general is effective, *correctional* management is not (Duffee 1986). We believe that for management to be more directive, task-oriented, and accountable, the communication skills of managers, especially writing, must improve.

The Role of the Manager in Criminal Justice

MANAGERS AND MANAGEMENT

In criminal justice, to manage means to control and direct, to administer, to take charge of a unit or a program. Managers blend resources—human, material, and financial—to achieve organizational goals of arrest, conviction, custody, and rehabilitation. Criminal justice managers should support the development of individual responsibility, permitting all their employees to achieve maximum potential while simultaneously supporting organizational needs. The terms *manager* and *supervisor* are used interchangeably throughout the criminal justice system.

AUTHORITY AND POWER

Authority is the ability to get things done through others by influencing behavior. *Power* is the ability to get things done with or without legal right: the ability to persuade people to do things they might not otherwise have done. Authority and power are alike in that both imply the ability to coerce compliance, to make subordinates carry out orders. Both are important to managers at all levels. They differ in that authority relies on force or on some sort of law or order, whereas power relies on persuasion and often lacks the support of law or rule.

LEVELS OF MANAGERS

- *CEO*: chief, sheriff, division directors, warden
- *Middle level*: captains, lieutenants
- *First line*: sergeants

BASIC MANAGEMENT TASKS

All basic management tasks require good writing and other communication skills. Managerial tasks are:

- Planning
- Organizing
- Directing
- Staffing
- Coordinating
- Reporting
- Budgeting

BASIC MANAGEMENT SKILLS

Management skills include technical skills, administrative skills, conceptual skills, and people skills (Drucker 1993).

- *Technical skills* include all procedures necessary to be a "good cop," such as interviewing, interrogating, searching, arresting, gathering evidence, recording, and reporting.
- *Administrative skills* refer to organizing, delegating, and directing the work of others.
- *Conceptual skills* is a phrase meaning the ability to solve problems, plan and see the big picture, and write and present effective programs, complete with acceptable budgets.
- *People skills* include being able to communicate clearly, to motivate, to discipline appropriately, and to inspire. For example, corrections managers, who are required to deal with both staff and inmates, must have mastered a range of communications skills, including:
  - Coordinating
  - Motivating
  - Leading

Criminal justice managers must also be interactors who work effectively with a number of groups. Law enforcement managers typically interact with politicians, community groups, the media, and executives of other law enforcement organizations, as well as individuals and groups within the agency itself.

Today, there are many types of careers, both frontline and management, available in all areas of criminal justice. The following job descriptions and advertisements are included by Stuart (1994) in his book *Inside Jobs: A Realistic Guide to Criminal Justice Careers for College Students.*

SOME FEDERAL POSITIONS IN CRIMINAL JUSTICE

ATF SPECIAL AGENT: Investigates violations of explosives, firearms, and illicit liquor and tobacco acts; prevents and solves bombings; detects illegal transportation of explosives and firearms; controls illegal possession of these items. *Agency:* ATF.

BORDER PATROL AGENT: Prevents smuggling and illegal entry of aliens into the United States; patrols border areas; inspects trains, vehicles, buses, airplanes, ships, and terminals. *Agency:* INS.

CORRECTIONAL OFFICER: Enforces rules governing confinement, safety, health, and protection of inmates; supervises inmate work assignments. *Agency:* Federal Prison System.

CRIMINAL INVESTIGATOR: Investigates violations of federal laws. *Agencies:* INS, Department Of Defense, Office of Personnel Management.

CUSTOMS INSPECTOR: Enforces laws governing imports and exports; weighs, gauges, measures, samples, and collects duties, taxes, and fees; searches violators of customs laws; seizes contraband; arrests violators. *Agency:* Customs Service.

CUSTOMS SPECIAL AGENT: Investigates fraud affecting customs revenue through underevaluation and smuggling of merchandise and contraband, Neutrality Act violations involving illegal shipment of arms, and violations involving customs employees. *Agency:* Customs Service.

INDUSTRIAL HYGIENIST: Inspects businesses to determine compliance with safety and occupational health regulations. *Agency:* OSHA.

INTERNAL REVENUE AGENT: Audits individual and corporate taxpayers to determine their tax liabilities. *Agency:* Internal Revenue Service (IRS).

INTERNAL REVENUE OFFICER: Collects taxes and secures tax returns; analyzes financial information on businesses and determines the methods to resolve tax liabilities. *Agency:* IRS.

IRS SPECIAL AGENT: Investigates criminal violations, particularly those relating to income and wagering or gaming devices; recommends criminal prosecution and the assertion of civil penalties against taxpayers; assists U.S. Attorneys in the preparation of trial cases. *Agency:* IRS.

PARK RANGER: Protects against structural forest fire and property damage; gathers and disseminates natural, historical, cultural, or scientific information; demonstrates folk art and crafts; enforces laws and regulations; investigates violations, complaints, trespasses, and accidents; conducts rescue missions. *Agencies:* Corps of Engineers, National Park Service.

SOME TYPICAL ADVERTISEMENTS FOR JOBS IN CRIMINAL JUSTICE

Local Law Enforcement

PROPERTY OFFICER: Evanston, IL. *Job description:* A variety of police work related to property and evidence necessary for police business in prosecutions. *Qualifications:* Two years' experience in property control, records inventory or related field; high school diploma preferably supplemented by two years of college with a concentration in criminal justice. *Annual salary:* $26,928 to $33,108 plus benefits.

PATROL OFFICER: Saginaw, MI. *Job description:* Community-oriented crime prevention. *Qualifications:* Must be certified or certifiable. *Annual salary:* Up to $30,699.

PUBLIC SAFETY OFFICER: Oklahoma City, OK. *Job description:* Perform duties of police officer and firefighter. *Qualifications:* Minimum of B.S./B.A. degree with police academy training preferred. *Annual salary:* Starting $23,442 to $35,413 after four years.

PUBLIC SAFETY OFFICER: Durham, NC. *Qualifications:* 60 semester/90 term hours of college credit, written and physical preemployment tests. *Annual salary:* $28,823 to $41,175 plus benefits.

POLICE OFFICER: Ann Arbor, MI. *Job description:* Basic police work. *Qualifications:* Must have passed the MLEOTC; related course work and/or experience is an advantage but is not required. *Annual salary:* Starts at $24,232; after one year $30,222 plus 3 percent with a four-year degree.

POLICE OFFICER: Aurora, CO. *Qualifications:* Three years' police experience in past four years. Minimum age 21, high school graduate or G.E.D.

PUBLIC SAFETY OFFICER: Toledo, OH. *Job description:* Must serve as police officer and firefighter, as required. *Qualifications:* Must be certified or certifiable.

POLICE CHIEF: Farley, WI. *Qualifications:* Associate's degree in law enforcement; two to five years' experience as supervisor in law enforcement. Certification is required. *Annual salary:* $21,000 to $35,000 plus benefits.

POLICE OFFICER FIRST YEAR: Pittsburgh, PA. *Qualifications:* Must become a city of Pittsburgh resident before appointment and remain a resident throughout employment; excellent physical condition; must have a valid class C (or class 1) driver's license at time of application. *Annual salary:* $24,553.

Law and Courts

LEGAL COORDINATOR: Maumee, OH. *Job description:* Coordinate legal resources with agency's needs. *Qualifications:* J.D. preferred, M.S.W., master's degree in public administration or related field, three years. Experience in children's services and legal issues. *Annual salary:* $35,071 to $54,709.

PARALEGAL: Newport News, VA. *Job description:* Coordinating court proceedings, litigation support, and client responsibilities.

LEGAL ASSISTANT/PARALEGAL: Detroit, MI. *Job description:* Prepare summary plan descriptions, planned amendments, resolutions, trust agreements, and IRS submissions. *Qualifications:* B.S., some computer experience. Legal assistant training an advantage. Will consider law school graduate.

LEGAL ASSISTANT: Baltimore, MD. *Job description:* Assist attorneys in collection, litigation, and other legal work. *Qualifications:* ABA-accredited paralegal program or equivalent, word processing. *Annual salary:* $24,128 plus benefits.

PRETRIAL OFFICER: Chicago, IL. *Job description:* Court-related work. *Qualifications:* Four-year degree with two years' experience.

LEGAL ASSISTANT: Toledo, OH. *Job description:* Working with general civil litigations, personal injury, medical litigation, and collections. *Qualifications:* Legal assistant degree/certificate preferred and computer skills required.

LEGAL ASSISTANT: Madison, WI. *Job description:* Litigation work with Madison law firm. *Qualifications:* B.A. and two to three years' litigation experience.

JUVENILE COURT REGISTER: Macon, GA. *Qualifications:* Five years' experience in legal environment (juvenile court preferred), four years of supervisory experience and computer literate.

COURT DEPUTY: Manchester, NH. *Job description:* Provide security for judges, court personnel, jurors, and public. Serve warrants for arrests, assist in placement, security, and transportation of criminals. *Qualifications:* Peace officer training certificate, three years' law enforcement experience, familiarity with court system and/or degree in law enforcement or criminal justice. *Annual salary:* $21,830 with full benefits.

Probation and Parole

PAROLE AND PROBATION: Assistant: State of Michigan. *Job description:* Parole and probation assistant for the state department of corrections. *Qualifications:* 60 college credit hours required.

VICTIM WITNESS ASSISTANT: Pittsburgh, PA. *Job description:* In-take and counseling work. *Qualifications:* Bachelor's degree in criminal justice, social work, human/social services, or psychology and one year of experience in social service or in-take in criminal justice program. *Annual salary:* $18,221.

DIVERSION SERVICES OFFICER: St. Paul, MN. *Job description:* Pretrial diversion program. *Qualifications:* Experience with probation, investigations, treatment plans, and community resources. Bachelor's degree required. *Annual salary:* Low 30s to start.

HISPANIC/LATINO OUTREACH SATELLITE COORDINATOR: Toledo, OH. *Job description:* Toledo–Lucas County Victim Witness Assistance Program, implement services to Hispanic/Latino victims of violent crime. *Qualifications:* Must speak, read, and write Spanish. Bachelor's degree preferred. *Annual salary:* $15,000 to $17,000 with benefits.

PROBATION OFFICER: Hartford, CT. *Job description:* Court probation officer. *Qualifications:* Bachelor's degree in sociology or related field. M.A. preferred or comparable experience. *Annual salary:* $25,000.

PROBATION COUNSELOR: Detroit, MI. *Job description:* Work with adjudicated youths. *Qualifications:* B.S./B.S.W. required and two years of experience.

PROBATION AND PAROLE OFFICER: Cheyenne, WY. *Job description:* Supervision of adults and juveniles on probation–parole, writing presentencing and predispositional reports, counseling of offenders and families, coordination of community resources, confer and cooperate with law enforcement agencies. *Qualifications:* B.A. and two years'. related experience. *Annual salary:* $21,564.

ADULT PROBATION OFFICER: Bowling Green, OH. *Qualifications:* Degree in criminal justice, psychology, or related field and one year of experience. *Annual salary:* $18,000 plus benefits.

Because people in need of treatment sometimes come in contact with the criminal justice system, the following job listings in the areas of substance abuse and human services are often pertinent to criminal justice students.

Substance Abuse

CHEMICAL DEPENDENCY COUNSELOR: Sandusky, OH. *Job description:* Provide counseling to adults and adolescents in both inpatient and outpatient settings. *Qualifications:* B.A./B.S. with two years' experience in chemical dependency counseling. Licensed or eligible CDC or CAC.

CHEMICAL DEPENDENCY COUNSELOR: Bridgeport, CT. *Job description:* Individual and group counseling, educational presentations, and case management. *Qualifications:* B.A. and substance abuse therapy certification.

SUBSTANCE ABUSE COUNSELOR: Athens, GA. *Job description:* Provide subacute 14-day program with didactic group, individual, and family therapy services. *Qualifications:* C.D. knowledge base with one year of experience preferred. M.S.W./M.A./B.A. and current licensure.

SUBSTANCE ABUSE THERAPIST: Coldwater, MI. *Job description:* Working with women inmates. *Qualifications:* B.A., M.A. preferred. Substance abuse therapy and relapse experience.

DRUG/ALCOHOL COUNSELOR: Mansfield, OH. *Job description:* Crisis intervention, counseling, after-care. *Qualifications:* Skilled chemical dependency counselor, experience with children, CAC or CCDC required, and M.S.W./M.A.

SUBSTANCE ABUSE COUNSELORS: Chicago, IL. *Job description:* Counselor for adolescents involved in substance abuse program. *Qualifications:* B.A./B.S.

SUBSTANCE ABUSE CLINICIAN: Macon, GA. *Job description:* Community coordinator for jail-based program. *Qualifications:* Master's degree preferred. Prior training and experience with ASI, SASSI, or McAndrews. Knowledge of available community resources.

PROGRAM DIRECTOR: Toledo, OH. *Job description:* Treatment Alternatives to Street Crime (TASC). *Qualifications:* Five years' experience in criminal justice or substance abuse field, two years' managerial experience, B.A., M.A., and CCDC certification. *Annual salary:* Mid-30s.

Human Services

DOMESTIC VIOLENCE TECHNICIAN: Buffalo, NY. *Job description:* Facilitate educational groups for batterers, conduct interviews and assessments. *Qualifications:* Group leadership knowledge in behavioral patterns of abusers and victims. Degree in psychology, social work, criminal justice, or related field and one year of experience. *Annual salary:* $29,332.

YOUTH CARE WORKER: Akron, OH. *Job description:* Residential work with adolescents. *Qualifications:* Bachelor's degree and/or experience. *Annual salary:* $13,000 to $14,500.

SOCIAL WORK SUPERVISOR: Toledo, OH. *Job description:* Live-in supervisor for small group of delinquent adolescents residing in transitional housing. *Qualifications:* B.S. in criminal justice, social work, and experience with adolescents. *Annual salary:* $17,500.

EEO INVESTIGATIVE CASE WORKERS: Warren, MI. *Job description:* Investigative/counseling in dispute settlement over EEO complaints for U.S. Army. Qualifications: Research, investigative experience, and good communication skills.

CASEWORKER: Lexington, KY. *Job description:* Investigate backgrounds of delinquent youths to assist court in determining disposition of cases, and counsel. *Qualifications:* Master's degree in social work or behavioral science and one year of experience.

CASE MANAGER: Birmingham, AL. *Job description:* Work with offenders, help them reintegrate, weekend and evening hours. *Qualifications:* B.A. in social work, criminal justice, or psychology. *Hourly wage:* $7.00.

CASEWORKER: Jacksonville, FL. *Job description:* Investigate backgrounds of delinquent youths to assist court in disposition of cases, and counsel. *Qualifications:* Master's degree in social work or behavioral science and one year of experience.

SOCIAL WORKER: College Park, MD. *Job description:* Work in adolescent girls' shelter. *Qualifications:* B.A. and one year of experience. *Annual salary:* $18,000 to $25,000.

THE NEED FOR CLEAR AND ACCURATE WRITING IN CRIMINAL JUSTICE

The more complex criminal justice systems become, the greater the need for clear, simple, direct communication. The sad reality is that many people have difficulty writing a simple declarative sentence. In all areas of criminal justice, no skill is recognized as more important than that of getting messages on paper clearly in order to get business done. If you learn to write well, you will be more valuable in whatever line of work you pursue.

Administrators in criminal justice agencies are looking for people who can condense a mass of data to one sheet of clear comment. They are looking for men and women who can report the day-to-day activities of a complex system concisely and accurately. They want more than undigested, descriptive data; they want to know what the experts in each area believe the data mean.

This book is designed to help you organize your thoughts and directions in order to write more clearly and accurately. You will find principles and guidelines to help you write complex reports as well as summarize information into condensed presentations. As you continue to use this manual throughout your college and professional career, we hope your writing skills evolve and aid you in attaining your professional goals and objectives.

PART I

A Handbook of Style for Criminal Justice

CHAPTER 1

Writing as Communication

WRITING TO LEARN

Writing is a way of ordering your experience. Think about it. No matter what you are writing—it may be a paper for your introductory criminal justice class, a short story, a limerick, or a grocery list—you are putting pieces of your world together in new ways and making yourself freshly conscious of these pieces. This is one of the reasons that writing is so difficult. From the infinite welter of data that your mind continually processes and locks in your memory, you are selecting only certain items significant to the task at hand, relating them to other items, and phrasing them in a new and coherent manner. You are mapping a part of your universe that has hitherto been unknown territory. You are gaining a little more control over the processes by which you interact with the world around you.

Writing is, therefore, one of the best ways to learn. This statement may sound odd at first. If you are an unpracticed writer, you may share a common notion that the only purpose that writing can have is to express what you already know or think. Any learning that you as a writer might do has already been accomplished by the time your pen meets the paper. In this view, your task is to inform and even surprise the reader. But if you are a practiced writer, you know that at any moment, as you write, you are capable of surprising yourself by discovering information you did not know you knew. It is surprise that you look for: the shock of seeing what happens in your own mind when you drop an old, established opinion into a batch of new facts or bump into a cherished belief from a different angle. Writing synthesizes new understanding for the writer. E. M. Forster's famous question—"How do I know what I think until I see what I say?"—is one that all of us could ask. We make meaning as we write, jolting ourselves by little discoveries into a larger and more interesting universe.

The Irony of Writing

Good writing helps the reader become aware of the ironies and paradoxes of human existence. One such paradox is that good writing expresses both that which is unique about the writer and at the same time, that which is common not to the writer alone, but to every human being. Many of our most famous political statements share this double attribute of mirroring the singular and the ordinary. For example, read the following excerpts from President Franklin Roosevelt's first inaugural address, spoken on March 4, 1933, in the middle of the Great Depression, then answer this question: Is what Roosevelt says famous in history because its expression is extraordinary, or because it appeals to something that is basic to every human being?

> This is pre-eminently the time to speak the truth, the whole truth, frankly and boldly. Nor need we shrink from honestly facing conditions in our country today. This great nation will endure as it has endured, will revive and will prosper.

> So first of all let me assert my firm belief that the only thing we have to fear is fear itself—nameless, unreasoning, unjustified terror which paralyzes needed efforts to convert retreat into advance.

> In every dark hour of our national life a leadership of frankness and vigor has met with that understanding and support of the people themselves which is essential to victory. I am convinced that you will again give that support to leadership in these critical days.

> In such a spirit on my part and on yours we face our common difficulties. They concern, thank God, only material things. Values have shrunken to fantastic levels; taxes have risen; our ability to pay has fallen, government of all kinds is faced by serious curtailment of income; the means of exchange are frozen in the currents of trade; the withered leaves of industrial enterprise lie on every side; farmers find no markets for their produce; the savings of many years in thousands of families are gone.

> More important, a host of unemployed citizens face the grim problem of existence, and an equally great number toil with little return. Only a foolish optimist can deny the dark realities of the moment.

> Yet our distress comes from no failure of substance. We are stricken by no plague of locusts. Compared with the perils which our forefathers conquered because they believed and were not afraid, we have still much to be thankful for. Nature still offers her bounty and human efforts have multiplied it. Plenty is at our doorstep, but a generous use of it languishes in the very sight of the supply....

> The measure of the restoration lies in the extent to which we apply social values more noble than mere monetary profit.

> Happiness lies not in the mere possession of money; it lies in the joy of achievement, in the thrill of creative effort.

> The joy and moral stimulation of work no longer must be forgotten in the mad chase of evanescent profits. These dark days will be worth all they cost us if they teach us that our true destiny is not to be ministered unto but to minister to ourselves and to our fellow-men. (Commager 1963:240)

The help that writing gives us with learning and with controlling what we learn is one of the major reasons why your criminal justice instructors will require a great deal of writing from you. Learning the complex and diverse world of the criminal justice professional takes more than a passive ingestion of facts. You have to come to grips with social issues and with your own attitudes toward them. When you write in a class on criminal justice or juvenile delinquency, you are entering into the world of professional researchers in the same way they do—testing theory against fact and fact against belief.

Virtually everything that happens in the discipline of criminal justice happens on paper first. Documents are wrestled into shape before their contents can affect the public. Meaningful social programs are written before they are implemented. The written word has helped bring slaves to freedom, end wars, create new opportunities in the workplace, and shape the values of nations. Often, gaining recognition for ourselves and our ideas depends less on what we say than on how we say it. Accurate and persuasive writing is absolutely vital to the criminal justice professional.

Challenge Yourself

There is no way around it: Writing is a struggle. Do you think you are the only one to feel this way? Take heart! Writing is hard for everybody, great writers included. Bringing order into the world is never easy. Isaac Bashevis Singer, winner of the 1978

E X E R C I S E

Learning by Writing

A way of testing the notion that writing is a powerful learning tool is by rewriting your notes from a recent class lecture. The type of class does not matter; it can be history, chemistry, criminal justice, whatever. If possible, choose a difficult class, one in which you are feeling somewhat unsure of the material and one for which you have taken copious notes.

As you rewrite, provide the *transitional elements* (connecting phrases such as *in order to, because of, and, but, however*) that you were unable to supply in class because of the press of time. Furnish your own examples or illustrations of the ideas expressed in the lecture.

This experiment will force you to supply necessary coherence out of your own thought processes. See if the loss of time it takes you to rewrite the notes is not more than compensated for by a gain in your understanding of the lecture material.

Nobel prize in literature, once wrote: "I believe in miracles in every area of life except writing. Experience has shown me that there are no miracles in writing. The only thing that produces good writing is hard work" (Lunsford and Connors 1992:2).

Hard work was evident in the words of John F. Kennedy's Inaugural Address. As you read the following excerpts from Kennedy's speech, what images come to mind? Historians tend to consider a president "great" when his words live longer than his deeds in the minds of the people. Do you think this will be—or has been—true of Kennedy?

> We observe today not a victory of party but a celebration of freedom—symbolizing an end as well as a beginning—signifying renewal as well as change. For I have sworn before you and Almighty God the same solemn oath our forebears prescribed nearly a century and three-quarters ago.
>
> The world is very different now. For man holds in his mortal hands the power to abolish all forms of human poverty and all forms of human life. And yet the same revolutionary beliefs for which our forebears fought are still at issue around the globe—the belief that the rights of man come not from the generosity of the state but from the hand of God.
>
> We dare not forget today that we are the heirs of that first revolution. Let the word go forth from this time and place, to friend and foe alike, that the torch has been passed to a new generation of Americans—born in this century, tempered by war, disciplined by a hard and bitter peace, proud of our ancient heritage—and unwilling to witness or permit the slow undoing of those human rights to which this nation has always been committed, and to which we are committed today at home and around the world....
>
> In the long history of the world, only a few generations have been granted the role of defending freedom in its hours of maximum danger. I do not shrink from this responsibility—I welcome it. I do not believe that any of us would exchange places with any other people or any other generation. The energy, the faith, the devotion which we bring to this endeavor will light our country and all who serve it—and the glow from that fire can truly light the world.
>
> And so, my fellow Americans: ask not what your country can do for you—ask what you can do for your country.
>
> My fellow citizens of the world: ask not what America will do for you, but what together we can do for the freedom of man. (Commager 1963:688–689)

One reason writing is difficult is that it is not actually a single activity at all but a process consisting of several activities that can overlap each other, with two or more sometimes operating *simultaneously* as you labor to organize and phrase your thoughts. (We discuss these activities later in this chapter.) The writing process tends to be sloppy for everyone, an often frustrating search for meaning and for the best way to articulate that meaning.

Frustrating though that search may sometimes be, it need not be futile. Remember this: The writing process makes use of skills that we all have. The ability to write, in other words, is not some magical competence bestowed on the rare, fortunate person. Although few of us may achieve the proficiency of Isaac Singer, we are all capable of phrasing thoughts clearly and in a well-organized fashion. But learning how to do so takes *practice*.

The one sure way to improve your writing is to write. One of the toughest but most important jobs in writing is to maintain enthusiasm for your writing project. Commitment may sometimes be hard to come by, given the difficulties that are inherent in the writing process and that can be made worse when the project is unappealing at first glance. How, for example, can you be enthusiastic about having to write a paper analyzing prison reform when you know little about the U.S. correctional system and see no real use in writing about it?

One of the worst mistakes that unpracticed student writers make is to fail to assume responsibility for keeping themselves interested in their writing. No matter how hard it may seem at first to drum up interest in your topic, *you have to do it*—that is, if you want to write a paper you can be proud of, one that contributes useful material and a fresh point of view to the topic. One thing is guaranteed: If you are bored with your writing, your reader will be, too. So what can you do to keep your interest and energy level high?

Challenge yourself. Think of the paper not as an assignment but as a piece of writing that has a point to make. To get this point across persuasively is the real reason why you are writing, *not* the simple fact that a teacher has assigned you a project. If someone were to ask you why you are writing your paper and your immediate, unthinking response is, "Because I've been given a writing assignment," or "Because I want a good grade," or some other nonanswer along these lines, your paper may be in trouble.

If, on the other hand, your first impulse is to explain the challenge of your main point—"I'm writing to show how prison reform will benefit both inmates and the U.S. taxpayer"—then you are thinking usefully about your topic.

Maintain Self-Confidence

Having confidence in your ability to write well about your topic is essential for good writing. This does not mean that you will always know what the end result of a particular writing activity will be. In fact, you have to cultivate your ability to tolerate a high degree of uncertainty while weighing evidence, testing hypotheses, and experimenting with organizational strategies and wording. Be ready for temporary confusion and for seeming dead ends, and remember that every writer faces these obstacles. It is from your struggle to combine fact with fact, to buttress conjecture with evidence, that order arises.

Do not be intimidated by the amount and quality of work that others have already done in your field of inquiry. The array of opinion and evidence that confronts you in the published literature can be confusing. But remember that no important topic is ever exhausted. *There are always gaps*—questions that have not yet been explored satisfactorily either in the published research on a subject or in the prevailing popular opinion. It is in these gaps that you establish your own authority, your own sense of control.

Remember that the various stages of the writing process reinforce each other. Establishing a solid motivation strengthens your sense of confidence about the project, which in turn influences how successfully you organize and write. If you start out well, using good work habits, and give yourself ample time for the various activities to coalesce, you should produce a paper that will reflect your best work, one that your audience will find both readable and useful.

THE WRITING PROCESS

Nature of the Process

As you engage in the writing process, you are doing many different things at once. While planning, you are no doubt defining the audience for your paper at the same time that you are thinking about the paper's purpose. As you draft the paper, you may organize your next sentence while revising the one you have just written. Different parts of the writing process overlap, and much of the difficulty of writing is that so many things happen at once. Through practice—in other words, through *writing*—it is possible to learn how to control those parts of the process that can in fact be controlled and to encourage those mysterious, less controllable activities.

No two people go about writing in exactly the same way. It is important for you to recognize routines—modes of thought as well as individual exercises—that help you negotiate the process successfully. It is also important to give yourself as much time as possible to complete the process. Procrastination is one of the writer's greatest enemies. It saps confidence, undermines energy, and destroys concentration. Working regularly and following a well-planned schedule as closely as possible often make the difference between a successful paper and an embarrassment.

Although the various parts of the writing process are interwoven, there is naturally a general order to the work of writing. You have to start somewhere! What follows is a description of the various stages of the writing process—*planning, drafting, revising, editing, proofreading*—along with suggestions on how to approach each most successfully.

PLANNING

Planning includes all activities that lead up to the writing of the first draft. The particular activities in this stage differ from person to person. Some writers, for instance, prefer to compile a formal outline before writing that draft. Some writers perform brief writing exercises to jump-start their imaginations. Some draw diagrams; some doodle. Later we look at a few starting strategies, and you can determine which may help you.

Now, however, let us discuss certain early choices that all writers must make during the planning stage. These choices concern *topic*, *purpose*, and *audience*, three elements that make up the *writing context*, or the terms under which we all write. Every time you write, even if you are writing a diary entry or a note to the milkman, these elements are present. You may not give conscious consideration to all of them in each piece of writing that you do, but it is extremely important to think carefully about them when writing a criminal justice paper. Some or all of these defining elements may be dictated by your assignment, yet you will always have a degree of control over them.

SELECTING A TOPIC

No matter how restrictive an assignment may seem, there is no reason to feel trapped by it. Within any assigned subject you can find a range of topics to explore. What you are looking for is a topic that engages your own interest. Let your curiosity be your guide. If, for example, you have been assigned the subject of prison reform, guide yourself to find some issue concerning prison reform that interests you. (How does inmate education—for example, taking college courses by correspondence or TV—affect recidivism? Should inmates incarcerated for violent offenses be allowed to "bulk up" by lifting weights?) Any good topic comes with a set of questions; you may well find that your interest picks up if you simply begin asking questions.

One strong recommendation: Ask your questions *on paper*. Like most other mental activities, the process of exploring your way through a topic is transformed when you write down your thoughts as they come instead of letting them fly through your mind unrecorded. Remember the old adage from Louis Agassiz: "A pen is often the best of eyes" (Pearce 1958:106).

Although it is vital to be interested in your topic, you do not have to know much about it at the outset of your investigation. In fact, having too heartfelt a commitment to a topic can be an impediment to writing about it; emotions can get in the way of objectivity. Better often to choose a topic that has piqued your interest yet remained something of a mystery to you: a topic discussed in one of your classes, perhaps, or mentioned on television or in a conversation with friends.

NARROWING A TOPIC

The task of narrowing your topic offers you a tremendous opportunity to establish a measure of control over the writing project. It is up to you to hone your topic to just the right shape and size to suit both your own interests and the requirements of the assignment. Do a good job of it, and you will go a long way toward guaranteeing yourself sufficient motivation and confidence for the tasks ahead of you. If you do not narrow your topic well, somewhere along the way you may find yourself directionless and out of energy.

Generally, the first topics that come to your mind will be too large to handle in your research paper. For example, the topic of gun control has generated a tremendous number of published news articles and reports recently by experts in the field. Despite all the attention turned toward this topic, however, there is still plenty of room for you to investigate it on a level that has real meaning to you and that does not merely recapitulate the published research. What about an analysis of how enactment of the Brady bill has affected hand gun crimes in your city?

The problem with most topics is not that they are too narrow or too completely explored, but rather that they are so rich it is difficult to choose the most useful ways to address them. Take some time to narrow your topic. Think through the possibilities that occur to you, and, as always, jot down your thoughts.

Students in an undergraduate course on criminology were told to write an essay of 2500 words on one of the following topics. Next to each general topic is an example of how students narrowed it to make a manageable paper topic.

General Topic	*Narrowed Topic*
Homicide	The effect of homicide on the black male population in the United States
Teenage crimes	The role of drug involvement in teenage crimes in the United ‣States
Prisons	Should U.S. prisons be run by the private sector?

E X E R C I S E

Narrowing Topics

Without doing research, see how you can narrow a general topic; for example,

- *General topic:*   Juvenile delinquency
- *Narrowed topics:* Labeling serious habitual offenders: harassment or public safety?

    Substance abuse and delinquent behavior

    Kids that kill: juvenile delinquents or adult murderers?

General Topics

Crime in America	Political corruption
International terrorism	Costs of incarceration
Education	Training police officers
Freedom of speech	Freedom to bear arms
Gun control	Attorney–client privileges

Finding a Thesis

As you plan your writing, be on the lookout for an idea that can serve as your *thesis*. A thesis is not a fact, which can be immediately verified by data, but an assertion worth discussing, an argument with more than one possible conclusion. Your thesis sentence will reveal to your reader not only the argument you have chosen but also your orientation toward it and the conclusion that your paper will attempt to prove.

In looking for a thesis, you are doing many jobs at once:

1. You are limiting the amount and kind of material that you must cover, thus making it manageable.
2. You are increasing your own interest in the narrowing field of study.
3. You are working to establish your paper's purpose, the *reason* why you are writing about your topic. (If the only reason you can see for writing is to earn a good grade, you probably won't!)
4. You are establishing your notion of who your audience is and what sort of approach to the subject might best catch their interest.

In short, you are gaining control over your writing context. For this reason it is a good idea to come up with a thesis early on, a *working thesis*, which will very probably change as your thinking deepens but which will allow you to establish a measure of order in the planning stage.

THE THESIS SENTENCE

The introduction of your paper will contain a sentence that expresses the task that you intend to accomplish. This *thesis sentence* communicates your main idea, the one you are going to prove, defend, or illustrate. The thesis sets up an expectation in the reader's mind which it is your job to satisfy. But in the planning stage a thesis sentence is more than just the statement that informs your reader of your goal. It is a valuable tool to help you narrow your focus and confirm in your own mind your paper's purpose.

DEVELOPING A THESIS

A class on crime and society was assigned to write a 20-page paper studying a problem currently being faced by the municipal authorities in their own city. The choice of the problem was left up to the students. One class member, Mark Gonzales, decided to investigate the problem posed to the city by the large number of abandoned buildings in a downtown neighborhood that he drove through on his way to the university. His first working thesis read as follows:

> Abandoned houses breed crime.

The problem with this thesis, as Mark found out, was that it was not an idea that could be argued but rather a fact that could easily be corroborated by the sources he began to consult. As Mark read reports from such sources as the Urban Land Institute and the City Planning Commission and talked with representatives from the Community Planning Department, he began to get interested in the dilemma his city faced in responding to the problem of abandoned buildings. Here is Mark's second working thesis:

> Removal of abandoned buildings is a major problem facing the city.

This thesis narrowed the topic somewhat and gave Mark an opportunity to use material from his research, but there was still no real comment attached to it. It still stated a bare fact, easily proved. At this point, Mark became interested in the still narrower topic of how to reduce criminal activity associated with abandoned buildings. He found that the major issue was crimes against homeless people who sleep in abandoned buildings. As Mark explored the means of reducing crimes against homeless people, he began to feel that one of them might be best for the city. Mark's third working thesis:

> Providing alternative shelter for homeless people reduces crime associated with abandoned buildings.

Note how this thesis narrows the focus of Mark's paper even further than the other two while also presenting an arguable hypothesis. It tells Mark what he has to do in his paper, just as it tells his reader what to expect.

At some time during your preliminary thinking on a topic, you should consult the library to see how much published work has already been done. This search is beneficial in at least two ways:

1. It acquaints you with a body of writing that will become very important in the research phase of the paper.
2. It gives you a sense of how your topic is generally addressed by the community of scholars you are joining. Is the topic as important as you think it is? Has there already been so much research on the topic as to make your inquiry, in its present formulation, irrelevant?

As you go about determining your topic, remember that one goal of criminal justice writing in college is to enhance your own understanding of the social and social–psychological process, to build an accurate model of the way that social institutions work. Let this goal help you to aim your research into those areas that you know are important to your knowledge of the discipline.

DEFINING A PURPOSE

There are many ways to classify the purposes of writing, but in general most writing is undertaken either to inform or to persuade an audience. The goal of informative or *expository writing* is, simply, to impart information about a particular subject, while the aim of *persuasive writing* is to convince your reader of your point of view on an issue. The distinction between expository and persuasive writing is not hard and fast, and most criminal justice writing has elements of both types. Most effective writing, however, is clearly focused on either exposition or persuasion. When you begin writing, consciously select a primary approach of exposition or persuasion and then set out to achieve that goal.

Suppose you have been required to write a paper explaining how perceptions of danger affect the volume of traffic violations. If you are writing an expository paper, your task could be to describe in as coherent and impartial a way as possible people's perceptions of danger when driving automobiles. If, however, your paper attempts to convince your reader that perceptions of a lack of danger often result in increasesd traffic violations, you are now writing to persuade, and your strategy is radically different. You will now need to explain the negative effects of certain perceptions. Persuasive writing seeks to influence the opinions of its audience toward its subject.

Know what you want to say. By the time of your final draft, you must have a very sound notion of the point you wish to argue. If, as you write that final draft, someone were to ask you to state your thesis, you should be able to give a satisfactory answer with a minimum of delay and no prompting. If, on the other hand, you have to hedge your answer because you cannot easily express your thesis, you may not yet be ready to write a final draft.

Watch out for bias! There is no such thing as pure objectivity. You are not a machine. No matter how hard you may try to produce an objective paper, the fact is that every choice you make as you write is influenced to some extent by your personal beliefs and opinions. What you tell your readers is *truth*, in other words, is influenced, sometimes without your knowing, by a multitude of factors: your environment, upbringing, and education; your attitude toward your audience; your political affiliation; your race and gender; your career goals; and your ambitions for the paper you are writing. The influence of such factors can be very subtle, and it is something you must

---

EXERCISE

Knowing What You Want to Say

Two writers have been asked to state the theses of their papers. Which of the writers better understands the writing task?

- *Writer 1:* "My paper is about police–community relations."
- *Writer 2:* "My paper argues that improving communication between the police and citizens in the community raises morale among police officers and helps people take greater responsibility for important issues within the community."

The second writer has a clear view of her task. The first knows what her topic is—police–community relations—but may not yet know what it is about these relations that fosters important changes within the community. It may be that you will have to write a rough draft or two or engage in various prewriting activities in order to arrive at a secure understanding of your task.

---

work to identify in your own writing as well as in the writing of others in order not to mislead or be misled. Remember that one of the reasons for writing is *self-discovery*. The writing you will do in criminal justice classes—as well as the writing you will do for the rest of your life—will give you a chance to discover and confront honestly your own views on your subjects. Responsible writers keep an eye on their own biases and are honest about them with their readers.

Defining Your Audience

In any class that requires you to write, it may sometimes be difficult to remember that the point of your writing is not simply to jump through the technical hoops imposed by the assignment. The point is *communication*, the transmission of your knowledge and your conclusions to the reader in a way that suits you. Your task is to pass to your reader the spark of your own enthusiasm for your topic. Readers who were indifferent to your topic should look at it in a new way after reading your paper. This is the great challenge of writing: to enter into your reader's mind and leave behind both new knowledge and new questions.

It is tempting to think that most writing problems would be solved if the writer could view the writing as if it had been produced by another person. The discrepancy between the understanding of the writer and that of the audience is the single greatest impediment to accurate communication. To overcome this barrier, you must consider your audience's needs. By the time you begin drafting, most if not all of your ideas will have begun to attain coherent shape in your mind, so that virtually any words in which you try to phrase those ideas will reflect your thought accurately—*to you*. Your readers, however, do not already hold the conclusions that you have so painstakingly achieved. If you omit from your writing the material that is necessary to complete your readers' understanding of your argument, they may well not be able to supply that information themselves.

The potential for misunderstanding is present for any audience, whether it is made up of general readers, experts in the field, or your professor, who is reading, in part, to see how well you have mastered the constraints that govern the relationship between writer and reader. Make your presentation as complete as possible, bearing in mind your audience's knowledge of your topic.

Invention Strategies

We have discussed various methods of selecting and narrowing the topic of a paper. As your focus on a specific topic sharpens, you will naturally begin to think about the kinds of information that will go into the paper. In the case of papers not requiring formal research, that material comes largely from your own recollections. Indeed, one of the reasons instructors assign such papers is to convince you of the incredible richness of your memory, the vastness and variety of the "database" you have accumulated and which, moment by moment, you continue to build.

So vast is your horde of information that it is sometimes difficult to find within it the material that would best suit your paper. In other words, finding out what you already know about a topic is not always easy. *Invention*, a term borrowed from classical rhetoric, refers to the task of discovering, or recovering from memory, such information. As we write, we go through some sort of invention procedure that helps us explore our topic. Some writers seem to have little problem coming up with material; others need more help. Over the centuries writers have devised different exercises that can help locate useful material housed in memory. We shall look at a few of these briefly.

FREEWRITING

Freewriting is an activity that forces you to get something down on paper. There is no waiting around for inspiration. Instead, you set yourself a time limit—perhaps 3 or 5 minutes—and write for that length of time *without stopping*, not even to lift the pen from the paper or your hands from the keyboard. Focus on the topic, and don't let the difficulty of finding relevant material stop you from writing. If necessary, you may begin by writing, over and over, some seemingly useless phrase, such as, "I cannot think of anything to write about," or perhaps the name of your topic. Eventually, something else will occur to you. (It is surprising how long a 3-minute freewriting can seem to last!) At the end of the freewriting, look over what you have produced for anything of use. Much of the writing will be unusable, but there may be an insight or two that you did not know you possessed.

In addition to its ability to help you recover from your memory usable material for your paper, freewriting has certain other benefits. First, it takes little time to do, which means that you may repeat the exercise as often as you like within a relatively short span of time. Second, it breaks down some of the resistance that stands between you and the act of writing. There is no initial struggle to find something to say; you just *write*.

E X E R C I S E

Freewriting

The teacher in Shelby Johnson's second-year family as a social institution class assigned Shelby a paper to write focusing on some aspect of family life in the United States. Shelby, who felt that her understanding of the family as an institution was slight, tried to get her mind started on the job of finding a topic that interested her with a 2-minute freewriting. Thinking about the family and child development, Shelby wrote steadily for 3 minutes without lifting her pen from the paper. Here is the result of her freewriting:

> Family family family family family family family what do I know? My family—father mother sister. Joely. Parents Mom and Dad. Carole and Don. Child development. My development. Okay okay okay okay okay. Both parents were present all my life. Both worked. Professionals. Dad at the school, Mom at the office. Sometimes we wished Mom was at home. The bedtimes she missed, Joely griping and that night she cried. That old empty feeling. Emptinesssssss. The way the air conditioner sounded when the house was quiet. That might be interesting: working parents, the effects on kids. A personal view. Two-paycheck families. Necessary nowadays—why not before? What's happened to make two jobs necessary? No. Back up. Go back to life in two-income family. I like it. Where to start. I could interview Mom. Get recent statistics on two-paycheck families. Where???? Ask in library tomorrow.

BRAINSTORMING

Brainstorming is simply making a list of ideas about a topic. It can be done quickly and at first without any need to order items into a coherent pattern. The point is to write down everything that occurs to you quickly and as briefly as possible, using individual words or short phrases. Once you have a good-sized list of items, you can then group the items according to relationships that you see among them. Brainstorming thus allows you to uncover both ideas stored in your memory and useful associations among those ideas.

ASKING QUESTIONS

It is always possible to ask most or all of the questions on page 17 about any topic: *Who? What? When? Where? Why? How?* These questions force you to approach the topic as a journalist does, setting it within different perspectives that can then be compared.

MAINTAINING FLEXIBILITY

As you engage in invention strategies, you are also doing other work. You are still narrowing your topic, for example, as well as making decisions that will affect your choice

EXERCISE

Brainstorming

A professor in a criminal justice class asked her students to write a 700-word paper in the form of a letter to be translated and published in a Warsaw newspaper, giving Polish readers useful advice about living in a democracy. One student, Chelsea Blake, started thinking about the assignment by brainstorming. First, she simply wrote down anything that occurred to her:

Voting rights	Welfare	Freedom of the press
Protest movements	Everybody equal	Minorities
Racial prejudice	The American Dream	Injustice
The individual	No job security	Lobbyists and PACs
Justice takes time	Psychological factors	Aristocracy of wealth
Size of bureaucracy	Market economy	Many choices

Thinking through her list, Chelsea decided to rearrange it into two lists, one devoted to positive aspects of life in a democracy, the other to negative aspects. At this point she decided to discard some items that were redundant or did not seem to have much potential. As you can see, Chelsea had some questions about where some of her items would fit.

POSITIVE	NEGATIVE
Voting rights	Aristocracy of wealth
Freedom of the press	Justice takes time
Everybody equal	Racial prejudice
The American Dream	Welfare
Psychological factors	Lobbyists and PACs
Protest movements (positive?)	Size of bureaucracy

At this point, Chelsea decided that her topic would be the ways in which money and special interests affect a democratically elected government. Which items on her lists would be relevant to Chelsea's paper?

of tone or audience. You are moving forward on all fronts, with each decision you make affecting the others. This means that you must be flexible to allow for slight adjustments in your understanding of the paper's development and of your goal.

ASKING QUESTIONS

For a class in the criminal justice of law, a professor asked her class to write a paper describing the impact of Supreme Court clerks on the decision-making process. One student developed the following questions as he began to think about a thesis:

- *Who* are the Supreme Court's clerks? (How old? What racial and gender mix are they? What are their politics?)
- *What* are their qualifications for the job?
- *What* exactly is their job?
- *When* during the court term are they most influential?
- *Where* do they come from? (Is any geographical pattern discernible in the way they are chosen? Any pattern regarding religion? Do certain law schools contribute a significantly greater number of clerks than any others?)
- *How* are they chosen? (Are they appointed? elected?)
- *When* in their careers do they serve?
- *Why* are they chosen as they are?
- *Who* have been some influential court clerks? (Have any gone on to sit on the bench themselves?)

Can you think of other questions that would make for useful inquiry?

Never be so determined to prove a particular theory that you fail to notice when your own understanding of it changes. *Stay objective.*

Organizing Your Writing

A paper that has all the facts but gives them to the reader in an ineffective order will confuse rather than inform or persuade. Although there are various methods of grouping ideas, none is potentially more effective than *outlining*. Unfortunately, no organizing process is more often misunderstood.

OUTLINING FOR YOURSELF

Outlining can do two jobs. First, it can force you, the writer, to gain a better understanding of your ideas by arranging them according to their interrelationships. There is one primary rule of outlining: Ideas of equal weight are placed on the same level within the outline. This rule requires you to determine the relative importance of

EXERCISE

Organizing Thoughts

Garcia, a student in a second-year criminal justice class, researched the impact of a worker-retraining program in his state and came up with the following facts and theories. Number them in logical order.

_____ A growing number of workers in the state do not possess the basic skills and education demanded by employers.

_____ The number of dislocated workers in the state increased from 21,000 in 1982 to 32,000 in 1992.

_____ A public policy to retrain uneducated workers would allow them to move into new and expanding sectors of the state economy.

_____ Investment in high technology would allow the state's employers to remain competitive in the production of goods and services in both domestic and foreign markets.

_____ The economy is becoming more global and more competitive.

your ideas. You have to decide which ideas are of the same type or order and into which subtopic each idea best fits.

If, in the planning stage, you carefully arrange your ideas in a coherent outline, your grasp of your topic will be greatly enhanced. You will have linked your ideas together logically and given a basic structure to the body of the paper. This sort of subordinating and coordinating activity is difficult, however, and as a result, inexperienced writers sometimes begin to write their first draft without an effective outline, hoping for the best. This hope is usually unfulfilled, especially in complex papers involving research.

OUTLINING FOR YOUR READER

The second job an outline can perform is to serve as a reader's blueprint to the paper, summarizing its points and their interrelationships. A busy person can quickly get a sense of your paper's goal and the argument you have used to promote it by consulting your outline. The clarity and coherence of the outline helps to determine how much attention your audience will give to your ideas.

While neither the American Psychological Association (APA) nor the American Sociological Association (ASA) in their style guides formally require the inclusion of an outline with a paper submitted for publication to a professional journal, both the *Publication Manual of the American Psychological Association* (4th ed., 1994:90–93) and the *ASA Style Guide* (1996:19–20) advocate the use of organizational headings, based on formal outline patterning, within the paper's text. Indeed, such a useful tool is a formal outline that your criminal justice instructor may require you to submit one. A look at the model presented in other chapters of this book will show you how strictly these formal outlines are structured. But while you must pay close attention to the requirements of the accompanying outline, do not forget how powerful a tool an outline can be in the early planning stages of your paper.

FORMAL OUTLINE PATTERN

Following this pattern accurately during the planning stage of your paper helps to guarantee that your ideas are placed logically:

Thesis sentence (prefaces the organized outline)

    I. First main idea
        A. First subordinate idea
            1. Reason, example, or illustration
            2. Reason, example, or illustration
                a. Detail supporting reason 2
                b. Detail supporting reason 2
                c. Detail supporting reason 2
        B. Second subordinate idea
    II. Second main idea

Notice that each level of the paper must have more than one entry; for every A there must be at least a B (and if required, a C, D, etc.), for every 1 there must be a 2. This arrangement forces you to compare ideas, looking carefully at each to determine its place among the others. The insistence on assigning relative values to your ideas is what makes your outline an effective organizing tool.

THE PATTERNS OF CRIMINAL JUSTICE PAPERS

The structure of any particular type of criminal justice paper is governed by a formal pattern. When rigid external controls are placed on their writing, some writers tend to feel stifled, their creativity impeded by this kind of "paint-by-numbers" approach to structure. It is vital to the success of your paper that you never allow yourself to be overwhelmed by the pattern rules for any type of paper. Remember that such controls exist not to limit your creativity but to make the paper immediately and easily useful to its intended audience. It is as necessary to write clearly and confidently in a case study or a policy analysis paper as in a term paper for English literature, a résumé, a short story, or a job application letter.

Drafting

THE ROUGH DRAFT

The planning stage of the writing process is followed by the writing of the first draft. Using your thesis and outline as direction markers, you must now weave your amalgam of ideas, researched data, and persuasion strategies into logically ordered sentences and paragraphs. Although adequate prewriting may facilitate the drafting, it still will not be easy. Writers establish their own individual methods of encouraging themselves to forge ahead with the draft, but here are some tips to bear in mind.

1. Remember that this is a *rough draft*, not the final paper. At this stage it is not necessary that every word be the best possible. Do not put that sort of pressure on yourself. You must not allow anything to slow you down now. Writing is not like sculpting in stone, where every chip is permanent; you can always go back to your draft later and add, delete, reword, or rearrange. *No matter how much effort you have put into planning, you cannot be sure how much of this first draft you will eventually keep.* It may take several drafts to get one that you find satisfactory.

2. Give yourself sufficient time to write. Don't delay the first draft by telling yourself that there is still more research to do. You cannot uncover all the material there is to know on a particular subject, so don't fool yourself into trying. Remember that writing is a process of discovery. You may have to begin writing before you can see exactly what sort of final research you need to do. Keep in mind that there are other tasks waiting for you after the first draft is finished, so allow for them as you determine your writing schedule. It is also very important to give yourself time to write, because the more time that passes after you have written a draft, the better your ability to view it objectively. It is very difficult to evaluate your writing accurately soon after you complete it. You need to cool down, to recover from the effort of putting all those words together. The "colder" you get on your writing, the better able you are to read it as if it were written by someone else and thus acknowledge the changes you will need to make to strengthen the paper.

3. Stay sharp. Keep in mind the plan you created for yourself as you narrowed your topic, composed a thesis sentence, and outlined the material. But if you begin to feel a strong need to change the plan a bit, do not be afraid to do so. Be ready for surprises dealt you by your own growing understanding of your topic. Your goal is to record your best thinking on the subject as accurately as possible.

LANGUAGE CHOICES

To be convincing, your writing needs to be *authoritative*. That is, you have to sound as if you have confidence in your ability to convey your ideas in words. Sentences that sound stilted or that suffer from weak phrasing or the use of clichés are not going to win supporters for the positions that you express in your paper. So a major question becomes: How can I sound confident? Following are some points to consider as you work to convey to your reader that necessary sense of authority.

LEVEL OF FORMALITY.   Tone is one of the primary methods by which you signal to readers who you are and what your attitude is toward them and your topic. Your major decision is which level of language formality is most appropriate to your audience.

The informal tone you would use in a letter to a friend might well be out of place in a paper on police corruption written for your criminal justice professor. Remember that tone is only part of the overall decision that you make about how to present your information. Formality is, to some extent, a function of individual word choices and phrasing. Is it appropriate to use contractions such as *isn't* or *they'll*? Would the strategic use of a sentence fragment for effect be out of place? The use of informal language, the personal *I*, and the second person *you* is traditionally forbidden—for better or worse—in certain kinds of writing. Often part of the challenge of writing a formal paper is simply how to give your prose bite while staying within the conventions.

JARGON. One way to lose readers quickly is to overwhelm them with jargon—phrases that have a special, usually technical meaning within your discipline but which are unfamiliar to the average reader. The occasional use of jargon may add an effective touch of atmosphere, but anything more than that will severely dampen a reader's enthusiasm for the paper. Often, a writer uses jargon in an effort to impress the reader by sounding lofty or knowledgeable. Unfortunately, all jargon usually does is cause confusion. In fact, the use of jargon indicates a writer's lack of connection to the audience.

Criminal justice writing is a haven for jargon. Perhaps writers of professional journals and certain policy analysis papers believe their readers are all completely attuned to their terminology. It may be that these writers occasionally hope to obscure damaging information or potentially unpopular ideas in confusing language. In other cases the problem could simply be unclear thinking by the writer. Whatever the reason, the fact is that criminal justice papers too often sound like prose made by machines to be read by machines.

Students may feel that, to be accepted as criminal justice professionals, their papers should conform to the practices of their published peers. *This is a mistake.* Remember that it is never better to write a cluttered or confusing sentence than a clear one, and that burying your ideas in jargon defeats the effort that you went through to form them.

CLICHÉS. In the heat of composition, as you are looking for words to help you form your ideas, it is sometimes easy to plug in a cliché—a phrase that has attained universal recognition by overuse.

EXERCISE

Revising Jargon

What words in the following sentence, from a published article in a journal, are jargon? Can you rewrite the sentence to clarify its meaning?

The implementation of statute-mandated regulated inputs exceeds the conceptualization of the administrative technicians.

Note: Clichés differ from jargon in that clichés are part of the general public's everyday language, whereas jargon is specific to the language of experts in a particular field.) Our vocabularies are brimming with clichés:

- It's *raining cats and dogs*.
- That issue is *dead as a doornail*.
- It's time for the governor to *face the music*.
- Angry voters *made a beeline* for the ballot box.

The problem with clichés is that they are virtually meaningless. Once vivid means of expression, they have lost their impact through overuse, and they tend to bleed energy and color from the surrounding words. When revising, replace clichés with wording that conveys your point more accurately.

DESCRIPTIVE LANGUAGE

Language that appeals to the readers' senses will always engage their interest more fully than language that is abstract. This is especially important for writing in disciplines that tend to deal in abstracts, such as criminal justice. The typical criminal justice paper, with its discussions of abstract principles, demographics, or deterministic outcomes, is usually in danger of floating off into abstraction, with each paragraph drifting farther away from the felt life of the readers. Whenever appropriate, appeal to your readers' sense of sight, hearing, taste, touch, or smell.

BIAS-FREE AND GENDER-NEUTRAL WRITING

Language can be a very powerful method of either reinforcing or destroying cultural stereotypes. By treating the sexes in subtly different ways in your language, you may unknowingly be committing an act of discrimination. A common example is the use of the pronoun *he* to refer to a person whose gender has not been identified. But there are many other writing situations in which sexist and/or ethnic bias may appear. To avoid gender bias, the *American Sociological Association Style Guide* (1996) recommends replacing words like *man*, *men*, or *mankind* with *person*, *people*, or *humankind*. When

---

EXERCISE

Using Descriptive Language

Which of the following two sentences is more effective?

1. The housing project had deteriorated since the last inspection.
2. Since the last inspection, deterioration of the housing project had become evident in stench rising from the plumbing, grime on the walls and floors, and the sound of rats scurrying in the hallways.

both sexes must be referred to in a sentence, use *he or she, her or him,* or *his or hers* instead of *he/she, him/her,* or *his/hers.*

Some writers, faced with this dilemma, alternate the use of male and female personal pronouns; others use the plural to avoid the need to use a pronoun of either gender:

- *Sexist:*   A lawyer should always treat his client with respect.
- *Nonsexist:* A lawyer should always treat his or her client with respect.
- *Nonsexist:* Lawyers should always treat their clients with respect.
- *Sexist:*   Man is a political animal.
- *Nonsexist:* People are political animals.

Remember that language is more than the mere vehicle of your thought. Your words shape perceptions for your readers. How *well* you say something will profoundly affect your readers' response to *what* you say. Sexist language denies to a large number of your readers the basic right to fair and equal treatment. Be aware of this subtle form of discrimination.

Revising

Revising is one of the most important steps in assuring the success of your essay. Unpracticed writers often think of revision as little more than making sure that all the *i*'s are dotted and *t*'s are crossed, but it is much more than that. Revising is *re-seeing* the essay, looking at it from other perspectives, trying always to align your view with the one that will be held by your audience. Research indicates that we are actually revising all the time, in every phrase of the writing process, as we reread phrases, rethink the placement of a item in an outline, or test a new topic sentence for a paragraph. Subjecting your entire hard-fought draft to cold, objective scrutiny is one of the toughest activities to master, but it is absolutely necessary. You must make sure that you have said everything that needs to be said clearly and in logical order. One confusing passage and the reader's attention is deflected from where you want it to be. Suddenly the reader has to become a detective, trying to figure out why you wrote what you did and what you meant by it. You do not want to throw such obstacles in the path of understanding.

Here are some tips to help you with revision.

1. *Give yourself adequate time for revision.* As discussed above, to analyze a paper objectively, you need time to become "cold" on the paper. After you have written your draft, spend some time away from it. Try to come back to it as if it had been written by someone else.

2. *Read the paper carefully.* This is tougher than it sounds. One good strategy is to read it aloud or to have a friend read it aloud while you listen. (Note, however, that friends are usually not the best critics. They are rarely trained in revision techniques and are often unwilling to risk disappointing you by giving your paper a really thorough examination.)

3. *Have a list of specific items to check.* It is important to revise in an orderly fashion, in stages, looking first at large concerns, such as the overall structure, and then rereading for problems with smaller elements such as paragraph organization or sentence structure.

4. *Check for unity*, the clear and logical relation of all parts of the essay to its thesis. Make sure that every paragraph relates well to the whole of the paper and is in the right place.

5. *Check for coherence.* Make sure that there are no gaps between the various parts of the argument. Look to see that you have adequate *transition* everywhere it is needed. Transitional elements are markers indicating places where the paper's focus or attitude changes. Transitional elements can be one word long—*however, although, unfortunately, luckily*—or as long as a sentence or a paragraph: *To appreciate fully the importance of democracy as a shaping presence in post–cold war Polish politics, it is necessary to examine briefly the Poles' last historical attempt to implement democratic government.*

Transitional elements rarely introduce new material. Instead, they are direction pointers, either indicating a shift to new subject matter or signaling how the writer wishes certain material to be interpreted by the reader. Because you, the writer, already know where and why your paper changes direction and how you want particular passages to be received, it can be very difficult for you to catch those places in your paper where transition is needed.

6. *Avoid unnecessary repetition.* Two types of repetition that can annoy a reader: repetition of content and repetition of wording.

Repetition of content occurs when you return to a subject that you have already discussed. Ideally, you should deal with a topic *once*, memorably, and then move on to your next topic. Organizing a paper is a difficult task, however, that usually occurs through a process of enlightenment in terms of purposes and strategies, and repetition of content can happen even if you have used prewriting strategies. What is worse, it can be difficult for you to be aware of the repetition in your own writing. As you write and revise, remember that any unnecessary repetition of content in your final draft is potentially annoying to your readers, who are working to make sense of the argument they are reading and do not want to be distracted by a passage repeating material they have already encountered. You must train yourself, through practice, to look for material that you have repeated unnecessarily.

Repetition of wording occurs when you overuse certain phrases or words. This can make your prose sound choppy and uninspired, as the following examples demonstrate:

- The subcommittee's report on prison reform will surprise a number of people. A number of people will want copies of the report.
- The chairman said at a press conference that he is happy with the report. He will circulate it to the local news agencies in the morning. He will also make sure that the city council has copies.
- I became upset when I heard how the committee had voted. I called the chairman and expressed my reservations about the committee's decision. I told him I felt that he had let the teachers and students of the state down. I also issued a press statement.

The last passage illustrates a condition known by composition teachers as the *I-syndrome*. Can you hear how such duplicated phrasing can hurt a paper? Your language should sound fresh and energetic. Before you submit your final draft, make sure to read through your paper carefully, looking for such repetition.

Not all repetition is bad. You may wish to repeat a phrase for rhetorical effect or special emphasis: *I came. I saw. I conquered.* Just make sure that any repetition in your paper is intentional, placed there to produce a specific effect.

Editing

Editing is sometimes confused with the more involved process of revising. But editing happens later, after you have wrestled through your first draft—and maybe your second and third—and arrived at the final draft. Even though your draft now contains all the information you want to impart and has arranged the information to your satisfaction, there are still many factors to check, such as sentence structure, spelling, and punctuation. It is at this point that an unpracticed writer might be less than vigilant. After all, most of the work on the paper is finished; the big jobs of discovering material and organizing and drafting it have been completed. But watch out! Editing is as important as any other job in the writing process. Any error that you allow in the final draft will count against you in the mind of the reader. It may not seem fair, but a minor error—a misspelling or the confusing placement of a comma—will make a much greater impression on your reader than perhaps it should. Remember that everything about your paper is *your* responsibility, including getting even the supposedly little jobs right. Careless editing undermines the effectiveness of your paper. It would be a shame if all the hard work you put into prewriting, drafting, and revising were to be damaged because you carelessly allowed a comma splice!

Most of the tips given above for revising hold for editing as well. It is best to edit in stages, looking for only one or two kinds of errors each time you reread the paper. Focus especially on errors that you remember committing in the past. If, for instance, you know you have a tendency to misplace commas, go through your paper looking at each comma carefully. If you have a weakness for writing unintentional sentence fragments, read each sentence aloud to make sure that it is indeed a complete sentence. Have you accidentally shifted verb tenses anywhere, moving from past to present tense for no reason? Do all the subjects in your sentences agree in number with their verbs? Now is the time to find out.

Watch out for *miscues*—problems with a sentence that the writer simply does not see. Remember that your search for errors is hampered in two ways:

1. As the writer, you hope *not* to find any errors with your writing. This desire not to find mistakes can cause you to miss sighting them when they occur.
2. Since you know your material so well, it is easy as you read to supply a missing word or piece of punctuation *unconsciously*, as if it is present.

How difficult is it to see that something is missing in the following sentence:

Unfortunately, legislators often have too little regard their constituents.

We can even guess that the missing word is probably *for*, which should be inserted after *regard*. It is quite possible, however, that the writer of the sentence would automatically supply the missing *for*, as if it were on the page. This is a miscue, which can be hard for writers to spot because they are so close to their material.

One tactic for catching mistakes in sentence structure is to read the sentences aloud, starting with the last one in the paper and then moving to the next to last, then the previous sentence, thus going backward through the paper (reading each sentence in the normal, left-to-right manner, of course) until you reach the first sentence of the introduction. This backward progression strips each sentence of its rhetorical context and helps you to focus on its internal structure.

Editing is the stage where you finally answer those minor questions that you put off earlier when you were wrestling with wording and organization. Any ambiguities regarding the use of abbreviations, italics, numerals, capital letters, titles (When do you capitalize the title "president," for example?), hyphens, dashes (usually created on a typewriter or computer by striking the hyphen key twice), apostrophes, and quotation marks have to be cleared up now. You must also check to see that you have used the required formats for footnotes, endnotes, margins, and page numbers.

Guessing is not allowed. Sometimes unpracticed writers who realize that they don't quite understand a particular rule of grammar, punctuation, or format do nothing to fill that knowledge gap. Instead, they rely on guesswork and their own logic—which is not always up to the task of dealing with so contrary a language as English—to get them through problems that they could solve if they had only referred to a writing manual. Remember that it does not matter to the reader why or how an error shows up in your writing. It only matters that you have dropped your guard. You must not allow a careless error to undo the good work that you have done.

Proofreading

Before you hand in your final version of the paper, it is vital that you check it over one more time to make sure that there are no errors of any sort. This job is called *proofreading* or *proofing*. In essence, you are looking for many of the same things you checked for during editing, but now you are doing it on the last draft, which is about to be submitted to your audience. Proofreading is as important as editing; you may have missed an error that you still have time to find, or an error may have been introduced when the draft was recopied or typed for the last time. Like every other stage of the writing process, proofreading is your responsibility.

At this point, you must check for typing mistakes: transposed or deleted letters, words, phrases, or punctuation. If you have had the paper professionally typed, you still must check it carefully. Do not rely solely on the typist's proofreading. If you are creating your paper on a computer or a word processor, it is possible to unintentionally insert a command that alters your document drastically by slicing out a word, line, or sentence at the touch of a key. Make sure that such accidental deletions have not occurred.

Above all else, remember that your paper represents you. It is a product of your best thinking, your most energetic and imaginative response to a writing challenge. If you have maintained your enthusiasm for the project and worked through the various stages of the writing process honestly and carefully, you should produce a paper that you can be proud of and one that will serve its readers well.

CHAPTER 2

Writing Competently

GUIDELINES FOR THE COMPETENT WRITER

Good writing places your thoughts in your readers' minds in exactly the way you want them to be there. It tells your readers just what you want them to know without telling them anything you do not wish to say. That may sound odd, but the fact is that writers have to be careful not to let unwanted messages slip into their writing. Look, for example, at the passage in below, taken from a paper analyzing the impact of a worker-retraining program in the writer's state. Hidden within the prose is a message that jeopardizes the paper's success. Can you detect the message?

> Recent articles written on the subject of dislocated workers have had little to say about the particular problems dealt with in this paper. Since few of these articles focus on the problem at the local level.

Chances are that when you reached the end of the second "sentence," you felt that something was missing and perceived a gap in logic or coherence, so you went back through both sentences to find the place where things had gone wrong. The second sentence is actually not a sentence at all. It does have certain features of a sentence—a subject, for example (*few*), and a verb (*focus*)—but its first word (*Since*) subordinates the entire clause that follows, taking away its ability to stand on its own as a complete idea. The second "sentence," which is properly called a *subordinate clause*, merely fills in some information about the first sentence, telling us why recent articles about dislocated workers fail to deal with problems discussed in the present paper.

The sort of error represented by the second "sentence" is commonly called a *sentence fragment*, and it conveys a message to the reader that no writer wants to send: that the writer either is careless or—worse—has not mastered the language. Language errors such as fragments, misplaced commas, or shifts in verb tense send out warnings in readers' minds. As a result, readers lose a little of their concentration on the issue being discussed. They become distracted and begin to wonder about the language competency of the writer. The writing loses effectiveness.

NOTE: Whatever goal you set for your paper, whether you want it to persuade, describe, analyze, or speculate, you must also set another goal: to *display language competence*. If your paper does not meet this goal, it will not completely achieve its other aims. Language errors spread doubt like a virus; they jeopardize all the hard work you have done on your paper.

Credibility in the job market depends upon language competence. Anyone who doubts this should remember the beating that Vice President Dan Quayle took in the press for misspelling the word *potato* at a spelling bee in 1992. His error caused a storm of humiliating publicity for the hapless Quayle, adding to an impression of general incompetence.

Correctness is relative. Although they may seem minor, the sort of language errors we are discussing—often called *surface errors*—can be extremely damaging in certain kinds of writing. Surface errors come in a variety of types, including misspellings, punctuation problems, grammar errors, and the inconsistent use of abbreviations, capitalization, or numerals. These errors are an affront to your reader's notion of correctness, and therein lies one of the biggest problems with surface errors. Different audiences tolerate different levels of correctness. You know that you can get away with surface errors in, say, a letter to a friend, who will not judge you harshly for them, while those same errors in a job application letter might eliminate you from consideration for the job. Correctness depends to an extent upon context.

Another problem is that the rules governing correctness shift over time. What would have been an error to your grandmother's generation—the splitting of an infinitive, for example, or the ending of a sentence with a preposition—is taken in stride today by most readers. So how do you write correctly when the rules shift from person to person and over time? Here are some tips.

Consider Your Audience

One of the great risks of writing is that even the simplest of choices regarding wording or punctuation can sometimes prejudice your audience against you in ways that may seem unfair. For example, look again at the old grammar rule forbidding the splitting of infinitives. After decades of counseling students to *never* split an infinitive (something this sentence has just done), composition experts now concede that a split infinitive is not a grammar crime. But suppose you have written a position paper trying to convince your city council of the need to hire security personnel for the library, and half of the council members—the people you wish to convince—remember their eighth-grade grammar teacher's outdated warning about splitting infinitives. How will they respond when you tell them, in your introduction, that librarians are compelled "to always accompany" visitors to the rare book room because of the threat of vandalism? How much of their attention have you suddenly lost because of their automatic recollection of what is now a nonrule? It is possible, in other words, to write correctly and still offend your readers' notions of language competence.

Make sure that you tailor the surface features and the degree of formality of your writing to the level of competency that your readers require. When in doubt, take a conservative approach. Your audience might be just as distracted by contractions as by a split infinitive.

Aim for Consistency

When dealing with a language question for which there are different answers, such as whether or not to place a comma after the second item in a series of three ("The mayor's speech addressed taxes, housing for the poor, and the job situation"), always use the same strategy. If, for example, you avoid splitting one infinitive, avoid splitting all infinitives in your paper.

Have Confidence in What You Already Know about Writing!

It is easy for unpracticed writers to allow their occasional mistakes to shake their confidence in their writing ability. The fact is, however, most of what we know about writing is correct. We are all capable, for example, of writing grammatically sound phrases, even if we cannot list the rules by which we achieve coherence. Most writers who worry about their chronic errors have fewer than they think. Becoming distressed about errors makes writing more difficult.

Grammar

As various composition theorists have pointed out, the word *grammar* has several definitions. One meaning is "the formal patterns in which words must be arranged in order to convey meaning." We learn these patterns very early in life and use them spontaneously without thinking about them. Our understanding of grammatical patterns is extremely sophisticated, despite the fact that few of us can actually cite the rules by which the patterns work. Patrick Hartwell tested grammar learning by asking native English speakers of different ages and levels of education, including high school teachers, to arrange these words in natural order:

French   the   young   girls   four

Everyone could produce the natural order for this phrase: "the four young French girls." Yet none of Hartwell's respondents said they knew the rule that governs the order of the words (Hartwell 1985:111).

Eliminate Chronic Errors

But if just thinking about our errors has a negative effect on our writing, how do we learn to write more correctly? Perhaps the best answer is simply to write as often as possible. Give yourself practice in putting your thoughts into written shape—and get lots of practice in revising and proofing your work. As you write and revise, be honest with yourself—and patient. Chronic errors are like bad habits; getting rid of them takes time.

You probably know of one or two problem areas in your writing that you could have eliminated but have not. Instead, you have "fudged" your writing at the critical points, relying upon half-remembered formulas from past English classes or trying to come up with logical solutions to your writing problems. (*Warning:* The English language does not always work in a way that seems logical.) You may simply have decided that comma rules are unlearnable or that you will never understand the difference between the verbs *lay* and *lie*. So you guess, and come up with the wrong answer a good part of the time. What a shame, when just a little extra work would give you mastery over those few gaps in your understanding and boost your confidence as well.

Instead of continuing with this sort of guesswork and living with the gaps in your knowledge, why not face the problem areas now and learn the rules that have heretofore escaped you? What follows is a discussion of those surface features of writing where errors most commonly occur. You will probably be familiar with most if not all of the rules discussed, but there may well be a few you have not yet mastered. Now is the time to do so.

PUNCTUATION

Apostrophes

An apostrophe is used to show possession; when you wish to say that something belongs to someone or to something, you add either an apostrophe and an *s* or an apostrophe alone to the word that represents the owner.

When the owner is *singular* (a single person or thing), the apostrophe precedes an added *s*:

- According to Mr. Pederson's secretary, the board meeting has been canceled.
- The school's management team reduced crime problems last year.
- Somebody's briefcase was left in the classroom.

The same rule applies if the word showing possession is a plural that does not end in *s*:

- The women's club provided screening services for at-risk youth and their families.
- Professor Logan has proven himself a tireless worker for children's rights.

When the word expressing ownership is a *plural* ending in *s*, the apostrophe follows the *s*:

- The new procedure was discussed at the youth workers' conference.

There are two ways to form the possessive for two or more nouns:

1. To show joint possession (both nouns owning the same thing or things), the last noun in the series is possessive:

   • Billy and Richard's first draft was completed yesterday.

2. To indicate that each noun owns an item or items individually, each noun must show possession:

   • Professor Wynn's and Professor Camacho's speeches took different approaches to the same problem.

The apostrophe is important, an obvious statement when you consider the difference in meaning between the following two sentences:

1. Be sure to pick up the psychiatrist's things on your way to the airport.
2. Be sure to pick up the psychiatrists' things on your way to the airport.

In the first of these sentences, you have only one psychiatrist to worry about, while in the second, you have at least two!

Capitalization

WHEN TO CAPITALIZE

Here is a brief summary of some hard-to-remember capitalization rules.

1. You may, if you choose, capitalize the first letter of the first word in a sentence that follows a colon, but you do not have to do so. Make sure, however, that you use one pattern consistently throughout your paper:

   a. Our instructions are explicit: Do not allow anyone into the conference without an identification badge.
   b. Our instructions are explicit: do not allow anyone into the conference without an identification badge.

2. Capitalize *proper nouns* (nouns naming specific people, places, or things) and *proper adjectives* (adjectives made from proper nouns). A common noun following the proper adjective is usually not capitalized, nor is a common adjective preceding the proper adjective (such as *a*, *an*, or *the*):

Proper Nouns	*Proper Adjectives*
England	English sociologists
Iraq	the Iraqi educator
Shakespeare	a Shakespearean tragedy

Proper nouns include:

• *Names of monuments and buildings:* the Washington Monument, the Empire State Building, the Library of Congress
• *Historical events, eras, and certain terms concerning calendar dates:* the Civil War, the Dark Ages, Monday, December, Columbus Day
• *Parts of the country:* North, Southwest, Eastern Seaboard, the West Coast, New England.

NOTE: When words like *north*, *south*, *east*, *west*, and *northwest* are used to designate direction rather than geographical region, they are not capitalized: "We drove *east* to Boston and then made a tour of the *East Coast*."

- *Words referring to race, religion, or nationality:* Islam, Muslim, Caucasian, White (or white), Oriental, Negro, Black (or black), Slavic, Arab, Jewish, Hebrew, Buddhism, Buddhists, Southern Baptists, the Bible, the Koran, American
- *Names of languages:* English, Chinese, Latin, Sanskrit
- *Titles of corporations, institutions, businesses, universities, organizations:* Dow Chemical, General Motors, the National Endowment for the Humanities, University of Tennessee, Colby College, Kiwanis Club, American Association of Retired Persons, the Oklahoma State Senate

NOTE: Some words once considered proper nouns or adjectives have, over time, become common, such as: *french fries, pasteurized milk, arabic numerals, italics*.

3. Titles of individuals may be capitalized if they precede a proper name; otherwise, titles are usually not capitalized.

- The committee honored Dean Furmanski.
- The committee honored the deans from the other colleges.
- We phoned Doctor MacKay, who arrived shortly afterward.
- We phoned the doctor, who arrived shortly afterward.
- A story on Queen Elizabeth's health appeared in yesterday's paper.
- A story on the queen's health appeared in yesterday's paper.
- Pope John Paul's visit to Colorado was a public relations success.
- The pope's visit to Colorado was a public relations success.

WHEN NOT TO CAPITALIZE

In general, you do not capitalize nouns when your reference is nonspecific. For example, you would not capitalize the phrase *the senator*, but you would capitalize *Senator Smith*. The second reference is as much a title as it is a mere term of identification, while the first reference is a mere identifier. Similarly, there is a difference in degree of specificity between the phrase *the state treasury* and *the Texas State Treasury*.

NOTE: The meaning of a term may change somewhat depending on capitalization. What, for example, might be the difference between a *Democrat* and a *democrat*? When capitalized, the word refers to a member of a specific political party; when not capitalized, it refers to someone who believes in a democratic form of government.

Capitalization depends to some extent on the context of your writing. For example, if you are writing a policy analysis for a specific corporation, you may capitalize words and phrases referring to that corporation—such as *Board of Directors, Chairman of the Board*, and *the Institute*—that would not be capitalized in a paper written for a more general audience. Similarly, in some contexts it is not unusual to see titles of certain powerful officials capitalized even when not accompanying a proper noun: The President's visit to the Oklahoma City bombing site was considered a success.

Colons

We all know certain uses for the colon. A colon can, for example, separate the parts of a statement of time (4:25 A.M.), separate chapter and verse in a biblical quotation (John 3:16), and close the salutation of a business letter (Dear Senator Keaton:). But the colon has other uses that can add an extra degree of flexibility to sentence structure.

The colon can introduce into a sentence certain kinds of material, such as a list, a quotation, or a restatement or description of material mentioned earlier:

- *List:* The committee's research proposal promised to do three things: (1) establish the extent of the problem, (2) examine several possible solutions, and (3) estimate the cost of each solution.
- *Quotation:* In his speech, the mayor challenged us with these words: "How will your council's work make a difference in the life of our city?"
- *Restatement or description:* Ahead of us, according to the senator's chief of staff, lay the biggest job of all: convincing our constituents of the plan's benefits.

Commas

The comma is perhaps the most troublesome of all marks of punctuation, no doubt because its use is governed by so many variables, such as sentence length, rhetorical emphasis, and changing notions of style. The most common problems are outlined below.

THE COMMA SPLICE

A *comma splice* is the joining of two complete sentences by only a comma:

- An impeachment is merely an indictment of a government official, actual removal usually requires a vote by a legislative body.
- An unemployed worker who has been effectively retrained is no longer an economic problem for the community, he has become an asset.
- It might be possible for the city to assess fees on the sale of real estate, however, such a move would be criticized by the community of real estate developers.

In each of these passages, two complete sentences (also called *independent clauses*) have been spliced together by a comma, which is an inadequate break between the two sentences.

One foolproof way to check your paper for comma splices is to read carefully the structures on both sides of each comma. If you find a complete sentence on each side, and if the sentence following the comma does not begin with a coordinating connective (*and, but, for, nor, or, so, yet*), you have found a comma splice.

Simply reading the draft through to try to "hear" the comma splices may not work, since the rhetorical features of your prose—its "movement"—may make it hard to detect this kind of sentence completeness error. There are five commonly used ways to correct comma splices.

1. Place a period between the two independent clauses:

    - *Incorrect:*   Physicians receive many benefits from their affiliation with clients, there are liabilities as well.

    - *Correct:*   Physicians receive many benefits from their affiliation with clients. There are liabilities as well.

2. Place a comma and a coordinating conjunction (*and, but, for, or, nor, so, yet*) between the sentences.

    - *Incorrect:*   The chairperson's speech described the major differences of opinion over the department situation, it also suggested a possible course of action.

    - *Correct:*   The chairperson's speech described the major differences of opinion over the departmental situation, and it also suggested a possible course of action.

3. Place a semicolon between the independent clauses.

    - *Incorrect:*   Some people believe that the federal government should play a large role in establishing a housing policy for the homeless, many others disagree.

    - *Correct:*   Some people believe that the federal government should play a large role in establishing a housing policy for the homeless; many others disagree.

4. Rewrite the two clauses of the comma splice as one independent clause.

    - *Incorrect:*   Television programs play a substantial part in the development of delinquent attitudes, however, they were not found to be the deciding factor in determining the behavior of juvenile delinquents.

    - *Correct:*   Television programs were found to play a substantial but not a decisive role in determining the delinquent behavior of juveniles.

5. Change one of the two independent clauses into a dependent clause by beginning it with a *subordinating word* (for example, *although, after, as, because, before, if, though, unless, when, which, where*), which prevents the clause from being able to stand on its own as a complete sentence.

- *Incorrect:*   The student meeting was held last Tuesday, there was a poor turnout.

- *Correct:*   When the student meeting was held last Tuesday, there was a poor turnout.

COMMAS IN A COMPOUND SENTENCE

A compound sentence is comprised of two or more independent clauses—two complete sentences. When these two clauses are joined by a coordinating conjunction, the conjunction should be preceded by a comma to signal the reader that another independent clause follows. (This is method 2 for fixing a comma splice described above.) When the comma is missing, the reader is not expecting to find the second half of a compound sentence and may be distracted from the text.

As the following examples indicate, the missing comma is especially a problem in longer sentences or in sentences in which other coordinating conjunctions appear. Notice how the comma sorts out the two main parts of the compound sentence, eliminating confusion.

- *Without the comma:* The senator promised to visit the hospital and investigate the problem and then he called the press conference to a close.
- *With the comma:* The senator promised to visit the hospital and investigate the problem, and then he called the press conference to a close.
- *Without the comma:* The water board can neither make policy nor enforce it nor can its members serve on auxiliary water committees.
- *With the comma:* The water board can neither make policy nor enforce it, nor can its members serve on auxiliary water committees.

An exception to this rule arises in shorter sentences, where the comma may not be necessary to make the meaning clear:

- The mayor phoned and we thanked him for his support.

However, it is never wrong to place a comma after the conjunction between the independent clauses. If you are the least bit unsure of your audience's notions about what makes for "proper" grammar, it is a good idea to take the conservative approach and use the comma:

- The mayor phoned, and we thanked him for his support.

COMMAS WITH RESTRICTIVE AND NONRESTRICTIVE ELEMENTS

A *nonrestrictive element* is part of a sentence—a word, phrase, or clause—that adds information about another element in the sentence without restricting or limiting its meaning. Although this information may be useful, the nonrestrictive element is not needed for the sentence to make sense. To signal its inessential nature, the nonrestrictive element is set off from the rest of the sentence with commas.

The failure to use commas to indicate the nonrestrictive nature of a sentence element can cause confusion. See, for example, how the presence or absence of commas affects our understanding of the following sentence:

1. The judge was talking with the policeman, who won the outstanding service award last year.

2. The judge was talking with the policeman who won the outstanding service award last year.

Can you see that the comma changes the meaning of the sentence? In the first version, the comma makes the information that follows it incidental: *The judge was talking with the policeman, who happens to have won the service award last year.* In the second version of the sentence, the information following the word *policeman* is important to the sense of the sentence; it tells us specifically *which* policeman—presumably there is more than one—the judge was addressing. Here the lack of a comma has transformed the material following the word *policeman* into a *restrictive element*, which means that it is necessary to our understanding of the sentence.

Be sure that in your paper you make a clear distinction between nonrestrictive and restrictive elements by setting off the nonrestrictive elements with commas.

COMMAS IN A SERIES

A series is any two or more items of a similar nature that appear consecutively in a sentence. The items may be individual words, phrases, or clauses. In a series of three or more items, the items are separated by commas:

- *The senator, the mayor*, and *the police chief* all attended the ceremony.
- Because of the new zoning regulations, *all trailer parks must be moved out of the neighborhood, all small businesses must apply for recertification and tax status*, and *the two local churches must repave their parking lots.*

The final comma in the series, the one before the *and*, is sometimes left out, especially in newspaper writing. This practice, however, can make for confusion, especially in longer, complicated sentences such as the second example above. Here is the way that sentence would read without the final, or *serial*, comma:

- Because of the new zoning regulations, all trailer parks must be moved out of the neighborhood, all small businesses must apply for recertification and tax status and the two local churches must repave their parking lots.

Notice that without a comma the division between the second and third items in the series is not clear. This is the sort of ambiguous structure that can cause a reader to backtrack and lose concentration. You can avoid such confusion by always using that final comma. Remember, however, that if you do decide to include it, do so *consistently*; make sure it appears in every series in your paper.

Dangling Modifiers

A *modifier* is a word or group of words used to describe, or modify, another word in the sentence. A *dangling modifier* appears either at the beginning or ending of a sentence and seems to be describing some word other than the one the writer obviously intended. The modifier therefore "dangles," disconnected from its correct meaning. It is often hard for the writer to spot a dangling modifier, but readers can—and will—find them, and the result can be disastrous for the sentence, as the following examples demonstrate:

- *Incorrect:* Flying low over Washington, the White House was seen.
- *Correct:* Flying low over Washington, we saw the White House.
- *Incorrect:* Worried at the cost of the program, sections of the bill were trimmed in committee.
- *Correct:* Worried at the cost of the program, the committee trimmed sections of the bill.
- *Incorrect:* To lobby for prison reform, a lot of effort went into the TV ads.
- *Correct:* The lobby group put a lot of effort into the TV ads advocating prison reform.
- *Incorrect:* Stunned, the television broadcast the defeated senator's concession speech.
- *Correct:* The television broadcast the stunned senator's concession speech.

Note that in the first two incorrect sentences above, the confusion is largely due to the use of *passive-voice verbs*: "the prison *was seen*," "sections of the proposal *were trimmed*." Often, although not always, a dangling modifier results from the fact that the actor in the sentence—*we* in the first sentence, *the committee* in the second—is either distanced from the modifier or obliterated by the passive-voice verb. It is a good idea to avoid passive voice unless you have a specific reason for using it.

One way to check for dangling modifiers is to examine all modifiers at the beginnings or endings of your sentences. Look especially for *to be* phrases (*to lobby*) or for words ending in *-ing* or *-ed* at the start of the modifier. Then check to see if the word being modified is always in plain sight and close enough to the phrase to be properly connected.

Parallelism

Series of two or more words, phrases, or clauses within a sentence should have the same grammatical structure, which is called *parallelism*. Parallel structures can add power and balance to your writing by creating a strong rhetorical rhythm. Here is a famous example of parallelism from the Preamble to the U.S. Constitution. (The capitalization follows that of the original eighteenth-century document. Parallel structures have been italicized.)

> We the People of the United States, in Order to *form a more perfect Union,*
> *Establish Justice, insure Domestic Tranquillity, provide for the common defence, promote*

the general Welfare, and secure the Blessings of Liberty to ourselves and our Posterity, do *ordain and establish* this Constitution for the United States of America.

There are actually two series in this sentence, the first composed of six phrases that each complete the infinitive phrase beginning with the word *to* (*to form*, *[to] Establish*, *[to] insure*, *[to] provide*, *[to] promote*, *[to] secure*), the second consisting of two verbs (*ordain* and *establish*). These parallel series appeal to our love of balance and pattern, and they give an authoritative tone to the sentence. The writer, we feel, has thought long and carefully about the matter at hand, and has taken firm control of it.

Because we find a special satisfaction in balanced structures, we are more likely to remember ideas phrased in parallelisms than in less highly ordered language. For this reason, as well as for the sense of authority and control that they suggest, parallel structures are common in well-written speeches:

> We hold these truths to be self-evident, that all men are created equal, that they are endowed by their Creator with certain unalienable Rights, that among these are Life, Liberty, and the pursuit of Happiness.

Declaration of Independence, 1776

> But, in a larger sense, we can not dedicate—we can not consecrate—we can not hallow—this ground. The brave men, living and dead, who struggled here, have consecrated it, far above our poor power to add or detract. The world will little note, nor long remember what we say here, but it can never forget what they did here.

Abraham Lincoln, Gettysburg Address, 1863

> Let us never negotiate out of fear. But never let us fear to negotiate....Ask not what your country can do for you; ask what you can do for your country.

John F. Kennedy, Inaugural Address, 1961

FAULTY PARALLELISM.   If the parallelism of a passage is not carefully maintained, the writing can seem sloppy and out of balance. Scan your writing to make sure that all series and lists have parallel structure. The following examples show how to correct faulty parallelism:

- *Incorrect:*   The mayor promises not only to reform the police department, but also *the giving of raises* to all city employees. [Connective structures such as *not only...but also*, and *both...and* introduce elements that should be parallel.]
- Correct: The mayor promises not only *to reform* the police department, but also *to give* raises to all city employees.
- Incorrect: The cost *of doing* nothing is greater than the cost *to renovate* the apartment block.
- Correct: The cost of *doing* nothing is greater than the cost *of renovating* the apartment block.

- Incorrect: Here are the items on the committee's agenda: (1) *to discuss* the new property tax, (2) *to revise* the wording of the city charter, (3) *a vote* on the city manager's request for an assistant.
- Correct: Here are the items on the committee's agenda: (1) *to discuss* the new property tax, (2) *to revise* the wording of the city charter, (3) *to vote* on the city manager's request for an assistant.

Fused (Run-on) Sentences

A *fused sentence* is one in which two or more independent clauses (passages that can stand as complete sentences) have been joined together without the aid of any suitable connecting word, phrase, or punctuation. The sentences have been run together. As you can see, there are several ways to correct a fused sentence:

- *Incorrect:* The council members were exhausted they had debated for two hours.
- *Correct:* The council members were exhausted. They had debated for two hours. [The linked independent clauses have been separated into two sentences.]
- *Correct:* The council members were exhausted; they had debated for two hours. [A semicolon marks the break between the two clauses.]
- *Correct:* The council members were exhausted, having debated for two hours. [The second independent clause has been rephrased as a dependent clause.]
- *Incorrect:* Our policy analysis impressed the committee it also convinced them to reconsider their action.
- *Correct:* Our policy analysis impressed the committee and also convinced them to reconsider their action. [The second clause has been rephrased as part of the first clause.]
- *Correct:* Our policy analysis impressed the committee, and it also convinced them to reconsider their action. [The two clauses have been separated by a comma and a coordinating word.]

Although a fused sentence is easily noticeable to the reader, it can be maddeningly difficult for the writer to catch in proofreading. Unpracticed writers tend to read through the fused spots, sometimes supplying the break that is usually heard when sentences are spoken. To check for fused sentences, read the independent clauses in your paper *carefully*, making sure that there are adequate breaks among all of them.

Pronoun Errors

ITS VERSUS *IT'S*

Do not make the mistake of trying to form the possessive of *it* in the same way that you form the possessive of most nouns. The pronoun *it* shows possession by simply adding an *s*:

- The prosecuting attorney argued the case on *its* merits.

The word *it's* is a contraction, meaning *it is*:

- *It's* the most expensive program ever launched by the prison.

What makes the *its/it's* rule so confusing is that most nouns form the singular possessive by adding an apostrophe and an *s*:

- The *jury's* verdict startled the crowd.

When proofreading, any time you come to the word *it's*, substitute the phrase *it is* while you read. If the phrase makes sense, you have used the correct form. If you have used the word *it's*:

- The newspaper article was misleading in *it's* analysis of the election.

Then read it as *it is*:

- The newspaper article was misleading in *it is* analysis of the election.

If the phrase makes no sense, substitute *its* for *it's*:

- The newspaper article was misleading in *its* analysis of the election.

VAGUE PRONOUN REFERENCE

Pronouns are words that stand in place of nouns or other pronouns that have already been mentioned in your writing. The most common pronouns include *he, she, it, they, them, those, which,* and *who*. You must make sure that there is no confusion about the word to which each pronoun refers:

- The mayor said that *he* would support our bill if the city council would also back *it*.
- The piece of legislation *that* drew the most criticism was the bill concerning housing for the poor.

The word that is replaced by the pronoun is called its *antecedent*. To check the accuracy of your pronoun references, ask yourself this question: *To what does the pronoun refer?* Then answer the question carefully, making sure that there is not more than one possible antecedent.

Consider the following example:

- Several special-interest groups decided to defeat the new health care bill. *This* became the turning point of the government's reform campaign.

To what does the word *This* refer? The immediate answer seems to be the word *bill* at the end of the preceding sentence. It is more likely that the writer was referring to the attempt of the special-interest groups to defeat the bill, but there is no word in the first sentence that refers specifically to this action. The reference is unclear. One way to clarify the reference is to change the beginning of the second sentence:

- Several special-interest groups decided to defeat the new health care bill. *Their attack on the bill* became the turning point of the government's reform campaign.

Here is another example:

- When John F. Kennedy appointed his brother Robert to the position of U.S. Attorney General, *he* had little idea how widespread the corruption in the Teamsters Union was.

To whom does the word *he* refer? It is unclear whether the writer is referring to John or to Robert Kennedy. One way to clarify the reference is simply to repeat the antecedent instead of using a pronoun:

- When President John F. Kennedy appointed his brother Robert to the position of U.S. Attorney General, *Robert* had little idea how widespread the corruption in the Teamsters Union was.

PRONOUN AGREEMENT

Remember that a pronoun must agree with its antecedent in both gender and number, as the following examples demonstrate:

- Mayor Smith said that *he* appreciated our club's support in the election.
- One reporter asked the senator what *she* would do if the President offered *her* a cabinet post.
- Having listened to our case, the judge decided to rule on *it* within the week.
- Engineers working on the housing project said *they* were pleased with the renovation so far.

The following words, however, can become troublesome antecedents. They may look like plural pronouns but are actually singular:

Anyone	Each	Either	Everybody	Everyone
Nobody	No one	Somebody	Someone	

A pronoun referring to one of these words in a sentence must be singular, too.

- *Incorrect:* *Each* of the women in the support group brought *their* children.
- *Correct:* *Each* of the women in the support group brought *her* children.
- *Incorrect:* Has *everybody* received *their* ballot?
- *Correct:* Has *everybody* received *his or her* ballot? [The two gender-specific pronouns are used to avoid sexist language.]
- *Correct:* Have *all* the delegates received *their* ballots? [The singular antecedent has been changed to a plural one.]

SHIFT IN PERSON

It is important to avoid shifting among first person (*I, we*), second person (*you*), and third person (*she, he, it, one, they*) unnecessarily. Such shifts can cause confusion:

- *Incorrect:*   *Most people* [third person] who seek a job find that if *you* [second person] tell the truth during *your* interviews, *you* will gain the voters' respect.
- *Correct:*   *Most people* who seek a job find that if *they* tell the truth during *their* interviews, *they* will win the voters' respect.
- *Incorrect:*   *One* [first person] cannot tell whether *they* [third person] are cut out for public office until *they* decide to run.
- *Correct:*   *One* cannot tell whether *one* is cut out for public office until *one* decides to run.

Quotation Marks

It can be difficult to remember when to use quotation marks and where they go in relation to other marks of punctuation. When faced with these questions, unpracticed writers often try to rely on logic rather than on a rule book, but the rules do not always seem to rely on logic. The only way to make sure of your use of quotation marks is to *memorize* the rules. Luckily, there are not many.

QUOTATION MARKS AND DIRECT QUOTATIONS

Use quotation marks to enclose direct quotations that are not longer than four typed lines:

> In his farewell address to the American people, George Washington warned, "The great rule of conduct for us, in regard to foreign nations, is, in extending our commercial relations, to have with them as little political connection as possible" (U.S. Senate, 1991).

Longer quotes, called *block quotes*, are handled in different ways according to the style guide you are using. For example, the American Sociological Association's *ASA Style Guide*, which is often used by criminal justice professionals, requires that block quotes appear, in smaller type, in an indented block without quotation marks:

Sowell's position is summarized by Scott (1997):

> The constrained vision sees people as fundamentally limited in terms of their abilities to live peaceful, cooperative, public-spirited lives. People are morally limited, and therefore, although they may do a good deed, they are not to be trusted to act as they ought to toward one another. If we hear of a disaster in another part of the world, we may take a moment to feel sorry for the victims, but then we proceed with our lives as if nothing had happened. (P. 46)

In this example, the author's name and the date of publication appear within the paper's text, while the page number of the quote is given, in parentheses, following the quote. (Note that the *p* representing *page number* is capitalized when it is the first item in the parentheses.) You may, if you wish, include the author's name and date within the parentheses instead of in your text.

The block quote format in the *Publication Manual of the American Psychological Association*, another style guide often used by criminal justice professionals, requires quotations of 40 words or longer to be indented and presented without quotation marks just as the *ASA Style Guide* does, but does not require a change of type size for the quote. Also, the APA *Publication Manual* does not capitalize the *p* representing *page number* if it appears at the beginning of the parenthetical reference following the quote: (p. 46)

NOTE: Bibliographical formatting styles for both the *ASA Style Guide* and the *Publication Manual of the American Psychological Association* are given in Chapter 4. Whichever bibliographical format you use, *be consistent*.

Use single quotation marks to set off quotations within quotations:

- "I intend," said the professor, "to use in my lecture a line from Frost's poem, 'The Road Not Taken.'"

When the interior quote occurs at the end of the sentence, both single and double quotation marks are placed outside the period.

Use quotation marks to set off titles of the following:

- A short poem (one not printed as a separate volume)
- A short story
- An article or essay
- A song title
- An episode of a television or radio show

Use quotation marks to set off words or phrases used in special ways:

- *To convey irony:* The "liberal" administration has done nothing but cater to big business.
- *To set off a technical term:* To have "charisma," Weber would argue, is to possess special powers. Many believe that John F. Kennedy had great charisma.

Note that once the term is defined, it is not placed in quotation marks again.

QUOTATION MARKS IN RELATION TO OTHER PUNCTUATION

Always place commas and periods *inside* closing quotation marks:

- "My fellow Americans," said the President, "there are tough times ahead of us."

Place colons and semicolons *outside* closing quotation marks:

- In his speech on voting, the sociologist warned against "an encroaching indolence"; he was referring to the middle class.
- There are several victims of the government's campaign to "Turn Back the Clock": the homeless, the elderly, and the mentally impaired.

Use the context to determine whether to place question marks, exclamation points, and dashes inside or outside closing quotation marks. If the punctuation is part of the quotation, place it *inside* the quotation mark:

- "When will the tenure committee make up its mind?" asked the dean. The demonstrators shouted, "Free the hostages!" and "No more slavery!"

If the punctuation is not part of the quotation, place it *outside* the quotation mark:

- Which president said, "We have nothing to fear but fear itself"? [Although the quote is a complete sentence, you do not place a period after it. There can only be one piece of "terminal" punctuation, punctuation that ends a sentence.]

Semicolons

The semicolon is another little-used punctuation mark you should learn to incorporate into your writing strategy because of its many potential applications. For example, a semicolon can be used to correct a comma splice:

- *Incorrect:*   The union representatives left the meeting in good spirits, their demands were met.
- *Correct:*   The union representatives left the meeting in good spirits; their demands were met.
- *Incorrect:*   Several guests at the fund-raiser had lost their invitations, however, we were able to seat them, anyway.
- *Correct:*   Several guests at the fund-raiser had lost their invitations; however, we were able to seat them, anyway. [Conjunctive adverbs such as *however, therefore*, and *thus* are not coordinating words (such as *and, but, or, for, so, yet*) and cannot be used with a comma to link independent clauses. If the second independent clause begins with *however*, it must be preceded by either a period or a semicolon.]

As you can see from the second example above, connecting the two independent clauses with a semicolon instead of a period strengthens the relationship between the clauses.

Semicolons can also separate items in a series when the series themselves contain commas:

- The newspaper account of the rally stressed the march, which drew the biggest crowd; the mayor's speech, which drew tremendous applause; and the party afterwards in the park.

Avoid misusing semicolons. For example, use a comma, not a semicolon, to separate an independent clause from a dependent clause:

- *Incorrect:*   Students from the college volunteered to answer phones during the pledge drive; which was set up to generate money for the new arts center.
- *Correct:*   Students from the college volunteered to answer phones during the pledge drive, which was set up to generate money for the new arts center.

Do not overuse semicolons. Although they are useful, too many semicolons in your writing can distract your readers' attention. Avoid monotony by using semicolons sparingly.

Sentence Fragments

A *fragment* is a part of a sentence that is punctuated and capitalized as if it were an entire sentence. It is an especially disruptive kind of error, because it obscures the connections that the words of a sentence must make in order to complete the reader's understanding.

Students sometimes write fragments because they are concerned that a particular sentence is growing too long and needs to be shortened. Remember that cutting the length of a sentence merely by adding a period somewhere along its length often creates a fragment. When checking your writing for fragments, it is essential that you read each sentence carefully to determine whether it has (1) a complete subject and a verb, and (2) a subordinating word before the subject and verb, which makes the construction a subordinate clause rather than a complete sentence.

TYPES OF SENTENCE FRAGMENTS.   Some fragments lack a verb:

- *Incorrect:*   The chairperson of our committee, having received a letter from the mayor. [The word *having*, which can be used as a verb, is here being used as a gerund introducing a participial phrase. *Watch out* for words that look like verbs but are being used in another way.]
- *Correct:*   The chairperson of our committee received a letter from the mayor.

Some fragments lack a subject:

- *Incorrect:*   Our study shows that there is broad support for improvement in the health care system. And in the unemployment system.
- *Correct:*   Our study shows that there is broad support for improvement in the health care system and in the unemployment system.

Some fragments are subordinate clauses:

- *Incorrect:*   After the latest edition of the newspaper came out. [This clause has the two major components of a complete sentence: a subject (*edition*) and a verb (*came*). Indeed, if the first word (*After*) were deleted, the clause would be a complete sentence. But that first word is a *subordinating word*, which acts to prevent the following clause from standing on its own as a complete sentence. *Watch out* for this kind of construction. It is called a *subordinate clause*, and it is not a sentence.]

- *Correct:*   After the latest edition of the newspaper came out, the mayor's press secretary was overwhelmed with phone calls. [A common method of correcting a subordinate clause that has been punctuated as a complete sentence is to connect it to the complete sentence to which it is closest in meaning.]

- *Incorrect:*   Several congressmen asked for copies of the Vice President's position paper. Which called for reform of the Environmental Protection Agency.

- *Correct:*   Several congressmen asked for copies of the Vice President's position paper, which called for reform of the Environmental Protection Agency.

SPELLING

All of us have problems spelling certain words that we have not yet committed to memory. But most writers are not as bad at spelling as they believe themselves to be. Usually, it is a handful of words that a person finds troubling. It is important to be as sensitive as possible to your own particular spelling problems—and to keep a dictionary handy. There is no excuse for failing to check spelling.

Do not rely on your computer's spell checker. There are certain kinds of spelling errors that computers cannot catch, as the following two sentences demonstrate:

- Wilbur wood rather dye than admit that he had been their. When he cited the bare behind the would pile, he thought, "Isle just lye hear until he goes buy."

Following are a list of commonly confused words and a list of commonly misspelled words. Read through the lists, looking for words that tend to give you trouble. If you have any questions, *consult your dictionary*.

Commonly Confused Words

accept/except	bare/bear
advice/advise	brake/break
affect/effect	breath/breathe
aisle/isle	buy/by
allusion/illusion	capital/capitol
an/and	choose/chose
angel/angle	cite/sight/site
ascent/assent	complement/compliment

conscience/conscious
corps/corpse
council/counsel
dairy/diary
descent/dissent
desert/dessert
device/devise
die/dye
dominant/dominate
elicit/illicit
eminent/immanent/imminent
envelop/envelope
every day/everyday
fair/fare
formally/formerly
forth/fourth
hear/here
heard/herd
hole/whole
human/humane
its/it's
know/no
later/latter
lay/lie
lead/led
lessen/lesson
loose/lose
may be/maybe
miner/minor
moral/morale
of/off
passed/past
patience/patients

peace/piece
personal/personnel
plain/plane
precede/proceed
presence/presents
principal/principle
quiet/quite
rain/reign/rein
raise/raze
reality/realty
respectfully/respectively
reverend/reverent
right/rite/write
road/rode
scene/seen
sense/since
stationary/stationery
straight/strait
taught/taut
than/then
their/there/they're
threw/through
too/to/two
track/tract
waist/waste
waive/wave
weak/week
weather/whether
were/where
which/witch
whose/who's
your/you're

Commonly Misspelled Words

a lot
acceptable
accessible
accommodate
accompany
accustomed
acquire
against
annihilate
apparent

arguing
argument
authentic
before
begin
beginning
believe
benefited
bulletin
business

cannot	license
category	likelihood
committee	maintenance
condemn	manageable
courteous	meanness
definitely	mischievous
dependent	missile
desperate	necessary
develop	nevertheless
different	no one
disappear	noticeable
disappoint	noticing
easily	nuisance
efficient	occasion
environment	occasionally
equipped	occurred
exceed	occurrences
exercise	omission
existence	omit
experience	opinion
fascinate	opponent
finally	parallel
foresee	parole
forty	peaceable
fulfill	performance
gauge	pertain
guaranteed	practical
guard	preparation
harass	probably
hero	process
heroes	professor
humorous	prominent
hurried	pronunciation
hurriedly	psychology
hypocrite	publicly
ideally	pursue
immediately	pursuing
immense	questionnaire
incredible	realize
innocuous	receipt
intercede	received
interrupt	recession
irrelevant	recommend
irresistible	referring
irritate	religious
knowledge	remembrance

reminisce
repetition
representative
rhythm
ridiculous
roommate
satellite
scarcity
scenery
science
secede
secession
secretary
senseless
separate
sergeant
shining
significant
sincerely
skiing
stubbornness
studying
succeed

success
successfully
susceptible
suspicious
technical
temporary
tendency
therefore
tragedy
truly
tyranny
unanimous
unconscious
undoubtedly
until
vacuum
valuable
various
vegetable
visible
without
women
writing

CHAPTER 3

GETTING ST

Your fo   not, accurately or not, it
announc   ence. A well-executed format impl   t, however, proper format
brings in   s the effect of setting their
minds at   ders with your academic
competer   r criminal justice writing.
Like the s   nicates messages that are
often mo~~~~~~~~ ~~~~~~~~~~ received than the content of the document itself.
This chapter contains instructions for the following format elements:

- General page format
- Title page
- Abstract
- Executive summary/outline summary
- Table of contents
- List of tables and figures
- Text
- Headings and subheadings
- Illustrations and figures
- Referencing sources
- Appendices

There are many format styles available to the criminal justice professional and no consensus as to which is most appropriate. The majority of journals in the discipline have established their own style. A case in point is the *Justice Quarterly*, the official journal of the Academy of Criminal Justice Sciences, which requires its contributors to use a format comprised of elements from the *ASA Style Guide* (1996), published by the American Sociological Association, and the fourth edition of the *Publication Manual of the American Psychological Association* (1994). The format described in this chapter is also based on elements from these two comprehensive sources, but it is styled more for the student writer than for the professional.

When preparing a paper for submission to an accredited journal in criminal justice, you should always carefully follow that journal's guidelines for submitting manuscripts; but for now, unless you receive instructions to the contrary from your course instructor, follow the format directions in this manual exactly. Guidelines for citing and referencing sources are explained in Chapter 4.

GENERAL PAGE FORMAT DIRECTIONS

Criminal justice assignments should be typed or printed on 8½-by-11-inch premium white bond, 20 lb or heavier. Do not use any other color or size except to comply with special instructions from your instructor, and do not use off-white or poor-quality (draft) paper. A criminal justice paper that is worth the time to write and read is worth good paper.

Always submit to your instructor an original typed or computer (preferably laser)-printed manuscript. Do not submit a photocopy! Always make a second copy to keep for your own files and to keep in case the original is lost. If you are using a computer—and we highly recommend that you do—it's a good idea to keep a copy of your paper on the hard drive, another on a disk you can store in a safe place, and a hard copy of the paper in case the computer "crashes" and the disk is lost.

Margins, except for theses and dissertations, should be 1 inch from all sides of the paper. [*Note:* The *ASA Style Guide* (1996) requires margins to be no less than 1¼ inches from all sides of the paper.] Unless otherwise instructed, all paper submissions should be *double-spaced* in a 12-point word-processing font or typewriter pica type (10 cpi). Typewriter elite type may be used if other fonts or typefaces are not available. Select a font that is plain and easy to read, such as Helvetica, Courier, Garamond, or Times Roman. Do not use script, stylized, or elaborate fonts.

Page numbers should appear in the upper right-hand corner of each page, starting immediately after the title page. No page number should appear on the title page or on the first page of the text. Page numbers should appear 1 inch from the right side and ½ inch from the top of the page. (If you are using a computer or word processor, you may need to set the top margin at 0.5 inch to achieve this spacing.) Page numbers should proceed consecutively beginning with the title page (although the first number is not actually printed on the title page). You may use lowercase roman numerals (i, ii, iii, iv, v, vi, vii, viii, ix, x, etc.) for pages such as the title page, table of contents, and table of figures that precede the first page of text; but if you use them the numbers must be placed at the center of the bottom of the page.

In special cases, as when your instructor wants no pages preceding the first page of text, the title of the paper should appear 1 inch from the top of the first page, centered, followed by your name and course information. Most formats omit placing the page number on this first page of text, but some instructors may require it to be placed at the bottom center. All other page numbering should follow the guidelines above.

Do not bind your paper or enclose it within a plastic cover sheet unless instructed to do so. Place one staple in the upper left corner, or use a paper clip at the top of the paper. Note that a paper to be submitted to a journal for publication should not be clipped, stapled, or bound in any form.

TITLE PAGE

The following information should be centered on the title page:

- Title of the paper
- Name of writer
- Course name and section number
- Name of instructor
- Name of college or university
- Date

As the sample title page shows, the title should clearly describe the problem addressed in the paper. If the paper discusses juvenile recidivism in Muskogee County jails, for example, the title "Recidivism in the Muskogee County Juvenile Justice System" is professional, clear, and helpful to the reader. "Muskogee County," "Juvenile Justice," or "County Jails" are all too vague to be effective. Also, the title should not be "cute." A cute title may attract attention for a play on Broadway, but it will detract from the credibility of a paper in criminal justice. "Inadequate Solid Waste Disposal Facilities in Norman" is professional. "Down in the Dumps" is not.

ABSTRACT

An abstract is a brief summary of a paper written primarily to allow potential readers to see if the paper contains information of sufficient interest for them to read. People conducting research need specific kinds of information, and they often read dozens of abstracts looking for papers that contain information relevant to their research topic. Abstracts have the designation "Abstract" centered near the top of the page. Next is the title, also centered, followed by a paragraph that precisely states the paper's topic, research and analysis methods, and results and conclusions. The abstract itself should be written in one paragraph that does not exceed 150 words. Remember that an abstract is not an introduction but instead, a very succinct summary of your paper, as demonstrated in the sample.

A Comparison of the Theories of Deviant Behavior

of

Karl Marx and Emile Durkheim

by

Lawanda Sheffield

Criminology

Criminal Justice 4473 Section 5233

Professor Reneé Shelby

Middlebury College

May 12, 1998

Sample Title Page

EXECUTIVE SUMMARY

An executive summary, like an abstract, summarizes the content of a paper but does so in more detail. Whereas abstracts are read by people who are doing research, executive summaries are more likely to be read by people who need information in the paper in order to make a decision. Many people, however, will read the executive summary to fix clearly in mind the organization and results of a paper before reading the paper itself.

Abstract

College Students' Attitudes on Capital Punishment

A survey of college students on the topic of

capital punishment was undertaken in October of

1994 at Pueblo State University. The sample was

comprised of forty-two students in a criminal justice

research methods class. The purpose was to deter-

mine the extent to which students believe it is accept-

able for the state to take the life of individuals who

commit certain crimes. Variables tested for associa-

tion with capital punishment attitudes were age, sex,

and ethnicity. Results indicated that students tend to

favor the use of capital punishment, and that among

these students, age, sex, and ethnicity are all signifi-

cant predictors of capital punishment attitudes.

The length of the executive summary is dictated to some extent by the length of the document being summarized. For example, a 150- to 200-page grant report might be summarized in a 10- to 12-page executive summary, whereas a 25-page research paper might need only a page or two of summary. The lengthier executive summary might also contain headings and subheadings similar to those used in the actual report. By following the outline of the actual paper, the executive summary serves as a sort of summary of each of the sections in the much lengthier report.

The executive summary on page 55 summarizes a 130-page report on the second year of a *Drug Assessment Study with Juvenile Offenders in a Secure Detention Setting*. It is an example of the lengthier type of executive summary. Executive summaries of papers you write will probably be shorter.

Executive Summary

This summary of a *Drug Assessment Study* is written for practitioners who deal with drug-involved juvenile offenders repeatedly cycling through detention centers. The assessment process was initiated sometime after they were placed in detention. Two psychologists interviewed 198 youths over a six-month period and recorded the information they obtained on a specially designed "assessment" instrument. They also administered an instrument designed to measure the level of alcohol and other drug use, coupled with an unobtrusive measurement of denial and other underlying manifestations of substance abuse. The results of this study are summarized below.

One important finding had to do with interpersonal relationships. Those who used and abused alcohol and/or drugs were generally friends of users and abusers. Those who did not use and abuse these substances almost always reported much less association with those who use and abuse drugs. Young people on probation and parole for substance abuse-related offenses probably should be restrained by the court from association with those who have serious alcohol and/or drug histories.

The findings from this study support the hypothesis that where youths are distanced from the family, in terms of communication, feelings, and disorganized relationships, their chances of alcohol and/or other drug involvement increase, at times dramatically. Significant progress in helping delinquents change and adjust might be attained by a serious commitment to family therapy and family development, especially with the cooperation and insistence of the court.

There is good reason to believe that significant differences exist between white and minority families with respect to child-rearing philosophy and practice. If this is true, it may well affect alcohol and/or other drug use, attitudes towards families, school, and other areas of juvenile misbehavior. It would follow that detention treatment plans, court-ordered probation, and aftercare alternatives should be differentiated where feasible and legal to respond to minority families at the point of their needs.

Findings from this study imply that for those youths who come in contact with the juvenile justice system: (1) blacks are much less addicted than either whites or other minorities, at least in very early adolescence, (2) black parents are significantly more concerned with their children's use of alcohol and/or other drugs when compared with white parents, (3) blacks report much more emotional support from their family members, and there appears to be, at least on the surface, more dysfunctional family interaction among white families than black. Perhaps the juvenile justice system should develop neighborhood programs to provide positive support within the strong kinshp networks already in place in the black culture; early intervention could reach black children *before* they fully enter the rebellious youth culture.

There is nothing in the data to support a connection between alcohol and/or other drug use on the part of black youth and the violent offenses they tend to commit when compared with white youth. They have fewer nondangerous options for acting out behavior than whites, and their families have fewer societal-economic support systems available to them.

Older black youth from lower socioeconomic backgrounds are suscep-tible to self-enhancement through deviate activities. Court personnel might consider the realistic pressures on blacks, especially when most of these families are almost always lacking in financial resources.

While female detainees comprise only about ten percent of the detention population, they have their own set of needs that must be addressed. They manifest lower self-concept, report more family dysfunc-tion and receive much less emotional support from family. This leads to significantly higher suicide attempts. Counselors should work hard for family resolution and restoration among the female population, perhaps developing special programs that address their unique circumstances.

Educational and support groups are impacting low self-esteem and self-concept according to our *Program Evaluation*. These groups have been an excellent expenditure of grant funds. Certainly the guided group experience has the potential to enable youth to share feelings, give and receive positive feedback, and learn to feel better about themselves.

Finally, advocacy for success in school must be emphasized if delinquency and drug abuse are minimized. A positive link between the court and school systems need to be forged. Otherwise, the juvenile court becomes a dumping ground for youth who encounter difficulty in school, bring drugs on campus, and act out in a disruptive manner.

The body of literature cited in this report is fairly unified in assert-ing that common etiological roots cannot be shown between substance abuse and delinquency. Even the relationship between violent crime and substance abuse remains clouded (Inciardi 1981). A relationship between substance use and more serious delinquency appears to be developmental rather than causal (Huizinga et al. 1989). More than ever this suggests that attention should be given to the National Council of Juvenile and Family Court Judges' report, which argues from a systemic and holistic perspective (*Criminal Justice Newsletter* 1986). Drug use and abuse, child neglect, abandonment, sexual, physical and emotional abuse, family violence, family dysfunction, and juvenile delinquency are interactive variables that cannot be clearly identified, diagnosed, or treated without addressing them together.

Our study supports a vast body of literature that suggests meaningful intervention in the lives of juveniles at risk should include, whenever possible, a holistic approach. Not only must each youth be requested to take responsibility for his behavior and work toward resolution of his problems, but family members should also be called to account for their responsibility, and compelled when necessary to participate in treatment.

OUTLINE SUMMARY

An outline page is a specific style of executive summary. It clearly shows the sections into which the paper is divided and the content of the information in each section. An outline summary is an asset to busy decision makers because it allows them to understand the entire content of a paper without reading it, or to refer quickly to a specific part of the paper for more information.

TABLE OF CONTENTS

A table of contents does not provide as much information as an outline but does include the headings of the major sections and subsections of a paper. Tables of contents are not normally required in student papers or papers presented at professional meetings,

Outline Summary

I. *The problem* is that picnic and rest room facilities at Hafer Community Park have deteriorated.

    A. Only one major renovation has occurred since 1967, when the park was opened.

    B. The Park Department estimates that repairs would cost about $33,700.

II. Three possible solutions have been given extensive consideration.

    A. One option is to do nothing. Area residents will use the park less as deterioration continues.

    B. The first alternative solution is to make all repairs immediately, which will require a total of $33,700.

    C. A second alternative is to make repairs according to a priority list over a five-year period.

III. The recommendation of this report is that alternative C be adopted by the city council. The benefit/cost analysis demonstrates that residents will be satisfied if basic improvements are made immediately.

but may be included. (The *ASA Style Guide* does not require a table of contents for manuscripts submitted for publication consideration.) Tables of contents are normally required, however, in books, theses, and dissertations. The table of contents should consist of the chapter or main section titles, the headings used in the text, with one additional level of titles, along with their page numbers, as the accompanying example demonstrates.

LISTS OF TABLES AND FIGURES

A list of tables or list of figures contains the titles of the tables or figures included in the paper in the order in which they appear, along with their page numbers. You

Table of Contents

may list tables, illustrations, and figures together under the title "Figures" (and call them all "Figures" in the text), or, if you have a list with more than a half-page of entries, you may have separate lists of tables, figures, and illustrations (and title them accordingly in the text). The format for all such tables should follow the accompanying example.

TEXT

Ask your instructor for the number of pages required for the paper you are writing. The text should follow the directions explained in Chapters 1 and 2 and should conform to the format of the accompanying facsimile page.

HEADINGS AND SUBHEADINGS

Generally, three heading levels should meet your organizational needs when writing criminal justice papers:

1. *Primary headings* should be centered and printed in all capital letters.

There is some evidence that the idea "you can never be too rich or too thin" (Rockett and McMinn 1990:278) has been taken to heart by many American women. Of 33,000 females responding to a survey published in *Glamour* (1984:200) magazine, when asked what would make them happy, 42 percent marked losing weight as their first choice. Interestingly, in addition to overweight females, women of normal weight marked this response most often, as did many underweight women.

Dissatisfaction with body often translates into dissatisfaction with self (Freedman, 1984:34). It is important to investigate the factors that lead to feelings of inferiority about body in order to deal effectively with women who suffer the often painful consequences associated with this dilemma.

This paper examines the relationship between women's body image and the following variables: (1) age, (2) self-esteem, (3) locus of control, (4) body weight, (5) opinion of ideal female body weight, and (6) opinion of the male's view of ideal female body weight.

2. *Secondary headings* should be centered on the page and italicized, with only the first letter in each word capitalized, excluding articles, prepositions, and conjunctions.

3. *Tertiary headings* should be indented and lead into the paragraph. They should be italicized and followed by a colon. The text should follow.

The example on page 63 has three heading levels that follow the guidelines described above.

TABLES

Tables are used in the text to show relationships among data to help the reader come to a conclusion or understand a certain point. Tables that show simple results or "raw" data should be placed in an appendix. Tables should not reiterate the content of the text. They should say something new, and they should stand on their own. That is, the

```
                          RESULTS

                 Alcohol and/or Other Drugs

         Risk Factors: Characteristics of risk can be found in...
```

Sample: Three Levels of Headings

reader should be able to understand the table without reading the text. Clearly label the columns and rows in each table. Each word in the title (except articles, prepositions, and conjunctions) should be capitalized. The source of the information should be shown immediately below the table, not in a footnote or end note. See the sample table.

ILLUSTRATIONS AND FIGURES

Illustrations are not normally inserted in the text of a criminal justice paper, and they are not included even in the appendix unless they are necessary to explain the material in the text. If illustrations are necessary, do not paste or tape photocopies of photographs or similar materials to the text or the appendix. Instead, photocopy each one on a separate sheet of paper and center it, along with its typed title, within the normal margins of the paper. The format of the illustration titles should be the same as that for tables and figures.

TABLE 1   Population Change in Ten U.S. Cities, 1980–1986

City	1986 Rank	1980 Population	1986 Population	Percentage Change, 1980 to 1986
New York	1	7,071,639	7,262,700	2.7
Los Angeles	2	2,968,528	3,259,300	9.8
Chicago	3	3,005,072	3,009,530	.2
Houston	4	1,611,382	1,728,910	7.3
Philadelphia	5	1,688,210	1,642,900	-2.3
Detroit	6	1,203,369	1,086,220	-9.7
San Diego	7	875,538	1,015,190	16.0
Dallas	8	904,599	1,003,520	10.9
San Antonio	9	810,353	914,350	12.8
Phoenix	10	790,183	894,070	13.1

Source: U.S. Bureau of the Census, 1988, *County and City Data Book*.

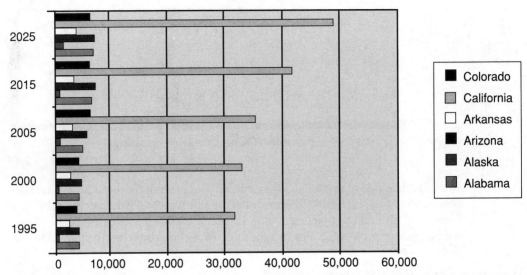

Projections of the Total Population of Selected States: 1995 to 2025 (all population figures in thousands)

Source: U.S. Census Data.

Figures in the form of charts and graphs may be very helpful in presenting certain types of information, as the accompanying example demonstrates.

REFERENCE PAGES

In Chapter 4 we discuss and give models of two standard citation systems for referencing the sources cited in your paper: the ASA style and the APA style.

APPENDICES

Appendices are reference materials for the convenience of the reader at the back of the paper, after the text. Providing information that supplements the important facts contained in the text, they may include maps, charts, tables, and selected documents. Do not include in an appendix materials that are merely interesting or decorative. Include only items that will answer questions raised by the text or that are necessary to explain the text. Follow the format guidelines for illustrations, tables, and figures when adding material in an appendix. At the top center of the page, label your first appendix "Appendix A," your second appendix "Appendix B," and so on. Do not append an entire government report, journal article, or other publication, only the portions of such documents that are necessary to support your paper. The source of the information should always be evident on the appended pages. An example of an appendix follows.

Appendix A
Projections of the Total Population of States: 1995 to 2025
(all population figures in thousands)

State	1995	2000	2005	2015	2025
Alabama	4,253	4,451	4,631	4,956	5,224
Alaska	604	653	700	791	885
Arizona	4,218	4,798	5,230	5,808	6,412
Arkansas	2,484	2,631	2,750	2,922	3,055
California	31,589	32,521	34,441	41,373	49,285
Colorado	3,747	4,168	4,468	4,833	5,188
Connecticut	3,275	3,284	3,317	3,506	3,739
Delaware	717	768	800	832	861
District of Columbia	554	523	529	594	655
Florida	14,166	15,233	16,279	18,497	20,710
Georgia	7,201	7,875	8,413	9,200	9,869
Hawaii	1,187	1,257	1,342	1,553	1,812
Idaho	1,163	1,347	1,480	1,622	1,739
Illinois	11,830	12,051	12,266	12,808	13,440
Indiana	5,803	6,045	6,215	6,404	6,546
Iowa	2,842	2,900	2,941	2,994	3,040
Kansas	2,565	2,668	2,761	2,939	3,108
Kentucky	3,860	3,995	4,098	4,231	4,314
Louisiana	4,342	4,425	4,535	4,840	5,133
Maine	1,241	1,259	1,285	1,362	1,423
Maryland	5,042	5,275	5,467	5,862	6,274
Massachusetts	6,074	6,199	6,310	6,574	6,902
Michigan	9,549	9,679	9,763	9,917	10,078
Minnesota	4,610	4,830	5,005	5,283	5,510
Mississippi	2,697	2,816	2,908	3,035	3,142
Missouri	5,324	5,540	5,718	6,005	6,250
Montana	870	950	1,006	1,069	1,121
Nebraska	1,637	1,705	1,761	1,850	1,930
Nevada	1,530	1,871	2,070	2,179	2,312
New Hampshire	1,148	1,224	1,281	1,372	1,439
New Jersey	7,945	8,178	8,392	8,924	9,558
New Mexico	1,685	1,860	2,016	2,300	2,612
New York	18,136	18,146	18,250	18,916	19,830
North Carolina	7,195	7,777	8,227	8,840	9,349

Appendix A
Projections of the Total Population of States: 1995 to 2025
(all population figures in thousands)
(cont'd)

State	1995	2000	2005	2015	2025
North Dakota	641	662	677	704	729
Ohio	11,151	11,319	11,428	11,588	11,744
Oklahoma	3,278	3,373	3,491	3,789	4,057
Oregon	3,141	3,397	3,613	3,992	4,349
Pennsylvania	12,072	12,202	12,281	12,449	12,683
Rhode Island	990	998	1,012	1,070	1,141
South Carolina	3,673	3,858	4,033	4,369	4,645
South Dakota	729	777	810	840	866
Tennessee	5,256	5,657	5,966	6,365	6,665
Texas	18,724	20,119	21,487	24,280	27,183
Utah	1,951	2,207	2,411	2,670	2,883
Vermont	585	617	638	662	678
Virginia	6,618	6,997	7,324	7,921	8,466
Washington	5,431	5,858	6,258	7,058	7,808
West Virginia	1,828	1,841	1,849	1,851	1,845
Wisconsin	5,123	5,326	5,479	5,693	5,867
Wyoming	480	525	568	641	694

Source: U.S. Bureau of the Census.

CHAPTER 4

Citing Sources

PRELIMINARY DECISIONS

One of your most important jobs as a research writer is to document your use of source material carefully and clearly. Failure to do so will cause your reader confusion, damage the effectiveness of your paper, and perhaps make you vulnerable to a charge of plagiarism. Proper documentation is more than just good form. It is a powerful indicator of your own commitment to scholarship and the sense of authority that you bring to your writing. Good documentation demonstrates your expertise as a researcher and increases your reader's trust in you and your work.

Unfortunately, as anybody who has ever written a research paper knows, getting the documentation right can be a frustrating, confusing job, especially for the novice writer. Positioning each element of a single reference citation accurately can require what seems an inordinate amount of time spent thumbing through the style manual. Even before you begin to work on specific citations, there are important questions of style and format to answer.

What to Document

Direct quotes must always be credited, as must certain kinds of paraphrased material. Information that is basic—important dates, facts, or opinions universally acknowledged—need not be cited. Information that is not widely known, whether fact or opinion, should receive documentation.

What if you are unsure whether or not a certain fact is widely known? You are, after all, very probably a newcomer to the field in which you are conducting your research. If in doubt, supply the documentation. It is better to overdocument than to fail to do justice to a source.

The Choice of Style

Although the question of which documentation style to use may be decided for you in some classes by your instructor, others may allow you a choice. Several styles are available, each designed to meet the needs of writers in particular fields. As mentioned earlier, many journals within the field of criminal justice establish their own documentation styles. Perhaps the two styles most widely accepted within the discipline are those of the American Sociological Association, published in the *ASA Style Guide* (1996), and the American Psychological Association (APA), published in the fourth edition of the *Publication Manual of the American Psychological Association* (1994). In this chapter we describe both styles in sufficient detail for you to use either one.

The chapter also includes for your consideration the Student Citation System (SCS), which has been developed for use in all undergraduate college classes, regardless of discipline. The advantage of the SCS is that it may be used in any college class (English, physics, psychology, criminal justice, political science, journalism, economics, etc.) in which it is permitted by the instructor. In addition, it is a simple system with few rules. It is easy to type, and its punctuation is familiar to students who use the Internet. You will find the SCS described at the conclusion of the sections below, which describe, respectively, the ASA and the APA citation systems.

Read through the following pages before trying to use them to structure your notes. Unpracticed student researchers tend to ignore the documentation section of their style manual until the moment the first note has to be worked out, and then they skim through the examples looking for the one that perfectly corresponds to the immediate case in hand. But most style manuals do not include every possible documentation model, so the writer must piece together a coherent reference out of elements from several models. Reading through all the models before using them gives you a feeling for where to find different aspects of models as well as for how the referencing system works in general.

CITING SOURCES IN ASA STYLE

The ASA Style Guide (1996) presents what is generally called an *author–date system* or alternatively a *parenthetical-reference system*. Such a system requires two components for each significant reference to a source: (1) a note placed within the text, in parentheses, near where the source material occurs, and (2) a full bibliographical reference for the source, placed in a list of references following the text and keyed to the parenthetical reference within the text. In order not to distract the reader from the argument, the parenthetical citation within the text is as brief as possible, containing just enough information to refer the reader to the full reference. As indicated by the models below, this information can be given in a number of ways.

NOTE: To provide a wider range of models than is found in the *ASA Style Guide*, the sections below are augmented by material from the fourteenth edition of the *Chicago Manual of Style*, which was used in compiling the *ASA Style Guide*. References to the *Chicago Manual of Style* in the models below are designated CMS and accompanied by the relevant section numbers. For example, the phrase "CMS (16.40)" refers to chapter 16, section 40 of the *Chicago Manual of Style* (1993).

Models of bibliographical entries that correspond to the following parenthetical text references are given in Section 4.2.2.

ASA Style: Parenthetical Reference Citations

Citations within the text should include the author's last name and the year of publication—hence the phrase *author–date* system. Subsequent citations of the same source should be identified the same way as the first.

Author's name in text; year of publication in parentheses

Freedman (1984) postulates that when individuals…

Author's name and year of publication in parentheses

…encourage more aggressive play (Perrez 1979).

Note that when it appears at the end of a sentence, the parenthetical reference is placed inside the period.

Reference including page numbers

Thomas (1961:741) builds on this scenario…

Page numbers should be included only when quoting directly from a source or referring to specific passages. The page number should follow the publication year and be preceded by a colon with no space between the colon and the page number.

Source with two authors

…establish a sense of self (Holmes and Bacon 1872:114–116).

Source with three authors. For the first citation

…found the requirements very restrictive (Mollar, Querley, and McLarry 1926).

For all subsequent citations:

…proved to be quite difficult (Mollar et al. 1926).

In the second and all subsequent references to a source with three authors, place the Latin phrase *et al.*, meaning "and others," after the name of the first author. Note that the phrase appears in roman type, not italics, and is followed by a period.

Source with more than three authors

Kinneson et al. (1933) made the following suggestion…

In all references, including the first, *et al.* should follow the name of the first author.

Two authors with the same last name

...the new budget cuts (K. Grady 1991).

...stimulate economic growth (B. Grady 1991).

Two works by the same author

George (1992, 1994) argues for...

If the two citations appear in the same note, place a comma between the publication dates of the works. If the two works were published in the same year, differentiate them by adding lowercase letters to the publication dates. Be sure to add the letters to the references in the bibliography, too.

...the city government (Estrada 1994a, 1994b).

Work with no author given.   According to the *CMS* (16.40), if the author's name is not provided within the work but you know the author's identity, you may give the name in brackets:

...cannot be held accountable ([Logan] 1994).

If you cannot ascertain the author's name, the *CMS* (16.41) suggests you begin the citation with the work's title, followed by the date of publication. Do not use the phrase *Anonymous* or *Anon.*

...a logical starting point (*Saving the Underclass* 1985).

Direct quotations.   Direct quotes of less than four lines should be placed in the text with quotation marks at the beginning and end. The citation should include the page number:

The majority of these ads promote the notion that "If you are slim, you will also be beautiful and sexually desirable" (Rockett and McMinn 1990:278).

A direct quote of four lines or more is called a *block quote*. Such a quote is presented in a separate, indented block and, when possible, in a smaller font or type:

According to Brown (1985):

There are few girls and women of any age or culture raised in white America, who do not have some manifestation of the concerns discussed here, i.e., distortion of body image, a sense of "out-of-control" in relationship to food, addiction to dieting, bingeing, or self-starvation. (P. 61)

Note that the parenthetical reference following the block quote is placed after the final period. When the page number in parentheses appears alone without the author and date, as in the example above, the "P" for "page" is capitalized.

Chapters, tables, appendices, etc.

...(Johnson 1995, chap. 6).

or

...(Blake 1985, table 4:34).

or

...(Cleary 1976, appendix C:177).

Reprints

...(Baldwin [1897] 1992) interpreted this as...

Give the earliest date of publication in brackets, followed immediately by the date of the version you have used.

More than one source in a reference

...are related (Harmatz 1987:48; Marble et al. 1986:909; Powers and Erickson 1986:48; Rackley et al. 1988:10; Thompson and Thompson 1986:1067).

Separate citations by a semicolon and order them in a manner of your choice. You may place them in alphabetical order, date order, or order of importance to your argument, but whatever order you choose, apply it consistently throughout your paper.

Unpublished materials. Use the word *forthcoming* when the source is scheduled for publication at a later time:

A study by Barkley (forthcoming) lends support...

Give the date for dissertations and other unpublished materials:

In her dissertation Albright (1989) contends...

Undated materials. Use *n.d.* (no date) in place of the date.

...except that Fox (n.d.) disagrees.

Archival sources

...declined the invitation (Wharton Archives, RPL, Box 12, June 15, 1924).

Abbreviate the parenthetical citations. The reference above refers to material dated June 15, 1924, in the Wharton Archives house in the Raleigh Public Library.

Classic texts. When citing classic texts, such as the Bible, standard translations of ancient Greek texts, or numbers of the *Federalist Papers*, you may cite the date and page numbers of the particular edition you are using. Or you may refer to these texts by using the systems by which they are subdivided. Since all editions of a classic text employ the standard subdivisions, this reference method has the advantage of allowing your reader to find the source passage in any published edition of the text. You may cite a biblical passage by referring to the particular book, chapter, and verse, all in roman type, with the translation given after the verse number:

> "But the path of the just is as the shining light, that shineth more and more unto the perfect day" (Proverbs 4:18 King James Version).

The *Federalist Papers* may be cited by their standard numbers:

> Madison addresses the problem of factions in a republic (Federalist 10).

Newspapers.   According to the *CMS* (16.117), references to material in daily newspapers should be handled within the syntax of your sentence:

> In an August 10, 1993, editorial, the *New York Times* painted the new regime in glowing colors.
>
> An article entitled "Abuse in Metropolis," written by Harry Black and published in the *Daily News* on December 24, 1996, took exception to Alderman Jones's remarks.

Usually, according to the *CMS*, references to newspaper items are not included in the bibliography. If you wish to include newspaper references, however, there is a model of a bibliographical entry in the next section of this chapter.

Public documents.   The *CMS* (15.322–15.411 and 16.148–16.179) gives detailed information on how to create parenthetical references for public documents published at the national, state, county, or city government level, as well as documents published by foreign governments.

Congressional journals.   Parenthetical text references to either the *Senate Journal* or the *House Journal* start with the journal title in place of the author, the session year, and if applicable, the page:

> ...as reworded by Senator Edward's committee (*Senate Journal* 1993, 24).

Congressional debates.   Congressional debates are printed in the daily issues of the *Congressional Record*, which are bound biweekly and then collected and bound at the end of the session. Whenever possible, you should consult the bound yearly collection instead of the biweekly compilations. Your parenthetical reference should begin with the title *Congressional Record* (or *Cong. Rec.*) in place of the author's name and include the year of the congressional session, the volume and part of the *Congressional Record*, and finally, the page:

> ...addressed the question of funding for secondary education (*Cong. Rec.* 1930, 72, pt.8:9012).

Congressional reports and documents.   References to these reports and documents, which are numbered sequentially in one- or two-year periods, include the
name of the body generating the material, the year, and the page:

> …to answer the charges against him next week (U.S. House 1993, 12).

NOTE: Any reference that begins with *U.S. Senate* or *U.S. House* may omit the *U.S.* if it
is clear from the context that you are referring to the United States. Whichever form you
use, be sure to use it *consistently*, in both the parenthetical notes and the bibliography.

Bills and resolutions.   According to the *CMS* (15.347–15.348), bills and resolutions, which are published in pamphlets called "slip bills," on microfiche, and in the
Congressional Record, are not always given a parenthetical text reference and a corresponding bibliography entry. Instead, the pertinent reference information appears in
the syntax of the sentence. If, however, you wish to cite such information in a text reference, the form depends on the source from which you took your information.
    When citing to a slip bill:

> …cannot reject visa requests out of hand (U.S. Senate 1996).

> …cannot reject visa requests out of hand (*Visa Formalization Act of 1996*).

You may cite either the body that authored the bill or the title of the work itself.
Whichever method you choose, remember to begin your bibliography entry with the
same material.
    When citing to the *Congressional Record*:

> … cannot reject visa requests out of hand (U.S. Senate 1996, S7658).

The number following the date and preceded by an *S* (for Senate; *H* for House) is the
page in the *Congressional Record*.

Laws.   As with bills and resolutions, laws (also called *statutes*) are not necessarily
given a parenthetical text reference and a bibliography entry. Instead, the identifying
material is included in the text. If you wish to make a formal reference for a statute,
you must structure it according to the place where you found the law published.
Initially published separately in pamphlets as slip laws, statutes are eventually collected
and incorporated, first into a set of volumes called *U.S. Statutes at Large* and later into
the *United States Code*, a multivolume set that is revised every six years. You should use
the latest publication.
    When citing to a slip law, you should either use *U.S. Public Law*, in roman type,
and the number of the piece of legislation, or the title of the law:

> …be rebound in library cloth (U.S. Public Law 678, 16–17).

> …be rebound in library cloth (*Library of Congress Book Preservation Act of 1997*,
> 16–17).

When citing to the *Statutes at Large*, include the page number after the year:

> …be rebound in library cloth (*Statutes at Large* 1997, 466).

When citing to the *United States Code*:

> ...be rebound in library cloth (*Library of Congress Book Preservation Act of 1997*, *U.S. Code*. Vol. 38, Sec. 1562).

United States Constitution.   According to the *CMS* (15.367), references to the U.S. Constitution include the number of the article or amendment, the section number, and the clause, if necessary:

> ...to convene or to dismiss Congress (U.S. Constitution, art. 3, sec. 3).

It is not necessary to include the Constitution in the bibliography.

Executive department documents.   A reference to a report, bulletin, circular, or any other type of material issued by the executive department starts with the name of the agency issuing the document, although you may use the name of the author, if known:

> ...businesses flee downtown areas for the suburbs (Department of Labor 1984, 334).

Legal references.

Supreme Court.   As with laws, court decisions are rarely given their own parenthetical text reference and bibliography entry, but are instead identified in the text. If you wish to use a formal reference, however, you may place within the parentheses the title of the case, in italics, followed by the source (for cases after 1875 this is the *United States Supreme Court Reports*, abbreviated *U.S.*), which is preceded by the volume number and followed by the page number. You should end the first reference to the case that appears in your paper with the date of the case in brackets. You need not include the date in subsequent references:

> ...which she failed to meet (*State of Nevada v. Goldie Warren* 324 U.S. 123 [1969]).

Before 1875, Supreme Court decisions were published under the names of official court reporters. The reference below is to William Cranch, *Reports of Cases Argued and Adjudged in the Supreme Court of the United States, 1801–1815*, 9 vols. (Washington, DC, 1804–1817). The number preceding the clerk's name is the volume number; the last number is the page:

> ...as famous a case as *Marbury v. Madison*, in 1803 (1 Cranch 137).

For most of these parenthetical references, it is possible to move some or all of the material outside the parentheses simply by incorporating it in the text:

> In 1969, in *State of Nevada v. Goldie Warren* (324 U.S. 123), the judge ruled that...

Lower courts.   Decisions of lower federal courts are published in the *Federal Reporter*. The note should give the volume of the *Federal Reporter* (*F.*), the series if it is other than the first (*2d*, in the model below), the page, and in brackets, an abbreviated reference to the specific court (the example below is to the Second Circuit Court) and the year:

> ...in certain types of personal injury lawsuits (*United States v. Sizemore*, 183 F. 2d 201 [2d Cir. 1950]).

Publications of government commissions.   According to the *CMS* (15.368), references to bulletins, circulars, reports, and study papers that are issued by various government commissions should include the name of the commission, the date of the document, and the page:

> ...to the new tax law (Securities and Exchange Commission 1985, 57).

Corporate authors.   Because government documents are often credited to a corporate author with a lengthy name, you may devise an acronym or a shortened form of the name and indicate in your first reference to the source that this name will be used in later citations:

> ...a rise in the inflation rate (*Bulletin of Labor Statistics* 1997, 1954; *hereafter BLS*).

The practice of using a shortened name in subsequent references to any corporate author, whether a public or private organization, is sanctioned in most journals, including the *American Business Review*, and approved in the *CMS* (15.252). Thus, if you refer often to the *U.N. Monthly Bulletin of Statistics*, you may, after giving the publication's full name in the first reference, use a shortened form of the title—perhaps an acronym such as *UNMBS*—in all later cites.

Publications of state and local governments.   According to the *CMS* (15.377), references to state and local government documents are similar to those for the corresponding national government sources:

> ...served as a deterrent to crime (Oklahoma Legislature 1995, 24).

The *CMS* (16.178) restricts bibliographical information concerning state laws or municipal ordinances to the running text.

Interviews.   According to the *CMS* (16.127, 16.130), citations to interviews, in the author–date system, should be handled by references within the text, in the syntax of a sentence, rather than in parentheses.
For published interviews:

> In a March 1997 interview with Councilwoman Barnes, Jennifer Witson asked questions that seemed to upset and disorient the former mayor.

For published or broadcast interviews, no parenthetical reference is necessary because there has been sufficient information given for the reader to find the complete citation, which in the example above will be alphabetized under Witson's name in the bibliography.

For unpublished interviews:

> In an interview with the author on April 23, 1993, Dr. Kennedy expressed her disappointment with the new court ruling.

If you are citing material from an interview that you conducted, you should identify yourself as the author and give the date of the interview.

ASA Style: References

Parenthetical citations in the text point the reader to the fuller source descriptions at the end of the paper known as the references, or bibliography. This reference list, which always directly follows the text under the heading *References*, is arranged alphabetically according to the first element in each citation. As with most alphabetically arranged bibliographies, there is a kind of reverse-indentation system: After the first line of a citation, all subsequent lines are indented five spaces. The entire references section is double-spaced.

The *ASA Style Guide* (1996) uses standard, or "headline style," capitalization for titles in the reference list. In this style, all first and last words in a title, and all other words except articles (*a, an, the*), coordinating words (*and, but, or, for, nor*), and all prepositions (*among, by, for, of, to, toward*, etc.), are capitalized.

Remember that every source cited in the text, with those exceptions noted in the examples below, must have a corresponding entry in the references section. Do not include references to any work not cited in the text of your paper.

Most of the following formats are based on those given in the *ASA Style Guide*. Formats for bibliographical situations not covered by the ASA guide are taken from the fourteenth edition of the *Chicago Manual of Style* (1993), referred to below as the *CMS*.

BOOKS

One author

> Northrup, A. K. 1997. *Living High off the Hog: Recent Pork Barrel Legislation in the Senate*. Cleveland, OH: Johnstown.

First comes the author's name, inverted, then the date of publication, followed by the title of the book, the place of publication, and the name of the publishing house. Use first names for all authors or initials if no first name is provided. Add a space after each initial, as in the example above. For place of publication, always identify the state unless the city is New York City. Use postal abbreviations to denote the state (*OK, AR*).

Periods are used to divide most of the elements in the citation, although a colon is used between the place of publication and publisher. Custom dictates that the main title of a book and its subtitle are separated by a colon, even though a colon may not appear in the title as printed on the title page of the book.

Two authors. Only the name of the first author is reversed, since it is the one by which the citation is alphabetized. Note that there is no comma between the first name of the first author and the *and* following:

> Spence, Michelle and Kelly Rudd. 1996. *Hiring and the Law*. Boston, MA: Tildale.

Three or more authors

> Moore, J. B., Jeannine Macrory, Allen Rice and Natasha Traylor. 1998. *Down on the Farm: Culture and Folkways*. Norman, OK: University of Oklahoma Press.

The use of *et al.* is not acceptable in the references section; list the names of all authors of a source. While the ASA style places commas between all names in the parenthetical text citation—(Moore, Rice, Macrory, and Traylor 1998)—it deletes the comma separating the next-to-last and last names in the bibliographical reference. Note also that the ASA does not advocate abbreviating the word *University* in the name of a press, as indicated in the model above.

Group as author. According to the *CMS* (16.52), if no specific author is named for a publication issued by a corporation or association, cite the issuing body as the author:

> National Association of Food Retailers. 1994. *Standardization Practices among New Jersey Beef Retailers*. Trenton, NJ: Arkway.

Alphabetize according to the first significant word in the group's title.

Work with no author given. Section 16.40 of the *CMS* states that if you can ascertain the name of the author when that name is not given in the work itself, you should place the author's name in brackets:

> [Morey, Cynthia]. 1977. *How We Mate: American Dating Customs, 1900–1955*. New York: Putney.

Do not use the phrase *anonymous* to designate an author whose name cannot be determined; instead, according to the *CMS* (16.41), begin your citation with the title of the book, followed by the date. You may move initial articles (*a, an, the*) to the end of the title:

> *Worst Way to Learn: The Government's War on Education, The*. 1997. San Luis Obispo, CA: Blakeside.

Editor, compiler, or translator as author. When no author is listed on the title page, begin the citation with the name of the editor, compiler, or translator:

> Trakas, Dylan, comp. 1998. *Making the Road-Ways Safe: Essays on Highway Preservation and Funding*. El Paso, TX: Del Norte.

Editor, compiler, or translator with author

> Pound, Ezra. 1953. *Literary Essays*. Edited by T. S. Eliot. New York: New Directions.
> Stomper, Jean. 1973. *Grapes and Rain*. Translated by John Picard. San Francisco, CA: Baldock.

Translated book

> Zapata, Emile M. 1948. *Beneath the Wheel: Exploitation of the Native Population in Northern Mexico, 1900–1940.* Translated by A. M. Muro. El Paso, TX: Del Norte.

Untranslated book.   If your source is in a foreign language, it is not necessary, according to the *CMS* (15.118), to translate the title into English. Use the capitalization format of the original language.

> Picon-Salas, Mariano. 1950. *De la Conquesta a la Independéncia.* Mexico D.F.: Fondo de Cultura Económica.

If you wish to provide a translation of the title, do so in brackets or parentheses following the title. Set the translation in roman type, and capitalize only the first word of the title and subtitle, proper nouns, and proper adjectives:

> Wharton, Edith. 1916. *Voyages au front* (Visits to the Front). Paris: Plon.

Two or more works by the same author.   The author's name in all citations after the first may be replaced, if you wish, by a three-em dash (six strokes of the hyphen):

> Russell, Henry. 1978. *Famous Last Words: Notable Supreme Court Cases of the Last Five Years.* New Orleans, LA: Liberty Publications.
> ———. 1988. *Great Court Battles.* Denver, CO: Axel & Myers.

Author of a foreword or introduction.   According to the *CMS* (16.51), there is no need to cite the author of a foreword or introduction in your bibliography unless you have used material from that author's contribution to the volume. In that case, the bibliography entry is listed under the name of the author of the foreword or introduction. Place the name of the author of the work itself after the title of the work:

> Farris, Carla. 1998. Foreword to *Marital Stress among the Professoriat: A Case Study,* by Basil Givan. New York: Galapagos.

The parenthetical text reference cites the name of the author of the foreword or introduction, not the author of the book:

> ...(Farris 1998)

Selection in a multiauthor collection

> Gray, Alexa North. 1998. "Foreign Policy and the Foreign Press." Pp. 188–204 in *Current Media Issues,* edited by Barbara Bonnard and Luke F. Guinness. New York: Boulanger.

The parenthetical text reference may include the page reference:

> ...(Gray 191, 195–97)

You *must* repeat the name if the author and the editor are the same person:

> Farmer, Susan A. 1995. "Tax Shelters in the New Dispensation: How to Save Your Income." Pp. 58–73 in *Making Ends Meet: Strategies for the Nineties,* edited by Susan A. Farmer. Nashville, TN: Burkette and Hyde.

Articles in encyclopedias and other reference books.
According to the *CMS* (15.293), well-known reference books such as the *Encyclopedia Britannica* or the *American Heritage Dictionary* are not given a citation in the references list. They should be credited within the running text of the paper:

> …in Ronald Gould's article on welfare in the twelfth edition of *Collier's Encyclopedia*…

Subsequent editions.
If you are using an edition of a book other than the first, you must cite the number of the edition or the status, such as *Rev. ed.* for revised edition, if there is no edition number:

> Hales, Sarah. 1994. *The Coming Water Wars*. 2d ed. Pittsburgh, PA: Blue Skies.

Multivolume work.
If you are citing a multivolume work in its entirety, use the following format:

> Graybosch, Charles. 1988–89. *The Rise of the Unions*. 3 vols. New York: Starkfield.

If you are citing only one of the volumes in a multivolume work, use the following format:

> Graybosch, Charles. 1988. *Bloody Beginnings*. Vol. 1 of *The Rise of the Unions*. New York: Starkfield.

Reprints.

> Adams, Sterling R. [1964] 1988. *How to Win an Election: Promotional Campaign Strategies*. New York: Alexander.

Classic texts.
According to the *CMS* (15.294, 15.298), references to classic texts such as sacred books and Greek verse and drama are usually confined to the text and not given citations in the bibliography.

PERIODICALS

JOURNAL ARTICLES.   Journals are periodicals, usually published either monthly or quarterly, that specialize in serious scholarly articles in a particular field.

Journal with continuous pagination.
Most journals are paginated so that each issue of a volume continues the numbering of the previous issue. The reason for such pagination is that most journals are bound in libraries as complete volumes of several issues; continuous pagination makes it easier to consult these large compilations:

> Hunzecker, Joan. 1987. "Teaching the Toadies: Cronyism in Municipal Politics." *Review of Local Politics* 4:250–262.

Note that the name of the journal, which is italicized, is followed without punctuation by the volume number, which is itself followed by a colon and the page numbers. There should be no space between the colon and the page numbers, which are *inclusive*. Do not use *p.* or *pp.* to introduce the page numbers.

Journal in which each issue is paginated separately

> Skylock, Browning. 1991. "'Fifty-Four Forty or Fight!': Sloganeering in Early
> America." *American History Digest* 28(3):25–34.

The issue number appears in parentheses immediately following the volume number.

Article published in more than one journal issue

> Crossitch, Vernelle, Lawrence K. Harpe, Charlene B. Randelle, Nathan Lanier Godey
> and Frances Bills. 1997. "Evaluating Evidence: Calibrating Ephemeral Phenomena,"
> parts 1–4. *Epiphanic Review* 15:22–29; 16:46–58; 17:48–60.

Remember to include first and last names for all authors.

Articles published in foreign-language journals

> Sczaflarski, Richard. 1986. "The Trumpeter in the Tower: Solidarity and Legend" (in
> Polish). *World Political Review* 32:79–95.

MAGAZINE ARTICLES.   Magazines, which are usually published weekly, bimonthly,
or monthly, appeal to the popular audience and generally have a wider circulation than
journals. *Newsweek* and *Scientific American* are examples of magazines.

Monthly magazine

> Stapleton, Bonnie and Ellis Peters. 1981. "How It Was: On the Trail with Og
> Mandino." *Lifetime Magazine*, April, pp. 23–24, 57–59.

Weekly or bimonthly magazine

> Bruck, Connie. 1997. "The World of Business: A Mogul's Farewell." *The New Yorker*,
> October 18, pp. 12–15.

NEWSPAPER ARTICLES

> Everett, Susan. 1996. "Beyond the Alamo: How Texans View the Past." *Carrollton
> Tribune*, February 16, D1, D4.

The article *The* is omitted from the newspaper's title.

SOURCES STORED IN ARCHIVES

> Clayton Fox Correspondence, Box 12. July–December 1903. File: Literary Figures 2.
> Letter to Edith Wharton, dated September 11.

According to the *ASA Style Guide* (1996), if you refer to a number of archival sources,
you should group them in a separate part of the references section and name it
"Archival Sources."

PUBLIC DOCUMENTS

Since the *ASA Style Guide* (1996) gives formats for only two types of government publications, the following bibliographical models are based not only on practices from the ASA guide but also on formats used in the *CMS* (15.322–15.411, 16.148–16.179).

Congressional journals. References to either the *Senate Journal* or the *House Journal* begin with the journal's title and include the years of the session, the number of the Congress and session, and the month and day of the entry:

> *U.S. Senate Journal.* 1997. 105th Cong., 1st sess., 10 December.

The ordinal numbers *second* and *third* may be represented as *d* (52d, 103d) or as *nd* and *rd*, respectively.

Congressional debates

> *Congressional Record.* 1930. 71st Cong., 2d sess. Vol. 72, pt. 8.

Congressional reports and documents

> U.S. Congress. 1997. House Subcommittee on the Study of Governmental/Public Rapport. *Report on Government Efficiency As Perceived by the Public.* 105th Cong., 2d sess., pp. 11–26.

Bills and resolutions. When citing to a slip bill:

> U.S. Senate. 1996. *Visa Formalization Act of 1996.* 105th Cong. 1st sess. S.R. 1437.

or

> *Visa Formalization Act of 1996. See* U.S. Senate. 1996.

The abbreviation *S.R.* in the first model above stands for *Senate Resolutions*, and the number following is the bill or resolution number. For references to House bills, the abbreviation is *H.R.* Notice that the second model refers the reader to the more complete entry above. The choice of formats depends on the one you used in the parenthetical text reference.

When citing to the *Congressional Record*:

> Senate. 1997. *Visa Formalization Act of 1997.* 105th Cong., 1st sess., S.R. 1437. *Congressional Record* 135, no. 137, daily ed. (10 December): S7341.

Laws. When citing to a slip law:

> U.S. Public Law 678. 105th Cong., 1st sess., 4 December 1997. *Library of Congress Book Preservation Act of 1997.*

or

> *Library of Congress Book Preservation Act of 1997.* U.S. Public Law 678. 105th Cong., 1st sess., 4 December 1997.

When citing to the *Statutes at Large*:

> *Statutes at Large*. 1998. Vol. 82, p. 466. *Library of Congress Book Preservation Act of 1997.*

or

> *Library of Congress Book Preservation Act of 1997*. Statutes at Large 82:466.

When citing to the *United States Code*:

> *Library of Congress Book Preservation Act, 1997*. U.S. Code. Vol. 38, sec. 1562.

United States Constitution.   According to the *CMS* (16.172), the Constitution is not listed in the bibliography.

Executive department documents

> Department of Labor. 1998. *Report on Urban Growth Potential Projections*. Washington, DC: GPO.

The abbreviation for the publisher in the model above, *GPO*, stands for *Government Printing Office*, which prints and distributes most government publications. According to the *CMS* (15.327), you may use any of the following formats to refer to the GPO:

> Washington, DC: U.S. Government Printing Office, 1984.
> Washington, DC: Government Printing Office, 1984.
> Washington, DC: GPO, 1984.
> Washington, 1984.
> Washington 1984.

Remember to be *consistent* in using the form you choose.

Legal references

Supreme Court.   According to the *CMS* (16.174), Supreme Court decisions are only rarely listed in bibliographies. If you do wish to include such an entry, here is a suitable format:

> *State of Nevada v. Goldie Warren*. 1969. 324 U.S. 123.

For a case prior to 1875, use the following format:

> *Marbury v. Madison*. 1803. 1 Cranch 137.

Lower courts

> *United States v. Sizemore*. 1950. 183 F. 2d 201 (2d Cir.).

Publications of government commissions

> U.S. Securities and Exchange Commission. 1984. *Annual Report of the Securities and Exchange Commission for the Fiscal Year*. Washington, DC: GPO.

Publications of state and local governments.   Remember that references for state and local government publications are modeled on those for corresponding national government documents:

> Oklahoma Legislature. 199 1. Joint Committee on Public Recreation. *Final Report to the Legislature, 1995*, Regular Session, on Youth Activities. Oklahoma City.

INTERVIEWS

According to the *CMS* (16.130), interviews need not be included in the bibliography, but if you or your instructor wants to list such entries, here are possible formats.

Published interview. **For an untitled interview in a book:**

> Jorgenson, Mary. 1998. Interview by Alan McAskill. Pp. 62–86 in *Hospice Pioneers*, edited by Alan McAskill. Richmond, VA: Dynasty Press.

For a titled interview in a periodical:

> Simon, John. 1997. "Picking the Patrons Apart: An Interview with John Simon," by Selena Fox. *Media Week*, March 14, pp. 40–54.

Interview on television

> Snopes, Edward. 1998. Interview by Kent Gordon. *Oklahoma Politicians*. WKY Television, 4 June.

Unpublished interview

> Kennedy, Melissa. 1997. Interview by author. Tape recording. Portland, ME, 23 April.

UNPUBLISHED SOURCES

Personal communications.   According to the *CMS* (16.130), references to personal communications may be handled completely in the text of the paper:

> In a letter to the author, dated 16 July 1997, Mr. Bentley admitted the organizational plan was flawed.

If, however, you wish to include a reference to an unpublished communication in the references section, you may do so using one of the following models:

> Bentley, Jacob. 1997. Letter to author, 16 July.
> Duberstein, Cindy. 1996. Telephone conversation with the author, 5 June.
> Timrod, Helen. 1997. E-mail to author, 25 April.

Theses and dissertations

> Hochenauer, Klint. 1980. "Populism and the Free Soil Movement." Ph.D. dissertation, Department of Sociology, Lamont University, Cleveland, OH.

Paper presented at a meeting

Zelazny, Kim and Ed Gilmore. 1997. "Art for Art's Sake: Funding the NEA in the Twenty-First Century." Presented at the annual meeting of the Conference of Metropolitan Arts Boards, June 15, San Francisco, CA.

Unpublished manuscripts

Borges, Rita V. 1993. "Mexican–American Border Conflicts, 1915–1970." Department of History, University of Texas at El Paso, El Paso, TX. Unpublished manuscript.

Working and discussion papers

Blaine, Emory and Ralph Cohn. 1995. "Analysis of Social Structure in Closed Urban Environments." Discussion Paper No. 312, Institute for Sociological Research, Deadwood College, Deadwood, SD.

ELECTRONIC SOURCES

ON-LINE SOURCES.   The need for a reliable on-line citation system continues to grow, but attempts to establish one are hampered by a number of factors. For one thing, there is no foolproof method of clearly reporting even such basic information as an on-line page's author(s), title, or date of establishment. Occasionally, authors identify themselves clearly; sometimes they place a link to their home page at the bottom of the site. But it is not always easy to determine exactly who authored a particular page. Similarly, it can be difficult to determine whether a Web page has its own title or exists as a subsection of a larger document with its own title. Perhaps the biggest problem facing on-line researchers is the instability of Internet sites. Although some sites may remain in place for weeks or months, many either move to another place on the Web—not always leaving a clear path for you to find them—or disappear.

You can watch bibliographical history being made on a day-to-day basis on the Internet, where a number of researchers are attempting to establish workable electronic citation formats. See what you can find, for example, on the following site on the World Wide Web:

http://www.fis.utoronto.ca/internet/citation.htm

This site offers links to several pages where bibliographers are coming to grips with the problems of Internet referencing.

The *ASA Style Guide* (1996) acknowledges that the American Sociological Association has not yet endorsed a standard referencing system for on-line sources and points the reader to other style sheets, including the fourth edition of the *Publication Manual of the American Psychological Association* (1995:218–212). However, placing APA-style citations for electronic sources within an ASA-style references list might make for confusion, since the standard items reported in one style are not formatted in the same way as those reported in the other. Therefore, until such time as an authoritative ASA-style citation system for electronic sources is available, we suggest the following simple formats, based in part on the work of other researchers currently available on the Internet.

REFERENCE FOR A SITE ON THE WORLD WIDE WEB.   Place the following information in this order, separating most of the elements with periods:

- Name of author (if known), reversed
- Title of document (in quotation marks)
- Edition, revision, or version information
- Date of document
- Site address, starting on the next line and enclosed in v-brackets (< and >), followed by the date upon which you last accessed the site (in parentheses)

> Page, Melvin E. "A Brief Citation Guide for Internet Sources in History and the Humanities." Ver. 2.1. 20 February 1996. <http://www.nmmc.com/libweb/employee/citguide.him> (13 April 1997).

The two symbols < and > which surround the site address are not part of the address; they serve merely to differentiate the address from the rest of the citation. It is important not to break the often lengthy information string that constitutes the site address, hence the relatively short second line of the citation. Note that there is no period between the > and the access date, in parentheses.

REFERENCE FOR AN FTP SITE:

> Dodd, Sue A. "Bibliographic References for Computer Files in the Social Sciences: A Discussion Paper." Rev. May 1990. <ftp://ftp.msstate.edu/pub/docs/history/netuse/electronic.biblio.cite> (13 April 1997).

Remember, the one thing that is absolutely required in order to find a site on the Internet is the site address, so make sure that you copy it accurately.

REFERENCE FOR A CD-ROM.   The following model is for a source with an unascertainable author. Identify the source as a CD-ROM and identify the publisher. Note that it is still necessary to include, in parentheses, the latest date on which you accessed the database:

> *Dissertation Abstracts Ondisc.* 1861–1994. CD-ROM: UMI/Dissertation Abstracts Ondisc. (December 15, 1996).

REFERENCE FOR AN E-MAIL DOCUMENT AND MATERIAL FROM BULLETIN BOARDS AND DISCUSSION GROUPS.   Due to the ephemeral nature of e-mail sources, most researchers recommend not including citations to e-mail in the bibliography. Instead, you may handle e-mail documentation within the text of the paper.

> In an e-mail message dated 22 March 1997, Bennett assured the author that the negotiations would continue.

If, however, you would like to include an e-mail citation in your references section, here is a possible format:

> Bothey, Suzanne. <sbb@mtsu.edu>. 15 March 1997. RE: Progress on education reform petition [e-mail to Courtney Cline <clinecl@usc.cola.edu>].

The name of the author of the e-mail message is placed first, followed by the author's e-mail address and the date of the message. Next comes a brief statement of the subject of the message, followed finally by the name of the person who originally received the message and that person's e-mail address.

CITING SOURCES IN APA STYLE

The following formats are taken from the fourth edition of the *Publication Manual of the American Psychological Association* (1994), a style guide that is frequently used by

REFERENCES

Adams, Daniel D., Thomas C. Johnson and Steven P. Cole. 1989. "Physical Fitness, Body Image, and Locus of Control in First-Year College Men and Women." *Perceptual and Motor Skills* 68:400–402.

Becker, Howard S. 1963. *The Outsiders*. New York: Free Press of Glencoe.

Brown, Laura S. 1985. "Women, Weight, and Power: Theoretical and Therapeutic Issues." *Women and Therapy* 4(1):61–71.

Burr, Wesley R., Geoffrey K. Leigh, Randall D. Day and John Constantine. 1979. "Symbolic Interaction and the Family." Pp. 42–111 in *Contemporary Theories about the Family*, edited by W. R. Burr, F. I. Nye and I. Reiss. New York: Free Press.

Chavis, Christopher F. "Pumping Iron in Prison: A Hierarchy of Values." *Penology: On-Line Issues* <http://www.penol.usil.edu.htm> (3 July 1997).

Cooley, Charles H. 1981. "The Social Self." Pp. 822–828 in *Theories of Society*, edited by T. Parsons, E. Shils, K. D. Naegele and J. R. Pitts. New York: Free Press.

_____. 1985. "Sex Differences in Perceptions of Desirable Body Shape." *Journal of Abnormal Psychology* 94(1):102–105.

ASA Style: Sample References Page

criminal justice professionals. Like the ASA style, the APA style employs an *author–date system*, also known as a *parenthetical–reference system* of referencing. Such a system requires two components for each significant reference to a source: (1) a note placed within the text, in parentheses, near where the source material occurs, and (2) a full bibliographical reference for the source, placed in a list of references following the text and keyed to the parenthetical reference within the text. Models for both parenthetical notes and full references are given below.

The Publication Manual of the American Psychological Association (1994) suggests that you not use italics in your paper if it is going to be set in type for publication. For this reason, and to help differentiate the ASA formats given earlier in this chapter from the APA formats that follow, this manual will underline material that in published form would be italicized.

APA Style: Parenthetical Reference Citations

Author's name and year of publication in text

…was challenged by Lewissohn in 1995.

Author's name in text; year of publication in parentheses

Freedman (1984) postulates that when individuals…

Author's name and year of publication in parentheses

…encourage more aggressive play (Perrez, 1979).

When it appears at the end of a sentence, the parenthetical reference is placed inside the period. Note that the primary difference between the format above and the format in ASA style is that the author's name is followed by a comma in the APA style.

Reference including page numbers

Thomas (1961, p. 741) builds on this scenario…
… in the years to come" (Dixon, 1997, pp. 34–35).

Page numbers should only be included when quoting directly from a source or referring to specific passages. Use *p.* or *pp.* in roman type, to denote page numbers.

Source with two authors. When the authors' names are given in the running text, separate them by the word *and*:

…and, according to Holmes and Bacon (1872, pp. 114–116), establish a sense of self.

When the authors' names are given in the parentheses, separate them by an ampersand:

...establish a sense of self (Holmes & Bacon, 1872, pp. 114–116).

NOTE: For all sources with more than one author, separate the last two names with the word *and* if they are given within the text and by an ampersand if within parentheses.

Source with three, four, or five authors. For the first citation:

...found the requirements very restrictive (Mollar, Querley, & McLarry, 1926).

For all subsequent citations:

...proved to be quite difficult (Mollar et al., 1926).

...according to Mollar et al. (1926)...

In the second and all subsequent references to a source with three, four, or five authors, place the Latin phrase *et al.*, meaning "and others," after the name of the first author. Note that the phrase appears in roman type, not italics, and is followed by a period.

Source with more than five authors

Kinneson et al. (1933) made the following suggestion...

In all references, include only the name of the first author, followed by *et al.*

NOTE: When references to two multiple-author sources shorten to the same abbreviated format, cite in your reference as many of the authors as needed to differentiate the sources. Example:

Keeler, Allen, Pike, Johnson, and Keaton (1994)

Keeler, Allen, Schmidt, Wendelson, Crawford, and Blaine (1994)

Using the standard method for abbreviating citations, these two sources would both shorten to the same format: (Keeler et al., 1994). In such situations, shorten the citation as follows:

(Keeler, Allen, Pike, et al., 1994)

(Keeler, Allen, Schmidt, et al., 1994)

Group as author.   Use the complete name of the group author in the first citation:

...to raise the standard of living (National Association of Food Retailers, 1994).

If the name of the group is lengthy, and if it is easily identified by the general public, you may abbreviate the group name in citations after the first one. In such a case, provide the abbreviation in the first reference, in brackets. For the first citation:

...usually kept in cages (Society for the Prevention of Cruelty to Animals [SPCA], 1993).

For all subsequent citations:

...which, according to the SPCA (1990)...

Two authors with the same last name

...the new budget cuts (K. Grady, 1991).
...stimulate economic growth (B. Grady, 1991).

Two works by the same author

George (1992, 1994) argues for...

If the two citations appear in the same note, place a comma between the publication dates of the works. If the two works were published in the same year, differentiate them by adding lowercase letters to the publication dates. Be sure to add the letters to the references in the bibliography, too.

...the city government (Estrada, 1994a, 1994b).

Work with no author given. Begin the parenthetical reference with the first few words of the bibliographical citation in the reference list at the back of the paper, underlining the words if they are part of the title of a book, or placing them in quotation marks if they are part of the title of an essay or chapter:

...recovery is unlikely (<u>Around the Bend,</u> 1990).

Note that a comma immediately following an underlined title is also underlined.

...will run again in the next election ("Problems for Smithson," 1996).

Direct quotations. Direct quotes of fewer than 40 words should be placed in the text with quotation marks at the beginning and end. The citation should include the page number:

The majority of these ads promote the notion that "If you are slim, you will also be beautiful and sexually desirable" (Rockett & McMinn, 1990, p. 278).

Direct quotes of 40 words or more should be indented five spaces from the left margin and double spaced. The first line of any new paragraph beginning within a block quote should be indented five spaces from the margin of the quote.

According to Brown (1985):

There are few girls and women of any age or culture raised in white America who do not have some manifestation of the concerns discussed here, i.e., distortion of body image, a sense of "out-of-control" in relationship to food, addiction to dieting, bingeing, or self-starvation. (p. 61)

Note that the parenthetical reference following the block quote is placed after the final period.

Chapters, tables, appendices, etc.

...(Johnson, 1995, chap. 6).

or

...(See Table 4 of Blake, 1985, for complete information).

or

(See Appendix B of Shelby, 1976).

Reprints

Daniels (1922/1976) takes a different view...

More than one source in a reference

...are related (Harmatz, 1987, p. 48; Marble et al., 1986, p. 909; Powers & Erickson, 1986, p. 48; Rackley et al., 1988, p.10; Thompson & Thompson, 1986, p. 62).

Separate citations by a semicolon and order them alphabetically by author.

Unpublished materials.   If the source is scheduled for publication at a later time:

A study by Barkley and Ford (in press) lends support...

Personal communications.   Materials such as letters to the author, memos, phone conversations, e-mail messages, and messages from electronic discussion groups should be cited within the text but not recorded among the references. Include in the textual note the last name and initials of the person with whom you communicated, and include as exact a date as possible:

...that the work was flawed (P. L. Bingam, personal communication, February 20, 1995).

Undated materials.   Use *n.d.* (no date) in place of the date:

...except that Fox (n.d.) disagrees.
...cannot be ascertained (Fox, n.d.).

Classic texts.   Refer to classic texts, such as the Bible, standard translations of ancient Greek texts, or numbers of the *Federalist Papers*, by using the systems by which they are subdivided instead of by the publication information of the edition you are using. Since all editions of a classic text employ the standard subdivisions, this reference method has the advantage of allowing your reader to find the source passage in any published edition of the text. You may cite a biblical passage by referring to the particular book, chapter, and verse, all in roman type, with the translation given after the verse number:

> "But the path of the just is as the shining light, that shineth more and more unto the perfect day" (Prov. 4:18, King James Version).

The *Federalist Papers* may be cited by their standard numbers:

> Madison addresses the problem of factions in a republic (Federalist 10).

If you are using a work whose date is not known or is inapplicable, cite the year of the translation or the version you are using, preceded by *trans.* or *version*, respectively:

> Plato (trans. 1908) records that...
>
> ...disagrees with the formulation in Aristotle (1892 version).

Newspaper article with no author.   Use a shortened form of the title of the article, or the entire title if it is short:

> ...painted the new program in glowing colors ("Little Left to Do," 1995).

Public documents.   Pages 224 through 234 of the fourth edition of the APA Manual (1994) give detailed information on how to create parenthetical and bibliographical references for public documents. These formats are taken from the fifteenth edition of *The Bluebook: A Uniform System of Citation* (1991). Here are models for some sources frequently used by criminal justice professionals.

Legislative hearings.   Information concerning a hearing before a legislative subcommittee is published in an official pamphlet. A parenthetical reference to such a pamphlet begins with a shortened form of the pamphlet's title and includes the year in which the hearing was held:

> ...the dangers of underfunded school programs (Funding for Inner City Schools, 1990).

Bills and resolutions.   For unenacted federal bills and resolutions:

> ...cannot reject visa requests out of hand (S. 7658, 1996).

Both of the references above refers to Senate Bill number 7658, originating in the Senate in 1996. The number of a bill originating in the House of Representatives should be preceded by *H.R.* instead of *S*. For enacted federal bills and resolutions:

> ...only to U.S. citizens (H.R. Res. 94, 1993).
>
> According to House Resolution 94 (1993)...

The parenthetical note above are to resolution number 94, originated in the House of Representatives in 1993.

Statutes.   In the parenthetical note in the text, cite either the popular or official name of the act and the year:

>   ...in order to obtain a license (Fish and Game Act of 1990).

Federal reports

>   ...as explained in Senate Report No. 85 (1989), the...
>   ...was finally clarified (S. Rep. No. 114, 1989).

Court decisions

>   ...which she failed to meet (State of Nevada v. Goldie Warren, 1969).

Executive orders

>   Executive Order No. 13521 (1993) states that...
>   It was decided (Executive Order No. 13521, 1993) that...

APA Style: References

Parenthetical citations in the text point the reader to the fuller source descriptions at the end of the paper, known as the references or bibliography. According to the fourth edition of the APA *Manual* (1994, p. 174), there is a difference between a reference list and a bibliography of sources consulted for a paper: A reference list comprises only those sources used directly in the paper for support, whereas a bibliography may include materials used indirectly, for background, perhaps, or further reading. Check with your instructor to make sure which type of source listing you are to provide for your class paper.

   As with most reference lists, entries in an APA-style reference list are double-spaced and alphabetized by the first element in each citation. The APA reference system uses "sentence-style" capitalization for titles of books and articles: Only the first word of the title and of the subtitle (if present) and all proper names are capitalized. Titles of periodicals, including journals and newspapers, are given standard, or "headline style," capitalization. In this style, all first and last words in a title, and all other words except articles (*a, an, the*), coordinating words (*and, but, or, for, nor*), and all prepositions (*among, by, for, of, to, toward*, etc.) are capitalized.

   While titles of journals and books are underlined, titles of chapters or articles are neither underlined nor enclosed in quotation marks. The APA *Manual* (1994, p. 239) suggests that you not use italics in your paper if it is going to be set in type for publication. For this reason, and to help differentiate the ASA formats given earlier in this chapter from the APA formats that follow, in this book we underline material that in published form would be italicized.

   The APA *Manual* (1994, p. 251) requires researchers who are typing on a computer a paper that will eventually be published to indent the first line of each item in the reference list five to seven spaces, paragraph style, rather than use the hanging indention common to bibliographies and reference lists. The reason for this is that the typesetter used later in the process of preparing the paper for publication will convert the reference entries to hanging style. Ask your instructor which indention style you should use. The models that follow employ the traditional hanging style—with the first line extended—since that is the standard format for a published essay and also the style most college instructors prefer.

BOOKS

One author

>   Northrup, A. K. (1997). <u>Living high off the hog: Recent pork barrel legislation in the senate</u>. Cleveland, OH: Johnstown.

First comes the author's last name, then the initials of the first and middle names. Add a space after each initial, as in the example above. The date of publication follows, in parentheses and followed by a period, and then the title of the book, underlined. Note that the underlining extends past the period following the title. The city of publication is cited next, then the state (or country if not the United States) unless the city is known for publishing. Cities that need not be accompanied by state or country include Baltimore, Boston, Chicago, Los Angeles, New York, Philadelphia, San Francisco, Amsterdam, Jerusalem, London, Paris, Rome, Stockholm, and Tokyo. Use postal abbreviations to denote the state (*OK, AR*). Finally comes the name of the publisher.

Periods are used to divide most of the elements in the citation, although a colon is used between the place of publication and publisher. Custom dictates that the main title of a book and its subtitle are separated by a colon, even though a colon may not appear in the title as printed on the title page of the book.

Two authors

>   Spence, M. L., & Rudd, K. M. (1996.) <u>Hiring and the law</u>. Boston: Tildale.

Reverse both names, placing a comma after the initials of the first name. Separate the names by an ampersand.

Three or more authors

>   Moore, J. B., Macrory, K. L., Rice, A. D., & Traylor, N. P. (1998). <u>Down on the farm: Culture and folkways</u>. Norman, OK: University of Oklahoma Press.

List the names and initials, in reversed order, of all authors of a source.

Group as author

>   National Association of Food Retailers. (1994). <u>Standardization practices among New Jersey beef retailers</u>. Trenton, NJ: Arkway.

Alphabetize according to the first significant word in the group's title.

Work with no author given

>   <u>Around the bend: Insanity among civic administrators</u>. (1981). Dallas, TX: Turbo.

Begin the citation with the title of the work, alphabetizing according to the first significant word.

Editor or compiler as author

Yarrow, P. T., & Edgarton, S. P. (Eds.). (1987). <u>Moonlighting in earnest: Second jobs and family instability</u>. New York: Halley.

Jastow, X. R. (Comp.). (1990). <u>Saying good-bye: Intimations of apocalypse in Soviet literature</u>. New York: Broadus.

Book with author and editor

Scarborough, D. L. (1934). <u>Written on the wind: Maxims</u> (E. K. Lightstraw, Ed.). Beaufort, SC: Juvenal.

Note that there is no comma between the title and the parentheses enclosing the editor's name, and that the editor's last name and initials are not reversed.

Translated book

Zapata, E. M. (1948). <u>Beneath the wheel: Exploitation of the native population in Northern Mexico, 1900–1940</u> (A. M. Muro, Trans.). El Paso, TX: Del Norte.

Do not reverse the last name and initials of the translator.

Untranslated book

Wharton, E. N. (1916). <u>Voyages au front</u> [Visits to the front]. Paris: Plon.

Provide a translation of the title, in brackets, following the title.

Two works by the same author

George, J. B. (1989). <u>They often said so: Repetition and obfuscation in nineteenth-century politics</u>. Stroud, OK: Casten.

George, J. B. (1981). <u>Who shot John: A profile of gunshot victims in the midwest, 1950–1955</u>. Okarche, OK: Flench & Stratton.

Do not use hyphens in place of the author's name in the second and subsequent entries; always state the author's name in full.

Author of a foreword or introduction

Farris, C. J. (1995). Foreword. In <u>Marital stress among the professariat: A case study</u> by B. Givan. New York: Galapagos.

The parenthetical text reference cites the name of the author of the foreword or introduction, not the author of the book.

Selection in a multiauthor collection

Gray, A. N. (1998). Foreign policy and the foreign press. In B. Bonnard & L. F. Guinness (Eds.), <u>Current media issues</u> (pp. 188–204). New York: Boulanger.

NOTE: When citing two or more selections in a multiauthor collection you must provide complete reference material for each selection in the references.

Signed article in a reference book

> Jenks, S. P. (1983). Fuller, Buckminster. In L. B. Sherman & B. H. Sherman
> (Eds.), <u>International dictionary of the humanities</u> (pp. 204–205). Boston: R. R.
> Hemphill.

Unsigned article in an encyclopedia

> Bill of rights. (1968). In <u>Encyclopedia Americana</u> (Vol. 1, pp. 521–522). Boston:
> Encyclopedia Americana.

Subsequent editions.   If you are using an edition of a book other than the first, you
must cite the number of the edition or the status, such as *Rev. ed.* for revised edition,
if there is no edition number:

> Hales, S. A. (1994). <u>The coming water wars</u> (2d ed.). Pittsburgh, PA: Blue Skies.
> Peters, D. K. (1972). <u>Social cognition in early childhood</u> (Rev. ed.). Riverside, CA:
> Ingot.

Multivolume work.   If you are citing a multivolume work in its entirety, use the following format:

> Graybosch, C. S. (1988). <u>The rise of the unions</u> (vols. 1–3). New York: Starkfield.

If you are citing only one volume in a multivolume work, use the following format:

> Graybosch, C. S. (1988). <u>The rise of the unions: Vol. 1. Bloody beginnings</u>. New York:
> Starkfield.

Reprints

> Adams, S. R. (1988). <u>How to win an election: Promotional campaign strategies</u>. New
> York: Alexander. (Original work published in 1964)

Modern editions of classics.   According to the APA *Manual* (1994, p. 173), references to classic texts such as sacred books and Greek verse and drama are usually confined to the text and not given a citation in the references list.

PERIODICALS

JOURNAL ARTICLES.   Most journals are paginated so that each issue of a volume
continues the numbering of the previous issue. The reason for such pagination is that
most journals are bound in libraries as complete volumes of several issues; continuous
pagination makes it easier to consult these large compilations:

> Hunzecker, J. (1987.) Teaching the toadies: Cronyism in police departments. *Review of*
> *Local Politics, 4,* 250–262.

Note that while the name of article appears in sentence-style capitalization, the name
of the journal is capitalized in standard, or headline, style. Do not use *p.* or *pp.* to
introduce the page numbers.

Journal in which each issue is paginated separately

> Skylock, B. L. (1991). "Fifty-four forty or fight!": Sloganeering in early America. American History Digest, 28(3), 25–34.

The issue number appears in parentheses immediately following the volume number. In this particular citation the quotation marks are necessary only because the title includes a quoted slogan.

English translation of a journal article

> Sczaflarski, Richard. (1990). The trumpeter in the tower: Solidarity and legend. World Political Review, 32, 79–95.

MAGAZINE ARTICLES.   Magazines, which are usually published weekly, bimonthly, or monthly, appeal to the popular audience and generally have a wider circulation than journals. *Newsweek* and *Scientific American* are examples of magazines.

Monthly magazine

> Stapleton, B., & Peters, E. L. (1981, April). How it was: On the trail with Og Mandino. Lifetime Magazine, 131, 24–23, 57–59.

Weekly or bimonthly magazine

> Bruck, C. (1997, October 18). The world of business: A mogul's farewell. The New Yorker, 73, 12–15.

NEWSPAPER ARTICLES

Newspaper article with no author named

> Little left to do says new justice chair. (1996, January 16). The Vernon Times-Democrat, p. A7.

Newspaper article with discontinuous pages

> Everett, S. (1996, February 16). Beyond the Alamo: How Texans view the past. The Carrollton Tribune, pp. D1, D4.

PERSONAL COMMUNICATIONS

According to the APA *Manual* (1994, pp. 173–174), personal communications such as letters, memos, and telephone and e-mail messages are not given a citation in the references list but are cited within the text.

PUBLIC DOCUMENTS

Pages 224 through 234 of the fourth edition of the APA *Manual* (1994) give detailed information on how to create parenthetical and bibliographical references for public documents. These formats are taken from the fifteenth edition of *The Bluebook: A Uniform System of Citation* (1991).

Legislative hearings. Information concerning a hearing before a legislative subcommittee is published in an official pamphlet. Your citation should refer to this pamphlet.

> Funding for inner city schools: Hearing before the Subcommittee on Education Reform of the Education Committee, House of Representatives, 103d Cong., 2d Sess. 1 (1993).

This citation refers to the official pamphlet reporting on the hearing named, which was held in the U.S. House of Representatives during the second session of the 103d Congress. The report of the hearing begins on page 1 of the pamphlet.

Bills and resolutions. For unenacted federal bills and resolutions:

> Visa Formalization Act of 1993, S. 1437, 103d Cong., 1st Sess. (1993).

The citation refers to a bill, from the U.S. Senate, created in the first session of the 103d Congress and assigned the bill number 1437. For enacted federal bills and resolutions:

> H.R. Res. 192, 104th Cong., 2d Sess. 152 Cong. Rec. 4281 (1994).

This citation refers to House Resolution number 192, reported on page 4281 of volume 152 of the *Congressional Record*.

Statute in a federal code

> Fish and Game Act of 1990, 51 U.S.C.A. § 1043 et seq. (West 1993).

The entry refers to an act located at section (§) 1043 of title 51 of the *United States Code Annotated*, the unofficial version of the United States Code. The phrase *et seq.*, Latin for "and following," indicates that the act recurs in later sections of the volume.

Federal reports

> S. Rep. No. 85, 99th Cong., 1st Sess. 4 (1989).

This citation refers to material found on page 4 of the report.

Court decisions. For unpublished cases:

> United States v. Vandelay Industries, No. 46-297 (U.S. filed Oct. 3, 1992).

The citation refers to a case filed in the U.S. Supreme Court. The docket number is 46-297.

> For published cases:

> Jacob v. Warren, 102 F. Supp. 482 (W. D. Nev. 1969).

The citation refers to a case published in volume 102 of the *Federal Supplement*, beginning on page 482. The decision in the case was rendered by the federal district court for the Western District of Nevada in 1969.

Executive orders

> Exec. Order No. 13521, 3 C.F.R. 305 (1993).

Executive orders are reported in volume 3 of the *Code of Federal Regulations*. This order appears on page 305. You should also include, if available, a parallel citation to the *United States Code* (U.S.C.).

ELECTRONIC SOURCES

CITING ON-LINE SOURCES.   The APA is working to establish a standard for citing on-line materials, but the attempt is hampered by a number of factors. For one thing, there is no foolproof method of clearly reporting even such basic information as the site's author(s), title, or date of establishment. Occasionally, authors identify themselves clearly; sometimes they place a link to their home page at the bottom of the site. But it is not always easy to determine exactly who authored a particular site. Similarly, it can be difficult to determine whether a site has its own title or exists as a subsection of a larger document with its own title. Perhaps the biggest problem facing on-line researchers is the instability of Internet sites. Although some sites may remain in place for weeks or months, many either move to another site—not always leaving a clear path for you to find them—or disappear.

You can watch bibliographical history being made on a day-to-day basis on the Internet, where a number of researchers are attempting to establish workable electronic citation formats. See what you can find, for example, on the following site on the World Wide Web:

http://www.fis.utoronto.ca/internet/citation.htm

This site offers links to several pages where bibliographers are coming to grips with the problems of Internet referencing.

In general, a reference for an on-line source should include as much as possible of the information that would be present in a printed citation, such as the name(s) of the author(s), the date of publication, and title (or titles, if the source is an article within a larger work). If the source is a periodical article, include volume number and page numbers; if the source is a separate publication (such as a book or pamphlet), include the place of publication and publisher. If the source needs further description, provide a brief one, in brackets, as illustrated in the examples below. Complete the citation by noting the date on which you retrieve the source from the Web and the Web address where you found it. Because a final period may be misinterpreted as part of the path, do not place one at the end of the citation.

REFERENCE FOR A SITE ON THE WORLD WIDE WEB

Reid, D.H., & Parsons M.B. (1995). Comparing choice and questionnaire measures of the acceptability of a staff training procedure. <u>Journal of Applied Behavior Analysis, 28</u>, 95-96. Retrieved July 7, 1996 from the World Wide Web: http://www.envmed.rochester.edu/wwwrap/behavior/jaba_htm/28/_28-095.htm

REFERENCE FOR AN *FTP* SITE

> Squires, C. (1997, August). Crime and punishment in the academy: A survey. Justice and the Law, 2, 25-34. Available: ftp://eastanglia.edu/pub/harnad/justlaw/vol.2[1998, February 21].

Note that for an FTP site, the date of access appears, in brackets, at the end of the citation.

REFERENCE FOR A *CD-ROM*   The following model is for a source with an unascertainable author. Identify the source as a CD-ROM and identify the publisher. Include the latest date on which you accessed the database, in parentheses:

> Oxford English dictionary computer file: On compact disk (2nd ed.), [CD-ROM]. (1992). Available: Oxford UP [1997, July].

E-MAIL MESSAGES AND CONVERSATIONS VIA BULLETIN BOARD AND DISCUSSION GROUPS.   According to the APA *Manual* (1994, p. 218), these types of material are cited as personal communication in the text and are not given a citation in the reference list.

CITING SOURCES USING THE STUDENT CITATION SYSTEM

As an alternative to the ASA and APA citation systems, you may want to use the Student Citation System (SCS). Be sure to get your instructor's approval before doing so. Why, you may ask, would anyone want another citation system, especially since so many disciplines already have their own? It is precisely because college students are currently required to use several different citation systems that the SCS was created. SCS was the first system specifically designed for use in all undergraduate college courses. Students can use it in their English, psychology, sociology, math, science, history, political science, and other courses.

How is the SCS different from other citation systems? In addition to its multidisciplinary applications, SCS has several other distinctive features:

- SCS is made for students, not academics. It is simpler, has fewer rules to learn, and is easier to type than other systems.
- SCS uses the punctuation and syntax of a new grammar that students are quickly learning around the world: the universal language of the Internet. The Internet is rapidly becoming the foremost means of a wide range of research and communication activities. SCS symbols are familiar to anyone who has used the Internet: / @ + . They allow citations to be constructed with a minimum of space, effort and confusion.

References

Adams, D. D., Johnson, T. C., & Cole, S. P. (1989). Physical fitness,
     body image, and locus of control in first-year college men and
     women. <u>Perceptual and Motor Skills</u>, *68*, 400–402.

Becker, H. S. (1963). <u>The outsiders</u>. New York: Free Press of Glencoe.

Brown, L. S. (1985). Women, weight, and power: Theoretical and
     therapeutic issues. <u>Women and Therapy</u>, 4(1), 61–71.

Burr, W. R., Leigh, G. K., Day, R. D., & Constantine, J. (1979).
     Symbolic interaction and the family. In W. R. Burr, F. I. Nye, &
     I. Reiss (Eds.), <u>Contemporary theories about the family</u> (pp.
     42–111). New York: Free Press.

Chavis, C. F. (1997, April). Pumping iron in prison: A hierarchy of
     values. <u>Penology: On-Line Issues 2</u> [On-line journal]. Retrieved
     November 16, 1997 from the World Wide Web:
     http://www.penol.usil.edu.htm

Cooley, C. H. (1981). The social self. In T. Parsons, E. Shils, K. D.
     Naegele, & J. R. Pitts (Eds.), <u>Theories of Society</u> (pp. 822–828).
     New York: Free Press.

Cooley, C. H. (1985). Sex differences in perceptions of desirable
     body shape. <u>Journal of Abnormal Psychology</u>, 94(1), 102–105.

APA Style: Sample References Page

SCS Style: Reference Citations

Like other citation systems, SCS requires that each source citation include (1) a note in the text in which the reference to the source cited occurs, and (2) an entry in a reference page. Notes in the text always appear at the end of the sentence in which the reference is made. Study the models that accompany the following list of rules for notes.

Rule	*Example*
1. Notes in the text always contain, in this order: a forward slash (/); a source reference numeral (1, 2, 3, etc.); a dot (.) that ends the sentence.	Reagan waved to the convention /1. (Notice that there is a space before the /, but no spaces between the / and the 1, or between the 1 and the dot.)
2. Direct quotes and references to materials on a specific page both require a page number. Note that no space appears between the dots and the page number.	Reagan waved to the convention /1.23.
3. You may indicate a range of pages or a page and a range of pages.	Reagan waved to the convention /1.23-25. Reagan waved to the convention /1.19.23-25.
4. Indicate chapters, sections, parts, and volumes in the note with appropriate abbreviations. Note that there is no dot between the abbreviation and the number of the chapter, section, part, or volume.	Reagan waved to the convention /1.c3. Reagan waved to the convention /1.s3. Reagan waved to the convention /1.pt3. Reagan waved to the convention /1.v3.
5. You may cite more than one source in a single note. Separate sources use a /, without spaces between any of the characters.	Reagan waved to the convention 1.v3.23/4/13c6. (This note refers to source 1, volume 3, page 23; source 4; and source 13, chapter 6.)
6. Once used, reference numbers always refer to the same source. They may be used again to refer to a quote or idea from that same source.	Reagan waved to the convention /1.19. Nancy, who had had a severe headache the evening before, came to join him /5/7. One source reported that they had argued about the color suit he was to wear /1.33. (The second note in this passage refers the reader to two difference sources, numbers 5 and 7. The third note is another reference to the first source used in the paper.)
7. Refer to Constitutions with article and section number.	Bill Clinton fulfilled his obligation to address the state of the nation /18.3.

Rule	*Example*
8. Refer to passages in the Bible, the Koran, and other ancient texts that are divided into standard verses with the verse citation in the note.	Jake forgot that "the seventh day shall be your Holy day" /6.Exodus 35.2. (This example refers to the book of Exodus, chapter 35, verse 2. The 6 indicates that this is the sixth source cited in the paper. There is a dot between the source number and the verse citation.)

SCS Style: References

GENERAL FORMAT RULES

The reference list is usually the final element in the paper. It is entitled *References*. Its entries are arranged in the order that citations appear in the paper. The reference page has standard page margins. All lines are double spaced. Model reference pages appear at the end of this chapter.

RULES OF PUNCTUATION AND ABBREVIATION

1. Punctuation imitates the format used on the Internet.
2. No spaces appear between entry elements (author, date, and so on) or punctuation marks (/ . + @ ").
3. Dots (.) always follow entry elements with exceptions for punctuation rules 6 and 7.
4. The source number is always followed immediately by a dot.
5. Dots are also used to separate volume and edition numbers in journals.
6. Additional authors are denoted by a plus (+) sign.
7. Subtitles of books and articles are separated from main titles by a colon and a single space: "Crushing Doubt: Pascal's Bleak Epiphany."
8. Book chapters and periodical articles are enclosed in quotation marks (" ").
9. The following abbreviations are used:

      c   chapter

      comp   compiler

      ed   editor

      NY   New York (Use postal abbreviations for all states. Note that NY is unique in that when it is used alone it always means New York City. Cite other New York state locations in this form: "Oswego NY." Cite cities in other states similarly: "Chicago IL" "Los Angeles CA" "Boston MA.")

      pt   part

      s   section

sess	session
tr	translator
v	volume
S	September (Months: Ja F Mr Ap My Je Jl Au S Oc N D)
C	College
I	Institute
U	University

10. Full names instead of initials of authors are used whenever they are used in the original source. When listing publishers, you may use the commonly used names instead of full titles. For example, use "Yale" for "Yale University Press"; use "Holt" for "Holt, Rinehart and Winston." Use Internet abbreviations when known, such as "Prenhall" for "Prentice Hall." When abbreviating universities in dissertation and thesis citations, place no dot between the names of the state or city and the university. For example, use "MaIT" for the Massachusetts Institute of Technology and "UMa" for the University of Massachusetts. Always use the second letter of the state abbreviation, in lower case, to avoid the following type of confusion: "OSU" could be a university in Ohio, Oklahoma, or Oregon.

RULES OF ORDER

Elements are always entered in the order shown in the following list of examples. Not all elements are available for every citation. For example, authors are sometimes not provided in source documents. Also, an element may be inappropriate for a certain type of citation. Cities of publication, for instance, are not required for magazines. Carefully examine the order of elements in the following examples.

BOOKS

One author

3.Edna Applegate.1995.My Life on Earth.4th ed.Howard Press.St. Louis MO.

Note the order of elements:

- Reference number of note (1, 2, 3, etc.), followed by a dot
- Author's name
- Year of publication
- Title of book
- Number of edition, if other than the first
- Name of publisher
- City of publication
- State of publication (not necessary for New York City)

Two to three authors

> 10.William Grimes+Joan Smith+Alice Bailey.1996.Philosophy and Fire.Harvard.Cambridge MA.

More than three authors

> 42.Lois Mills+others.1989.Revolution in Thought.Agnew.NY.

Editor, compiler, or translator in place of an author

> 1.Michael Schendler ed.1992.Kant's Cosmology.Bloom.NY.

Remember that the citation for New York City does not require a state abbreviation.

Editor, compiler, or translator with author

> 9.Elena White.1997.Nietzsche Was Right.Alexander Nebbs tr.Spartan.Biloxi MS.

No author, editor, compiler, or translator

> 5.The Book of Universal Wisdom.1993.4th ed.Northfield Publications.Indianapolis IN.

Reverse the placement of the date and title of the book, beginning the entry with the title.

Separately authored foreword, afterword, or preface as source

> 17.Beulah Garvin.1992.Preface.Down in the Hole by James Myerson.Philosopher's Stone Press.Boston MA.

Separately authored chapter, essay, or poem as source

> 5.Jack Wittey.1994."Chickens and People."Animal Rights Anthology.3rd ed.Gene Cayton comp.Palo Duro Press.Canyon TX.73-90.

One volume in a multivolume work

> 9.Astrid Schultz+others.1991.The Myth of the West.v3 of The Development of European Thought.8 vols.Muriel Hodgson ed.University of Rutland Press.Rutland ME.

ENCYCLOPEDIAS

Citation from an encyclopedia that is regularly updated

> 24.Ronald Millgate.1985."Mill, John Stuart."Encyclopedia Americana.

The date refers to the edition of the encyclopedia. Cite the name of the article exactly as it appears in the encyclopedia.

When no name is given for the article's author

> 2. "Mill, John Stuart."1946.Hargreave's Encyclopedia.

ANCIENT TEXTS

Bible, Koran, etc.

> 24.Holy Bible.New International Version.

Because the book, chapter, and verse numbers are given in the textual reference, it is not necessary to repeat them here. Remember to cite the traditional divisions of the work instead of the page number and publication information of the specific edition you used.

PERIODICALS

JOURNAL ARTICLES

Article with author or authors named

> 30.Ellis Michaels+Andrea Long.1996."How We Know: An Exercise in Cartesian Logic."Philosopher's Stone.12.4.213-227.

This citation refers to an article published in a journal entitled *Philosopher's Stone*, volume 12, number 4, pages 213-227.

Article with no author named

> 7."Odds and Ends."1995.Philosopher's Stone.12.4.198-199.

MAGAZINE ARTICLES

Article in a weekly or biweekly magazine

> 11.Lorraine Bond.1994."The Last Epicurean."Mental Health.6Je.34-41.

This citation refers to an article published in the June 6, 1994, issue of *Mental Health*.

Article in a monthly magazine

> 3.Allan Hull.1996."My Secret Struggle."Pathology Digest.Mr.17-30.

The difference between a citation for a monthly magazine and one for a weekly or biweekly magazine is that the former does not include a reference to the specific day of publication.

NEWSPAPERS

Article with named author

> 10.Anne Bleaker.1995."Breakthrough in Artificial Intelligence."New York Times.10My.14.

The word The is omitted from the newspaper's title.

Article with unnamed author

> 22."Peirce Anniversary Celebration Set."1996.Kansas City Times-Democrat.1Ap.14.

When city is not named in newspaper title

> 13.Boyd Finnell.1996."Stoic Elected Mayor."(Eugenia TX) Daily Equivocator.30D.1.

Place the name of the city, and the abbreviation for the state if the city is not well known, in parentheses before the name of the paper.

GOVERNMENT DOCUMENTS

Agency publications

> 28.U.S. Department of Commerce.1996.Economic Projections: 1995-2004.GPO.

Note that when no author's name is given, the government department is considered the author. Because the Government Printing Office (GPO), the government's primary publisher, is located in Washington, DC, you need not list the city of publication.

Legislative journals

> 31.Senate Journal.1993.103Cong.sess1.D10.

This citation refers to the record, published in the *Senate Journal*, of the first session of the 103rd Congress, held on December 10, 1993.

> 8.Congressional Record.71 Cong.sess.2.72.8.

This citation refers to the account of the second session (sess.2) of the 71st Congress, published in volume 72, part 8, of the *Congressional Record*.

Bills in Congress

> 13.U.S. Senate.1997.Visa Formalization Act of 1997.105Cong.sess1.SR.1437.

This citation refers to Senate Resolution 1437, originated in the first session of the 105th Congress. Bills originating in the House of Representatives are designed by the abbreviation HR.

Laws

> 17.U.S. Public Law 678.1993.Library of Congress Book Preservation Act of 1993.U.S.Code.38.1562.

The law referred to in this citation is recorded in section 1562 of volume 38 of the *U.S. Code*.

Constitutions

> 31.U.S.Constitution.
>
> 8.MO.Constitution.

The latter citation refers to the Missouri State Constitution.

INTERNET DOCUMENTS

> 4.Akiko Kasahara and K-lab,Inc.1995.ArtScape of the Far East:
> Seminar on the Philosophy of Art.Shinshu.University
> Nagano.Japan.@<http://Pckiso3.cs.Shinshu-
> u.ac.jp/artscape/index.html>Oct27.96.

The last two items in an Internet citation are always the web site at which the document was found, followed by the date upon which the site was accessed by the researcher. The Web site is enclosed within the symbols < and > in order to set it apart from punctuation marks that might be misleading.

UNPUBLISHED MATERIALS

Interview

> 12.Lily Frailey.1994.Interview with Clarence Parker.Santa Fe
> NM.10Au.

Thesis or dissertation

> 21.Gregory Scott.1973.Mysticism and Politics in the Thought of
> Bertrand Russell.MA thesis.UVa.

Paper presented at a meeting

> 5.Celia Hicks.1995."What Whitehead Would Say."Conference on
> the Western Imagination.14Ja.Boston MA.

The citation includes the name of the conference and the date on which the paper was presented, and ends with the city where the conference took place.

Manuscript housed in a collection

> 32.Jose Sanchez.1953?-1982.Journal.Southwest Collection.Arial
> Library.Chisum Academy.Canyon TX.

Unpublished manuscripts are sometimes left unnamed and undated by their authors. Use any relevant information supplied by the repository catalogue to complete the citation. When a date is hypothesized, as in the example above, place a question mark after it.

Manuscript in the author's possession

> 14.Jane Fried.1996.Life in California.UTx.Photocopy.

The citation includes the institution with which the author is affiliated and ends with a description of the format of the work: typescript, photocopy, and so on.

1.Amanda Collingwood.1993.Architecture and Philosophy.Carlington Press.Detroit MI.

2.Tom Barker+Betty Clay, eds.1987.Swamps of Louisiana.Holt.NY.

3.Joan Garth+Allen Sanford.1963."The Hills of Wyoming."Critical Perspectives on Landscape.Prentice Hall.Upper Saddle River NJ.49-75.

4.Hayley Trakas, ed.1994.Russell on Space.3rd ed.Harmony Press.El Paso TX.

5.Philippe Ariès.1962.Centuries of Childhood: A Social History of Family Life in the Northeastern Region of Kentucky.Robert Baldock tr.Knopf.NY.

6.Jesus Gonzolez.1995."The Making of the Federales."Mexican Stories Revisited.Jules Frank ed.Comanche Press.San Antonio TX.54-79.

7.Carla Harris.1994.Foreword.Marital Stress and the Philosophers: A Case Study by Basil Givan.Galapagos.NY.

8.Jasper Craig.1993."The Flight from the Center of the Cities."Time.10S.67-69.

9.Matthew Moen.1996."Evolving Politics of the Christian Right."PS:Political Science and Politics.29.3.461-464.

10.Patrick Swick.1996."Jumping the Gun on the Federal Reserve."New York Times.10My.78.

SCS Style: Sample References Page

11.Frances Muggeridge.1993."The Truth Is Nowhere."Conundrum Digest.Mr.40-54.

12.Alan McAskill.1994."Interview with Mary Jordan."Hospice Pioneers of New Mexico.Dynasty Press.Enid OK.62-86.

13.Jane Smith.1997.Interview with Jerry Brown.San Francisco CA.15Oc.

14.Jacob Lynd.1973.Perfidy in Academe: Patterns of Rationalization in College Administrations.Ph.D. diss.UVa.

15.Holy Bible.New King James Version.

16.Paula Thomas.1970-1976.Diary.Museum of the Plains.Fabens TX.

17.U.S. Department of Labor.1931.Urban Growth and Population Projections:1930-1939.GPO.

18.Senate Journal.1993.103Cong.sess1.D10.

19.U.S.Senate.1997.Visa Formalization Act of 1997.105Cong. sess1.SR.1437.

21.Peter Bolen.1995."Creating Designs in Social Systems."The Internet Journal of Sociological Welfare.14.6.http://www.carmelpeak.com.

22. U.S.Public Law 678.1993.Library of Congress Book Preservation Act of 1993.U.S.Code.38.1562.

23.U.S.Constitution.

Note: Most of the sources used as models in this chapter are not actual publications.

PART II

How to Conduct Research in Criminal Justice

CHAPTER 5

Organizing the Research Process

Don't waste any time mourning—organize!

Union organizer Joe Hill. Letter to W. D. Hayward, the day before being shot by a firing squad, Utah State Penitentiary, November 19, 1915.

GAINING CONTROL OF THE RESEARCH PROCESS

The research paper is where all your skills as an interpreter of details, an organizer of facts and theories, and a writer of clear prose come together. Building logical arguments with facts and hypotheses is the way things get done in criminal justice, and the most successful social scientists are those who master the art of research.

Students new to writing research papers sometimes find themselves intimidated by the job ahead of them. After all, the research paper adds what seems to be an extra set of complexities to the writing process. As any other expository or persuasive paper does, a research paper must present an original thesis using a carefully organized and logical argument. But a research paper often investigates a topic that is outside the writer's own experience. This means that writers of research papers must locate and evaluate information that is new to them, in effect educating themselves as they explore the topic. A beginning researcher sometimes feels overwhelmed by the basic requirements of the assignment or by the authority of the source material.

In the beginning it may be difficult to establish a sense of control over the different tasks you are undertaking in your research project. You may have little notion of which direction to search in for a thesis, or even where the most helpful sources of information might be located. If you fail to monitor your own work habits carefully, you may unwittingly abdicate responsibility for the paper's argument by borrowing it wholesale from one or more of your sources.

WHO IS IN CONTROL OF YOUR PAPER?

Although your instructor may have a specific purpose in assigning a topic and make meaningful suggestions on how to carry out the assignment, the answer must be *you*— not the instructor who assigned you the paper, and certainly not the published writers whose opinions you solicit. If all your paper does is paste together the opinions of others, it has little use. It is up to you to synthesize an original idea through evaluation of your source material. Although at the beginning of your research project you will be unsure about many elements of your paper—you will probably not yet have a definitive thesis sentence, for example, or even much understanding of the shape of your argument—you *can* establish a measure of control over the process you will go through to complete the paper. If you work regularly and systematically, keeping yourself open to new ideas as they present themselves, your sense of control will grow. Here are some suggestions to help you establish and maintain control of your paper.

UNDERSTAND YOUR ASSIGNMENT

A research assignment can fall short simply because the writer did not read the assignment carefully. Considering how much time and effort you are about to put into your project, it is a very good idea to make sure that you have a clear understanding of what it is your instructor wants you to do. Be sure to ask your instructor about any aspect of the assignment that is unclear to you, but only after you have thought about it carefully. Recopying the assignment in your own handwriting is a good way to start, even though your instructor may have given the assignment to you in writing. Before you begin the project, make sure that you have considered the following questions.

WHAT IS YOUR TOPIC?

It may be that the assignment gives you a great deal of specific information about your topic, or that you are allowed considerable freedom in establishing one for yourself. In a criminal justice class in which you are studying issues affecting the U.S. criminal justice system, your professor might give you a very specific assignment—a paper, for example, examining the difficulties involved in locating a halfway house in a suburban community—or you may be allowed to choose for yourself the issue that your paper will address. You need to understand the terms, set up in the assignment, by which you will design your project.

WHAT IS YOUR PURPOSE?

Whatever the degree of latitude you are given in the matter of your topic, pay close attention to the way in which your instructor has phrased the assignment. Is your primary job to describe a current issue in criminal justice or to take a stand on it? Are you to compare social systems, and if so, to what end? Are you to classify, persuade, survey, analyze? Look for such descriptive terms in the assignment to determine the purpose of the project.

WHO IS YOUR AUDIENCE?

Your own orientation to the paper is profoundly affected by your conception of the audience for whom you are writing. Granted, your number one reader is your instructor, but who else would be interested in your paper? Are you writing for the citizens of a community? a group of professionals? a city council? A paper that describes the difficulties involved in locating a halfway house in a suburban community may justifiably contain much more technical jargon for an audience of criminal justice professionals than for a citizens group made up of local business and civic leaders.

WHAT KIND OF RESEARCH ARE YOU DOING?

In your paper you will do one or both of two kinds of research, primary and secondary. *Primary research* requires you to discover information firsthand, often through the conducting of interviews, surveys, or polls. In primary research, you are collecting and sifting through raw data—data not already interpreted by researchers—which you will study, select, arrange, and speculate upon. This raw data may be the opinions of experts or people on the street, historical documents, the theoretical speculations of a famous criminologist, or material collected from other researchers. It is important to set up carefully the method(s) by which you collect your data. Your aim is to gather the most accurate information possible, from which sound observations may be made later, either by you or by other writers using the material you have uncovered.

    Secondary research uses published accounts of primary materials. Whereas the primary researcher might poll a community for its opinion on locating a halfway house in their community, the secondary researcher will use the material from the poll to support a particular thesis. Secondary research, in other words, focuses on *interpretations* of raw data. Most of your college papers will be based on your use of secondary sources.

© *Tribune Media Services. All Rights Reserved. Reprinted with permission.*

Primary Source	*Secondary Source*
A published collection of Thurgood Marshall's letters	A journal article arguing that the volume of letters illustrates Marshall's attitude toward the media
An interview with the police chief	A character study of the police chief based on the interview
Material from a questionnaire	A paper basing its thesis on the results of the questionnaire

The following is a list of *research approaches* commonly used to study and evaluate crime and other variables in criminal justice.

1. *Comparative research* is used to compare various explanations for crime, delinquency, and other important concerns in criminal justice. It also utilizes cross-cultural analysis. The comparative approach can help to generate explanations of how something like crime develops and how society reacts to criminal behavior.

2. *Historical research* evaluates the same society at different times and looks at how a societal component such as crime has changed with economic and social development.

3. *Biographical research* employs a case study approach to describe and analyze a certain type of criminal, such as a serial killer. The biographical approach can help to reveal the needs and motivations of the subject.

4. *Patterns of crime research* help determine where a particular kind of crime is typically committed, who commits it, who is victimized, and what the major dimensions of the criminal act are.

5. *Cohort research* examines the impact of certain cohorts on such subjects as crime and delinquency. The cohort approach is effective in delineating increases and decreases in crime rates. It attempts to isolate changes that are attributable to alterations in attitudes or behavior within an age group.

6. *Records research* uses official and unofficial records to examine such topics as how police arrest suspects, how racial discrimination affects sentencing, and how parole boards determine the release of inmates.

7. *Survey research* requires firsthand data to be gathered from prepared questions or statements and then often quantified for description or inference. This is usually done in interviews, especially with open-ended questions, or with such direct-sampling techniques as mail-outs or phone surveys. For example, a list of statements about how police officers should and should not behave might help determine citizens' opinions concerning the role of the police in their community or society. Or, in the case of interviews, the researcher might simply ask respondents the open-ended question, "How do you think police officers should behave?"

8. *Experimentation* uses direct observation and measurement to analyze the effects of different treatments on attitudes and behavior. Experiments are designed to control for the influence of outside variables.

9. *Direct observation* of social phenomena is conducted by trained observers who carefully record selected behaviors.

10. *Content analysis* is a method of analyzing written documents that allows researchers to transform nonquantitative data into quantitative data by counting and categorizing certain variables within the data. Content analysts look for certain types of words or references in the texts, then categorize them or count them.

Three of these methods—experimentation, observation, and content analysis—are discussed in greater detail in Chapter 8; survey research is described more completely in Chapter 15.

KEEP YOUR PERSPECTIVE

Whatever type of research you are performing, it is important to keep your results in perspective. There is no way in which you, as a primary researcher, can be completely objective in your findings. It is not possible to design a questionnaire that will net you absolute truth, nor can you be sure that the opinions you gather in interviews reflect the accurate and unchanging opinions of the people you question. Similarly, if you are conducting secondary research, you must remember that the articles and journals you are reading are shaped by the aims of their writers, who are interpreting primary materials for their own ends. The farther you get from a primary source, the greater the possibility for distortion. Your job as a researcher is to be as accurate as possible, and that means keeping in view the limitations of your methods and their ends.

EFFECTIVE RESEARCH METHODS

In any research project there will be moments of confusion, but establishing an effective procedure can prevent confusion from overwhelming you. You need to design a schedule for the project that is as systematic as possible, yet flexible enough so that you do not feel trapped by it. A schedule will help keep you from running into dead ends by always showing you what to do next. At the same time, the schedule helps you to retain the presence of mind necessary to spot new ideas and new strategies as you work.

GIVE YOURSELF PLENTY OF TIME

There may be reasons why you feel like putting off research: unfamiliarity with the library, the press of other tasks, a deadline that seems comfortably far away. Do not allow such factors to deter you. Research takes time. Working in a library often seems to speed up the clock, so that the hour you expected it to take to find certain sources becomes two hours. You should allow yourself time not only to find material but to read, assimilate, and set it in context with your own thoughts.

The following schedule lists the steps of a research project in the order in which they are generally accomplished. Remember that each step depends on the others, and that it is quite possible to revise earlier decisions in light of later discoveries. After some background reading, for example, your notion of the paper's purpose may change, which may, in turn, alter other steps. One of the strengths of a good schedule is its flexibility. The general schedule lists tasks for both primary and secondary research; you should use only those steps that are relevant to your project.

Task	*Date of Completion*
Determine topic, purpose, audience	_____
Do background reading in reference books	_____
Narrow your topic; establish a tentative hypothesis	_____
Develop a working bibliography	_____
Write for needed information	_____
Read and evaluate written sources, taking notes	_____
Determine whether to conduct interviews or surveys	_____
Draft a thesis and outline	_____
Write a first draft	_____
Obtain feedback (show draft to instructor, if possible)	_____
Do more research, if necessary	_____
Revise draft	_____
Correct bibliographical format of paper	_____
Prepare final draft	_____
Proofread	_____
Proofread again, looking for characteristic errors	_____
Deadline for final draft	_____

DO BACKGROUND READING

Whether you are doing primary or secondary research, you need to know what kinds of work have already been accomplished in your field of study. A good way to start is by consulting general reference works, although you do not want to overdo it (see below). Chapter 6 lists specialized reference works focusing on topics of interest to criminal justice students and professionals. You might find help in such volumes even for specific, local problems, such as how to restructure a juvenile treatment program or plan an antidrug campaign aimed at area schools.

Warning: Be very careful not to rely too exclusively on material taken from general encyclopedias. You may wish to consult one for an overview of a topic with which you are unfamiliar, but students new to research are often tempted to import large sections, if not entire articles, from such volumes, and this practice is not good scholarship. One major reason why your instructor has required a research paper from you is to let you experience the kinds of books and journals in which the discourse of criminal justice is conducted. General reference encyclopedias, such as *Encyclopedia Brittanica* or *Collier's Encyclopedia*, are good places for instant introductions to subjects; some encyclopedias even include bibliographies of reference works at the ends of their articles. But you will need much more detailed information about your subject to write a useful paper. Once you have learned what you can from a general encyclopedia, move on.

A primary rule of source hunting is to use your imagination. Determine what topics relevant to your study might be covered in general reference works. If, for example, you are looking for introductory readings to help you with the afore-mentioned research paper on antidrug campaign planning, you might look into such specialized reference tools as the *Encyclopedia of Social Work* (Edwards 1995). Remember to check articles in such works for lists of references to specialized books and essays.

NARROW YOUR TOPIC AND ESTABLISH A WORKING THESIS

Before beginning to explore outside sources, it would be a good idea for you to find out what you already know or think about your topic, a job that can only be accomplished well in writing. You might wish to investigate your own attitude toward the topic, your beliefs concerning it, using one or more of the prewriting strategies described in Chapter 1. You might also be surprised by what you know—or don't know—about the topic. This kind of self-questioning can help you discover a profitable direction for your research.

For a research paper in her criminal justice course, Blake Johnson was given the general topic of studying grassroots attempts to legislate morality in American society. She chose the topic of textbook censorship. Here is the course her thinking took as she looked for ways to limit the topic effectively and find a thesis:

General topic:	Textbook censorship
Potential topics:	How a local censorship campaign gets started
	Funding censorship campaigns
	Reasons behind textbook censorship
	Results of censorship campaigns
Working thesis:	It is disconcertingly easy in our part of the state to launch a textbook censorship campaign.

It is unlikely that you will come up with a satisfactory thesis at the beginning of your project. You need a way to guide yourself through the early stages of research toward a main idea that is both useful and manageable. Having in mind a *working thesis*—a preliminary statement of your purpose—can help you select material that is of greatest interest to you as you examine potential sources. The working thesis will probably evolve as your research progresses, and you need to be ready to accept such change. You must not fix on a thesis too early in the research process, or you may miss opportunities to refine it.

DEVELOP A WORKING BIBLIOGRAPHY

As you begin your research, look for published sources—essays, books, interviews with experts in the field—that may help you with your project. This list of potentially useful sources is your *working bibliography*. There are many ways to discover items for the bibliography. The cataloging system in your library will give you titles, as will specialized published bibliographies in your field. (Some of these bibliographies are listed in Chapter 6.) The general reference works in which you did your background reading may also list such sources, and each specialized book or essay you find will have a bibliography of sources its writer used that may be useful to you.

From your working bibliography you can select items for the final bibliography, which will appear in the final draft of your paper. Early in your research you may not know which sources will help you and which will not. It is important to keep an accurate description of each entry in your working bibliography in order to tell clearly which items you have investigated, which you will need to consult again, and which you will discard. Building the working bibliography also allows you to practice using the required bibliographical format for the final draft. As you list potential sources, include all the information about each source called for by your format, and place the information in the correct order, using the proper punctuation.

The bibliographical format of the American Sociological Association (ASA), a format required for criminal justice papers by many professional journals, is described in detail in Chapter 4 of this book. The format of the American Psychological Association (APA) is also used in criminal justice journals and is described in Chapter 4.

WRITE FOR NEEDED INFORMATION

In the course of your research you may need to consult a source that is not immediately available to you. Working on the antidrug campaign paper, for example, you might find that a packet of potentially useful information is available from a government agency or a public interest group at the state or federal level. Maybe a needed book is not held by your university library or by any other local library. Perhaps a successful antidrug program has been implemented in the school system of a city comparable in size to yours but located in another state. In such situations as these, it may be tempting to disregard potential sources because of the difficulty of consulting them. If you ignore the existence of material important to your project, however, you are not doing your job.

It is vital that you take steps to acquire the needed material. In the first case above, you can simply write the state or federal agency; in the second, you may use your library's interlibrary loan procedure to obtain a copy of the book; in the third, you can track down the council that manages the antidrug campaign by e-mail, mail, or phone and ask it for information. Remember that many businesses and government agencies want to share their information with interested citizens; some have employees or entire departments whose job is to facilitate communication with the public. Be as specific as possible when asking for information by mail. It is a good idea to outline your project—in no more than a few sentences—to help the respondent determine the types of information that will be useful to you.

Never let the immediate unavailability of a source stop you from trying to consult it. Also, be sure to begin the job of locating and acquiring such long-distance source material as soon as possible, to allow for the various types of delays that often occur while conducting a search from a distance.

EVALUATE WRITTEN SOURCES

Fewer research experiences are more frustrating than half-remembering something worth using found in a source that you are no longer able to identify. The potential usefulness of a source should be determined as quickly as possible. You need to establish an efficient method of evaluating the sources listed in your working bibliography. Here are some suggestions:

- By examining a book closely you can usually assess the quality of information presented. The preface and introduction give clues to who the author is, why the work was written, and what methodology and research tools were used in the book's preparation. If the author is an acknowledged authority in the field, this fact will often be mentioned in the preface or the foreword.

- The footnotes, in-text references, and the extent and quality of the bibliography (or in some cases, the lack of one) can also serve as clues about the reliability of the work. If few or no original documents have been used, or if major works in the field have not been cited and evaluated, you have reason to question the quality of the book.

- The reputation of the publisher, or organization that sponsors a particular book or periodical, says something about its value. Some publishers have rigid standards of scholarship and others do not. For example, the requirements of university presses are generally very high, and the major publishers, such as Cambridge, Chicago, Michigan, and Harvard, are discriminating about studies in criminal justice.

- A journal article should announce its intention in its abstract or introduction, which in most cases will be a page or less in length.

This sort of preliminary examination should tell you whether a more intensive examination is worthwhile.

NOTE: Whatever you decide about the source, copy the title page of the book or journal article on a photocopy machine, making sure that all important publication information (including title, date, author, volume number, and page numbers) is included. Write any necessary information that is not already printed there, on the photocopied page. Without such a record, later in your research you may forget that you have consulted a text, in which case you may find yourself repeating your examination of it.

When you have determined that a potential source is worth closer inspection, explore it carefully. If it is a book, determine whether you should invest the time it will take to read it in its entirety. Whatever the source, make sure you understand not only its overall thesis, but also each part of the argument that the writer sets up to illustrate or prove the thesis. You need to get a feeling for the shape of the writer's argument, how the subtopics mesh to form a logical defense of the main point. What do you think of the writer's logic and the examples used? Coming to an accurate appraisal may take more than one reading.

As you read, try to get a feeling for the larger argument in which the source takes its place. Its references to the works of other writers will show you where to look for additional material and indicate the general shape of scholarly opinion concerning your subject. If you can see the source you are reading as only one element of an ongoing dialogue instead of an attempt to have the last word on the subject, you can place the argument of the paper in perspective.

USE PHOTOCOPIES

Periodicals and most reference works cannot be checked out of the library. Before the widespread placement of photocopy machines, students could use these materials only by sitting in the library, reading sources, and jotting down information on note cards. Although there are advantages to using the old note-card method (see below), photo-copying saves you time in the library and allows you to take the source information home in its original shape, where you can decide how to use it at your convenience.

If you do decide to copy source material, you should do the following:

- Be sure to follow all copyright laws.
- Have the exact change for the photocopy machines. Do not trust the change machines at the library. They are usually battle-scarred and cantankerous.
- Record all necessary bibliographical information on the photocopy. If you forget to do this, you may find yourself making an extra trip to the library just to get an accurate date of publication or set of page numbers.

IMPORTANT: Remember that photocopying a source is not the same thing as examining it. You will still have to spend time going over the material, assimilating it in order to use it accurately. It is not enough merely to have the information close to hand or even to read it through once or twice. You should understand it thoroughly. Be sure to give yourself time for this kind of evaluation.

USE NOTE CARDS: A THING OF THE PAST?

In many ways note cards are an old-fashioned method of recording source material, and for unpracticed researchers, they may seem unwieldy and unnecessary, since the information jotted on them—one fact per card—will eventually have to be transmit-ted again, in the research paper. However, before you decide to abolish the note-card system once and for all, consider its advantages:

1. Using note cards is a way of forcing yourself to think productively as you read. In translating the language of the source into the language of your notes, you are assimilating the material more completely than you would by merely reading it.
2. Note cards give you a handy way to arrange and rearrange your facts, look-ing for the best possible organization for your paper. Not even a computer gives you the flexibility of a pack of cards as you try to order your paper.

DETERMINE WHETHER TO CONDUCT INTERVIEWS OR SURVEYS.

If your project calls for primary research, you may need to interview experts on your topic or to conduct a survey of opinions among a select group using a questionnaire. Be sure to prepare yourself as thoroughly as possible for any primary research. Here are some tips:

- Establish a purpose for each interview, bearing in mind the requirements of your working thesis. In what ways might your discussion with the subject benefit your paper? Write down your formulation of the interview's purpose. Estimate the length of time you expect the interview to take and inform your subject. Arrive for your scheduled interview on time and dressed appropriately. Be courteous.

- Learn as much as possible about your topic by researching published sources. Use this research to design your questions. If possible, learn something about the people you interview. This knowledge may help you establish rapport with your subjects and will also help you tailor your questions. Take a list of prepared questions to the interview. However, be ready to depart from your scheduled list of questions in order to follow any potentially useful direction that the interview takes.

- Take notes during the interview. Take along extra pens. The use of a tape recorder may inhibit some interviewees. If you wish to use audiotape, ask for permission from your subject. Follow up your interview with a thank-you letter and, if feasible, a copy of the published paper in which the interview is used.

If your research requires a survey or questionnaire, see Chapter 8 (page 191) for a brief explanation on how to design and conduct surveys.

DRAFT A THESIS AND OUTLINE

Since you will never be able to find and assimilate every source pertaining to your subject, especially if it is a popular or controversial one, you should not prolong your research unduly. You must bring this phase of the project to an end—with the option of resuming it later if the need arises—and begin to shape both the material you have gathered and your thoughts about it into a paper. During the research phase, you have been thinking about your working thesis, testing it against the material you have discovered, considering ways to improve it. Eventually, you must arrive at a formulation of the thesis that sets out an interesting and useful task, one that can be managed satisfactorily within the limits of your assignment and that effectively employs much, if not all, of the source material you have gathered.

Once you have formulated your thesis, it is a good idea to make an outline of the paper. In helping you determine a structure for your writing, the outline is also testing the thesis, prompting you to discover the kinds of work that your paper will have to do to complete the task set out by the main idea. Chapter 1 discusses the structural requirements of the formal and informal outline. (If you have used note cards, you may want to start outlining by organizing your cards according to the headings you have given them and looking for logical connections among the different groups of cards. Experimenting with structure in this way will lead you to discoveries that further improve your thesis.)

No thesis or outline is written in stone. There is always time to improve the structure or purpose of your paper even after you have begun to write your first draft, or, for that matter, your final draft. Some writers actually prefer to do a first draft of the paper before outlining, then study the draft's structure to determine what revisions need to be made. *Stay flexible*, always looking for a better connection, a sharper wording of your thesis. The testing of your ideas goes on the entire time you are writing.

WRITE A FIRST DRAFT

Despite all the preliminary work you have done on your paper, you may feel a resistance to beginning your first draft. Integrating all your material and ideas into a smoothly flowing argument is a complicated task. It may help to think of this first attempt as only a *rough draft*, which can be changed as necessary. Another strategy for reducing reluctance to starting is to begin with the part of the draft that you feel most confident about instead of with the introduction. You may write sections of the draft in any order, piecing the parts together later. But however you decide to start writing—START.

OBTAIN FEEDBACK

It is not enough that you understand your argument; others have to understand it, too. If your instructor is willing to look at your rough draft, you should take advantage of the opportunity and pay careful attention to any suggestions for improvement. Other readers may be of help, although having a friend or relative read your draft may not be as helpful as having it read by someone who is knowledgeable in your field. In any event, be sure to evaluate carefully any suggestions you receive for improvement. And always remember that the final responsibility for the paper rests with you.

ETHICAL USE OF SOURCE MATERIAL

You want to use your source material as effectively as possible. This will sometimes mean that you should quote from a source directly; at other times you will want to express source information in your own words. At all times, you should work to integrate the source material skillfully into the flow of your written argument.

When to Quote

You should quote directly from a source when the original language is distinctive enough to enhance your argument or when rewording the passage would lessen its impact. In the interest of fairness, you should also quote a passage to which your paper will take exception. Rarely, however, should you quote a source at great length (longer than two or three paragraphs). Nor should your paper, or any substantial section of it, be merely a string of quoted passages. The more language you take from the writings of others, the more disruptive the quotations are to the rhetorical flow of your own language. Too much quoting creates a choppy patchwork of varying styles and borrowed purposes in which your sense of your own control over the material is lost.

ACKNOWLEDGE QUOTATIONS CAREFULLY

Failing to signal the presence of a quotation skillfully can lead to confusion or choppiness:

> The U.S. Secretary of Labor believes that worker retraining programs have failed because of a lack of trust within the American business culture. "The

American business community does not visualize the need to invest in its workers" (Winn 1992:11).

The first sentence in the passage above seems to suggest that the quote that follows comes from the Secretary of Labor. Note how this revision clarifies the attribution:

According to reporter Fred Winn (1992), the U.S. Secretary of Labor believes that worker retraining programs have failed because of a lack of trust within the American business culture. Summarizing the Secretary's view, Winn writes, "The American business community does not visualize the need to invest in its workers" (p. 11).

The origin of each quote must be signaled within your text at the point where the quote occurs, as well as in the list of works cited, which follows the text. Chapter 4 describes documentation formats set forth by the American Sociological Association (ASA) and the American Psychological Association (APA).

QUOTE ACCURATELY

If your quotation introduces careless variants of any kind, you are misrepresenting your source. Proofread your quotations very carefully, paying close attention to such surface features as spelling, capitalization, italics, and the use of numerals. Occasionally, either to make a quotation fit smoothly into a passage, to clarify a reference, or to delete unnecessary material from a quotation, you may need to change the original wording slightly. You must signal any such change to your reader by using brackets:

"Several times in the course of his speech, the attorney general said that his stand [on gun control] remains unchanged" (McAffrey 1995:2).

Ellipses may be used to indicate that words have been left out of a quote:

"The last time voters refused to endorse one of the senator's policies...was back in 1982" (Law 1992:143).

When you integrate quoted material with your own prose, it is unnecessary to begin the quote with ellipses:

Benton raised eyebrows with his claim that "nobody in the mayor's office knows how to tie a shoe, let alone balance a budget" (Williams 1990:12).

Paraphrasing

Your writing has its own rhetorical attributes—its own rhythms and structural coherence. Inserting too many quotations into a section of your paper can disrupt the patterns you establish in your prose and diminish the effectiveness of your own language. Paraphrasing, or recasting source material in your own words, is one way of avoiding the risk of creating a choppy hodgepodge of quotations. Paraphrasing allows you to communicate ideas and facts from a source in your own prose, thereby keeping intact the rhetorical characteristics that distinguish your writing.

Remember that a paraphrase is to be written in *your* language; it is not a near copy of the source writer's language. Merely changing a few words of the original does justice to no one's prose and frequently produces stilted passages. This sort of borrowing is actually a form of plagiarism. To fully integrate the material you wish to use into your writing, *use your own language*.

Paraphrasing may actually increase your comprehension of source material, because in recasting a passage you have to think very carefully about its meaning, more carefully, perhaps, than you might if you merely copied it word for word.

Avoiding Plagiarism

Paraphrases require the same sort of documentation as direct quotes. The words of a paraphrase may be yours, but the idea belongs to someone else. Failure to give that person credit, in the form of references within the text and in the bibliography, may make you vulnerable to a charge of plagiarism.

Plagiarism is using someone else's words or ideas without giving them proper credit. Although some plagiarism is deliberate, produced by writers who understand that they are guilty of a kind of academic thievery, much of it is unconscious, committed by writers who are not aware of the varieties of plagiarism or who are careless in recording their borrowings from sources. Plagiarism includes:

- Quoting directly without acknowledging the source
- Paraphrasing without acknowledging the source
- Constructing a paraphrase that closely resembles the original in language and syntax

One way to guard against plagiarism is to keep careful records in your notes of when you have actually quoted source material directly and when you have paraphrased—making sure that the wording of the paraphrase is yours. Make sure that all direct quotes in your final draft are properly set off from your own prose, either with quotation marks or in indented blocks.

What kind of paraphrased material must be acknowledged? Basic material that you find in several sources need not be acknowledged by a reference. For example, it is unnecessary to cite a source for the information that Franklin Delano Roosevelt was elected to a fourth term as President of the United States shortly before his death, because this is a commonly known fact. However, Professor Smith's opinion, published in a recent article, that Roosevelt's winning of a fourth term hastened his death is not a fact but a theory based on Smith's research and defended by her. If you wish to use Smith's opinion in a paraphrase, you need to credit her, as you should all judgments and claims from another source. Any information that is not widely known, whether factual or open to dispute, should be documented. This includes statistics, graphs, tables, and charts taken from a source other than your own primary research.

CHAPTER 6

The Library and Other Sources
of Information

The resources of civilization are not yet exhausted.

William E. Gladstone, 1809–1898

GETTING STARTED

In this chapter we highlight methods of information retrieval for major sources in criminal justice. Let's assume for a moment that you have been assigned a paper on the alternatives to incarceration for nonviolent criminal offenders. With the materials introduced in this chapter, you should be able to find:

- Concise definitions for the terms *incarceration* and *nonviolent criminal offenses*
- Lists of articles and books written on these topics and offering hypotheses about their impact on American society
- Book reviews that will allow you to provide a balanced coverage of the relevant published research
- Government and other statistical sources that help document historical changes in our understanding of both phrases, while associating them with such variables as age, geographic region, race, and socioeconomic status

In some cases, for whatever topic you select, someone in a public agency or private organization has probably already conducted significant research. If you can find the right person, you may be able to secure much more information in much less time than you can by looking in your local library by yourself.

Did you know, for example, that the members of the U.S. Senate and House of Representatives constantly use the services of the Congressional Research Service (CRS), and that upon request to your congressperson or senator, materials from the

CRS may be sent to you on the topic of your choice? Further, every agency of government on the local, state, and national level has employees who are hired primarily for the purpose of gathering information that is needed to help their managers to make decisions. Much of the research that is done by these employees is available upon request.

Please note that the point of this discussion is not to keep you from going to the library but to encourage you to use other sources of information, such as government agencies. In fact, to find the right government agency or private research organization, you will need to go to the library first and consult the directories of organizations you will find there, examples of which are listed below.

This chapter is divided into sections, each describing a type of reference tool. The sections are arranged so that you can become familiar with the nature and uses of general reference works first, and then with the nature and use of specialized studies. Bibliographic examples were selected according to the following criteria:

1. All are available in English.
2. Most are available in college libraries.
3. All are examples of sources potentially useful to criminal justice students.

Publications that may seem unusually dated often represent the inaugural issue of the document or publication being described.

GUIDES TO THE LITERATURE

There are three principal categories of reference works:

1. *Finding aids* help you locate publications that contain information on your topic. Finding aids include bibliographies and periodical indexes.
2. *Content reference works* contain within them the type of factual information you are looking for about a particular topic or topics. Content reference works include handbooks, yearbooks, subject dictionaries, and subject encyclopedias.
3. *Guides to the literature* are books or articles that list—and usually describe— reference works that fit in one or both of categories 1 and 2. Some guides include discussions of various types of research materials, such as government publications, while others include lists of important book-length studies on topics in a subject field. Researchers can identify criminal justice reference publications by consulting a guide that covers a wide spectrum of fields related to their areas of interest.

Here is a list of general guides that can be of great benefit to student researchers.

Bray, R., ed. 1996. *Guide to Reference Books*. Chicago, IL: American Library Association.

Bray and his associates have compiled one of the most complete guides to reference sources in criminal justice and other areas. Many of the works we list in this chapter were obtained from Bray's guide. One of its strengths is its classification of works into many areas that fall under the umbrella of criminal justice, such as General Criminal Justice, Criminology, Probation and Parole, Police Community Relations, Prosecution and Defense, Juvenile Delinquency, and Alcohol and Other Drug Treatment. Bray's guide further classifies the type of reference work within each of these areas, such as guides, bibliographies, periodicals, indexes, encyclopedias, dictionaries, book reviews, directories, atlases, chronologies, biographies, terminology, quotations, handbooks, and statistics. We believe that this guide is probably the best on the market for the serious criminal justice student.

The New York Public Library Desk Reference. 1993. New York: Stonesong Press.

This reference book includes commonly needed material on a vast range of topics, some of interest to criminal justice students, such as the addresses of national, state, county, and city government consumer protection agencies; spoken and written forms of addressing government and military personnel; brief accounts of events in world history; and descriptions of international organizations. There is an index.

Sheehy, E. P., ed. 1986. *Guide to Reference Books*. 10th ed. Chicago, IL: American Library Association.

Like Bray's guide, the primary purpose of this volume is to list and evaluate reference sources. Individual books are grouped under these headings: General Reference Works, Humanities, Social Sciences, History and Area Studies, Pure and Applied Sciences. Within each group, titles are subdivided by subject, then by specific type of material (encyclopedia, dictionary, bibliography, etc.).

For most academic disciplines there are specialized guides to the literature. Given an unfamiliar topic in criminal justice or a related field, a student can consult a guide that focuses on the social sciences for titles of content reference works containing information on the topic. Several examples are:

Aby, S. H. 1987. *Sociology: A Guide to Reference and Information Sources*. Littleton, CO: Libraries Unlimited.

Part of the Reference Sources in the Social Sciences Series (No. 1), this excellent guide is divided into three sections: (1) works of use to all social sciences; (2) individual social science resources of use to sociologists; and (3) criminal justice sources, including general works and a section on resources especially useful in 22 subdivisions of criminal justice.

White, C. 1973. *Sources of Information in the Social Sciences*. 2d ed. Chicago, IL: American Library Association.

This one-volume guide covers eight social sciences, each in a separate chapter. The first part of each chapter introduces important monographs on the development, organization, and content of a discipline and its subfields; the second part lists and annotates major reference works in the discipline by type (dictionaries, encyclopedias, handbooks, etc.). There is an inclusive author–title–subject index.

Sometimes there are guides that reference all available information on a given subject or a constellation of subjects.

Selth, J. P. 1985. *Alternative Lifestyles: A Guide to Research Collections on Intentional Communities, Nudism, and Sexual Freedom*. Westport, CT: Greenwood.

This book describes 30 research collections on intentional communities, nudism, and sexual freedom in the United States, which total 120,000 volumes, 15,000 periodicals, 125,000 audiovisual items, over 3 million photographs, and many ephemeral materials.

As the Internet increasingly becomes a major source of information, guides like the following are needed:

Turecki, Given, ed. 1996. *Cyberhound's Guide to Internet Libraries*. Detroit, MI: Gale Research.

Handbooks

A handbook is a compact factbook designed for quick reference. Handbooks, sourcebooks, and factbooks usually deal with one broad subject area and emphasize generally accepted data rather than recent findings. In the latter respect, handbooks differ from yearbooks, although these reference tools overlap in the way they are used and the information they include. Two types of handbooks useful to criminal justice students are: (1) statistical handbooks, which provide data about a number of demographic and social characteristics, and (2) subject handbooks, which offer a comprehensive summary of research findings and theoretical propositions for broad substantive areas in a discipline.

STATISTICAL HANDBOOKS

Containing data gathered from numerous sources, statistical handbooks provide students with information necessary for the description and analysis of social trends and phenomena. Among the many statistical handbooks useful to students and professionals in criminal justice are:

Historical Statistics of the United States: Colonial Times to 1970. 1971. Washington, DC: Government Printing Office.

This two-volume work contains statistics on a wide spectrum of social and economic developments from the colonial period to the present. The tables are accompanied by explanatory notes and references to additional sources of statistical information. To use this work effectively, you may turn to the table of contents, which provides a broad subject access; the subject index, which offers a more narrow topical approach to the data; or the time period index, which provides access to statistics on major topics for individual decades.

Hurdle, Angela and Andrea Yurasits, eds. 1996. *Demographics USA: County Addition*. New York: Bill Communications.

The information in this guide is organized within a geographic hierarchy by region, state, metropolitan area, and county. Summaries are provided for each geographic area. You will find information dealing with the area's total population; its percentage of the U.S. total; and listings by age, sex, number of households, number of persons in household, and so on.

Morgan, Kathleen O'Leary, ed. 1995. *State Rankings: A Statistical View of the 50 United States*. 6th ed. Lawrence, KS: Morgan Quinto Corporation.

This book features a huge collection of up-to-date statistical information about the 50 United States. Five hundred and forty-six tables compare states in a wide variety of areas: agriculture, crime, defense, economy, government finance, health, housing, population, social welfare, and transportation.

Morgan, Kathleen O'Leary, Scott Morgan and Neal Quinto, eds. 1995. *City Crime Rankings: Crime in Metropolitan America*. Lawrence, KS: Morgan Quinto Corporation.

This reference tool gives current statistics (1993) on the incidence of reported crime for the 100 largest cities in the country. It includes population tables and cross-reference tools that describe which cities and counties make up specific metropolitan areas.

Simon Market Research Bureau. 1992. *The New American Family: Significant and Diversified Lifestyles*. New York: SMRB.

This book draws from government sources and from the publisher's study of media and markets. It provides tables, charts, and figures on income, shopping habits, marital status, mobility, and so on, for groups such as new mothers, singles, baby boomers, empty nesters, and teens.

Stanley, H. W. and R. G. Niemi, eds. 1993. *Vital Statistics on American Politics*. 5th ed. Washington, DC: Congressional Quarterly.

The charts and tables in this guide cover a wide range of topics related to U.S. politics, including the media (newspaper endorsements of presidential candidates from 1932 to 1988 are graphed), interest groups, and the geographical and ethnic composition of political bodies. An index is included.

U.S. Bureau of the Census. *County and City Data Book*. Washington, DC: Government Printing Office.

This handbook contains statistics on population, housing, income, education, and employment for counties, standard metropolitan statistical areas, cities, urbanized areas, and unincorporated places. Since there is no subject index, the only subject access to the tables is through the "Outline of Tabular Subject Content" located in the front of the volume. This handbook is published irregularly.

Walker, Monica A., ed. 1995. *Interpreting Crime Statistics*. New York: Oxford University Press.

This monograph explores statistics that are published (or easily accessible) relating to crime, criminals, and the criminal justice system in the United Kingdom. It is of particular value for students, educators, and professionals involved in criminal justice studies.

Students may also want to consult the following statistical guides:

Darnay, A. J., ed. 1994. *Statistical Record of Older Americans*. Detroit, MI: Gale Research.

Ficke, R. C. 1992. *Digest of Data on Persons with Disabilities*. Washington, DC: National Institute on Disability and Rehabilitation Research.

Gall, S. B. and Timothy L. Gall, eds. 1993. *Statistical Record of Asian Americans*. Detroit, MI: Gale Research.

Gall, Timothy L. and Daniel M. Lucus, eds. 1996. *Statistics on Alcohol, Drug, and Tobacco Use*. Detroit, MI: Gale Research.

Horton, C. P. and J. C. Smith, eds. 1990. *Statistical Record of Black America*. Detroit, MI: Gale Research.

Maguire, Kathleen and Ann L. Pastore, eds. 1995. *Sourcebook of Criminal Justice Statistics. Washington, DC: Bureau of Justice Statistics*, Office of Justice Programs.

National Data Book. 1992. 116th ed. Washington, DC: Statistical Abstract of the United States, U.S. Department of Commerce.

Reddy, Marlita A., ed. 1993. *Statistical Record of Hispanic Americans*. Detroit, MI: Gale Research.

Reddy, Marlita A., ed. 1993. *Statistical Record of Native North Americans*. Detroit, MI: Gale Research.

Schick, F. L. and R. Schick, eds. 1994. *Statistical Handbook on Aging Americans*. Phoenix, AZ: Oryx.

Uniform Crime Reports. 1995. Washington, DC: Federal Bureau of Investigation, U.S. Department of Justice.

SUBJECT HANDBOOKS

Subject handbooks in criminal justice provide a summary and a synthesis of concepts, research, and theoretical approaches to specific topical areas within the discipline, such as formal organizations, juvenile delinquency, and criminal justice management. Students who want a brief overview of well-established information or an explanation of major concepts in substantive areas such as forensics, evidence, or terrorism should find the subject handbooks listed below helpful.

NOTE: For students who are considering a career in writing about crime, from journalism to novels to screenplays, the following reference books should prove very helpful.

Becker, Ronald F. 1997. *Specific Evidence and Expert Testimony Handbook: A Guide for Lawyers, Criminal Investigators and Forensic Specialists*. Springfield, IL: Charles C Thomas.

This book offers valuable information for the advanced criminal justice student. While brief and to the point, it provides important insights and information concerning expert testimony.

Bentley, William K., and James M. Corbett. 1992. *Prison Slang: Words and Expressions Depicting Life Behind Bars.* Jefferson, NC: McFarland.

This work is an essential resource for students and personnel in corrections, criminal justice, and law, as well as a useful tool for journalists, etymologists, fiction writers, and anyone seeking a better understanding of prison life.

Friedman, Lawrence, Nicholes F. Fleming, David H. Roberts and Steven E. Hyman, eds. 1996. *Sourcebook of Substance Abuse and Addiction.* Baltimore, MD: Williams & Wilkins.

This book is designed to synthesize chemical dependency and substance abuse information. It includes an epidemiological evaluation of the impact of substance abuse and addiction on the individual, the family, and society.

Mullins, Waymon C. 1996. *A Sourcebook on Domestic and International Terrorism.* 2d ed. Springfield, IL: Charles C Thomas.

This sourcebook provides a discrete analysis of issues, organizations, tactics, and responses in the area of terrorism.

Roth, Martin. 1990. *The Writer's Complete Crime Reference Book.* Writer's Digest Books. Cincinnati, OH: F.W. Publications.

Today, there are many television shows, motion pictures, and novels dealing with crime and criminals. If you are planing to write about crime, you'll find this book an essential tool in helping you add credibility to your story or script. This reference source includes information and facts dealing with the fundamentals of investigation, as well as with the wide variety of law enforcement agencies and investigative services and their responsibilities and jurisdictions. Criminal motives, escape methods, weapons, rules of evidence, and slang are just a small portion of the research and reference material available in this book.

For the criminal justice student in need of current facts and details in the legal field, the following directory is an excellent source.

Wasserman, Sterss, Jacqueline Wasserman-O'Brian and Bosnia Shaw Pfaff, eds. 1991. *Law and Legal Information Directory.* Detroit, MI: Gale Research.

Almost everyone is aware of the impact of the law on everyday situations: malpractice for lawyers, dentists, doctors, and even clergy; compliance regulations to avoid gender, racial, or disabilities discrimination; waste disposal directives; and a myriad of other laws with ramifications for social, economic, and political activities. This book describes organizations, services, programs, and other sources of information about the legal field, bringing together in one work a large amount of information on an area of increasing significance to all walks of life.

Other subject handbooks of interest to criminal justice students and professionals include:

Adler, L. L. ed. 1993. *International Handbook on Gender Roles*. Westport, CT: Greenwood.

Baker, T.O. 1992. *Operator's Manual for a Witness Chair*. Kansas City, MO: Baker and Sterchi.

Bart, P. and L. Frankel. 1986. *The Student Sociologist's Handbook*. 4th ed. New York: Random House.

Bellenir, Karen. 1996. *Substance Abuse Sourcebook*. Detroit, MI: Omnigraphics.

Bellenir, Karen and Peter D. Dresser, eds. 1995. *AIDS Sourcebook*. Detroit, MI: Omnigraphics.

Binstock, R. H. and L. K. George, eds. 1990. *Handbook of Aging and the Social Sciences*. San Diego, CA: Academic Press.

Bintliff, Russell. 1990. *Training Manual for Law Enforcement Officers*. Upper Saddle River, NJ: Prentice Hall.

Bird, F.F. 1988. *Management Guide to Loss Control*. Loganville, LA: International Loss Control Institute.

Creating Safe and Drug Free Schools: An Action Guide. 1996. Washington, DC: U.S. Department of Education.

Desktop Guide to Good Juvenile Detention Practice. 1996. Rockville, MD: Juvenile Justice Clearinghouse.

Factbook on Intelligence. 1992. Washington, DC: Central Intelligence Agency.

Family Life, Delinquency, and Crime: A Policymaker's Guide. 1994. Rockville, MD: Juvenile Justice Clearinghouse.

F.B.I. Facts and History. 1992. Washington, DC: Federal Bureau of Investigation, U.S. Department of Justice.

Fennelly, L.J. 1992. *Handbook of Loss Prevention and Crime Prevention*. Newton, MA: Butterworth-Heinemann.

Guide for Implementing the Comprehensive Strategy for Serious, Violent, and Chronic Juvenile Offenders. 1995. Rockville, MD: Juvenile Justice Clearinghouse.

Handbook of Forensic Evidence. 1984. Washington, DC: Federal Bureau of Investigation, U.S. Department of Justice.

Handbook of Forensic Sciences. 1990. Washington, DC: Federal Bureau of Investigation, U.S. Department of Justice.

Helping Victims and Witnesses in the Juvenile Justice System: A Program Handbook. 1991. Rockville, MD: Juvenile Justice Clearinghouse.

Hurrelmann, K., ed. 1994. *International Handbook of Adolescence*. Westport, CT: Greenwood.

Questions and Answers on the Defense Industrial Security Program. 1991. Washington, DC: Defense Investigative Service, U.S. Department of Defense.

Resource Manual for Juvenile Detention and Corrections: Effective and Innovative Programs. 1995. Rockville, MD: Juvenile Justice Clearinghouse.

Smelser, Neil J., ed. 1988. *Handbook of Sociology*. Thousand Oaks, CA: Sage.

Woods, G. 1993. *Drug Abuse in Society: A Reference Handbook*. Santa Barbara, CA: ABC-Clio.

Zophy, A. H. and F. M. Karenik, eds. 1990. *Handbook of American Women's History*. New York: Garland.

Yearbooks

Although many yearbooks contain a good deal of background information, they are primarily fact books that focus on the developments and events of a given year. Unlike handbooks, they emphasize current information. Like handbooks, there are two types of yearbooks most useful for criminal justice students: (1) statistical yearbooks, which provide the most recent data on social and demographic characteristics, and (2) subject yearbooks, which review current theory and research.

STATISTICAL YEARBOOKS

You can turn to the most recent yearbook for the latest data available on topics such as population composition, fertility, and economic activity, and you can also use back issues to collect data for previous time periods. This is especially true in cases where no handbook presents data for a specific geographical or topical area. Among the general statistical yearbooks often used by criminal justice students are the following:

Statistical Yearbook. New York: United Nations Statistical Office.

Tables in this annual publication cover population, manpower, agriculture, production, mining construction, consumption, transportation, external trade, wages and prices, national income, finance, social statistics, and education and culture. Normally, a 10 to 20-year span is given for each series. The table of contents is the only subject access to this book. Sources are cited. Textual material, including indexes, is in French and English.

Statistical Yearbook. Paris: UNESCO.

The statistical charts in this annual publication are printed in three languages and cover aspects of education, science, and culture in 200 member nations of UNESCO. The data are generated from questionnaires given to a wide variety of respondents. There is no index.

Vital Statistics of the United States. 2 vols. Hyattsville, MD: U.S. Department of Health and Human Services.

This yearly series is published annually in two volumes. Volume 1 presents the year's birth statistics at the national and local levels, and Volume 2 covers death statistics.

Yearbook of Labour Statistics. Geneva: International Labour Office.

This book publishes statistical tables on the economic development of countries around the world. There is an index of countries.

Statistical yearbooks focusing on a special subject are often useful to criminal justice students interested in specific problems. Two yearbooks focusing on specific subjects are:

Demographic Yearbook. New York: United Nations Statistical Office.

This annual publication contains demographic statistics for over 200 separate geographic areas. Population and vital statistics appear in each annual volume, but the subject matter of the other statistical compilations varies from year to year. Each volume includes an introduction defining terms and describing the tables. The table of contents provides access to tables by broad categories. A cumulative index in each volume identifies the annual volumes in which statistics on individual topics are to be found and indicates the time span of the statistics in individual volumes.

U.S. Federal Bureau of Investigation. *Uniform Crime Reports for the United States*. Washington, DC: Government Printing Office.

This annual report contains statistics on crimes, offenders, and law enforcement personnel. Tables include statistics by type of offenses, geographical divisions, age groups, trends, and police employment. The table of contents provides the only subject access to the tables.

SUBJECT YEARBOOKS

The subject yearbook, also known as the annual review, is particularly useful because it contains information that gives a brief overview of recent major developments in the field. This allows a student beginning a research project to define and clarify the subject matter. The bibliographies appended to the articles can provide useful leads for further reading. The subject yearbook for criminal justice is:

Annual Review of Criminal Justice. Palo Alto, CA: Annual Reviews.

New developments in the field of criminal justice are discussed in approximately 16 essays covering 10 broad subject areas in this annual. Areas covered include formal organizations, social processes, urban criminal justice, and institutions. The essays average 25 to 30 pages in length and include extensive bibliographies. Each volume beginning with the second contains cumulative indexes that list essays by author and broad subject area.

Another annual publication that is potentially of interest to criminal justice students and professionals is:

Whitehead, Kenneth D. *Federal Personnel Guide*. Washington, DC: Key Communications Group.

This annual publication is a useful, accurate, timesaving source of valuable information on government personnel, organization, compensation, promotion, leave, retirement, insurance, health benefits, and other important and interesting subjects for the Civil Service, Postal Service, and all other civilian employees of the federal government.

Subject Dictionaries and Encyclopedias

DICTIONARIES

The primary purpose of a dictionary is to indicate the meanings and give accurate spellings of words. The words included, and the exhaustiveness of their definitions, depend on the type of dictionary. This discussion focuses on subject dictionaries.

Virtually all academic disciplines have their own specialized language. The function of a subject dictionary is to explain briefly the words, whether terms or names, that make up a particular subject's specialized jargon. Such a source lists terms unfamiliar in common usage, as well as rather ordinary terms that have taken on specialized and technical meanings within the context of a subject discipline.

Criminal justice is a broad field encompassing a wide span of human social behavior. Many concepts or terms that have a common usage take on a specialized meaning in criminal justice. The term *norm* is an example. In common usage the word refers to something common or normal. In criminal justice, however, *norm* refers to the rules or expectations that guide social behavior.

In addition to defining concepts, subject dictionaries are also useful for locating brief descriptions of methodological techniques or tests and definitions of major theories. When students are unsure of the exact meaning of a concept or theory, or of the function of a specific methodological technique, they can consult a criminal justice dictionary or a broader dictionary of the social sciences. Examples are:

Addictionary: A Primer of Recovery Terms and Concepts, from Abstinence to Withdrawal. 1992. New York: Fireside/Parkside, a division of Simon & Schuster.

This book is for anyone interested in the process of recovery from addiction to alcohol, drugs, food, overeating, purging, starving, gambling, sex, tobacco, exercise, work relationships, codependency, or any other addiction or its effects. Topics, or modules, are arranged alphabetically to make them easy for use in ongoing recovery or research.

Black, Henry Campbell. 1990. *Black's Law Dictionary*. 6th ed. St. Paul, MN: West Publishing.

For a century, *Black's Law Dictionary* has been the recognized standard for accurate, comprehensive, and current definitions of legal words and terms. This edition contains over 5000 new or revised terms as well as greatly expanded usage examples and cross-references to related terms. There are also new and updated references throughout to related federal statutes, court rules, model and uniform laws, the Internal Revenue Code, and many other authorities.

De Sala, Ralph. 1980. *Crime Dictionary*. New York: Facts on File.

The *Crime Dictionary* contains definitions relating to alcoholic and narcotic addiction, supplied mostly by the Drug Enforcement Administration of the U.S. Department of Justice. Some were rewritten and simplified from the many appearing in medical books and journals. Blood brotherhoods and crime syndicates flourish almost worldwide. They, too, have their own terminology, and every attempt was made to include multilingual terms of interest to general readers as well as law enforcement officers. The dictionary also includes criminal slang, historical and literary allusions, medical and psychiatric expressions, nicknames, and shortcuts which are characteristic of underground and underworld speech, along with many popular colloquialisms. Crime has been defined many times by great authors. Their works have also been included in the section entitled "Selected Sources."

Gould, J. and W. L. Kolb. 1964. *A Dictionary of the Social Sciences*. New York: Free Press.

This excellent dictionary includes approximately 1000 terms used in the social sciences. Selections were made from a study of the literature in political science, social anthropology, economics, social psychology, and criminal justice.

Johnson, Allan G. 1995. *The Blackwell Dictionary of Sociology*. Cambridge, MA: Blackwell.

In this "user's guide to sociological language," students will find major concepts that sociologists use in their professional writing, many of which are germane to criminal justice.

Rush, George E. 1986. *The Dictionary of Criminal Justice*. 2d ed. Guilford, CT: Dushkin Publishing Group.

The Dictionary of Criminal Justice, 2d ed., defines terms commonly used in the interdisciplinary field of criminal justice. The criminal justice student, researcher, or practitioner continually encounters certain words, names, personalities, court cases, events, phrases, and terms that by their selective nature have somewhat special meaning. Because the study of criminal justice and its processes cross, blend, and overlap several disciplines, this book attempts to compile in one reference volume information that could otherwise be found only through a tedious search through an endless amount of interdisciplinary literature. It represents an extensive effort to cover the terms associated with the wide spectrum of law enforcement, courts, probation, parole, and corrections and cites information and sources specific to each area.

Theodorson, G. A. and A. G. Theodorson. 1969. *A Modern Dictionary of Sociology*. New York: Barnes & Noble.

This comprehensive dictionary, prepared for students in sociology, contains extensive definitions of words as they are used by sociologists, especially those linked with the related fields of social psychology, demography, political science, and criminal justice.

Other examples of dictionaries that are germane to criminal justice, some of which are designed for specific areas within the discipline of criminal justice, include the following:

Abel, E. L. 1984. *A Dictionary of Drug Abuse Terms and Terminology*. Westport, CT: Greenwood.

Ellmore, R. T. 1991. *NTC's Mass Media Dictionary*. Lincolnwood, IL: National Textbook.

Fay, J. J., ed. 1988. *The Alcohol/Drug Abuse Dictionary and Encyclopedia*. Springfield, IL: Charles C Thomas.

Fay, J. J., ed. 1989. *Butterworth's Security Dictionary*. Newton, MA: Butterworth-Heinemann.

Harris, D. K. 1988. *Dictionary of Gerontology*. Westport, CT: Greenwood.

Lindsey, M. P. 1989. *Dictionary of Mental Handicap*. New York: Routledge.

Mills, J. 1992. *Womanwords: A Dictionary of Words about Women*. New York: Free Press.

Richter, A. 1993. *Dictionary of Sexual Slang*. New York: Wiley.

ENCYCLOPEDIAS

In contrast to dictionaries, which contain brief definitions of terms, encyclopedias include summary essays about individual topics. There are two types of encyclopedias: *general encyclopedias*, which are wide-ranging in topical coverage, and *subject encyclopedias*, which focus on topics within an individual subject discipline or a group of related disciplines. The rest of this discussion will deal with subject encyclopedias.

The essays in subject encyclopedias are often written by recognized scholars. They include bibliographies listing major topical studies and cross-references listing other essays that may contain useful additional information. You can use a subject encyclopedia in several ways: as an introduction to a topic, as a means of viewing a topic in a wider context, or as the starting point for research. You may find an essay helpful for clarification and definition of your research project, and the bibliography can provide valuable leads for further reading. The following subject encyclopedias are especially useful to criminal justice majors:

Borgatta, E. F. and M. L. Borgatta, eds. 1992. *Encyclopedia of Sociology*. New York: Macmillan.

This four-volume set is a comprehensive general sociology encyclopedia intended for a broad audience. It contains 370 articles written by 339 sociologists, each two to 18 pages in length and concluding with bibliographies.

Fay, J.J. ed., 1993. *Encyclopedia of Security Management*. Newton, MA: Butterworth-Heinemann.

This encyclopedia offers a collection of authoritative information that impinges directly on the security management function as it is performed in many different industries. Its purpose is to (1) make the novice aware of opportunities that are present in the diverse nature of security jobs, (2) make the retail store investigator aware of cash register auditing techniques used by his or her counterpart in the lodging industry, (3) make the electronic access control designer aware of group dynamics, (4) make the consultant knowledgeable about finance, and (5) give the top security executive improved insights into the work of the front-line technicians. In addition, this book endeavors to make all security practitioners aware of strides that have been made in electronic technology, the forensic sciences, human motivation, and the like.

McShane, M. D. and F. P. Williams III. 1996. *Encyclopedia of American Prisons*. New York: Garland Reference Library.

Many of the entries in this encyclopedia begin with a historical discussion to help frame the issues that are discussed. Each is written by an author who knows the subject matter well and, in many cases, is preeminent in the field.

The entries compose a comprehensive collection that tells the story of the people, places, and ideas behind the American prison system.

Nash, Jay R. 1989. *Encyclopedia of World Crime: Criminal Justice, Criminology, and Law Enforcement*. 7 vols. Wilmette, IL: Crime Books.

For historical research, this work offers detailed, extensive, international information in the areas of crime, criminal justice, and criminology. It is a comprehensive biographical and historical source.

Nash, Jay R., ed., 1992. *World Encyclopedia of Organized Crime*. 1989. New York: Paragon House.

Condensed from the *Encyclopedia of World Crime*, this encyclopedia examines the international scope of present-day organized crime, as well as its historical roots.

Sells, David A. 1979. *International Encyclopedia of the Social Sciences*. New York: Macmillan.

This 17-volume set contains articles covering the subject matter of the following fields, as well as some of the most important contributors in their development: anthropology, economics, geography, history, law, political science, psychiatry, psychology, criminal justice, and statistics. The treatment of individual topics is often divided into more than one essay, each approaching the topic from the perspective of a different social science. Although the encyclopedia is arranged alphabetically by subject, the articles are lengthy and cover broad areas. To find a specific topic, you should consult the index in the last volume. There is also a useful "Classification of Articles" section in the last volume. The essays themselves are carefully cross-referenced, and the bibliographies accompanying the articles, some of which are extensive although dated, remain useful.

Tierney, H., ed. 1989–1991. *Women's Studies Encyclopedia: Views from the Inside*. Westport, CT: Greenwood.

The major focus of this three-volume work is on the American experience. There is no single feminist perspective informing the articles. Contributors had the widest possible latitude in developing their articles.

The following encyclopedias deal with areas of potential interest to criminal justice students:

Bernes, William J., ed., 1989. *Personal Computer Programming Encyclopedia*. New York: McGraw-Hill.

Clark, R. E. and J. F. Clark, eds. 1989. *The Encyclopedia of Child Abuse*. New York: Facts on File.

DiCanio, M. 1993. *The Encyclopedia of Violence: Origins, Attitudes, Consequences*. New York: Facts on File.

Encyclopedia Dictionary of American Government. 1986. Guilford, CT: Dushkin Publishing Group.

Evans, G., R. O'Brien and S. Cohen, eds. 1991. *The Encyclopedia of Drug Abuse*. New York: Facts on File.

Heydel, C., ed. 1982. *The Encyclopedia of Management*. 3d ed. New York: Van Nostrand Reinhold.

Kadish, Sanford H., ed. 1983. *The Encyclopedia of Crime and Justice*. 3 vols. New York: Free Press.

Lerner, R., A. C. Petersen and J. Brooks-Gunn, eds. 1991. *Encyclopedia of Adolescence*. 2 vols. New York: Garland.

Maddox, G. L., ed. 1987. *The Encyclopedia of Aging*. New York: Springer.

Manstead, Anthony S. R. and Miles Hewstone. 1995. *The Blackwell Encyclopedia of Social Psychology*. 2 vols. Cambridge, MA: Blackwell.

Nash, Jay Robert. 1992. *World Encyclopedia of 20th Century Murder*. New York: Paragon House.

O'Brien, R. and M. Chafetz, eds. 1991. *The Encyclopedia of Alcoholism*. New York: Facts on File.

Roy, F. H. and C. Russell, eds. 1992. *The Encyclopedia of Aging and the Elderly*. New York: Facts on File.

Indexes and Abstracts

Indexes contain lists of citations of articles printed in journals, magazines, and other periodicals. The standard citation for articles in indexes includes the author's name, the date of the issue in which the article appears, the article title, the name of the journal, the volume and/or issue number, and page numbers. Abstracts contain short summaries of articles or books. Indexes and abstracts are important because the articles in scholarly journals often update information found in books or in some cases constitute the only published treatments of certain topics.

COMPUTER ON-LINE DATABASE SYSTEMS

Specialized indexes and abstracts list articles published in scholarly journals by subject and author. Most are now retrievable through computer on-line database systems located in the library. These CD-ROM networks index thousands of professional and popular articles in most academic areas. The most useful databases for criminal justice are stored in *Sociofile and Social Sciences Index*. *Sociofile* indexes over 1900 international journals in sociology, criminal justice, and related fields that are stored in two print indexes titled *Sociological Abstracts* (1974–present) and *Social Planning, Policy and Development Abstracts*. *Social Sciences Index* (1983–present) indexes journals in most of the social sciences, including anthropology, area studies, criminal justice, economics, environmental science, geography, law, political science, and sociology.

Other databases that offer potential sources for criminal justice studies are:

- *Eric*, an education database (1966–present) consisting of the *Resources in Education* file and the *Current Index to Journals in Education* file, compiling journal article citations with abstracts from over 750 professional journals.
- *Psyclit*, a psychology database (1974–present) that compiles summaries for literature in psychology and related disciplines and corresponds to *Psychological Abstracts*, which indexes about 1300 professional journals in 27 languages.

- *Readers' Guide to Periodical Literature*, a popular and general interest database (1983–present) that provides citations from more than 900 journals and magazines in the popular press.
- *United States Government Periodical Index*, a government periodicals database (November 1994–present) that indexes approximately 180 U.S. government sources covering a wide variety of subjects.

The reference department in many libraries also allows you to access over 40 other databases on FIRSTSEARCH.

DISCIPLINE INDEXES

While general indexes identify journal articles according to broad topical areas without a discipline focus, discipline indexes identify articles in journals by the discipline or group of related disciplines (such as social sciences) instead of by topic. An example of a discipline index that indexes by subject articles in social science, economics, and anthropology journals as well as those in criminal justice and sociology is:

Social Sciences Index. New York: H.W. Wilson.

A quarterly publication with annual cumulations, this index organizes—by subject and author—articles in some 260 journals in anthropology, sociology, law, and criminology. A helpful feature is the separate "Book Reviews" index at the back of each issue.

TOPICAL INDEXES

An important topic often becomes the focus of an index, which is generated to make all articles relevant to that topic available to researchers, regardless of field or discipline. An example of a topical index that might be helpful to criminal justice students is:

Population Index. Princeton, NJ: Office of Population Research, Princeton University and Population Association of America.

This quarterly indexes books, journals, and government publications. The annotated entries are arranged by broad subjects, such as mortality, internal migration, and spatial distribution. Each issue also contains several articles on topics of current interest. Geographical, author, and statistical indexes cumulate annually.

Statistical Reference Index Annual Abstracts. Bethesda, MD: Congressional Information Service.

This annual volume is a guide to American statistical publications produced by private organizations and state governments. Contents are organized by the type of organization publishing the reports, each of which is described briefly. An accompanying volume includes four indexes: subject and name, category, issuing sources, and title.

Other topical indexes of interest to criminal justice students are:

Inventory of Marriage and Family Literature. 1973. St. Paul, MN: National Council on
   Family Relations.
Kaiser Index to Black Resources: 1948–1986. 1992. Brooklyn, NY: Carlson.
Newman, R. 1981. *Black Index: Afro-Americana in Selected Periodicals, 1907–1949*. New
   York: Garland.
Women's Studies Index. 1991. Boston, MA: G.K. Hall Citation Indexes.

A third type of index, the citation index, lists articles that refer to previous
research by a particular author. When a researcher knows of one article—or author of
articles—on a particular topic, newer related materials can be found by locating articles
that cite the original work or author. Thus you can find articles without depending on
any subject classification system. This type of index is useful for determining the quality
of a specific key research paper or for tracing the developments in theory and methods
that were stimulated by this key paper. A student can determine the number of times
a key article has been used, as well as the names of the sociologists who have cited it.
One citation index useful to criminal justice students and professionals is:

Social Sciences Citation Index. Philadelphia, PA: Institute for Scientific Information.

Each issue of this index is divided into three parts. The *Citation Index*, arranged
alphabetically by cited author, lists articles in which a particular work was cited.
The *Source Index* lists the authors who are citing the original work alphabetically
and gives bibliographic information for each article that cites the original work.
The *Permaterm Subject Index* lists articles by all the significant words in the
titles. The index is issued three times a year and cumulates annually.

ABSTRACTS

Like indexes, abstracts provide a complete citation for each article and include a brief
summary of its contents. Abstracts enable researchers to determine whether or not an
article is useful without having to locate and read it. This can be important when students are working in a library with a small periodical collection and must depend on
interlibrary loans to acquire enough articles.

Criminal Justice Abstracts. Hackensack, NJ: National Council on Crime and Delinquency.

This quarterly publication (entitled *Crime and Delinquency Literature* through
1976) abstracts books and journals in the area of crime and delinquency.
Abstracts are arranged under broad subject areas such as correction and law
enforcement. There is a detailed subject index. Each issue also contains a
review of current developments in one area, such as aid to victims, employee
theft, and delinquency prevention.

Sociological Abstracts. New York: Sociological Abstracts.

This source indexes and summarizes over 6000 books and journal articles each
year. Within broad subject areas, such as deviance, group interaction, social

differentiation, and feminist studies, abstracts are arranged alphabetically by author. The last issue of each year contains cumulative author and subject indexes. The abstract is currently issued five times a year.

Examples of other abstracts within the broader discipline of criminal justice include:

Abstracts in Social Gerontology. Thousand Oaks, CA: Sage.
Child Development Abstracts and Bibliography. Chicago, IL: University of Chicago Press.
Sage Family Studies Abstracts. Thousand Oaks, CA: Sage.
Sage Race Relations Abstracts. Thousand Oaks, CA: Sage.
Women's Studies Abstracts. New York: Rush.

Bibliographies

Bibliographies constitute a particularly important category of finding aids. An individual bibliography might list any or all of the following: books, periodicals, periodical articles, published documents, unpublished documents, or unpublished manuscripts. Our focus is on bibliographies as finding aids for articles and for books other than reference books. Whenever you use a bibliography that does not list journal articles as well as book titles, you must also consult a periodical index or abstract in order to compile a thorough reading list on the topic.

Some bibliographies provide only citations for the books and articles they list; others provide annotations as well. Standard bibliographic citation form for journal articles includes author(s), date of publication, title, journal name, volume/number, and pages. Usually, the information is sufficiently complete to locate the item. Annotated bibliographies provide more information, helping you decide if an individual title might be useful. An annotation is a brief summary of the article or book's content, along with a comment on its quality.

Bibliographies come in two formats: (1) brief compilations appended to articles or books and (2) book-length works.

APPENDED BIBLIOGRAPHIES

Appended bibliographies identify titles that are either cited in the article or book or are relevant to the topic being discussed. You can use a bibliography appended to a reliable book or article as a guide to your readings on the topic. To identify appended bibliographies on a particular topic, you may consult:

Bibliographic Index. New York: H.W. Wilson.

Published in April and August and in a cumulated annual volume in December, this work lists, by subject, bibliographies with 50 or more entries that are published separately or as parts of books or periodicals in English and Western European languages. Citations specify whether or not the bibliographies are annotated. Each volume begins with a prefatory note that explains briefly the forms used in the entries.

BOOK-LENGTH BIBLIOGRAPHIES

Bibliographic indexes also identify book-length bibliographies. Their scope is ordinarily wider than that of appended bibliographies. Some book-length bibliographies are published only once and are retrospective in nature. An example of this type is:

> Aldous, Joan and Ruben Hill. 1989. *International Bibliography of Research in Marriage and the Family.* St. Paul, MN: Family Social Science, University of Minnesota.

Others are published periodically, sometimes annually, and are called *current bibliographies*. Each new edition lists titles that have appeared since the preceding edition. However, most current bibliographies allow a one- to two-year lag between the publication of a book and its citation.

Some useful current bibliographies cover a particular academic discipline, such as sociology, or a group of related disciplines, such as social sciences. Generally, the coverage includes articles as well as books, and the scope is international. An example is the following:

> *International Bibliography of Sociology.* London: Tavistock.

One of a set entitled *International Bibliography of the Social Sciences*, this volume attempts to provide comprehensive coverage of scholarly publications in the field, regardless of country of origin, language, or type. Three to five thousand citations are arranged in a detailed classification scheme, with author and subject indexes providing complete access. Citations are not annotated. All information is given in French and English. Although the volume is published each year, there is a one- to two-year time lag.

National libraries, such as the British Library or the Library of Congress, house copies of most of the important books on all subjects which are available in that country. Therefore, the subject catalog of the Library of Congress, available in most college and university libraries, can be used as a reasonably comprehensive current bibliography on most topics.

> U.S. Library of Congress. *Subject Catalog: A Cumulative List of Works Represented by Library of Congress Printed Cards.* Washington, DC: Library of Congress.

Published in quarterly, yearly, and five-year cumulative editions since 1950, the *Subject Catalog* lists books cataloged by the Library of Congress and other major libraries in the United States. Each edition offers the single most comprehensive bibliography of works on every subject (excluding works of fiction), and from all parts of the world, which have become available during the period it covers. Subject headings are cross-referenced.

The following bibliographies contain materials with potential use for criminal justice students:

> Aday, R. H. 1988. *Crime and the Elderly: An Annotated Bibliography.* Westport, CT: Greenwood.
> Berndt, J. 1986. Rural Sociology: *A Bibliography of Bibliographies.* Metuchen, NJ: Scarecrow.

Bruhn, J. G., B. U. Philips and P. L. Levine. 1985. *Medical Sociology: An Annotated Bibliography*. New York: Garland.

Dabney, M. L. 1984. *Incest: An Annotated Bibliography*. Jefferson, NC: McFarland.

De Young, M. 1987. *Child Molestation: An Annotated Bibliography*. Jefferson, NC: McFarland.

Engeldinger, E. A. 1986. *Spouse Abuse: An Annotated Bibliography of Violence Between Mates*. Metuchen, NJ: Scarecrow.

Ghorayshi, P. 1990. *The Sociology of Work: A Critical Annotated Bibliography*. New York: Garland.

Kinl, G. C. 1987. *Social Stratification: An Annotated Bibliography*. New York: Garland.

Nordquest, J. 1988. *The Homeless in America: A Bibliography*. Santa Cruz, CA: Reference and Research Services.

Nordquest, J. 1988. *Substance Abuse I: Drug Abuse: A Bibliography*. Santa Cruz, CA: Reference and Research Services.

Nordquest, J. 1990. *Substance Abuse II: Alcohol Abuse: A Bibliography*. Santa Cruz, CA: Reference and Research Services.

Nordquest, J. 1991. *The Elderly in America: A Bibliography*. Santa Cruz, CA: Reference and Research Services.

Soliday, G. L. et al., eds. 1980. *History of the Family and Kinship: A Select International Bibliography*. Millwood, NY: Kraus International.

General Periodicals and Newspapers

GENERAL PERIODICALS

General periodicals contain articles on a range of topics intended to attract general readers with varied interests. News magazines, hobby or recreational magazines, and a host of publications such as the *Atlantic Monthly* and the *New Yorker* are all classified as general periodicals. A student can find information on specific topics covered in general periodicals by consulting the *Readers' Guide to Periodical Literature* in printed format on the library shelf, going back for several decades, or on the *CD-ROM Database Network*, which goes back to 1983.

General periodicals not only broaden a student's knowledge and outlook, but can also serve a legitimate research function. Many general periodicals include regular features on important social issues (such as crime, poverty, unemployment, or busing) and public opinion (attitudes toward such topics as marijuana smoking, abortion, and capital punishment). Among the major general periodicals which emphasize social, legal and political affairs are the *New York Times Magazine, Atlantic Monthly, Newsweek, U.S. News and World Report, Time*, and *Harper's*. General periodicals reporting current events and issues of interest to criminal justice students usually do not analyze them from a criminal justice perspective. However, one general periodical that uses sociological and criminal justice models to analyze social, legal, and political issues is:

Society (Formerly: *Transaction: Social Science and Modern Society*). New Brunswick, NJ: Rutgers University Press.

Written for the layperson by well-known sociologists and other social scientists, this periodical, which began publication in 1967, covers a wide variety of topics in the areas of government, housing, welfare, law, race relations, and education. It is issued monthly.

Other examples of similar utility are *Business Week*, *Psychology Today*, and *Library Journal*. These periodicals cover professional news, trends, developments, and other events for the professions. Articles are often written by professionals in the field.

NEWSPAPERS

Newspapers are regularly issued publications (daily, weekly, semiweekly) that report events and discuss topics of current interest. The types of information that sociologists may find useful include news items comprising factual reporting of events, editorials representing the editor's thinking on current issues, feature articles presenting an investigation of a topic, and columns publishing comments or reports on current events or issues by journalists. In newspapers you can find factual information on topics such as crime or intergroup conflict. Also, you can identify attitudes of people toward important social issues.

Newspapers distinguished for the extensive coverage they give to national affairs include the *Washington Post* and *The New York Times*. You can find articles that cover specific topics in *The New York Times* by consulting its index:

New York Times Index. New York: New York Times.

First published in 1913, the *New York Times Index* provides subject access to *New York Times* news stories, editorials, and other features. Published every two weeks, it is cumulated annually. Each entry begins with a subject, followed by references to other sections in the index (if there are any). Then the article is summarized. For the sake of brevity, the citation identifies each month by one or two letters, followed by the date, a roman number for a section, an Arabic page number, and sometimes a column number prefaced by a colon. The year is always identified on the cover and title page and is essential information to record when copying citations. One important item to note in using this index is that the cross-references that directly follow the subject in each entry must be checked in the index to obtain a complete citation. You cannot identify the exact location of the articles noted in this section without doing so.

The following major newspapers have indexes available either in print or on microfilm:

- *Chicago Tribune*
- *Houston Post*
- *Los Angeles Times*
- *National Observer*
- *New Orleans Times–Picayune*
- *The New York Times*
- *The Times of London*

- *Wall Street Journal*
- *Washington Post*

You may need coverage of an important topic from a number of different perspectives. In such a research project a local newspaper or *The New York Times* would not suit your needs. For example, you may want to compare the coverage of right-to-work laws presented in a Southwestern newspaper to that presented in a Northern newspaper. For that type of project you should consult:

NewsBank. Greenwich, CT: Urban Affairs Library.

Begun in 1975, this publication not only indexes articles on subjects from over 150 daily and weekly urban newspapers but also includes the articles themselves on microfiche. The index is divided into 13 subject sections—Business and Economic Development, Consumer Affairs, Government Structure, Social Relations, Welfare and Poverty, Housing and Urban Renewal, Law and Order, Education, Political Development, Health, Transportation, Environment, and Employment—each contained in separate binders. The microfiche copies of the articles are located in the back of each binder. Note that there is a separate binder containing an Introduction, Guide to the Index, and an overall Name Index. The Guide to the Index section is designed as an aid to determine in which of the 13 major subject categories a particular topic is covered. A cumulative subject index for each topical area is provided annually.

Professional Journals

Articles in *scholarly journals*, written by specialists and critically evaluated (refereed) by other scholars prior to being accepted for publication, represent the most recent additions to an academic discipline's shared store of knowledge and to its debate on a particular topic. Students interested in compiling a well-rounded and up-to-date reading list on a topic should always consult the scholarly journals.

Criminal justice professionals publish numerous journals, some rather general in scope and some devoted to a particular subfield within the discipline, such as juvenile detention. Below is a list and description of several of these journals:

Corrections Today. Laurel, MD: American Correctional Association.

Corrections Today is an official publication of the American Correctional Association. Seven issues each year cover all aspects of adult and juvenile corrections and detention, from sentencing through parole or release. Articles are usually from four to 10 pages in length and tend to focus on applied concepts and perspectives.

Crime and Delinquency. Thousand Oaks, CA: Sage Periodicals Press.

A policy-oriented journal for the professional with direct involvement in the criminal justice field, *Crime and Delinquency* publishes articles that address specific policy or program implications. The editor welcomes submissions that fall into any of the following broad criminal justice areas: the social, political, and economic context; the victim and the offender; the criminal justice response; the setting of sanctions; and the implications of sanctions. This journal uses the citation and reference style guidelines of the American Sociological Association (ASA).

Criminal Law Bulletin. New York: Warren, Gorham & Lamont.

The *Criminal Law Bulletin* is published six times a year by the SUNY School of Criminal Justice. Articles of interest are directed to judges, practicing attorneys, prosecutors, administrators, correctional officials, and university students. Citing should conform to "a uniform system of citation."

Criminology. Columbus, OH: American Society of Criminology.

Published four times annually by the American Society of Criminology, *Criminology* is interdisciplinary in nature. Articles are devoted to crime and deviant behavior as they are defined in the disciplines of criminal justice, law, and the social and behavioral sciences. The journal emphasizes research and theoretical and historical issues, publishing articles that review and discuss current criminal justice issues and controversies.

Journal for Juvenile Justice and Detention Services. Frankfort, KY: National Juvenile Detention Association.

An official publication of the National Juvenile Detention Association and the Juvenile Justice Trainers Association, this journal provides high-quality articles about institutional practices.

Journal of Criminal Justice Education. Highland Heights, KY: Academy of Criminal Justice Sciences.

This journal, published by the John Jay College of Criminal Justice, is also an official publication of the Academy of Criminal Justice Sciences. It is a multidisciplinary journal that publishes articles written by scholars in all relevant disciplines. Issues covered include criminal justice education and teaching criminal justice.

Journal of Forensic Sciences. Mundelein, IL: Callagham.

The *Journal of Forensic Sciences* is the official publication of the American Academy of Forensic Sciences. It is devoted to the publication of original investigations, observations, scholarly inquiries, and reviews in the various branches of the forensic sciences. These include forensic pathology, toxicology, psychiatry, immunology, jurisprudence, criminalistics, and questioned documents. This quarterly journal has been published for over 40 years.

Journal of Gang Research. Chicago, IL: National Gang Crime Research Center.

A refereed journal now in its fourth volume, this journal publishes original gang research (quantitative and qualitative), views from the field, and gang profiles.

Journal of Research in Crime and Delinquency. Thousand Oaks, CA: Sage Periodicals Press.

This journal is devoted to reports of original research in crime and delinquency, new theory, and the critical analysis of theories and concepts especially pertinent to research development in this field. Published four times annually, in February, May, August, and November. Citations follow the style recommended by the American Sociological Association.

Justice Quarterly. Highland Heights, KY: Academy of Criminal Justice Sciences.

Justice Quarterly is an official publication of the Academy of Criminal Justice Sciences. It is a multidisciplinary journal publishing articles on criminal justice and related justice issues written by scholars in all relevant disciplines.

The following important journals in sociology and social psychology often deal with issues and concepts that are germane to criminal justice.

American Journal of Sociology. Chicago, IL: University of Chicago Press.

Begun in 1895, this bimonthly journal reports research and field work on a variety of topics in sociology. Short papers that summarize recent empirical research are included in a "Research Notes" section. Each issue also contains a comprehensive book review section with evaluative reviews.

American Sociological Review. Washington, DC: American Sociological Association.

The official journal of the American Sociological Association since 1936, this bimonthly publication contains articles that cover all areas of sociology. The journal also reports the activities of the association and contains a section for comments and discussions of previous articles.

Journal of Applied Social Psychology. Columbia, MD: Bellwether Publishing.

Articles in this journal, published four times annually, disseminate findings from behavioral science research that have applications to current social problems. Preference is given to manuscripts reporting laboratory and field research in areas such as health, race relations, discrimination, group processes, population growth, accelerated cultural change, violence, poverty, environmental stress, helping behavior, effects to the legal system on society and the individual, political participation and extremism, cross-cultural differences, communication, cooperative problem solving, negotiations among nations, socioeconomics, social aspects of drug action and use, organizational and industrial issues, behavioral medicine, and environmental psychology.

Journal of Personality and Social Psychology. Washington DC: American Psychological Association.

The Journal of Personality and Social Psychology publishes original papers in all areas of personality and social psychology. It emphasizes empirical reports but may include specialized theoretical, methodological, and review papers. The journal is divided into three independently edited sections: (1) Attitudes and Social Cognition, (2) Interpersonal Relations and Group Processes, (3) Personality Processes and Individual Differences.

Social Forces. Chapel Hill, NC: University of North Carolina Press.

This quarterly includes papers on all aspects of sociology. First published in 1922, the journal is international in scope, but articles about the United States predominate. Each issue contains a number of book reviews. Special issues, in which all the articles focus on a specific topic, appear at least once a year.

These major journals represent a fraction of the scholarly periodicals published by professionals in criminal justice and related areas. Students can find a brief description of other scholarly journals within criminal justice and other academic disciplines by consulting:

Katz, W. 1978. *Magazines for Libraries.* 3d ed. New York: Bowker.

This work contains publication information and descriptive and evaluative annotations for over 6500 periodicals and newspapers. Titles are organized into approximately 100 subject areas, such as Aeronautics Space Science, Africa, Business Education, General Magazines, Government Magazines, History, Opinion Magazines, and Newspapers. Because of this topical organization, the volume's index is particularly useful for locating individual titles.

The following is a list of professional social science journals that are potentially of interest to criminal justice students. Some are refereed, while others are not, but all contain articles with potential use for criminal justice students:

- *Addiction*
- *Addictive Behaviors*
- *Administration*
- *Administration and Society*
- *Administration in Social Work*
- *Administrative Science Quarterly*
- *Adolescence*
- *Africa Quarterly*
- *African Affairs*
- *African Studies*
- *Age and Aging*
- *Aging and Society*
- *AIDS and Public Policy Journal*

- *Alcohol Health and Research World*
- *Alcoholism Treatment Quarterly*
- *Alternatives: A Journal of World Policy*
- *American Anthropologist*
- *American Behavioral Scientist*
- *American Demographics*
- *American Economic Review*
- *American Educational Research Journal*
- *American Ethnologist*
- *American Indian Culture and Research Journal*
- *American Journal of Community Psychology*
- *American Journal of Drug and Alcohol Abuse*
- *American Journal of Economics and Sociology*
- *American Journal of Education*
- *American Journal of Family Therapy*
- *American Journal of Human Genetics*
- *American Journal of International Law*
- *American Journal of Orthopsychiatry*
- *American Journal of Philology*
- *American Journal of Physical Anthropology*
- *American Journal of Political Science*
- *American Journal of Psychiatry*
- *American Journal of Psychoanalysis*
- *American Journal of Psychology*
- *American Journal of Psychotherapy*
- *American Journal of Public Health*
- *American Journal of Sociology*
- *American Political Science Review*
- *American Politics Quarterly*
- *American Prospect*
- *American Psychologist*
- *American Scholar*
- *American Scientist*
- *American Society for Information Science Journal*
- *American Sociologician Review*
- *American Sociologist*
- *American Statistician*
- *Annals of the American Academy of Political and Social Science*
- *Annual Review of Anthropology*

- *Annual Review of Psychology*
- *Annual Review of Sociology*
- *Anthropological Quarterly*
- *Antioch Review*
- *Applied Psycholinguistics*
- *Archive of Sexual Behavior*
- *Argumentation and Advocacy*
- *Armed Forces and Society*
- *Asian Affairs*
- *Asian Quarterly*
- *Asian Survey*
- *Atlantic Community Quarterly*
- *Australian and New Zealand Journal of Sociology*
- *Australian Journal of Anthropology*
- *Australian Journal of Politics and History*
- *Australian Journal of Public Administration*
- *Australian Journal of Social Issues*
- *Behavior Research and Therapy*
- *Behavior Research Methods, Instruments, and Computers*
- *Behavior Science Research*
- *Behavior Therapy*
- *Behavioral Health Management*
- *Behavioral Neuroscience*
- *Behavioral Science*
- *Black Politician*
- *Black Scholar*
- *Brain*
- *British Journal of Clinical Psychology*
- *British Journal of Criminology*
- *British Journal of Educational Psychology*
- *British Journal of Educational Studies*
- *British Journal of International Studies*
- *British Journal of Law and Society*
- *British Journal of Political Science*
- *British Journal of Psychology*
- *British Journal of Social Psychology*
- *British Journal of Sociology*
- *Bulletin of the Association for Business Communication*
- *Bureaucrat*

- *Business*
- *Business and Society*
- *Cambridge Journal of Education*
- *Campaign and Elections*
- *Canadian Journal of Behavioral Science*
- *Canadian Journal of Criminology*
- *Canadian Journal of Economics*
- *Canadian Journal of Experimental Psychology*
- *Canadian Journal of Nursing Research*
- *Canadian Journal of Political Science*
- *Canadian Journal of Psychiatry*
- *Canadian Journal of Psychology*
- *Canadian Psychologist*
- *Canadian Psychology*
- *Canadian Public Administration*
- *Canadian Public Policy*
- *Canadian Review of Sociology and Anthropology*
- *Change*
- *Child Abuse and Neglect*
- *Child and Adolescent Social Work Journal*
- *Child Development*
- *Child Psychiatry and Human Development*
- *Child Study Journal*
- *Child Welfare*
- *Children's Literature in Education*
- *China Quarterly*
- *Church History*
- *Clinical Social Work Journal*
- *Cognition*
- *Cognitive Psychology*
- *Communication Quarterly*
- *Communication Reports*
- *Communication Research*
- *Communication Theory*
- *Communist Affairs*
- *Communist and Post-Communist Studies*
- *Communities*
- *Community Development Journal*
- *Community Mental Health Journal*

- *Comparative Education Review*
- *Comparative Political Studies*
- *Comparative Politics*
- *Comparative Strategy*
- *Comparative Studies in Society and History*
- *Computers and the Humanities*
- *Conflict*
- *Conflict Bulletin*
- *Conflict Management and Peace Science*
- *Conflict Studies*
- *Congress and the Presidency*
- *Contemporary China*
- *Contemporary Drug Problems*
- *Contemporary Economic Policy*
- *Contemporary Education*
- *Contemporary Sociology*
- *Cooperation and Conflict*
- *Corrections Today*
- *Counseling Psychologist*
- *Crime and Delinquency*
- *Criminal Justice and Behavior*
- *Criminal Justice Ethics*
- *Criminal Justice Review*
- *Criminal Law Bulletin*
- *Criminology*
- *Crisis*
- *Critical Quarterly*
- *Critical Review*
- *Critical Studies in Mass Communication*
- *Crossroads*
- *Cultural Anthropology*
- *Current Anthropology*
- *Current Sociology*
- *Current World Leaders*
- *Daedalus*
- *Day Care and Early Education*
- *Death Studies*
- *Democracy*
- *Demography*

- *Development and Change*
- *Developmental Psychology*
- *Diplomatic History*
- *Dissent*
- *Dissertation Abstracts International A: The Humanities and Social Sciences*
- *Dissertation Abstracts International B: Sciences and Engineering*
- *Drugs and Society*
- *East European Politics and Societies*
- *East European Quarterly*
- *Economic Development and Cultural Change*
- *Economic History Review*
- *Economic Inquiry*
- *Economic Journal*
- *Economic Outlook USA*
- *Economica*
- *Economist*
- *Economy and Society*
- *Education*
- *Education and Urban Society*
- *Educational and Psychological Measurement*
- *Educational Gerontology*
- *Educational Horizons*
- *Educational Psychology Review*
- *Educational Review*
- *Educational Studies*
- *Educational Theory*
- *Electoral Studies*
- *Environment and Behavior*
- *Environmental Ethics*
- *Environmental Policy and Law*
- *Environmental Politics*
- *Ethics*
- *Ethnic and Racial Studies*
- *Ethnic Groups*
- *Ethnohistory*
- *Ethnology*
- *Ethnology and Sociobiology*
- *European Economic Review*
- *European Journal of Political Research*

- *European Journal of Political Science*
- *European Studies Review*
- *Experimental Study of Politics*
- *Families in Society*
- *Family and Community Health*
- *Family Economics Review*
- *Family Planning Perspectives*
- *Family Process*
- *Family Relations*
- *FBI Law Enforcement Bulletin*
- *Federal Probation*
- *Feminist Issues*
- *Feminist Studies*
- *Foreign Affairs*
- *Foreign Policy*
- *Forum of Applied Research and Public Policy*
- *Free Inquiry in Creative Sociology*
- *Futurist*
- *Gender and Society*
- *General Systems*
- *Generations*
- *Geographical Journal*
- *Geographical Review*
- *George Washington Law Review*
- *Georgia Review*
- *German Life and Letters*
- *German Political Studies*
- *German Quarterly*
- *Gerontologist*
- *Global Political Assessment*
- *Global Risk Assessment: Issues, Concepts and Applications*
- *Governance: An International Journal of Policy and Administration*
- *Government and Opposition*
- *Government Finance*
- *Growth and Change*
- *Harvard Educational Review*
- *Harvard Journal on Legislation*
- *Health and Social Work*
- *Health Values*

- *Higher Education Quarterly*
- *Hispania*
- *Hispanic Journal of Behavioral Sciences*
- *History and Political Economy*
- *History and Theory*
- *History of Political Thought*
- *History of the Human Sciences*
- *Hudson Review*
- *Human Biology*
- *Human Communication Research*
- *Human Ecology*
- *Human Ecology Forum*
- *Human Organization*
- *Human Relations*
- *Human Rights*
- *Human Rights Quarterly*
- *Human Rights Review*
- *Humanist*
- *Identities*
- *Impact of Science in Society*
- *In the Public Interest*
- *Indian Journal of Political Science*
- *Indian Journal of Public Administration*
- *Indian Political Science Review*
- *Individual Psychology*
- *Industrial and Labor Relations Review*
- *Industrial Relations*
- *Information Sciences*
- *Innovation Higher Education*
- *Inter-American Economic Affairs*
- *Interchange*
- *Interfaces*
- *International Affairs*
- *International Criminal Justice Review*
- *International Development Review*
- *International Economic Review*
- *International Interactions*
- *International Journal of Aging and Human Development*
- *International Journal of Comparative Sociology*

- *International Journal of Eating Disorders*
- *International Journal of Group Psychotherapy*
- *International Journal of Health Services*
- *International Journal of Middle East Studies*
- *International Journal of Offender Therapy and Comparative Criminology*
- *International Journal of Political Education*
- *International Journal of Public Administration*
- *International Journal of Social Psychiatry*
- *International Journal of Sociology of Law*
- *International Journal of Sociology of the Family*
- *International Journal of Urban and Regional Research*
- *International Labour Review*
- *International Migration Review*
- *International Organization*
- *International Political Science Review*
- *International Relations*
- *International Review of Education*
- *International Review of Social History*
- *International Security*
- *International Social Science Journal*
- *International Social Science Review*
- *International Social Work*
- *International Studies*
- *International Studies Quarterly*
- *Interpretation: Journal of Political Philosophy*
- *Japan Quarterly*
- *Jerusalem Journal of International Relations*
- *Journal for the Scientific Study of Religion*
- *Journal of Abnormal Child Psychology*
- *Journal of Abnormal Psychology*
- *Journal of Addictive Diseases*
- *Journal of Adolescence*
- *Journal of Adolescent Chemical Dependency*
- *Journal of Adolescent Health*
- *Journal of Adolescent Research*
- *Journal of Advertising*
- *Journal of African Studies*
- *Journal of Aging and Social Policy*
- *Journal of Aging Studies*

- *Journal of American History*
- *Journal of American Indian Education*
- *Journal of Anthropological Research*
- *Journal of Applied Behavior Analysis*
- *Journal of Applied Behavioral Science*
- *Journal of Applied Communication Research*
- *Journal of Applied Gerontology*
- *Journal of Applied Psychology*
- *Journal of Applied Social Psychology*
- *Journal of Asian and African Studies*
- *Journal of Asian Studies*
- *Journal of Behavior Therapy and Experimental Psychiatry*
- *Journal of Black Psychology*
- *Journal of Black Studies*
- *Journal of Business Communication*
- *Journal of Child and Family Studies*
- *Journal of Child Psychology and Psychiatry and Allied Disciplines*
- *Journal of Clinical Child Psychology*
- *Journal of Clinical Psychiatry*
- *Journal of Clinical Psychology*
- *Journal of Common Market Studies*
- *Journal of Commonwealth and Comparative Politics*
- *Journal of Communication*
- *Journal of Community Health*
- *Journal of Comparative and Physiological Psychology*
- *Journal of Comparative Economics*
- *Journal of Comparative Family Studies*
- *Journal of Comparative Psychology*
- *Journal of Conflict Resolution*
- *Journal of Constitutional and Parliamentary Studies*
- *Journal of Consumer Research*
- *Journal of Contemporary Ethnography*
- *Journal of Contemporary History*
- *Journal of Counseling Psychology*
- *Journal of Creative Behavior*
- *Journal of Criminal Justice*
- *Journal of Criminal Justice Education*
- *Journal of Criminal Law and Criminology*
- *Journal of Cross-Cultural Psychology*

- *Journal of Democracy*
- *Journal of Developing Areas*
- *Journal of Development Economics*
- *Journal of Development Studies*
- *Journal of Divorce and Remarriage*
- *Journal of Drug Education*
- *Journal of Drug Issues*
- *Journal of Econometrics*
- *Journal of Economic History*
- *Journal of Economic Issues*
- *Journal of Economic Literature*
- *Journal of Economic Perspectives*
- *Journal of Economic Theory*
- *Journal of Education*
- *Journal of Educational Measurement*
- *Journal of Educational Research*
- *Journal of Elder Abuse and Neglect*
- *Journal of Environmental Economics and Management*
- *Journal of Environmental Management*
- *Journal of Ethnic Studies*
- *Journal of European Integration*
- *Journal of Experimental Child Psychology*
- *Journal of Experimental Education*
- *Journal of Experimental Social Psychology*
- *Journal of Extension*
- *Journal of Family History*
- *Journal of Family Issues*
- *Journal of Family Law*
- *Journal of Family Psychology*
- *Journal of Family Violence*
- *Journal of Fluency Disorders*
- *Journal of Forensic Sciences*
- *Journal of Gambling Studies*
- *Journal of Gang Research*
- *Journal of General Education*
- *Journal of General Psychology*
- *Journal of Genetic Psychology*
- *Journal of Gerontological Social Work*
- *Journal of Gerontology*

- *Journal of Group Psychotherapy, Psychodrama and Sociometry*
- *Journal of Health and Social Behavior*
- *Journal of Health Politics, Policy and Law*
- *Journal of Homosexuality*
- *Journal of Housing*
- *Journal of Housing and Community Development*
- *Journal of Human Resources*
- *Journal of Humanistic Psychology*
- *Journal of InterAmerican Studies and World Affairs*
- *Journal of Interdisciplinary History*
- *Journal of Interdisciplinary Studies*
- *Journal of International Affairs*
- *Journal of Interpersonal Violence*
- *Journal of Japanese Studies*
- *Journal for Juvenile Justice and Detention Services*
- *Journal of Labor Research*
- *Journal of Latin American Studies*
- *Journal of Law and Economics*
- *Journal of Law and Politics*
- *Journal of Learning Disabilities*
- *Journal of Legal Studies*
- *Journal of Leisure Research*
- *Journal of Libertarian Studies*
- *Journal of Management*
- *Journal of Management Studies*
- *Journal of Marital and Family Therapy*
- *Journal of Marriage and the Family*
- *Journal of Medical Ethics*
- *Journal of Memory and Language*
- *Journal of Modern African Studies*
- *Journal of Modern History*
- *Journal of Near Eastern Studies*
- *Journal of Negro Education*
- *Journal of Nonverbal Behavior*
- *Journal of Offender Rehabilitation*
- *Journal of Parapsychology*
- *Journal of Peace Research*
- *Journal of Peace Science*
- *Journal of Peasant Studies*

- *Journal of Pediatric Psychology*
- *Journal of Personal Assessment*
- *Journal of Personality*
- *Journal of Personality and Social Psychology*
- *Journal of Police Science and Administration*
- *Journal of Policy Analysis and Management*
- *Journal of Policy Modeling*
- *Journal of Political and Military Sociology*
- *Journal of Political Economy*
- *Journal of Political Science*
- *Journal of Politics*
- *Journal of Popular Culture*
- *Journal of Primary Prevention*
- *Journal of Psychiatric Research*
- *Journal of Psychohistory*
- *Journal of Psychology*
- *Journal of Psychosomatic Research*
- *Journal of Public Administration Research and Theory*
- *Journal of Public Policy*
- *Journal of Reading Behavior*
- *Journal of Rehabilitation*
- *Journal of Research and Development in Education*
- *Journal of Research in Crime and Delinquency*
- *Journal of School Psychology*
- *Journal of Sex Research*
- *Journal of Social History*
- *Journal of Social Issues*
- *Journal of Social Policy*
- *Journal of Social, Political and Economic Studies*
- *Journal of Social Psychology*
- *Journal of Social Work Education*
- *Journal of Special Education*
- *Journal of Specialists in Group Work*
- *Journal of Sport and Social Issues*
- *Journal of State Government*
- *Journal of Strategic Studies*
- *Journal of Studies on Alcohol*
- *Journal of Substance Abuse Treatment*
- *Journal of the American Academy of Child and Adolescent Psychiatry*

- *Journal of the American Geriatrics Society*
- *Journal of the American Oriental Society*
- *Journal of the American Planning Association*
- *Journal of the American Society for Information Science*
- *Journal of the Experimental Analysis of Behavior*
- *Journal of the History of Ideas*
- *Journal of the History of the Behavioral Sciences*
- *Journal of the Philosophy of Sport*
- *Journal of the Royal Anthropological Institute*
- *Journal of the Royal Society of Health*
- *Journal of Theoretical Politics*
- *Journal of Third World Studies*
- *Journal of Traumatic Stress*
- *Journal of Urban Affairs*
- *Journal of Urban Analysis*
- *Journal of Urban History*
- *Journal of Verbal Learning and Verbal Behavior*
- *Journal of Youth and Adolescence*
- *Journalism Quarterly*
- *Journals of Gerontology*
- *Journals of Gerontology (Series B: Psychological and Social Sciences)*
- *Justice Quarterly*
- *Landscape*
- *Language*
- *Language Learning*
- *Latin American Perspectives*
- *Latin American Research Review*
- *Law and Society Review*
- *Law and Contemporary Problems*
- *Law and Philosophy*
- *Law and Policy Quarterly*
- *Learning and Motivation*
- *Legislative Studies Quarterly*
- *Linguistic Inquiry*
- *Linguistics and Education*
- *Literature and Psychology*
- *Magazine of History*
- *Man*
- *Man–Environment Systems*

- *Management Communication Quarterly*
- *Management Science*
- *Mankind*
- *Marriage and Family Review*
- *Massachusetts Review*
- *Mathematical Social Sciences*
- *Meaning*
- *Media, Culture and Society*
- *Memory and Cognition*
- *Merill–Palmer Quarterly*
- *Micropolitics*
- *Mid-American Review of Sociology*
- *Middle East Journal*
- *Middle East Report*
- *Middle Eastern Studies*
- *Midwest Quarterly*
- *Millennium*
- *Mind*
- *Mississippi Quarterly*
- *Modern Asian Studies*
- *Modern China*
- *Modern Language Journal*
- *Modern Language Notes*
- *Modern Philology*
- *Monographs for the Society for Research in Child Development*
- *Monthly Labor Review*
- *Monthly Review*
- *Multivariate Behavioral Research*
- *National Interests*
- *New England Journal of Medicine*
- *New Literacy History*
- *New Perspectives*
- *New Political Science*
- *New Politics*
- *New Statesmen*
- *New Statesmen and Society*
- *Omega*
- *Orbis: A Journal of World Affairs*
- *Oxford Economic Papers*

- *Pacific Affairs*
- *Pacific Philosophical Quarterly*
- *Papers on Language and Literature*
- *Parliamentarian*
- *Parliamentary Affairs*
- *Parliaments, Estates and Representation*
- *Partisan Review*
- *Past and Present*
- *Peace and Change*
- *Peace Research*
- *Perception and Psychophysics*
- *Personality and Social Psychology Bulletin*
- *Perspectives*
- *Perspectives on Political Science*
- *Philological Quarterly*
- *Philosophical Quarterly*
- *Philosophical Review*
- *Philosophy and Phenomenological Research*
- *Philosophy and Public Affairs*
- *Philosophy and Rhetoric*
- *Philosophy and Science*
- *Philosophy of the Social Sciences*
- *Phylon*
- *Planning and Administration*
- *Police Chief*
- *Policy Analysis*
- *Policy and Politics*
- *Policy Review*
- *Policy Sciences*
- *Policy Studies*
- *Policy Studies Journal*
- *Policy Studies Review*
- *Political Anthropology*
- *Political Behavior*
- *Political Communication*
- *Political Communication and Persuasion*
- *Political Geography Quarterly*
- *Political Psychology*
- *Political Quarterly*

- *Political Research Quarterly*
- *Political Science*
- *Political Science Quarterly*
- *Political Science Review*
- *Political Science Reviewer*
- *Political Studies*
- *Political Theory*
- *Politics*
- *Politics and Society*
- *Politics and the Life Sciences*
- *Polity*
- *Population and Development Review*
- *Population Bulletin*
- *Presidential Studies Quarterly*
- *Proceedings of the Academy of Political Science*
- *Professional Psychology, Research and Practice*
- *Psychiatric Quarterly*
- *Psychiatry*
- *Psychoanalytic Review*
- *Psychobiology*
- *Psychological Assessment*
- *Psychological Bulletin*
- *Psychological Record*
- *Psychological Reports*
- *Psychological Science*
- *Psychology and Aging*
- *Psychology in the Schools*
- *Psychology of Women Quarterly*
- *Psychology Today*
- *Psychophysiology*
- *Psychosomatic Medicine*
- *Public Administration*
- *Public Administration (Australia)*
- *Public Administration Review*
- *Public Choice*
- *Public Finance*
- *Public Finance Quarterly*
- *Public Health Reports*
- *Public Interest*

- *Public Law*
- *Public Management*
- *Public Opinion*
- *Public Opinion Quarterly*
- *Public Policy*
- *Public Relations Quarterly*
- *Public Relations Review*
- *Public Welfare*
- *Publius: The Journal of Federalism*
- *Quarterly Journal of Administration*
- *Quarterly Journal of Economics*
- *Quarterly Journal of Speech*
- *Quarterly Review of Doublespeak*
- *Race and Class*
- *Radical America*
- *Radical History Review*
- *Ratio*
- *Reading Research Quarterly*
- *Regional Studies*
- *Research in Education*
- *Research in Higher Education*
- *Research in Nursing and Health*
- *Research on Aging*
- *Review of Black Political Economy*
- *Review of Economic Studies*
- *Review of Economics and Statistics*
- *Review of Educational Research*
- *Review of International Studies*
- *Review of Law and Social Change*
- *Review of Metaphysics*
- *Review of Politics*
- *Revolutionary World*
- *Romance Philology*
- *Romance Quarterly*
- *Round Table*
- *Rural Sociology*
- *Russian Review*
- *Sage*
- *SAIS Review*

- *Scandinavian Political Studies*
- *Science*
- *Science and Public Affairs*
- *Science and Public Policy*
- *Science and Society*
- *Sciences, The*
- *Sex Roles*
- *Signs*
- *Simulation*
- *Simulation and Games*
- *Simulation and Gaming*
- *Skeptical Inquirer*
- *Slavic Review*
- *Slavonic and East European Review*
- *Small Group Research*
- *Social Action*
- *Social and Economic Studies*
- *Social Behavior and Personality*
- *Social Biology*
- *Social Casework*
- *Social Forces*
- *Social History*
- *Social Indicators Research*
- *Social Justice*
- *Social Philosophy and Policy*
- *Social Policy*
- *Social Praxis*
- *Social Problems*
- *Social Psychology Quarterly*
- *Social Research*
- *Social Science and Medicine*
- *Social Science Information*
- *Social Science Journal*
- *Social Science Quarterly*
- *Social Science Research*
- *Social Science Review*
- *Social Theory and Practice*
- *Social Work*
- *Social Work Education*

- *Social Work with Groups*
- *Socialism and Democracy*
- *Socialists Review*
- *Society*
- *Sociological Analysis and Theory*
- *Sociological Inquiry*
- *Sociological Methods and Research*
- *Sociological Perspectives*
- *Sociological Quarterly*
- *Sociological Review*
- *Sociology*
- *Sociology and Social Research*
- *Sociology of Education*
- *Sociology of Religion*
- *Sociology of Sport Journal*
- *Soundings*
- *Southern Economic Journal*
- *Southern Exposure*
- *Southern Quarterly*
- *Soviet Review*
- *Soviet Studies*
- *Soviet Union*
- *Spectrum*
- *State Government*
- *Strategic Review*
- *Studies in Comparative Communism*
- *Studies in Comparative International Development*
- *Studies in Conflict and Terrorism*
- *Studies in Family Planning*
- *Studies in Philosophy and Education*
- *Suicide and Life-Threatening Behavior*
- *Survey*
- *Survival*
- *Symposium*
- *Talking Politics*
- *Technological Forecasting and Social Change*
- *Technology and Culture*
- *Terrorism*
- *Theory and Decision*

- *Theory and Society*
- *Third World*
- *Trial*
- *UN Chronicle*
- *Urban Affairs Quarterly*
- *Urban Affairs Review*
- *Urban and Social Change Review*
- *Urban Anthropologist*
- *Urban Anthropology and Studies of Cultural Systems and World Economic Development*
- *Urban Education*
- *Urban Life*
- *Urban Review*
- *Urban Studies*
- *Victimology*
- *Violence and Victims*
- *Volta Review*
- *War and Society*
- *Washington Quarterly: A Review of Strategic and International Studies*
- *West European Politics*
- *Western Journal of Communications*
- *Western Political Quarterly*
- *Wilson Quarterly*
- *Women and Environments*
- *Women and Health*
- *Women and Politics: A Quarterly Journal of Research and Policy Studies*
- *Women and Work*
- *Women's Studies International Forum*
- *Women's Studies Quarterly*
- *World Affairs*
- *World Development*
- *World Marxist Review*
- *World Policy Journal*
- *World Politics*
- *World Today*
- *World Watch*
- *Young Children*
- *Youth and Society*

RESEARCHING BOOKS

Academic books, along with articles from professional journals, will usually form the greater part of the criminal justice student's reading list on an individual research topic. If the sources of information used in book research are unreliable, the results will be unsatisfactory. There are two principal paths for a student to take in evaluating a book-length study: (1) rely upon book reviews, and (2) examine the bibliographic character of the book itself.

Most professional journals contain a book review section where scholars in the field present critiques of books recently published. These reviews usually give an accurate assessment of the book's quality from a criminal justice standpoint. When faced with a choice of several books, you can save time by reading book reviews to select the most useful, authoritative sources.

Since 1975, reviews appearing in most of the major journals that are germane to criminal justice have been indexed in the book review section of the *Social Sciences Index* (see above). The reviews are indexed by the name of the author of the book; the journal, volume, and date; and the page of the review. There is a time lag, however, sometimes more than a year, between a book's publication and the appearance of a review in a scholarly journal. The need for more current reviews has led to a new type of journal consisting entirely of scholarly book reviews. The journal for sociologists is:

> *Contemporary Sociology: A Journal of Reviews*. Washington, DC: American Sociological Association.

This journal, which began publication in 1971, reviews books published in every area of sociology plus many in related fields such as education. Each issue also contains feature essays that review several books on related topics or the works of one major author. The reviews are arranged by broad subject areas, and each issue also contains a list of new publications.

For reviews of books on the popular market, along with many very academic selections, the *New York Review of Books* (1976–present) and *New York Times Book Review* (1923–present) are two reliable sources.

UNITED STATES GOVERNMENT PUBLICATIONS

General Publications

United States government publications comprise all the printed public documents of the federal government. The materials include, for example, the official records of the meetings of the U.S. Congress; the text of laws, of court decisions, and of public hearings and rulings of administrative and regulatory agencies; studies of economic and social issues commissioned by official agencies; and the compilation of statistics on a number of social and demographic characteristics of the U.S. population.

Federal publications provide students and professionals with material for research in many criminal justice subfields, such as the educational attainment of minorities, sex discrimination, and drug and physical abuse. But *beware:* The fact that a document is "official" is no automatic guarantee of the accuracy of the information or data it might contain. Accuracy depends on the methods of information and data collection the agency uses. Therefore, the use of these publications, like the use of any other source material, requires good judgment. You can identify relevant late nineteenth- and twentieth-century federal government publications by consulting:

U.S. Superintendent of Documents. *Monthly Catalog of United States Government Publications*. Washington, DC: Government Printing Office.

Begun in 1885, this is the most complete catalog of federal documents available. The detailed indexes—subject, author/agency, and title—identify individual items by entry number. Entries identify individual author (if any), pagination, date, illustration notes, series title, serial number, any other publication superseded by this item, and the Superintendent of Documents number. (United States documents are cataloged by this number in many libraries, especially those that are depositories.)

Cumulative Subject Index to the Monthly Catalog of United States Government Publications, 1900–1971. 1973. Washington, DC: Carrollton Press.

This is a comprehensive subject index to more than 1 million publications listed in the *Monthly Catalog* from 1900 through 1971. To discover what has been published on a given subject, one first finds the topic and then goes to the appropriate subheading. This will be followed by one or more years in parentheses, each followed by one or more entry numbers, such as "(65) 14901." Then researchers must turn to the *Monthly Catalog* for the specified year (in this case, 1965) and locate the entry number (in this case, 14901) to find a complete citation for the publication.

The most useful list and discussion of finding aids for U.S. government publications in the social sciences is:

Lu, J. K. *U.S. Government Publications Relating to the Social Sciences*. Thousand Oaks, CA: Sage.

An awareness of the factors that influence U.S. government policies toward such social issues as crime, welfare, and minority rights is essential to sociologists. Political policy is formulated by political officials and influenced by citizens or groups of citizens, all of whom are concerned about a specific issue. For this reason, the records of congressional hearings are valuable sources of information to the criminal justice student. These records provide important policy-related information. They reveal the political stands that various citizens or groups take on a specific issue, and they demonstrate the influence these persons have on the formulation.

United States Census Publications

U.S. Census Bureau publications allow criminal justice students to summarize social and demographic characteristics of various population groups in the United States by using descriptive statistics. We frequently think of the Census Bureau as a government agency that collects census data every 10 years, but there are actually 10 categories of censuses, and data are collected and reported at different intervals. In addition to collecting data on national and state populations, the Census Bureau studies subpopulations that are of special interest. These studies are generally published in Current Population Reports. Recent reports, for example, have focused on the characteristics of blacks, persons of Hispanic origin, and poverty-level families.

Since the Census Bureau analyzes and publishes data, criminal justice students can locate relevant census materials by consulting guides and indexes to statistical reports published by the government. The following comprehensive volume indexes statistical studies by all government agencies. It can be used to locate a variety of statistics on a given topic:

American Statistics Index. Washington, DC: Congressional Information Service.

Since its first publication in 1973, this commercially produced abstract has become an important source for identifying statistical publications of the U.S. government. It indexes and abstracts statistics on numerous topics from the publications of many government agencies, describes these publications, and makes the material available on microfiche. This source is issued monthly in two sections—indexes and abstracts—and is cumulated annually. The index volume contains four separate indexes that list the publications by subject and name; by geographic, economic, and demographic categories; by title; and by agency report numbers. The abstract volume gives brief descriptions of the publications and their content.

The Census Bureau publishes an index to its own publications. If you require information on a topic that is routinely studied by the Census Bureau, you should consult:

U.S. Bureau of the Census. *Bureau of the Census Catalog*. Washington, DC: Government Printing Office.

An indispensable guide to materials issued by the Bureau of the Census and publications from other agencies which contain statistics, this catalog is published quarterly, updated with monthly supplements, and has annual cumulations. The basic volume is retrospective, covering the years 1790–1945 in part I, 1946–1972 in part II. The arrangement differs in each part. The material covered includes annotated lists of census publications for the years covered, followed by subject and geographical indexes. The annual cumulation lists and annotates only those publications issued during that year.

A number of reports or volumes published by the Census Bureau are useful to criminal justice students doing research. Several of these publications—the *County and City Data Book*, the *Statistical Abstracts of the United States*, and the *Historical Statistics of the United States*—have been discussed above under other subheadings. These publications summarize many of the important findings of past censuses, as well as more recent ones.

Besides the population census, the bureau conducts surveys of housing, business, and manufacturing. A student who wants information about the structural or industrial characteristics of the United States can use these decade censuses to find past and current statistics. These censuses have the advantages and disadvantages discussed earlier.

At little cost to the researcher, Census Bureau publications provide much descriptive information on various components of the American population. However, you should be aware of some serious problems with census data. Since most data are compiled every five or 10 years, often a researcher must either find more current information or use the somewhat dated statistics published by the Census Bureau. Also, the design of the census survey does not always include the type of questions or issues that are of interest to criminal justice students. For example, a student comparing the educational or employment status of blacks with that of persons of Hispanic origin for a period between 1970 and 1990 would not be able use 1970 census data because the 1970 Census of Population did not ask persons of Hispanic origin to identify their racial or ethnic background. Another disadvantage of census publications is that they use only descriptive statistics to summarize the data. Their analysis does not indicate the relevance or meaning of trends. You can determine social and demographic differences within populations but must look elsewhere for the causes of these differences.

CHAPTER 7

Criminal Justice on the World Wide Web

A WHIRLWIND INTRODUCTORY TOUR OF THE INTERNET

To understand the Internet and how to use it, we need to begin with the basics. Follow along on our whirlwind tour of the Internet. Let's let the symbol 🖥 represent a computer. Two or more computers linked by a telephone line, fiber optic line, radio wave, or satellite beam compose a network:

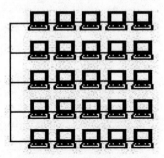

Let's call this dot [.] a symbol for a network composed of 10,000 computers and place a dot on a map of the world for every 10,000 computers.

The map would look something like the one that follows. This map represents, very imperfectly, the Internet. The *Internet* is a network of thousands of smaller computer networks that use a common computer language to communicate with each other, linked together by communications lines. The Internet was conceived in the late 1960s when the Advanced Research Projects Agency of the U.S. Department of Defense began to develop a military communications system that would be capable of surviving a nuclear war. The defense researchers produced a network of computers

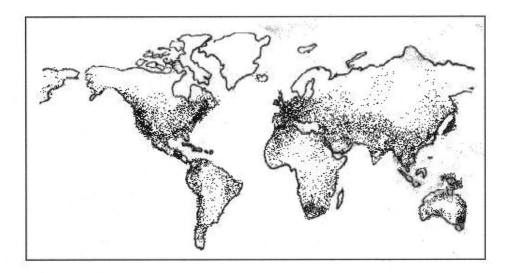

called the ARPANET, which at first included military research labs and universities but which later added many related computer systems.

Two decades later the National Science Foundation initiated a project called NSFNET, the purpose of which was to connect American supercomputer centers so that they could communicate with each other. Throughout the world similar networks were being established, and by the late 1980s, connections among these networks came to be known as the Internet, which is now growing at a phenomenal rate. In 1991 there were only about 700,000 people using the Internet. In 1998 that number is more than 50 million.

The World Wide Web (WWW) is an organized system for accessing the information on the Internet. Tim Berners-Lee of CERN, the European Laboratory for Particle Physics in Geneva, Switzerland, launched the WWW when he created a method for using a single means of access to the networks on the Internet. The WWW is now the primary vehicle for access to information on the Internet.

HOW DO I ACCESS THE INTERNET AND THE WORLD WIDE WEB?

The best way to access the Internet is to obtain access to a new computer with the latest communications software and follow the directions included in the software. Before long you will be "surfing the net" to your heart's content. In the pages that follow we examine briefly each stage of the process by which you may gain access to the Internet. To access the WWW on the Internet, you need four things:

1. A computer
2. A modem

3. A service provider
4. A browser

First, you need two pieces of *hardware*: a computer and a modem. We will assume that you know what a computer is, but you may not be aware that your local magazine stand or bookstore carries a wide variety of periodicals that review and rate them. When the time comes for you to purchase one, you will make a much more informed choice if you read the articles in such magazines as *Consumer Reports* and *Computer Shopper*. It is very important to buy a computer with the largest memory and hard drive disk capacity that you can afford. The Internet is getting more sophisticated every day, and many of the materials that you will want to *download* (a term meaning to transmit material electronically from a computer or computer system to another computer) from the Internet to your computer will require substantial space on your computer's hard drive.

A *modem* is a device that connects your computer to a telephone line or other line of communication. Because it can take time to download files, and because many Internet access programs charge their customers for the time they spend hooked up to the Internet, it is important that your modem be capable of running at a fast rate of speed. Both computers and modems require software containing operating instructions.

Next, you will need an Internet service, a commercial business that connects you to the Internet and charges you a monthly fee that varies with the service and the amount of time you spend using it. Some of the most popular Internet services, with telephone numbers you can use to contact them, are:

*   America Online: 1-800-827-3338
*   Compuserve: 1-800-848-8990
*   Earthlink Network: 1-213-644-9500
*   Global Network Navigator (GNN): 1-800-819-6112
*   Microsoft Network (MSN): 1-800-386-5550
*   Prodigy: 1-800-776-3449

Many smaller companies also provide Internet service, and you may be able to find rates more suited to your own pattern of Internet use from them. You will find these services listed in the Yellow Pages of your phone book. If you buy a new computer from a major manufacturer, you may find Internet service product brochures and software included with your computer. In addition to connecting you to the World Wide Web, some services also provide you with news, communications, and other services.

Finally, you need a *browser*, a software program that allows you to search for information on the Internet. In 1993 the National Center for Supercomputing Applications (NCSA) introduced Mosaic, a browser that greatly facilitated searching for information on the WWW and encouraged many people to gain access to the Internet, but since that time other commercial browsers have become more popular. At the moment this book is being written, *Netscape Navigator* is the most popular browser, but Microsoft's *Internet Explorer* is challenging Navigator's dominance with some success. If you contract with MSN for Internet service, you will be able to download *Internet Explorer* for free, and from time to time Netscape makes a special free offer of its *Navigator*.

You will experience a browser as a window, or *dialog box*, on your computer screen that assists you in finding information on the Internet. Once you have opened the *home page* (the starting page for a Web site) of your browser, you will notice that it offers you a number of *search engines*, which are programs that allow you to search the Internet using key words or phrases. Your browser will also provide a space in which you can type Internet addresses to access search engines and other Internet sites. Some of the most commonly used search engines and their Internet addresses are:

- AltaVista: http://altavista.digital.com
- EXCITE: http://www.excite.com
- LYCOS: http://www.lycos.com
- Webcrawler: http://webcrawler.com
- YAHOO!: http://www.*Yahoo!*.com

Let's suppose you use the *Yahoo!* search engine. In the search engine's dialog box you type in the words *criminal justice*. The search engine will then make several clickable links appear on the screen. A *clickable link* is an icon or line of text that is highlighted and programmed so that when you click your mouse button on it, you immediately go to a new Internet address.

CRIMINAL JUSTICE RESOURCES ON THE INTERNET

Thousands of sources of criminal justice information are already available on the Internet, and we will provide only a few examples here. Good sites have been established by

- government agencies
- nonprofit public interest groups
- private research organizations
- lobbyist and other private interest associations

If you visit the United States Department of Justice home page (http://www.usdoj.gov/alpha.html), for example, you will find links to bureaus and agencies with the Department which can provide you with statistics and a wide variety of other materials relating to issues within their particular jurisdictions. The Department's agencies include:

- Antitrust Division
- Bureau of Justice Assistance
- Bureau of Justice Statistics
- Civil Division
- Civil Rights Division
- Community Oriented Policing Office (COPS)
- Community-Relations Service

- Criminal Division
- Drug Enforcement Administration
- Environment and Natural Resources Division
- Executive Office for Immigration Review
- Executive Office for U.S. Attorneys
- Executive Office for U.S. Trustees
- Federal Bureau of Investigation
- Federal Bureau of Prisons
- Foreign Claims Settlement Commission of the United States
- Immigration and Naturalization Service
- INTERPOL—U.S. National Central Bureau
- Justice Management Division
- National Criminal Justice Reference Service
- National Drug Intelligence Center
- National Institute of Corrections
- National Institute of Justice
- Office for Victims of Crime
- Office of Associate Attorney General
- Office of Attorney General
- Office of Deputy Attorney General
- Office of Inspector General
- Office of Intelligence Policy and Review
- Office of International Programs
- Office of Justice Programs
- Office of Juvenile Justice and Delinquency Prevention
- Office of Legal Counsel
- Office of Legislative Affairs
- Office of Pardon Attorney
- Office of Professional Responsibility
- Office of Public Affairs
- Office of Solicitor General
- Office of Tribal Justice
- Tax Division
- United States Marshals' Service
- United States Parole Commission
- Violence Against Women Office

The Department of Justice is by no means the only government agency with criminal justice information, however. You can reach a wealth of information about the Supreme Court, the Federal Court system, Congress and other related sites by visiting a page entitled "THOMAS: Legislative Information on the Internet," and subtitled: "In the spirit of Thomas Jefferson, a service of the U.S. Congress through its Library" (http://thomas.loc.gov/). Agencies of the federal government of interest to criminal justice students that you can reach through *Thomas* or your search engine include:

- Bureau of Alcohol, Tobacco, and Firearms
- Bureau of Diplomatic Security, U.S. State Department
- Bureau of Justice Assistance
- Bureau of Justice Statistics
- Central Intelligence Agency
- Customs Service
- Drug Enforcement Administration
- Environmental Protection Administration (EPA)
- Federal Bureau of Investigation
- Federal Law Enforcement Training Center
- Federal Protective Service
- Federal Trade Commission
- Justice Technology Information Network
- Military Law Enforcement Sites
- National Institute of Justice
- National Law Enforcement Technology Center
- Office of Juvenile Justice and Delinquency Prevention
- Office of the Inspector General
- Secret Service
- Securities and Exchange Commission
- United States Marshals Service

In addition to government agencies, hundreds of private organizations provide criminal justice information. A good place to begin your search for private criminal justice sites is one of the many college and university criminal justice program sites. They often list numerous links to other resources. The home site of the criminal justice program at Florida State University (http://www.criminology.fsu.edu/) is a good example.

Although we cannot begin to list all of the important sites in this chapter, we do wish to conclude by providing some detail about some of the sites that you may find most helpful. As you explore these sites you will discover many more. Among the most helpful sites for criminal justice students are:

- *The Police Officer's Internet Directory*: http://www.officer.comv3.0/   This is the world's largest law enforcement Web site. You will find information on (1) Agencies, USA and International; (2) Associations, Unions, and Organizations; (3) Criminal Justice Resources; (4) Employment; (5) Leo Recruiting Sites; and over 100 additional areas of interest.

- *Federal Court's Home Page*: http://www.uscourts.gov/   This page is maintained by the Administrative Office of the U.S. Courts on behalf of the courts. Information, including historical and contemporary statistics (unclassified), is available to the public.
- *Judicial On-line Superhighway User Access System*: http://justice.courts.state.fl.us/ A nongeographical menu is available.
- *Juvenile Justice Clearinghouse*: http://ncjrs.org/ojjdp   The Office of Juvenile Justice and Delinquency Prevention (OJJDP), a branch of the U.S. Department of Justice, makes available statistical information, papers from the field and from academe, on current issues and programs. The agency is also the primary source for research funding in juvenile justice. Grants are given to graduate students from time to time upon request and screening. Every few months they publish a booklet outlining the various research areas they are willing to fund, along with the rules and regulations for submissions.
- *Prisons and Corrections*: http://www.mitretek.org/business_areas/justice/cjlinks/pri... Association of Correctional Officers Against Privatization. South Forty Corporation—an Avenue from Prison to Society.
- *Correctional Systems Incorporated*: http://www.crxs.com/   This is one of the largest private correctional companies in the world. They provide system information about their privately run jails, prisons, and community release centers. They also offer a Brief History of Privately Managed Secure Correctional Facilities Management Teams.
- *American Correctional Association Home Page*: http.//www.corrections.com/new-corrections/aca/indtex.html   The American Correctional Association is an organization of professionals representing all levels and sectors of corrections and criminal justice, including federal, state, military correctional facilities, prisons, and county jails. Through this group a myriad of information is readily available upon request.
- *Federal Bureau of Prisons Quick Facts*: http://www.bop.fct1097html#Inst Data presented here are extracted from Bureau of Prisons automated information systems.

    1. Number of Institutions
    2. Total Population
    3. Inmates by Security Level
    4. Inmates by Gender
    5. Inmates by Race
    6. Inmates by Ethnicity
    7. Inmates by Citizenship
    8. Average Inmate Age
    9. Sentence Imposed
    10. Type of Offense
    11. BOP Population over Time/Drug Offenders as a Percentage of All Sentenced Offenders

12. Staff by Gender
13. Staff by Race/Ethnicity
14. An Overview of the Federal Bureau of Prisons

- *The National Institute of Justice, Justice Information Center*: http://www.ncjrs.org
  The National Institute of Justice is a component of the Office of Justice
  Programs, which also includes the Bureau of Justice Assistance, the Bureau
  of Justice Statistics, the Office of Juvenile Justice and Delinquency
  Prevention, and the Office for Victims of Crimes. Created by the Omnibus
  Crime and Safe Streets Act of 1968, as amended, the National Institute of
  Justice is authorized to support research, evaluation, and demonstration
  programs, the development of technology, and both national and interna-
  tional information dissemination.

- *National Youth Gang Center*: http://www.iir.com/nygc/nygc.htm   This
  group works toward a balanced approach to the problem of gangs. It points
  to the need for comprehensive policies if we are to reduce the amount of
  delinquency and crime perpetrated by juvenile gang members. Many bulletins and papers are published each year.

- *United States Department of Education*: http://www.edgov/drugfree   A primary mission of this research is keeping kids in school and decreasing the
  dropout rate.

- *National Clearinghouse on Child Abuse and Neglect Information*:
  http://www.calib.com/nccanch   This clearinghouse provides access to the
  most extensive collection of information on child maltreatment in the
  world. Professionals and members of the general public can obtain up-to-
  date information on all aspects of child abuse and neglect from the
  Clearinghouse, which will provide annotated bibliographies on specific topics or a copy of the CDROM database on request.

- *National Archive of Criminal Justice Data at the University of Michigan*:
  http://www.ojp.usdoj.gov/bjs/   This archive contains a wealth of information on prosecution, courts, sentencing, and the theories and concepts
  behind the legal holdings followed by practitioners at all levels of the criminal justice system.

- *National Criminal Justice Reference Center*: http://www.ncjrs.org   This arm
  of the U.S. Department of Justice collects, produces, and disseminates a
  wide range of books, articles, data summaries, and films in areas such as
  criminal justice policy, the impact of crime, and crime and the media.

- *Institute for Intergovernmental Research*: http://www.iir.com/   Sponsors conferences and makes documents available, including *New Riders' Official
  World Wide Web Yellow Pages.*

- *The Police Pages*: http://www.mcs.net-jra/police/pages/whereisit.html   In
  addition to the many sections and listings that are provided on *The Police
  Pages*, there are other outstanding internet references on law enforcement
  and criminal justice–related subjects (e.g., Terror and Terrorists/Anarchy
  and Anarchists).

- *History of Correctional Education*: http://www.coe.utk.edu/literacy/corr_edu/ corrhist.html   Despite the fact that most prisons, reformatories, and training schools seem to be bleak environments more likely to impede student learning than encourage it, most correctional educational programs are judged success-ful according to the traditional measures of learning. Highlights of this period include the expansion of federal influence, the rise of postsecondary programs in corrections, and so on.

- *Division of Prisons Programs—DART* http://www.doc.state.nc.us/dop/ program/dart.htm   DART provides inmates with drug alcohol problems an initial opportunity to engage in treatment and early recovery.

- *Office of National Drug Control Policy (ONDCP)*: http://www.whitehousedrug-policy.gov/   ONDCP provides information for policymakers, grant applica-tions, legislators, criminal justice professionals and students, researchers, educators, and parents. Provides links to other valuable resources.

- *Zeno's Forensic Page*: http://zeno.simplenet.com/forensic.html   General information is provided on forensic sources, including forensic science, forensic medicine, forensic psychiatry/psychology, and forensic accounting. Contains hundreds of related links divided into clickable categories.

- *Other Internet Sites Related to Criminal Justice*: http://broadway.vera.org/pub/ocjsites.html   This is a civics and govern-ment archive that is maintained by the Internet Wiretap (gopher). FedStats has access to statistics and information produced by more than 70 agencies in the U.S. federal government.

Once you have begun, you will discover thousands of sites and dozens of types of information that we have not mentioned in this chapter. Some of the things you will find will include:

- *Mailing Lists.* You can join a mailing list and receive by e-mail or, in printed form, publications from a wide variety of organizations.

- *Bibliographies.* Numerous extensive bibliographies of criminal justice infor-mation already appear on the net.

- *Publishers and Bookstores.* You will find publishers offering to sell you virtual-ly any title in criminal justice, and you will find bookstores that offer not only new books, but also old, outdated, and rare editions of many texts.

- *Criminal Justice Projects.* Many criminal justice research and discussion pro-jects have home pages on the net, and sometimes you can join in the research and discussions.

- *Criminal Justice Resource Guides.* Guides to all these resources and more are on the net, with clickable links that take you directly to the sources they cite.

- *News Groups.* News Groups are Internet pages in which people exchange information on current events.

CHAPTER 8

Conducting Quantitative Research

Social analysis is the systematic attempt to explain social events by placing them within a series of meaningful contexts. We call this activity social science, and we conduct it using methods which are often quantitative in nature. These quantitative methods of research are much the same in social science as they are in any other scientific field. To understand them, we begin with a brief look at what we mean by the terms *science* and *scientific method*.

THINKING SCIENTIFICALLY

We tend to use the word *science* too loosely, referring to things that are not, strictly, science. Hoover and Donovan (1995:4–5) describe three common uses of the term *science* that divert our understanding from what science really is. First, people often—and wrongly—think of science as technology. In fact, technology is a product of science. Technology results from the application of science to different tasks. The technology involved, for instance, in sending people to the moon came into existence, over time, as people decided how to use discoveries they made through the application of scientific principles. While the lunar module that landed in the Sea of Tranquillity is definitely a piece of technology, it is not science.

A second misconception people have about the nature of science is that it is a specific body of knowledge that discloses to us the rules by which the natural world works. To say that "science tells us" something is misleading. For example, it is not science that "tells" us that smoking is dangerous to our health. It is people, who, investigating the effects of smoking tobacco on a variety of human pathologies, conclude that smoking is a very harmful practice. The body of knowledge that these people produce is evidence, accumulated through scientific inquiry, of the effects of smoking. It is important not to mistake the body of knowledge for the mode of inquiry that helps researchers to produce it.

Finally, Hoover and Donovan point out that it is also misleading to think of science as an activity conducted only by a specialized group of researchers called *scientists*. This notion implies that some people use the scientific approach to understanding reality, whereas others do not. In fact, all people use some form of scientific thinking to aid them in their struggle to deal with the uncertainty of life. Sometimes the thinking process is a bit crude, as when we decide what to eat by determining through trial and error what tastes good. But it is scientific thinking nonetheless.

So if science is not simply technology or a body of knowledge available only to people we call scientists, what is it? Let us define science as a *method of inquiry*, a process of thinking and asking questions by which we arrive at an understanding of the world around us. Conceived of in this way, science does not exist in machines or in books or even in the natural phenomena around us, but in the mind. More specifically, science is a way of formulating questions and investigating answers, a set of rules for inquiry created to help achieve valid and reliable answers.

Historically, the scientific approach to knowing has not done well when competing with other approaches. This is largely because, throughout the centuries, knowledge acquired through scientific investigation often threatened established values, norms, and institutions by which those in power maintained control of their world—values and institutions founded on such approaches to knowledge as myth, dogma, and superstition. Those who used science to understand and predict events were often viewed negatively by the powerful. Galileo was sanctioned by both church and state when he used the scientific method to arrive at conclusions that challenged existing beliefs about the "center" of the universe. Using science to support the conclusion that the sun was in fact the center around which all things revolved, his outcome flew in the face of the Roman Catholic dogma that held the earth to be the center.

So it is safe to say that science is never practiced in a social vacuum. Today, leaders in the developed world tend to rely on science, rather than superstition or dogma, to establish credibility for what they say and do. But the scientific approach to seizing and maintaining power is very new in the history of the world.

THE SCIENTIFIC METHOD

The goal of science is to explain reality. The *scientific method* attempts to explain reality through the development and testing of *theories*, which are general explanations for the existence or cause of certain classes of phenomena. Two centuries before Christ, for example, Ptolemy constructed a theory to explain the movement of the stars in the sky. His theory suggested that the sun and planets all revolve around the earth. Ptolemy's theory, which described the general relationship of the planets and stars to the earth, explained much of what could be observed in the sky at night. More precise observations, however, later began to cast doubt on Ptolemy's theory.

Once they are constructed, theories must be tested to see if they actually explain the phenomena they are intended to explain. We test theories in a two-step process:

1. We create specific statements that should be true if the theory is correct.
2. We then devise tests of these statements. A statement devised to test a theory is known as a *hypothesis*. A substantial part of what social science does is to test research hypotheses.

The development of this two-step scientific method was a historical and cultural breakthrough. Accomplished slowly at the end of the Middle Ages by brilliant thinkers in different European countries, it stands as one of the watershed events that differentiate the ancient world from the modern. We now briefly examine the elements of the scientific method.

Formulating and Testing Research Hypotheses

A *research hypothesis* is an educated guess. It is a declarative sentence stating that a specific relationship exists between two or more phenomena. Consider the following example of a research hypothesis:

When a person's anxiety rises, his or her intolerance of others increases.

This hypothesis states that there is a specific relationship between two variables: (1) a person's anxiety, and (2) the person's tolerance of other people. In addition, the hypothesis states the nature of the relationship between the two variables: an increase in the first is associated with an increase in the second.

A researcher constructs a hypothesis for the sole purpose of testing whether or not it is "true," that is, whether or not a certain relationship exists between two phenomena that the formulator of the hypothesis is interested in investigating. Hypotheses help define the question that our research is trying to answer. Suppose that we want to know if family relationships are affected by economic conditions. We would like, eventually, to develop a theory that will help explain how different economic conditions lead to different ways in which family members relate to each other. Before we can understand general patterns of relationships and create a theory to explain these patterns, we must become much more specific in our inquiry. Hypotheses help us to select specific aspects of a problem or question and explore them one at a time.

For instance, in our example of the economy and family relationships, we might propose the following hypothesis:

When the economy is strong, the divorce rate decreases, and when the economy is weak, the divorce rate increases.

We notice, however, that there will be difficulties in testing this hypothesis. What, for example, are "strong" and "weak" economies? Our hypothesis will need to be more specific. We will perhaps find that a combination of selected economic indicators, such as the rate of unemployment or the amount of manufacturing production, will help us to define strong and weak in economic terms. The problem has now become more rather than less complicated. How will we know if family relationships are influenced by only one of these factors and not by others? What if only certain combinations of these factors, and not other combinations, might have an effect on relationships? The answer to these questions is that we need to start with one simple hypothesis, then test others in a careful, systematic way. Our first hypothesis might be, "When the national unemployment rate is greater than 7 percent, the divorce rate will remain above 50 percent."

Two types of hypotheses are commonly used in social science. The first may be called causal, the second relational. *Causal* hypotheses attempt to show that one phenomenon causes another. *Relational* hypotheses, on the other hand, attempt to indicate whether or not two phenomena are related to one another in a specific way, without demonstrating that one causes the other. Testing the hypothesis above will only indicate whether a relationship exists between unemployment and divorce, not whether unemployment causes divorce. Relations between hypotheses may be either positive or negative. A *positive relation* exists when an increase in one variable is associated with an increase in another, while a *negative* or *inverse relation* occurs when an increase in one variable coincides with a decrease in another variable.

Once hypotheses are constructed, we test them by observing the behavior of the variables that they contain. For example, let us phrase our hypothesis like this:

Extended periods of unemployment increase the likelihood of divorce.

Variables

The phenomena being observed are designated as different types of variables:

- The *dependent variable* is the phenomenon that is in some way affected by other variables. In our example, divorce is the dependent variable.
- The *independent variable* is the phenomenon that may have some effect on the dependent variable. In our example, the time period in which a person is unemployed is the independent variable, and divorce is the dependent variable.
- *Antecedent variables* are phenomena that act upon or relate to independent variables. In our example, if we hypothesized that "extended periods of unemployment occur in states with fewer high-tech industries," the number of high-tech industries in a state would be an antecedent variable.
- *Intervening variables* are variables other than the independent variable that affect the dependent variable directly. In our example, if we said that "divorce rates decrease when it rains," then rain, in this case, would be an intervening variable.

Identifying the dependent, independent, antecedent, and intervening variables is very important in conducting research because it helps you to define carefully the relationships that you are examining.

Hypotheses are constructed to find out what relationship, if any, exists between the independent and dependent variables. To test a hypothesis, therefore, you need to measure the amount of change in the dependent variable as you observe change in the independent variable. To do this, you must complete two tasks.

The first task is to find accurate measurements of the dependent and independent variables as they vary over time or in different circumstances. For measurements to be accurate, they must be both valid and reliable. *Valid measurements* measure the effects they are supposed to measure instead of measuring something else. *Reliable measurements* are those that can be made under different conditions and still yield the same result.

The second task is to determine the effects of antecedent and intervening variables upon the dependent variable so that you will know how much effect the independent variable has had. For example, if the voter turnout is greater in one community than another and the communities have different registration time periods, you must determine how much of the difference in turnout was due to the registration periods as opposed to the percentage of independent voters or the occurrence of rain.

Conducting a study that is reliable and valid requires an analysis that utilizes accepted statistical methods. Your research methods instructor will help you determine the correct statistical applications for analyzing your criminal justice research problem.

Problems for the Scientific Study of Society

A hypothesis can often be difficult to test. When attempting to test hypotheses in criminal justice and other social sciences, we often encounter three general problems:

1. *Data insufficiency or incongruity.* Once we have stated our hypothesis, our investigation may find that sufficient data are not available. Sometimes the records that we need have not been kept consistently or accurately, or have been compiled according to different systems or categories. If we want to compare divorce rates in the United States and Italy, for example, we may find that the American and Italian governments have different reporting requirements and that the procedures used to validate data may be much more reliable in one country than in another.

2. *Multiplicity and ambiguity of variables.* It is often difficult to cope with the sheer number of variables that may or may not affect the result of our study; similarly, it can be difficult to isolate the effects of one variable from those of others. If we want to find out what decreases the divorce rate, for example, we may need to try to sort out the competing effects of family histories, customs, religious beliefs, and economic factors.

3. *Methodological uncertainty.* The third problem with the scientific study of society originates in epistemology, that is, the study of the nature of knowledge itself. Testing hypotheses, an approach fundamental to the scientific method, is an *inductive* process. One requirement of induction is the examination of numerous specific cases in hopes of finding general principles that help explain or predict behavior. For example, if all known cases of oak trees have acorns, one may conclude that all oak trees have acorns. But there may be a flaw in this sort of reasoning. In his book *The Logic of Scientific Discovery* (1959), Karl Popper pointed out that to show that some examples of a certain phenomenon behave in a certain manner is not to demonstrate that others will also. Even if all known examples of a phenomenon behave in a certain way, there may be examples in the

future that will deviate from the pattern. The fact that all known oak trees have acorns, for example, does not mean that an oak tree without acorns will never be found.

Furthermore, according to Popper, scientific observation is always *selective*. We must choose to observe before the actual observation takes place, and when we do observe, our observation will always take place within a particular context. This suggests that hypotheses are observations not of reality *per se*, but merely of one context, one view of reality. Hypotheses, therefore, are not genuine observations, only bold guesses. Since we can never say with certainty that a hypothesis is true, Popper explains that the *only* time we can be sure of a hypothesis is when it is disproved. Scientific progress, therefore, is made not by verifying hypotheses, but by refuting them. Because of Popper's works and those of others, this is indeed the way research often proceeds: by working not to prove hypotheses but to refute them.

A hypothesis established precisely for the purpose of being refuted is called a *null hypothesis*. Returning to our previous example, if we wanted to try to prove that extended registration periods increase voter turnout, we would begin by testing a null hypothesis: "Extended registration periods do not increase voter turnout." If we can find a case in which an extended registration period does increase voter turnout, we will have disproved the null hypothesis. We will not have proven that extended registration periods *always* increase voter turnout, but we will at least have taken the first step by showing that extended registration periods *can* increase voter turnout. Science thus proceeds by disproving successively specific null hypotheses.

No matter how we decide to treat hypotheses, there is still a question about how useful they are when it comes to major scientific discoveries. According to Thomas Kuhn (1970), even the refutation of null hypotheses is not a feasible strategy if one wants to achieve the occasional new perspective that revolutionizes science. When Copernicus proposed his heliocentric theory of astronomy, the Ptolemaic model of the solar system was well entrenched in the scientific community. Kuhn calls established patterns of scientific inquiry "paradigms" and says that they are essential to the progress of science. A paradigm establishes the foundations of knowledge in a particular discipline until the paradigm is displaced by a new one. Discrepancies in the Ptolemaic paradigm were met by increasingly complicated explanations devised to make observation conform to the theory. Copernicus' system was so different from Ptolemy's that it became a new scientific paradigm. At first Copernicus' theory had little evidence from observation to support it. Kuhn argues that Copernicus did not come up with his new theory by disputing the Ptolemaic system. Instead of gradually and successively refuting hypotheses, Copernicus had a flash of intuition. A paradigm, for Kuhn, is never refuted by evidence; it can only be overturned when another one takes its place.

Social science, says Kuhn, needs a paradigm to establish its identity, its mission. Not having one, social science winds its way endlessly through a series of disagreements over methods and goals. Therefore, while the scientific method remains the normal way of adding to our common store of knowledge about society, the great breakthroughs of the future may as likely come from exceptional moments of human creativity as from the steady testing of statements within our normal range of exploration.

The Stages of Social Research

How do those who practice scientific inquiry go about "doing" social research? What are the steps involved in approaching a research problem scientifically? Actually, as we have stated above, thinking scientifically and using science to help us make decisions are parts of our everyday life. However, if we wish to use this approach to aid in the investigation of problems that are germane to criminal justice, the scientific method is more structured and stepwise. Whether researchers are pursuing a problem in criminal justice, sociology, political science, psychology, or any area that relies on the scientific method, they take the following steps:

1. Define a research problem.
2. Formulate a meaningful hypothesis.
3. Conduct a literature review to determine what is known about the research problem.
4. Identify dependent, independent, and intervening variables.
5. Formulate a research design.
6. Conduct the study.
7. Analyze and interpret the results.

COMMON QUANTITATIVE RESEARCH DESIGNS

Since students and professionals in criminal justice investigate a wide variety of issues and problems, their quantitative research can take many forms. Four of the most common quantitative research designs are:

1. Surveys
2. Experiments
3. Scientific observation
4. Content analysis

Because the processes of conducting surveys and experiments, performing scientific observation, and making content analysis studies require extensive additional knowledge and are normally undertaken by students only at the graduate level, we have not devoted individual chapters to them. However, it is important for you as a student of criminal justice to have some basic knowledge about experiments, scientific observation, and content analysis. Therefore, we provide a brief introduction to these procedures here.

Surveys

A survey is simply a device for identifying and counting events, actions, perceptions, attitudes, or beliefs. Researchers usually conduct criminal justice surveys to find out how large groups of people, such as Americans in general, African Americans, women, or welfare recipients, behave in certain situations, or what they believe or feel about certain issues. Public and private organizations often conduct surveys on attitudes and preferences in order to make their services more effective and desirable.

It is normally unnecessary and too costly to obtain data on every member of the group under consideration, so most surveys question a small but representative percentage of the total group that is being studied. The individual units being studied in a criminal justice survey are usually called *elements*. An element might be a group—an ethnic group, a social organization, a church denomination—but it is most often an individual. The *population* is the total number of elements covered by the research question. If the research question is "Are left-handed fifth-grade boys more likely to identify with sports heroes than right-handed fifth-grade boys?", the population is all fifth-grade boys in the United States. The *sampling frame* consists of all fifth-grade boys that attend the school in which your survey will take place. The *sample* is the part of the population that is selected to respond to the survey. A *representative sample* includes numbers of elements in the same proportions as they occur in the general population. In other words, if 81 percent of the population of fifth-grade boys in America are right handed and 19 percent left handed, then 81 percent of a representative sample of fifth-grade boys will also be right handed and 19 percent will be left handed. *Nonrepresentative samples* do not include numbers of elements in the same proportions as they occur in the general population.

- *Research question:* Are seventh-grade boys more likely to be aware of the dangers of illegal drugs than fifth-grade boys?
- *Research hypothesis:* Seventh-grade boys are more likely than fifth-grade boys to be aware of the dangers of illegal drugs.
- *Elements:* Individual fifth- and seventh-grade boys.
- *Population:* Fifth- and seventh-grade boys in the United States.
- *Sampling frame:* Fifth-grade boys at Hoover Elementary School and seventh-grade boys at Hamilton Middle School.
- *Sample:* Eighty-four students in Mr. Wimbly's fifth-grade classes and Mrs. Baker's seventh-grade classes, out of the total population of 1276 boys at the two schools.

How large must a sample be to represent the population accurately? This question is difficult to answer, but two general principles apply. The first is that a large sample is more likely, simply by chance, to be more representative of a population than a small sample. The second is that the goal of a representative sample is to include within it representatives of all of the *strata* that are included in the whole population.

Sometimes the researcher is able to control error from certain variables by *stratifying the sample*, or subdividing it into different layers based on prior knowledge of how these variables are distributed in the population. For example, before sampling a university population, if we know that 58 percent of the student body is female, 13 percent are minorities, the average age is 28, and 54 percent of the students attend all or part of their program at night, we can stratify the sample according to these variables before making the random selections. Again, like the purely random sample, obtaining a stratified sample is very difficult, if not impossible, when the population in question is college students.

Faced with such problems, the most reasonable and economical question becomes: Can the survey be filled out in select classes that represent the student body? For example, would sampling classes that are diversified by such factors as age, gender, ethnic background, or major field lower the error enough to allow the researcher to feel comfortable generalizing to the target population as a whole? Our answer depends to some extent on the degree to which the makeup of the classes parallels the stratification of the university. Although this is often the best sampling procedure available in such a complex environment as a college or university, the problem with the method lies in our inability to gauge the amount of error. When we read about a ±3 or 4 percent error in samples that have been taken for opinion polls and other scientific endeavors, it is important to understand that the researchers have applied controlled procedures to judge the error involved in generalizing to the population being sampled. So while we may have given careful thought to selecting classes that are stratified much like the student body of the university, the absence of random selection prevents us from accurately measuring the error involved in generalizing to the population.

Surveys consist of two types of questions, closed and open. *Closed questions* restrict the response of the respondent to a specific set of answers, normally two to six. Multiple-choice examination questions are typical closed questions.

Open questions do not preselect certain answers but instead, allow the respondents to answer in any manner they choose. Open questions, therefore, call for a more active and thoughtful response than do closed questions. The fact that open questions require more time and effort may be a disadvantage because, in general, the more time and effort a survey demands, the fewer responses it is likely to get. Open questions do have an advantage, however, in providing an opportunity for unusual views to be expressed. You might, for example, get a response to the question "What should be done about gun control?" that is like the following:

> All firearms should be restricted to law enforcement agencies in populated areas. Special privately owned depositories should be established for hunters to be able to store rifles in hunting areas, where they can be used for target practice, or outdoors during hunting season.

Open questions are preferable to closed questions when you want to expand a range of possible answers to find out how much diversity there is among opinions on an issue. For practice working with open questions, you may want to include at least one in your survey questionnaire.

Perhaps the greatest difficulty with open questions is the problem of quantifying the results. The researcher must examine each answer and then group responses according to their content. For example, it might be possible to differentiate responses that are clearly in favor, clearly opposed, and ambivalent to gun control. Open questions are of particular value to researchers who are doing continuing research. The responses they obtain help them to create better questions for the next survey they conduct.

In addition to the regular open and closed questions on your survey questionnaire, you will want to add what are often called *identifiers*, questions that ask for personal information about the respondents. If you ask questions about gun control, for example, you may want to know if men respond differently from women, if Caucasians respond differently from African-Americans, or if young people respond differently from older people. Identifier questions ask about things such as the respondent's gender, age, political party, religion, income level, or other items that may be relevant to the particular survey topic.

Criminal justice surveys are the barometers of society. They describe a society's quality of life and the characteristics of its culture. They tell us who we are. There is little doubt that the skillful use of surveys dramatically increases the accuracy of our perceptions of ourselves.

Experiments

Experimentation is the fundamental method of acquiring knowledge in the physical sciences. As a research method it has one primary and substantial benefit: experiments allow the researcher to control the variables, making it easier than it might otherwise be to determine the effect of the independent variable on the dependent variable. Experiments are more difficult to conduct in the social sciences than in the physical sciences because the research subjects are human beings and the number of variables is normally large. Despite these difficulties, however, social scientists are now successfully conducting more experiments than they have in the past.

Experiments in the social sciences are set up according to several different basic designs. A simple one is the *post-test measurement*. For example, a lecture on the consequences of using marijuana may be followed by a test of the knowledge of the participants who heard the lecture. The *test–retest method* is more accurate. A researcher using this method might measure the effects of a lecture on the attitudes of the people in an audience by first having the members of the audience complete a survey, then listen to the lecture, and finally, complete the survey again. The researcher could then measure the differences in opinion registered before and after the survey. Without the first survey, the researcher cannot be sure of the level of knowledge or the respondents' attitudes before the test was given, and the effects of the lecture or speech, then, are less certain.

The *alternative-form* type of experiment uses two different measures of the same concept. In a research project concerning the effects of peer pressure on adolescents, for example, the analyst could measure subjects' propensity to conform in one test and then measure their desire for acceptance in another test. The *split-halves* device is similar to the alternative-form measurement, except that two measures of the concept under study are applied at the same time.

All experiment designs confront the following problems:

1. *Control of variables.* Can the environment be controlled to rule out other factors?
2. *Time passage.* People get tired, or for some other reason assume a different attitude.
3. *Varying acts of measurement.* Poll takers may record responses differently.

4. *Statistical regression*. Someone who is on the high end of a test score range may register a high score only temporarily.

5. *Experimental mortality*. Subjects drop out.

6. *Instrument decay*. The instrument may not be used as carefully the second time.

7. *Selection error*. Control and experimental groups may not be equivalent.

Researchers have developed a number of complex methodologies to overcome these problems. *Multigroup designs*, for example, test multiple independent variables against the same dependent variable. *Factorial designs* may test the effects of several independent variables in different combinations. A simple "2 × 2" factorial design, for example, might test combinations of four possible results from two different actions a researcher might take to test the social acceptability of her actions. Let's suppose that the researcher made an identical presentation of information on the health hazards of smoking to four different groups of people and later had the groups fill in a questionnaire that would indicate their acceptance of her presentation. Normally, the researcher would wear a traditional business suit when addressing a group, but the experiment's goal is to study how socially acceptable her appearance is to her audiences, so she decides to alter her customary appearance in each group setting, using a straw hat and a pink leotard. The chart below illustrates the four possible variations in her appearance:

	wear pink leotard	do not wear pink leotard
wear a straw hat	(1) both hat and leotard	(2) hat but no leotard
do not wear a straw hat	(3) leotard but not hat	(4) neither hat nor leotard

A factorial design based on the choices set forth in the chart would test the results of presentation participant acceptance according to each of the four situations.

Researchers conduct dozens of different types experimental designs, using different combinations of strategies. The factorial design above is designed to be used as part of a *field experiment*, an experiment conducted within a natural setting, which in our example above would be four regular high school health classes.

In the following example the groups who participate in the experiment have not been left in their natural setting but have been preselected by the researcher. Some researchers claim that this type of interference with subjects creates a quasi-experimental design.

Let us suppose that we design an experiment to test this research hypothesis: Students who are anxious because they believe their instructor will have access to their evaluations of the instructor's effectiveness before the assignment of the student's final grade will give the instructor a higher evaluation than if they had no such anxiety.

For our experiment the teacher will use two course sections of his criminology class, the sections being similar in size and student makeup. Section 1, the control group, will be given the teacher evaluation form in the usual manner. The teacher will leave the room while a monitor—a student in the class—dispenses the forms, reads the instructions, gathers the forms after they have been completed, seals them in an envelope, then leaves the room, supposedly to take them where they will be kept from the teacher until final grades have been assigned to transcripts. As part of the instruction, the teacher emphasizes the fact that he does not have access to the results until final grades have been recorded.

Section 2, the experimental group, will follow the same procedure with one exception. The monitor, again a student in the class, will first disclose information she has been given about teachers being allowed to look at the evaluations prior to the final grades being assigned. She will state that this is something she has heard from several reliable sources, but that she is unwilling to disclose those sources. Everything else in the evaluation process will be carefully controlled to emulate the procedure used with the control group. The evaluations are then tallied to determine if the experimental group's perception that the teacher has access to their evaluation before the final grade is assigned caused them to give their teacher significantly higher evaluations than the control group did.

Experiments in criminal justice such as the one above encounter certain difficulties. See if you can answer the following questions:

- What is the dependent variable of the experiment?
- What is the independent variable?
- What are the important antecedent and intervening variables?
- What else would need to be done to control the antecedent and intervening variables?
- What ethical issues might preclude running an experiment of this kind?

Content Analysis

Content analysis is a method of analyzing written documents that allows researchers to transform nonquantitative data into quantitative data by counting and categorizing certain variables within the data. Content analysts look for certain types of words or references in the texts, then categorize them or count them. A content analyst of news articles on women, for example, might count the number of times the authors of the articles portray women in a positive manner.

Content analysts of "events data" focus on a particular event or a series of events over time. A number of content analysts have examined the major wars of this century and have attempted to identify factors that are common in situations of war. Compilations of events data, such as the *World Handbook of Political and Social Indicators*, provide a listing of the important political events (elections, coups, wars) for most countries of the world. These listings help to compare trends in selected types of events from one country to another. Press reports, statistics, televised and radio media reports, personal records, newspapers, and magazines provide inexhaustible mines of data for content analysts.

Government documents are an especially rich source of material for political scientists. Different types of government documents include presidential papers; the *Code of Federal Regulations*; the *Congressional Record*; federal, state, and local election returns; historical records; judicial decisions; and legal records. The data analyzed in content analysis are most often the words contained in books, journals, magazines, newspapers, films, and radio or television broadcasts. But content analysis may also be conducted on photographs, cartoons, or music.

A recent example of content analysis design may be found in the research of Levin, Arluke, and Mody-Desbareau (1986), who coded 311 celebrity and non-celebrity profiles that appeared in the four most widely circulated gossip magazines—*The National Enquirer, The Star, The Globe*, and *The National Examiner*—from February through July 1983. The researchers concluded that while the profiles of noncelebrities mostly emphasized extraordinary acts of heroism, strength, or charity, celebrities were usually featured for some mundane or minor event, such as a shopping spree or quarrel with a spouse or lover. The researchers found a hidden message in the articles they reviewed: the ordinary, "little" person in the world should be content with his or her collective place in life (Levin and Fox 1997).

Direct Observation

A number of other techniques are used for data collection. *Direct observation* of social phenomena is conducted by trained observers who carefully record selected behaviors. Observation may be *structured*; that is, a definite list of phenomena is compiled and studied, including such items as number of social contacts or religious allusions in a speech. Or observation may be *unstructured*, in which case observation attempts to take in every action in a certain setting that may possibly be significant. In either case, successful observation for purposes of social science research always follows clear guidelines and standard procedures.

Direct scientific observation is difficult to conduct for several reasons. First, researchers usually consider observation data to be qualitative, and therefore subjective, in nature. Although many of the data can be quantified, qualitative considerations are hard to avoid. Another problem is that social events can be difficult, time consuming, and expensive to observe, and an entire event such as an election may require several observers whose activities are highly coordinated and regulated.

PART III

How to Write Different Types Of Criminal Justice Papers

CHAPTER 9

Two Brief Writing Assignments for Introductory Students

REACTION PAPERS

The purpose of this assignment is to develop and sharpen your critical thinking and writing skills. The model originated from Professor Stephen Jenks of the University of Central Oklahoma. Your objective in writing this assignment is to define an issue clearly and to formulate and clarify your position on that issue by reacting to a controversial statement. Completing this assignment requires accomplishing the following six tasks:

1. Select a suitable reaction statement.
2. Explain your selection.
3. Clearly define the issue addressed in the statement.
4. Clearly state your position on the issue.
5. Defend your position.
6. Conclude concisely.

Select a Suitable Reaction Statement

Your first task is to find or write a statement to which to react. Reaction statements are provocative declarations. They are controversial assertions that beg for either a negative or a positive response. Your instructor may assign a reaction statement, you may find one in a newspaper or on the Internet or hear one on television, or you may construct one yourself, depending on your instructor's directions. The following statements may elicit a polite reply but will probably not stir up people's emotions. They are, therefore, not good reaction statements:

- It's cold out today.
- My pants are too tight.

- Orange is not green.
- Saturday morning is the best time to watch cartoons.

The following statements, however, have the potential to be good reaction statements, because when you hear them you will probably have a distinct opinion about them:

- Abortion is murder.
- Capital punishment is necessary.
- Government is too big.

Such statements are likely to provoke a reaction, either negative or positive, depending on the person who is reacting to them. Although they may be incendiary, they are also both ordinary and vague. If your instructor assigns you a statement to which to react, you may proceed to the next step. If you are to select your own, select or formulate one that is provocative, imaginative, and appropriate to the course for which you are writing the paper. Professor Otto, for example, once assigned this statement in his Innovations in Corrections class:

- Prisons should be run by the private sector of society.

Consider the following examples of reaction statements for other criminal justice classes:

- Automatic weapons should be banned.
- Criminals should be punished, not rehabilitated.
- The United States should be a Christian nation.
- Juveniles who commit heinous crimes should be certified and tried as adults.
- Criminal justice agencies ought to be run more like businesses.
- The U.S. Supreme Court should take an active role in determining social policy.
- Police officers should not carry weapons of deadly force.

Where do you find good reaction statements? A good way is to think about subjects that interest you. When you hear something in class that sparks a reaction because you either agree or disagree with it, you know you are on the right track. Be sure to write your statement and ask your instructor for comments on it before beginning your paper. Once you have completed your selection, state it clearly at the beginning of your paper.

Explain Your Selection

After you have written the reaction statement, write a paragraph that explains why it important to you. Be as specific as possible. Writing "I like it" does not tell the reader anything useful, but sentences like the following are informative: "Innocent people are being shot down by violent gangs in the inner city. We must crack down on gang violence to make the inner city safe for all who live there."

Clearly Define the Issue Addressed in the Statement

Consider the statement assigned by Professor Otto: "Prisons should be run by the private sector of society." What is the most important issue addressed in this statement? Is it the notion that punishment and/or rehabilitation can be handled more efficiently by private business? Or is it the question of whether or not government can run a prison as eco_____Perhaps some aspects of the statement are more import_____essed in the statement, you provide yourself with som_____that will help you state your position.

Clearly St_____ssue

In response t_____ might begin by saying, "Much waste and corrupti_____vere run like private businesses. The money saved_____on management could be returned to taxpayers in_____of this response will have no doubt about where

Defend Yo

You should n_____ur stand on the issue. When evaluating your pa_____extent to which you:

- Iden_____needed to support your position. (When arguing for the privat_____prisons, did you cite examples of how this had worked efficiently in history?)
- Provided facts and information, when appropriate. (When arguing that prison expenditures are too high, you should state the actual amounts of recent expenditures and how the money was used in a wasteful manner.)
- Introduced new arguments to those traditionally made on this issue. (Have new developments in technology enabled private business?)
- Presented your case accurately, coherently, logically, consistently, and clearly.

Conclude Concisely

Your concluding paragraph should sum up your argument clearly, persuasively, and concisely. When writing this assignment, follow the format directions in Chapter 3. Ask your instructor for directions concerning the length of the paper, but in the absence of further directions, your paper should not exceed five pages (typed, double-spaced).

SAMPLE REACTION PAPERS

The following sample reaction papers were selected from a criminal justice class instructed by Professor Rettig at the University of Central Oklahoma. Two of them are for prisons being run by the private sector, and one is opposed. Read them and assess their strengths and weaknesses. How well does each meet the criteria outlined above? Is one paper better than the others? Why?

A Positive Response to the Reaction Statement:

"Prisons should be run by the private sector."

by

Aleksandar Ristich

University of Central Oklahoma

January 1998

In the past 15 years, the United States has witnessed unprecedented increases in prison populations; conservative estimates indicate that 1.5 million Americans are incarcerated in state and federal prisons nation-wide. Reasons for the dramatic escalation of prison inmate populations in recent years can be attributed, in large part, to society's embrace of the retributive philosophy toward crime control. The phenomenon of prison overcrowding that resulted has had a sobering effect on this nation's policymakers, forcing them to seriously examine various alternatives to this problem. One option that state governments should consider in their struggle to manage prison overflows is to allow the private sector to construct and operate minimum- and medium-security prisons.

In an effort to relieve the current crisis of overcrowding, these additional private facilities can prove worthwhile. Such private minimum and medium prisons would not replace comparable state correction facilities; they would only enhance the services provided by the public sector. A private prison would be ideal for housing parole violators, inmates close to being released, white-collar criminals, and other inmates determined to be nonviolent offenders. The management of these types of offenders can be as effective in a private facility as in a public one.

In the past, state prisons have been pressured by judicial mandate to reduce prison populations due to overcrowding. In lieu of a premature release initiative, state prison authorities can look to the private sector for expedient construction of additional prisons to ameliorate such emergency situations. Typically, a private-sector prison is able to open a facility rather quickly because it is not subject to elaborate and time-consuming bidding procedures common when the state is involved in similar matters. Furthermore, minimal, if any, tax dollars would be expended in such an endeavor, thereby satisfying both the populace and state governments, which often lack money in their budgets to fund construction of additional prison facilities. Monies saved in the process could then be diverted to bolster existing programs, initiatives, and services of the state prisons.

The introduction of a private prison to the community generates economic growth by offering additional job opportunities. Naturally, a need for various prison personnel, such as guards, special service personnel, and food service workers, would become available to the surrounding community. Prior to employment, correction officers in this private setting would have to become certified by the state in the same manner as public correction officers.

Because a private-sector prison is a business enterprise, citizens of the state would have the opportunity to invest through the purchase of stock. Taxpayers, who are usually reluctant to spend additional dollars for state prison construction, could conceivably earn handsome dividends with a successful private prison as a result of their ownership in that business. If the current high rates of incarceration continue into the next century, the private prison industry and its investors will virtually be guaranteed generous profits.

Finally, privatization would stimulate competition with state prisons. Private prisons, especially those that are successful at managing costs more efficiently and effectively than comparable state facilities, would force government to reevaluate existing management methods and practices and alter them accordingly to remain competitive. A direct result of this vigorous competition would be improved correctional services across the board. Thus, a partnership with the private sector should be sought by government to aid in its seemingly endless battle against prison overflows. Implicit in this argument is the shift from a government monopoly on corrections to a system where market forces will have the opportunity to provide dynamic and vigorous competition among all providers. Such developments offer considerable promise for the future of correctional management.

A Negative Response to the Reaction Statement:

"Prisons should be run by the private sector."

by

Scott M. Houck

University of Central Oklahoma

January 1998

Privatization of prisons is a mistake. Almost all private-sector industries and corporations are motivated toward the goal of making a profit. Private-sector management is mostly, if not totally, concerned with the reduction of overhead and increase in the profit margin. In the prison setting, it would be too much of a temptation to cut overhead to such an extent that it violates the civil rights of offenders and/or threatens the health and safety of employees, offenders, and the community.

Although the current system is certainly not perfect, government-run prisons are not designed to make a profit for an individual or a group of individuals. A tax cut to the constituency is the main selling point of privatization. However, no matter what you do, it will still cost a lot of money to keep a person incarcerated. That inmate is still entitled to certain rights and liberties that have been granted by the constitution and upheld in various court decisions. In general, the provisions of many of the rights granted by the constitution require some form of funding. A profit-based company will test the very limits of humane incarceration by cutting costs on primary and secondary services and necessities provided to inmates. Services such as health programs, food necessities (quantitative and qualitative), treatment programs, vocational training, education, and religious provisions would be cut to increase the profit margin.

In the never-ending struggle for increased profits, personnel expenditures are the first items to be cut back. The result is lower salaries for entry-level employees, lack of or decreased in-service training events, decreased promotional opportunities, short staffing of shifts, increased potential for sick leave abuse, lack of or decreased health and retirement benefits, and reductions in various other personnel benefits.

The problem will begin in the recruitment process. Currently, it is very difficult to recruit qualified people into this thankless profession while paying a modest salary. The correctional officer position is one of the least respected, most underpaid, and most important job classifications in the prison environment. Not only must the correctional officer supervise offender activity, maintain facility security, update or create reports, communicate with offenders, and defuse potentially violent situations, but he or she must also try to maintain some form of a family and personal life. It is very difficult to maintain a decent family life when shift work constantly interferes with holidays, birthdays, weekends, and anniversaries. Compound that with minimal financial compensation for this often unrewarding job and it's easy to see the difficulty in attracting qualified people. Private-sector prison management's concern with profit will make prison life even more demanding on everyone by employing just about anyone who applies for a job for as little as possible.

Another major consideration or argument against privatization of prisons is health care provisions. Due to the fact that a privatized prison is a profit-based organization, it is very likely that basic and preventive health care would be drastically reduced. Such procedures or items that are necessary to the survival of the offender would not be implemented. If they were provided, the cost would certainly be passed back to the taxpayer. Usually, if not always, when a contract is written by a private company to the government, certain items are included in the basic contract for the housing of the offender, such as bed space, clothing, sundry items, and food. Other items that are not included, but provided at the cost of the state, are things like major surgery, kidney dialysis, some minor surgery, emergency room costs, and other medical items that possibly come up during a person's incarceration. These "extras" add up quickly to be a major expense, one that is not included in the original contract.

There is much more to privatization of prisons than what meets the eye. On the surface it seems to sound great. However, once one reads "the fine print" of private-sector prisons, it will probably cost the taxpayer more in the long run, while jeopardizing the rights of inmates. Privatization of prisons is a mistake; no one but the "company" will benefit!

A Positive Response to the Reaction Statement:

"Prisons should be run by the private sector."

by

Ken McDonald

University of Central Oklahoma

January 1998

The time has come for the public and society to deal effectively with the issue of corrections. The government has proven that it is ineffective in rehabilitating criminal offenders using the existing system. Furthermore, the emphasis on punishment has resulted in costs to the taxpayers of billions of dollars annually. The bureaucracy inherent in government operations has contributed to the rising costs and the inability to establish effective rehabilitation-oriented programs. It's time to give the private sector a chance to run our prisons.

Privatizing corrections provides an opportunity for creativity, innovation, and more efficient utilization of taxpayer dollars. The most important goal of any correctional program should be the reduction in recidivism. The important factor cannot be ignored, and it must be one criterion for which a privatized correctional facility is judged.

According to recent statistics, 1.5 million people are behind bars on any given day in the United States. The vast majority of those offenders will, at some point, be released. Government-operated corrections has proven to be both ineffective in reducing the recidivism rate and economically inefficient.

The issue of privatizing corrections must be played out in an organized manner. Private corporations will only be involved as long as there is a profit to be made. This should not be surprising, not that it is necessarily negative. The cost of construction for new prisons is virtually prohibitive for government entities. Inherent bureaucracy, purchasing policies, procurement issues, and so-called "red tape" all serve to drastically inflate construction costs per inmate bed. Private corporations have developed efficient ways to build new facilities, and they are generally operated more efficiently with fewer personnel than similar government operations.

Although money is important, rehabilitation efforts are the key and should be the deciding factor. Society cannot afford, economically or socially, to disregard this aspect of corrections. Privatizing corrections should be oriented toward developing rehabilitation programs to provide offenders with the skills they need to return to society in a productive manner. Failure to do so perpetuates crime and requires more and more resources for warehousing offenders.

As of 1995, 32 states, Puerto Rico, and the District of Columbia had contracts with 19 private corrections corporations. At this time it was estimated that over $150 billion taxpayer dollars had been saved in construction and operation costs compared to government operations. It seems clear that corporations can build and operate facilities more efficiently than government. What is still to be determined is how privatizing will affect recidivism.

Although many people will tolerate the private sector running low- and medium-security prisons, they question the private sector's control of maximum-security facilities. Employees of private corporations are private citizens, and their utilization in a maximum-security facility increases the chance that force will be used. When private citizens use force on other private citizens, the dilemma of deadly force must ultimately be dealt with.

Failure to try something different in corrections constrains and condemns society to the existing inefficient structure. While privatizing corrections may not be the ultimate answer to the corrections problem in this country, it does offer the possibility of innovation, and with proper governmental control, it could greatly reduce the burden on society.

ARTICLE CRITIQUES

An article critique evaluates an article published in an academic journal. A good critique tells the reader what point the article is trying to make and how convincingly it makes this point. Writing an article critique achieves three purposes. First, it provides you with an understanding of the information contained in a scholarly article and familiarity with other information written on the same topic. Second, it provides an opportunity to apply and develop your critical thinking skills as you attempt to critically evaluate the work of a criminal justice professional. Third, it helps you to improve your own writing skills as you attempt to describe the selected article's strengths and weaknesses so that your readers can understand them.

The first step in writing an article critique is to select an appropriate article. Unless your instructor specifies otherwise, select an article from a scholarly journal (such as

Justice Quarterly, Criminology, The Justice Professional, or *Journal of Criminal Justice*) and not a popular or journalistic publication (such as *Time* or *The National Review*). Chapter 6 contains a substantial list of academic journals that pertain to criminals. Your instructor may also accept appropriate articles from academic journals in other disciplines, such as history, political science, or sociology, many of which are also contained in this list.

Choosing an Article

Three other considerations should guide your choice of an article. First, browse article titles until you find a topic that interests you. Writing a critique will be much more satisfying if you have an interest in the topic. Hundreds of interesting journal articles are published every year. The following articles, for example, appeared in a 1997 issue (Volume 10, Number 1) of *The Justice Professional*:

- "Scamming: An Ethnographic Study of Workplace Crime in the Retail Food Industry"
- "A Writing-Intensive Approach to Criminal Justice Education"
- "Future Trends in Terrorism"
- "Problem-Oriented Policing: Assessing the Process"
- "The Legal Ramifications of Student Internships"
- "Retiring from Police Service: Education Needs and Second Career Planning"

The second consideration in selecting an article is your current level of knowledge. Many criminal justice studies, for example, employ sophisticated statistical techniques. You may be better prepared to evaluate them if you have studied statistics.

The third consideration is to select a current article, one written within the 12 months prior to making your selection. Much of the material in criminal justice is quickly superseded by new studies. Selecting a recent study will help ensure that you will be engaged in an up-to-date discussion of your topic.

Writing the Critique

Once you have selected and read your article carefully, you may begin to write your critique, which should cover the following four areas:

1. Thesis
2. Methods
3. Evidence or thesis support
4. Recommendation

THESIS

Your first task is to find and clearly state the thesis of the article. The thesis is the main point the article is trying to make. In an article selected from a 1997 issue (Volume 10, Number 1) of *The Justice Professional* (see above), Professors Michael Doyle and

Robert Meadows of California Lutheran University's Department of Sociology and Criminal Justice examine "A Writing-Intensive Approach to Criminal Justice Education: The California Lutheran University Model." In this article, coincidentally on the importance of helping criminal justice students become better thinkers through writing, Doyle and Meadows state their thesis very clearly:

> The purpose of Criminal Justice education is to develop in students the knowledge, judgment, values, and ethical consciousness essential to becoming responsible citizens and leaders in the Criminal Justice system. Equally important is preparing students to critically evaluate and analyze justice issues through a variety of writing assignments...By exposing students to a number of reflective, documentary, and analytical writing assignments, a better understanding of the justice process is achieved. (P. 19)

Sometimes the thesis is more difficult to ascertain. Do you have to hunt for the thesis of the article? Comment about the clarity of the author's thesis presentation, and state the author's thesis in your own paper. Before proceeding with the remaining elements of your paper, consider the importance of the topic. Has the author of the article written something that is important for us as criminal justice students or professionals to read?

METHODS

What methods did the author use to investigate the topic? In other words, how did the author go about supporting the thesis? In your critique, carefully answer the following two questions. First, were appropriate methods used? In other words, did the author's approach to supporting the thesis make sense? Second, did the author employ correctly the methods selected? Did you discover any errors in the way that he or she conducted her research?

EVIDENCE OF THESIS SUPPORT

In your critique, answer the following questions: What evidence did the author present in support of the thesis? What are the strengths of the evidence presented by the author? What are the weaknesses of the evidence presented? On balance, how well did the author support the thesis?

RECOMMENDATION

In this section, summarize your evaluation of the article. Tell your readers several things. Who will benefit from reading this article? What will the benefit be? How important and extensive is that benefit? Clearly state your evaluation of the article, in the form of a thesis for your own critique. Your thesis might be something like the following:

> Doyle and Meadows' article "A Writing-Intensive Approach to Criminal Justice Education: The California Lutheran University Model" is an excellent

presentation on both the need for criminal justice students to become better writers and how variety in writing assignments in the curriculum can enhance a "better understanding of the justice process." If they wish to ensure that students are able to critically evaluate and analyze important issues, those involved in criminal justice education would be well advised to consider adopting this model.

When writing this assignment, follow the directions for formats in Chapter 3. Ask your instructor for directions concerning the length of the paper, but in the absence of further directions, your paper should not exceed five pages (typed, double-spaced).

CHAPTER 10

Book Reviews

OBJECTIVES OF A BOOK REVIEW

Successful book reviewers answer two questions for their readers:

1. What is the book trying to do?
2. How well is it doing it?

People who read a book review want to know if a particular book is worth reading, for their own particular purposes, before buying or beginning to read it. These potential book readers want to know the book's subject and its strengths and weaknesses, and they want to gain this information as easily and quickly as possible. Your goal in writing a book review, therefore, is to help people decide efficiently whether or not to buy or read a book. Your immediate objectives may be to please your instructor and get a good grade, but these objectives are most likely to be met if you focus on a book review's audience: people who want help in selecting books to read. In the process of writing a review that reaches this primary goal you will also:

- Learn about the book you are reviewing.
- Learn about professional standards for book reviews in criminal justice.
- Learn the essential steps to reviewing books that apply in any academic discipline.

This final objective, learning to review a book properly, has more applications than you may imagine. First, it helps you to focus quickly on the essential elements of a book, to draw from a book its informational value for yourself and others. Some of the most successful professional and business people speed-read many books. They read these books less for enjoyment than to assimilate knowledge quickly. These readers then apply this knowledge to substantial advantage in their professions. It is normally not wise to speed-read a book you are reviewing because you are unlikely to gain from such a fast reading enough information to evaluate the book's qualities fairly. Writing book reviews, however, helps you to become proficient in quickly locating the book's most valuable information and paring away material that is of secondary importance. The ability to make such discriminations is of fundamental importance to academic and professional success.

In addition, writing book reviews for publication allows you to participate in the discussions of the broader intellectual and professional community of which you are a part. People in law, medicine, teaching, engineering, administration, and other fields are frequently asked to write reviews of books to help others in their professions assess the value of newly released publications.

SAMPLE BOOK REVIEWS

Before beginning your book review, read the following samples. Both were selected because they represent recent, typical, academic reviews of books of interest to criminal justice students and professionals. The first is University of Wisconsin–Milwaukee Professor Eleanor M. Miller's review published in volume 25 of *Contemporary Sociology* (1996), of Mark S. Fleisher's *Beggars and Thieves: Lives of Urban Street Criminals.* Miller's review has been selected because it is a recent, typical, academic book review useful to criminal justice scholars and practitioners. The second review of the same book was taken from volume 102:2 of the *American Journal of Sociology* (1996). In this journal Fleisher's book is reviewed by John M. Hagedorn, also of the University of Wisconsin–Milwaukee. Although both reviews do certain things well, they, like all reviews, have both strengths and weaknesses, which we discuss in the directions for writing book reviews in this chapter.

Fleisher, Mark S. 1995. Beggars and Thieves: Lives of Urban Street Criminals. Madison, WI: University of Wisconsin Press.

Mark Fleisher has a lot of experience studying and working with street criminals. He is an anthropologist by training, has spent many years doing prison-based research, and has been employed as a correctional programs specialist in the federal correctional system. He has strong and passionately felt opinions about what is wrong with the way the United States deals with street criminals. *Beggars and Thieves* is his soapbox. This is not to say that the book is sheer demagoguery or that the author's recommendations are not grounded in social science research or worthy of a forum. It is by way of trying to understand why the work has the peculiar character it has.

Fleisher claims that the research described in this book is ethnographic and, in fact, spends a great deal of time trying to convince the reader of the importance and usefulness of ethnography as a technique for understanding the behavior of street criminals, as well as for program evaluation and policy formation. However, although Fleisher employs some of the same field methods that ethnographers do (e.g., participant observation, life-history interviews), technically speaking, Beggars and Thieves is not an ethnography. It is both more and less than an ethnography: more because he draws on all sorts of sources and interview material from other settings (Seattle, Arizona, California, Oregon, Washington, D.C., and several other places in the state of Washington) and time periods, and less, because he fails to acknowledge the nature, requirements, or limits of this method.

It seems, in fact, that what he means by ethnography is the whole grab bag of qualitative methods available to those who do field research. The reader is not helped by statements such as these: "Criminological research and ethnography are dissimilar," or "Criminology and ethnography can complement each other" (p. 14). I think what he means to do is defend the nonquantitative nature of his data and the use of induction as an analytical strategy, but the fact that it is difficult to tell is disturbing.

Nor is Fleisher particularly sensitive to the array of ethical issues that plague ethnographers, such as informed consent. For example, some of his data were gathered while he was working for the U.S. Bureau of the Census as part of an attempt to understand the social and attitudinal aspects of the undercount, but in search of interviews and rapport with street criminals, he presented himself as a worker with this goal. When discussing the decision of whether or not to tape-record snippets of conversation, he says: "A large pocket concealed a microcassette tape recorder. When conversations were taped, I imagined myself in an informant's position: Would I allow a stranger to tape record the facts about yesterday's drug sales?" (p. 44). Finally, he assured informants "that law enforcement officials would not see [his] interview notes. I trusted them; they had to trust me" (pp. 35–36). Given all the ways that researchers can lose control of their fieldnotes, more cautious reassurances might have been in order.

The interview data themselves and the descriptions of the day-to-day interaction and behavior of Fleisher's informants are fascinating. It makes for gripping reading, not unlike the experience of reading Richard Price's

Clockers (New York: Avon, 1992): Fleisher's portraits are filled with detail; he paints his informants so well that one can easily picture them in one's mind and, having done so, try to anticipate their behavior. He captures their outlooks and motivations particularly well because of his interest in and attention to language. And yet, like a skillful novelist, he keeps the reader hanging so that s/he reads on to discover what's going to happen to Miss Ann, Wolf Man, Popcorn, Itch, T-Cool, Shy, CJ, and the others. At the same time, however, there is little attempt to analyze discrete sets of related data in order to build an argument. The data are presented in moving vignettes, grouped by street life-cycle stage, the policy recommendations comprise the last chapter of the book and are peppered throughout, and the theoretical basis for interpreting the data is introduced at the outset. The reader is left to impute causality via juxtaposition because there is no attempt to use the data to buttress, build, refute, or extend particular aspects of the theory as the book progresses. When it comes to the interplay of theory and method, Fleisher uses a very broad brush.

The book contains two sorts of theory. There is a theory of psycholinguistics outlined toward the beginning of the book which suggests that the author has paid particular attention to linguistic patterns and speech variations in analyzing his data. He says, for example: "Transcription of taped and natural conversations in the International Phonetic Alphabet was useful in capturing speech variations" (p. 44). However, there is no evidence in the book of linguistic analysis or analysis of speech variation. What there is is attention to word choice as an indicator of cognitive framing and worldview. Fleisher believes that "worldviews can be metaphorically divided into two complementary components: a 'sociocultural' grammar, a set of tacit rules that guide behaviors and interpretations of those behaviors; and a 'sociolinguistic' grammar, a set of tacit rules that generate utterances in social contexts" (p. 12).

This linguistic theorizing is loosely connected to the explanatory theory that undergirds the whole book. I will summarize it briefly. Children who are abused permanently acquire sociocultural and sociolinguistic grammars as part of their "enculturating environment." These grammars, in turn, lead these children to develop a particular cognitive frame and worldview, behaviors, and patterns of speech characterized by Fleisher as "defensive." Such a worldview is predicated on fear and manifest in six traits: a feeling of vulnerability, a willingness to use violence, an attraction to those with similar worldviews, a need to maintain social distance, a lack of trust, and an expectation that no one will provide aid. These traits "bind street hustlers together into a recognizable yet diffusely dispersed subgroup" (p. 104). Once abused children escape their home, this worldview and concomitant behaviors become the basis for the development of concrete survival skills on the streets. However, as youths age, this worldview retards social maturation and leaves them, as adults, in a prolonged state of adolescent dependency, without the requisite cognitive and social skills to live as law-abiding, independent Americans. As parents who cannot empathize with their children or realistically assess their needs or abilities, such adults will semantically miscue their children's behaviors and interpret them as signs of rejection. Rage and violent behavior will result, starting the cycle anew. Fleisher concludes that: "A defensive worldview isn't abnormal; it isn't a mental illness; it isn't psychopathy; and it can't easily be fixed or replaced with grammatical rules that lead to behavior and speech that are more acceptable to lawful society" (p. 107).

The problems with this theory are myriad, but returning to ethnographic method, the most damaging critique is that Fleisher is extrapolating a hypothetical life cycle from the memories of criminals who purportedly have defensive worldviews. And, yet, one of the reasons why these worldviews are so pernicious is that "rehabilitation efforts may be hampered if informants can't retrieve recollections of early life and feelings accompanying those thoughts, as psychotherapy requires" (p. 65).

Despite the fact that the field research used to write *Beggars and Thieves* falls short as the scholarly basis for the policy recommendations that are the clear raison d'être for the book, Fleisher's wealth of experience, including this fieldwork, combined with his good sense and wisdom make his treatment of an array of pressing policy issues related to street crime worthy of attention and debate—even though some may find them radical or naive, and they certainly are controversial. They include: removing children from abusive and neglectful homes and placing them until majority in long-term residential homes overseen by the federal government and funded via a reallocation from federal and state correctional budgets; establishing two community-based programs, one school-based whose purpose would be to identify, diagnose, and treat children who have been abused, and another to treat alcohol- and drug-addicted delinquents; building as many prisons as necessary to house violent adolescents and adults in separate facilities; turning all prisons into factories and insisting that all prisoners work as part of their rehabilitation; providing remedial education, vocation training, and substance-abuse treatment in prison with an eye to producing a worthy prison worker; paying inmate workers minimum-wage salaries, out of which they must pay for their board and keep and whatever other education or training they would like to pursue; releasing from secure facilities all nonviolent drug offenders and placing them in minimum-security community work camps.

There is no discussion of the fact that in a democracy there might be some problems in the area of due process and civil rights with some of these policies. They are a natural outgrowth of Fleisher's belief that rehabilitation of violent criminals has been a miserable and costly failure, that we have overly romanticized the family as the site of all prosocial impulses and attempted with limited success to make families that just don't work as nurturing havens for children become such, that we cannot afford to sustain the high level of incarceration we are currently committed to for nonviolent drug offenders, and that public opinion is probably more likely at this point in history than at any point in recent years to support such an agenda. There are many who would agree.

Below is John M. Hagedorn's somewhat different review of the same book. Compare and contrast the two reviews using the criteria we have suggested in this chapter.

Fleisher, Mark S. 1995. *Beggars and Thieves: Lives of Urban Street Criminals. Madison, WI: University of Wisconsin Press.*

With the right dominating today's politics, C. Wright Mill's admonition for social scientists to criticize "official definitions of reality" has renewed meaning. In that spirit, Herbert Gans has called for a "debunking ethnography" to dispel media stereotypes of poor people. But, given the power of the conservative revolution, are you surprised that some ethnographers are studying the poor in a manner that reinforces stereotypes? Consider Mark Fleisher's *Beggars and Thieves.*

First, Fleisher's book is devoid of structural context. Unlike Bourgeois's recent ethnography (*In Search of Respect: Selling Crack in El Barrio* [Cambridge University Press, 1995]), which is peppered with economic and social statistics about East Harlem, Fleisher says his book "isn't about" racism or poverty (p. 4).

Basically, the street criminals he studied "choose to be outlaws" (p. 16) and their lives are described with no other context than their common history of child abuse: "Their life trajectory was set in motion decades earlier in early childhood, and they can't stop it now" (p. 184). His respondents uniformly adopt a "defensive world-view" related to Hirschi and Gottfredson's low self-control.

Fleisher states that he is studying a "subpopulation" of urban criminals (p. 6), but he later implies he is generalizing to "ordinary criminals standing on street corners" (p. 259). This is especially problematic because of selectivity and lack of variation in his sample. Many refused his requests for interviews, and it was the police and prison officials, not street contracts, who helped him find his informants. He does not say whether he followed accepted practices in snowball sampling and looked for people who might, in some key respects, be "different." He also does not report how he analyzed his data, but I doubt he used analytic induction or other methods based on searching for negative cases. Are most street criminals with an abused family background similar to Fleisher's subjects? We cannot draw that conclusion from this study.

Other studies dispute many of Fleisher's findings. After an abused early childhood, Fleisher's subjects are rejected by their schoolmates and then form gangs. This may be plausible, but writers such as Thrasher (*The Gang* [University of Chicago Press, 1963]), Short and Strodtbeck (*Group Process and Gang Delinquency* [University of Chicago Press, 1965]), Klein (*The American Street Gang: Its Nature, Prevalence, and Control* [Oxford University Press, 1995]), and Moore (*Homeboys: Gangs, Drugs, and Prison in the Barrios of Los Angeles* [Temple University Press, 1978]) have found gang formation is less related to family factors than to ecological variables and group process. Most gang research also finds wider variation in the family background of gang members.

As Fleisher's abused subjects become adults, they stay uniformly deviant: "My informants never considered the option of getting a straight job...nor did they seriously consider asking someone to help them create a straight lifestyle" (p. 208). While there are undoubtedly some street criminals who disdain work, classic studies from Valentine (*Hustling and Other Hard Work* [Free Press, 1978]) to Bourgeois find most adult street criminals, even those from troubled families, go in and out of low-paying jobs and want a share of the American dream, not a deviant lifestyle.

Beggars and Thieves' view of prison may be too extreme even for some on the right. For Fleisher, who earlier had studied prisons while working as a guard, prisons are "sanctuaries," where street criminals want to be (p. 172) and are "comfortably imprisoned" (p. 179). The harried and hazardous lives of some might cause prison at times to be seen as a relief. However, the consensus from both criminals and criminologists is that U.S. prisons are brutal and overcrowded.

Finally, Fleisher never discusses why he thinks his respondents were truthful. Could his informants have told him what he wanted to hear to get the "street money" he liberally handed out? "Listen darling, you telling him bullshit?" Miss Ann asks T-Cool (p. 59). "For all they knew, I was a new associate warden or the FBI," Fleisher says (p. 59), but does not explore. Of his informants, I was most sympathetic to T-Cool, who once complained (p. 73): "I told you everything you wanted to know. You write a book about me, you get rich, and what the fuck do I get?" Fleisher said he was "annoyed" and "bored" by such questions, which I think social scientists ought to take very seriously.

This is a book avowedly aimed at influencing social policy and selectively supports the right-wing political agenda. Fleisher recommends stepped up removal of poor children from their families and creation of orphanages, called "residential homes." While he opposes incarcerating drug offenders and nonviolent criminals, he simultaneously opposes closing prisons: "Prisons are good business; they employ thousands of lawful citizens and keep violent criminals off the street" (p. 263). Neanderthal politicians can easily ignore the few spots where Fleisher says that his subjects are a small fraction of street criminals and use the book as "social science" to support their demeaning caricatures of the poor. It is not exactly what Gans meant, but I think social scientists need to be "debunking ethnographies" like *Beggars and Thieves*.

ELEMENTS OF A BOOK REVIEW

Book reviews in criminal justice contain the essential elements of all book reviews. Since social science is nonfiction, book reviews within the disciplines focus less upon writing style and more upon content and method than reviews of works of fiction. Your book review should generally contain four basic elements, although not always in this order:

1. Enticement
2. Examination
3. Elucidation
4. Evaluation

Enticement

The first sentence should entice people to read your review. Criminal justice studies do not have to be dull. Start your review with a sentence that both (1) sums up the objective of the book, and (2) catches the reader's eye. Miller's opening paragraph, for example, makes it very difficult for the reader to resist reading further: "He [Mark Fleisher] has strong and passionately felt opinions about what is wrong with the way the United States deals with street criminals." This sort of emphatic statement draws the attention of the reader. Be sure, however, that your opening remarks, like Miller's, offer an accurate description of the book as well as an enticement to the reader.

Examination

Your book review should encourage the reader to join you in examining the book. One of the greatest strengths of Miller's review is that her first paragraph immediately reinforces her enticing early sentence with a brief summary of the content and character of Fleisher's book

When you review a book, write about what is actually in the book, not what you think is probably there or what ought to be there. Do not tell how you would have written the book, but tell instead how the author wrote it. Describe the book in clear, objective terms. Tell enough about the content to identify for the reader the major points that the book's author is trying to make. A strength of Miller's review is her apparent objectivity and her constructively critical remarks. Compare Hagedorn's article to Miller's with respect to objectivity. Do you find one review to be more objective?

Elucidation

Elucidation means to give a clarifying explanation. Clarify for the reader the book's value and contribution by defining (1) what the author is attempting to do, and (2) how his work fits within current similar efforts in the discipline or scholarly inquiry in general.

Notice how Miller describes what Fleisher's book is attempting to do. Miller follows her definition of Fleisher's scope and method by placing his work within the context of basic concepts of ethnographic work. Although she questions aspects of his methodology and finds some insensitively to ethical concerns, she always points to the outstanding and "fascinating" aspects of his work.

The elucidation portion of a book review often provides additional information about the author. Miller has not included information about Fleisher in her review, but it would be helpful to know, for example, if the author has written other books or articles on the same subject, developed a reputation for exceptional expertise in a certain subject, or is known to have a particular ideological bias. How would your understanding of a book be changed, for example, if you knew that its author is a leader in the radical movement? Always include in your book review information about the author that helps the reader understand how the book fits within the broader picture of social science.

Evaluation

Once your readers understand what a book is attempting to do, they will want to know the extent to which the book has succeeded. To evaluate a book effectively, you should establish evaluation criteria and then compare the book's content to those criteria. You do not need to define your criteria in your review specifically, but they should be evident to the reader. The criteria will vary according to the book you are reviewing, and you may discuss them in any order that is helpful to the reader. Note how carefully Miller has constructed her review around a set of criteria:

- How important is the subject matter to the study of culture and society?
- How complete and thorough is the author's coverage of the subject?
- How carefully is the author's analysis constructed?
- What are the strengths and limitations of the author's methodology?
- What is the quality of the writing in the book? Is it clear, precise, and interesting?
- How does this book compare with other books on the same subject?
- What contribution does this book make to criminal justice, and more specifically, to understanding street gangs?
- Who will enjoy and benefit from this book?

When giving your evaluation according to such criteria, be specific. When you write, "This is a good book; I liked it very much," you have told the reader nothing of interest or value. Notice, however, the specific character of Miller's evaluatory comments on Fleisher's book: "Fleisher's wealth of experience, including this fieldwork, combined with his good sense and wisdom make his treatment of an array of pressing policy issues related to street crime worthy of attention and debate."

Hagedorn's review as a whole and his conclusion in particular are sharply critical of *Beggars and Thieves*. Hagedorn lists several specific deficiencies of Fleisher's book. *Beggars and Thieves*, Hagedorn claims, is "devoid of structural context," and deficient in its sampling methodology. Furthermore, Fleisher's conclusions are refuted by a number of notable studies. Overall, Fleisher's work is flawed, according to Hagedorn, by being extremely ideological: it "selectively supports the right-wing political agenda." For each of these criticisms Hagedorn provides specific examples. Your review should follow Hagedorn's example in this respect.

TYPES OF BOOK REVIEWS: REFLECTIVE AND ANALYTICAL

Two types of book reviews are normally assigned by instructors in the humanities and social sciences: the reflective and the analytical. Ask your instructor which type of book review she or he wants you to write. The purpose of a *reflective* book review is for the student reviewer to exercise creative analytical judgment without being influenced by the reviews of others. Reflective book reviews contain all the elements covered in this chapter—enticement, examination, elucidation and evaluation—but they do not include the views of others who have also read the book.

Analytical book reviews contain all the information provided by reflective book reviews but add an analysis of the comments of other reviewers. The purpose is to review not only the book itself, but also its reception in the professional community. To write an analytical book review, insert a review analysis section immediately after your summary of the book. To prepare this review analysis section, use the *Book Review Digest* and *Book Review Index* in the library to locate other reviews of the book that have been published in journals and other periodicals. As you read these reviews:

1. List the criticisms (strengths and weaknesses) of the book that are made in these journals.
2. Develop a concise summary of these criticisms, indicate the overall positive or negative tone of the reviews, and discuss some of the most frequent comments.
3. Evaluate the criticisms of the book found in these reviews. Are they basically accurate in their assessment of the book?
4. Write a review analysis of two pages or less that states and evaluates steps 2 and 3 above, and place it in your book review immediately after your summary of the book.

FORMAT AND LENGTH OF A BOOK REVIEW

The directions for writing papers provided in Parts One and Two apply to book reviews as well. Unless your instructor gives you other specifications, a reflective book review should be three to five pages in length, and an analytical book review should be from five to seven pages. In either case, a brief, specific, concise book review is almost always preferred over one of greater length.

CHAPTER 11

Criminal Justice Agency Case Studies

DEFINITION AND PURPOSE OF A CASE STUDY

A case study is an in-depth investigation of a social unit such as a police department, a group of prisoners, or a juvenile detention agency, undertaken to identify the factors that influence the manner in which the unit functions. Some examples of case studies are:

- An evaluation of the comparative effectiveness of behavior modification methods in maximum-security facilities
- A study of management practices at Capricola State Penitentiary
- A study of the personality types of juvenile justice officers

Case studies have long been used in law schools, where students learn how the law develops by reading actual court case decisions. Business schools began to develop social service agency case studies to help students understand actual management situations. Courses in social organization, public administration, and social institutions adopt the case study method as a primary teaching tool less often than business or law schools, but case studies have become a common feature of many courses in these areas.

Psychologists have used the case histories of mental patients for many years to support or negate a particular theory. Criminologists and sociologists use the case study approach to describe and draw conclusions about a wide variety of subjects, such as labor unions, police departments, medical schools, gangs, public and private bureaucracies, religious groups, cities, and social class (Philliber et al. 1980:64). The success of this type of research depends heavily on the openmindedness, sensitivity, insights, and integrative abilities of the investigator.

Case studies fulfill many educational objectives in the social sciences. As a student in a criminal justice course, you may write a case study to improve your ability to:

- Analyze information carefully and objectively.
- Solve problems effectively.
- Present your ideas in clear written form, directed to a specific audience.

In addition, writing a case study allows you to discover some of the problems you will face if you become involved in an actual social situation that parallels your case study. For example, writing a case study like the forthcoming example, which focuses on a government organization, can help you to understand:

- Some of the potentials and problems of society in general
- The operation of a particular cultural, ethnic, political, economic, or religious group
- The development of a particular problem, such as crime, alcoholism, or violence within a group
- The interrelationships, within a particular setting, of people, structures, rules, politics, relationship styles, and many other factors

USING CASE STUDIES IN RESEARCH

Isaac and Michael (1981:48) suggest that case studies offer several advantages to the investigator. For one thing, they provide useful background information for researchers planning a major investigation in the social sciences. Case studies often suggest fruitful hypotheses for further study, and they provide specific examples by which to test general theories. Philliber et al. (1980:64) believe that through the intensive investigation of only one case the researcher can gain more depth and detail than might be possible by examining many cases briefly. Also, the depth of focus in the study of a single case allows investigators to recognize certain aspects of the object being studied that would otherwise go unobserved. For example, Becker et al. (1961) noticed that medical students tend to develop a "slang" that Becker and his associates refer to as "native language." Only after observing the behavior of the students for several weeks were the researchers able to determine that the slang word *crocks* referred to those patients who were of no help to the students professionally because they did not have an observable disease. The medical students felt that the crocks were robbing them of their important time.

Bouma and Atkinson (1995:110–114) call attention to the exploratory nature of some case studies. Researchers, for example, may be interested in what is happening within a juvenile detention center. Before beginning the project, they may not know enough about what they will find in order to formulate testable hypotheses. The researchers' purpose in doing a case study may be to gather as much information as possible in order to help in the formulation of relevant hypotheses. Or the researchers may intend simply to observe and describe all that is happening within the case being studied. Or, as is the case in our juvenile detention study described later in this chapter, the intention may be to observe, describe, and measure certain behaviors within the case being studied in order to test predetermined hypotheses statistically.

LIMITATIONS OF THE CASE STUDY METHOD

Before writing a case study you should be aware of the limitations of the methods you will be using, to avoid drawing conclusions that are not justified by the knowledge you acquire. First, case studies are relatively subjective exercises. When you write a case study, you select the facts and arrange them into patterns from which you may draw conclusions. The quality of the case study will depend largely on the quality of the facts you select and the way in which you interpret those facts.

A second potential liability to the case study method is that every case study, no matter how well written, is in some sense an oversimplification of the events that are described and the environment within which those events take place. To simplify an event or series of events makes it easier to understand but at the same time distorts its effect and importance. It can always be argued that the results of any case study are peculiar to that one case and, therefore, offer little as a rationale for a general explanation or predic-tion (Philliber et al. 1980:65). A third caution about case studies pertains strictly to their use as a learning tool in the classroom: Remember that any interpretations you come up with for a case study in your class, no matter how astute or sincere, are essentially parts of an academic exercise and therefore may not be applicable in an actual situation.

TYPES OF CASE STUDIES WRITTEN IN CRIMINAL JUSTICE

Criminal justice cases usually take one of two basic forms. The first might be called a *didactic case study*, because it is written for use in a classroom. It describes a situation or a problem in a certain setting but performs no analysis and draws no conclusions. Instead, a didactic case study normally lists questions for the students to consider and then answer, either individually or in class discussion. This sort of case study allows the teacher to evaluate student analysis skills, and, if the case is discussed in class, to give students an opportunity to compare ideas with other students.

The second form, an *analytical case study*, provides not only a description but an analysis of the case as well. This is the form of case study most often assigned in a criminal justice class, and it is the form described in detail in this chapter.

Criminal justice professionals conduct case studies for a variety of specific pur-poses. An *ethnographic case study*, for example, is an in-depth examination of a group of people or an organization over time. Its major purpose is to lead the researchers to a better understanding of human behavior through observations of the interweaving of people, events, conditions, and means in natural settings or subcultures.

Ethnographic case studies examine behavior in a community or, in the case of some technologically primitive societies, an entire society. The term *ethnography* means "a portrait of a people," and the ethnographic approach was historically an anthropolog-ical tool for describing societies whose cultural evolution was very primitive when compared to the "civilized" world (Hunter and Whitten 1976:147). Anthropologists would sometimes live within the society under scrutiny for several months or even years, interviewing and observing the people being studied. The in-the-field nature of ethnographies has caused them to be referred to occasionally as field studies.

HOW TO CONDUCT A CRIMINAL JUSTICE AGENCY CASE STUDY

Unlike an ethnographic study, which looks at a community or a society as a whole, a *social service agency case study* focuses on a formal organization that provides a specific service or set of services either to a section of a society or society as a whole. A social service agency case study usually describes and explains some aspect of a social service agency's operation. Case studies do not attempt to explain everything there is to know about the organization. To conduct a social service agency case study, you undertake the following tasks:

1. Select a particular social service agency to study.
2. Formulate a general goal, for example, to better understand how the agency works.
3. Describe in general terms the agency and how it operates.
4. Describe the structure, practices, and procedures of the agency.
5. Select a specific objective, for example, to discover the responsiveness to the agency's programs of the people the agency serves.
6. Describe your methodology, that is, the procedures you will use to conduct your investigation.
7. Describe the results of your study, the observations you have made.
8. Draw conclusions about your findings.

The specific goal of your case study is to explain the effectiveness or ineffectiveness of some aspect of the agency's operation. This focused inquiry will, in turn, contribute to a general understanding of how the agency selected works. You may select any social service agency, such as the United Way, the Social Security Administration, the American Red Cross, or your state's department of human services. Its personnel, however, should be directly accessible to you for interviews.

Once you have chosen a social service agency to examine, you need to focus on a specific topic related to the agency—some characteristic procedure or situation—and write a description of how that topic has developed within the agency. For example, if your agency focus is a county health department and your topic focus is recruitment problems, you might choose to describe how the recruitment problems evolved within the overall operations of the department.

Most social service agency case studies assigned in criminal justice classes are not fictional. They are based on your investigation of an actual current or recent situation in a public or private agency.

Selecting a Topic

In seeking a topic, you are looking for a situation that is likely to provide some interesting insights about how social service agencies affect people's lives. There are two ways to begin your search. The first is to contact an agency involved with a matter that interests you and then inquire about recent events. If, for example, you are interested in the court system, you would contact a local court administrator's office. Tell the secretary who answers the phone that you are a student who wants to write a college term paper about the agency and ask to talk to someone who can explain the organization's current programs. Ask for an appointment for an interview with the person to whom you are referred by the secretary. When you arrive for the interview, tell the agency official to whom you are speaking that you are interested in doing a case study on some aspect of the agency's operations and that your purpose is to understand better how government agencies operate. Then ask a series of questions aimed at helping you find a topic to pursue. These questions might include:

- "What recent successes has your agency had?"
- "What is the greatest challenge facing your agency at the moment?"
- "What are some of the agency's goals for this year?"
- "What are some of the obstacles to meeting these goals?"

You should follow up these questions with others until you identify a situation in the agency appropriate for your study. There will probably be many. Consider the following examples: The agency faces budget cuts, and the director may have to decide among competing political pressures which services she must reduce.

- The agency faces a reorganization.
- The agency receives criticism from the people it serves.
- The agency has initiated a controversial policy.

Another way to select a topic is to find an article of interest in your local newspaper. The successes, failures, challenges, and mistakes of government and private agencies are always in the news. The benefit of finding a topic in the newspaper is that when you contact the agency involved, you will already have a subject to discuss. The disadvantage is that on some publicized topics, agency officials may be reluctant to provide detailed information.

The Importance of Interviews

The goal of your first interview is to obtain enough information to request a series of other interviews. The answers to questions you pose in these interviews will allow you to understand the course of events and the agency interactions that have resulted in the situation you are studying. Remember that you are writing a story, but the story you are writing is accurate and factual. Do not accept the first version of a course of events that you hear. Ask several qualified people the same basic questions.

Take notes constantly. Do not use a tape recorder, because tape recorders tend to inhibit people from giving you as much information as they would without one present. At every interview ask about documents relevant to the case. These documents may include committee reports, meeting minutes, letters, or organizational rules and procedures. Sort out fact from appearance. When the facts are straight you will be ready to organize your thoughts first into an outline and then into a first draft of your paper.

Elements of the Case Study Paper

OVERVIEW OF THE CONTENTS

Your case study will consist of four basic parts:

1. Title page
2. Executive summary
3. Text
4. Reference page

The text, executive summary, and reference page should all conform to the directions in the preceding chapters of this manual.

THE TEXT

The text of a social service agency case study includes the following elements:

- The facts of the case
- The environment, context, and participants of the case
- Topic analysis
- Conclusions

Although the content of the text should adhere to this general order, elements will overlap. Ask your instructor for the assigned length of the paper. In general, case studies should be brief and concise. They may include material from numerous interviews and documents—but only material essential to understanding the case. A case study can be any length, but a paper of about 15 pages, double-spaced, is usually adequate to describe and analyze a case situation accurately.

THE FACTS   Write the facts of the case in story-narrative form. Although accuracy is the most important quality that a case study should have, writing style will determine in large part the benefit the reader receives from reading it. The facts of the case that you will reveal in your story include a description of the events, the major actors and their relationships with one another, and the external and internal agency environments and contexts within which the events of the situation you are describing developed.

THE ENVIRONMENT AND CONTEXT   In your account, consider the following aspects of a situation and relate to your readers those items that are relevant to the case at hand:

- The law under which the agency operates
- Political and economic factors of the agency's internal environment: power and influence, budget constraints, agency structure, rules, role, and mission
- Factors of the agency's internal social service agency environment: social service agency style, tone, preferences, and procedures

Without altering the essential facts of the course of events, alter or delete the names of the actors and the agencies for which they work. Accuracy of facts in a case study is essential for a correct interpretation, but the actual identities of the people involved is irrelevant, and they may want their property protected. Any change of facts for this purpose should be done in a manner that does not alter the content of the story of the case at hand.

A well-written criminal justice agency case study will reveal much about how public and private agencies conduct business in the United States and even more about the agency selected for study. Public and private administrators face many of the same problems: They must recruit personnel, establish goals and objectives, account for expenditures, and abide by hundreds of rules and regulations. In several important respects, however, public agencies are very different from private businesses. A public administrator will often serve several bosses (governor, legislators) and have several competing clienteles (interest groups, the general public). Public officials are more susceptible than private business to changes in political administrations. They also face more legal constraints and are held accountable to higher ethical standards. In addition, public administrators are more likely to be held under the light of public surveillance; and finally, they are held accountable to a different "bottom line."

The goal of most businesses is, first and foremost, to earn profits for their owners. The amount of these profits is normally easy to quantify. The success of public agencies, however, can be hard to measure. Criteria used to evaluate public programs, such as effectiveness and efficiency, often contradict one another. For example, the nation's space program has accomplished some remarkable achievements, but not many people commend the program's economic efficiency.

TOPIC ANALYSIS   Your analysis should explore and explain the events in your selected situation, concentrating on the social service agency strategies and practices used by the primary actors. Your analysis should answer questions such as the following:

- How did the situation or problem at the heart of the case arise?
- What important external and internal factors directed what transpired?
- What were the major sources of power and influence in the situation, and how were they used?
- What social service agency styles and practices were employed, and were they effective and appropriate within the situation described?
- How did relationships within the organization affect the conduct of other public or private programs?

CONCLUSIONS

To the fullest extent possible, your conclusions should use what you have learned about the nature of administrative practices to explain causes and effects, summarize events and their results, and interpret the actions of administrators. One major purpose of a social service agency case study is to give its readers an opportunity to benefit from the successes and mistakes of others. In your conclusion, tell the reader what you have learned from this situation, what you would imitate in your own social service agency practice, and what you would do differently if you found yourself in a similar situation.

A SAMPLE CASE STUDY

Notice how the following sample case study, which addresses the topic of how incidents of negative behavior affect program implementation in a juvenile detention center, accomplishes the following goals:

- The problem being investigated is introduced along with a rationale for doing the case study.
- The professional literature is reviewed to see what is already known about the issue or problem.
- The design of the study is explained: data collection and analysis procedures.
- The results and conclusions are given: limitations of the study; interpretation of the results; discussion of how this interpretation affects the detention center; suggestions or recommendations for future studies.

An Analysis of Negative Behavior Incidents and Their Impact on Program

Implementation at the Oklahoma County Juvenile Detention Center.

Johnson, William A. and Richard P. Rettig. 1990.

Journal for Juvenile Justice and Detention Services. 5(2):13–20.

INTRODUCTION

Over the past twenty years there has been a major effort within the juvenile justice system to treat delinquent offenders within confined settings from the fundamental assumptions of the rehabilitation model. Here the major assumption about juvenile offenders is that they are experiencing one or more acute problems, i.e., emotional distress, conflicts with other family members, difficulties in school, underdeveloped social skills, low ability to cope with failure or stress, or lack of job skills. Furthermore, it is also assumed that any assistance in meeting these needs, whether the juvenile offender is detained, confined or in the community, might prevent him or her from committing more delinquency in the future (Glaser 1969). Gendreau and Ross (1987:395) feel that offender rehabilitation has had many successes in the past and will continue to be successful in the future. However, there have been a number of significant attacks on this perspective (Lipton et al. 1975; Martinson 1974:181; Rubin 1979:280).

From a different perspective, Schwartz (1988) argues that the "get tough" policy of the Reagan years has infiltrated the juvenile court principally through the judges who are "either incompetent or ill-suited for the job," and tend to disregard or violate the rights of children in making detention decisions, as well as in all other segments of the juvenile court process.

The youth that come before the Oklahoma County Juvenile Court and are considered for preventive detention are either adjudicated delinquent or are alleged to have committed an offense, which would be a felony, were they an adult. Additionally, they usually fall into two broad categories: (1) those who are no longer subject to the guidance or effective control of their parents or guardians, and (2) those who have no custodians at all. These conditions have contributed to their delinquency to the extent that the court often must exercise a substitute form of protective control. In some sense these youth are victims. But it is also clear that sometimes they are the perpetrators of homicides, robberies, burglaries, assaults and rapes that seriously threaten our communities.

The argument here is that there is in fact a legitimate basis for treating juveniles differently from adults with respect to openness of the courts, privacy of records, length of incarceration, right to treatment and presumption of release. Therefore, it should be clearly recognized that there are valid reasons for detaining them when detention is in the best interest of society or the particular juvenile involved.

If the detention authorities are to provide a socially and psychologically healthy climate, and discharge their responsibilities to the youth and the community, then several opportunities for furthering the youth's growth and development must be made available. The nature and quality of the detention experience rather than its limited or extended duration must be the prime consideration.

Rettig (1980) maintains that when the detention community is fulfilling its philosophy and stated purposes in helping adolescents, the following contributions are possible:

- A system of controls or limits to protect both the child and the community while ensuring the child's legal rights.

- A life experience, which enables the child to be studied in his physical, social, emotional, and spiritual dimensions.

- Resources such as program, personnel, and facilities especially equipped and oriented to meet both the normal and special physical, social and emotional needs during a time of crisis in the child's life.

- A sociological climate conducive to working on the problems of the detained child through understanding, acceptance, consistency, limits, structure, and individual and group counseling which together provide emotional security and first aid enabling the emotional security and first aid enabling the child to have constructive experiences contributing to personality growth.

- A sound and integrated detention program outlining and specifying the limited treatment goals for each detainee. (P. 453)

Among juvenile justice practitioners, detention refers to pretrial and predispositional confinement (Rubin 1979:86). Norman (1960) states that "the detention of children awaiting juvenile court disposition has been a problem ever since juvenile courts were established" (p. 1). The U.S. Department of Justice defines the detention center as "a short-term facility that provides custody in a physically restricting environment pending adjudication or, following adjudication disposition, placement, or transfer" (Office of Justice Programs 1989:4).

The development of residential short-term programs for juvenile offenders is among the most challenging problems confronting juvenile justice administrators today. Detention programs around the country range from very inadequate custodial arrangements, like "boob-tube therapy," to very complex and sophisticated intervention strategies, such as behavioral management (Whitehead and Lab 1990:244-256).

During the 70's and 80's the courts repeatedly affirmed the rights of juveniles to services at the pretrial level. All juveniles in custody must now have clear access to educational, recreational, and other therapeutic services while in detention care. Both case law and national standards have supported this, and any program which can be construed as punitive in and of itself is no longer acceptable in any juvenile facility.

Presently, the juvenile justice system is involved in an era of accelerated change in response to rapidly advancing juvenile case law, federal and local legislation, improved standards of practice, more sophisticated training, increasing experience in the field, and modifications in the juvenile population itself. For example, the preventive detention of juvenile offenders awaiting court disposition is now reserved for more serious offenders (Bynum and Thompson 1989:413), while truants, runaways, and out-of-parental-control youth—status offenders—are often diverted away from detention. Statistics show that youth referred for violent offenses are twice as likely to be detained as youth charged with non-violent offenses (Juvenile Justice Bulletin 1989:1).

Therefore, the population at detention facilities has come to assume a more serious character than in the past. Young felons and serious misdemeanants, overrepresented by blacks and Hispanics, now comprise a much larger percentage of the detention population (Office of Justice Programs, 1989:1). Distribution of detainees by race is a critical variable. While white youths make up the vast majority of all arrestees (74.9%) and all Part 1 property offenses (72.1%), personal offenses, i.e., murder, rape, robbery and aggravated assault, are committed more by black juveniles (52%) than any other racial group. This overrepresentation of blacks in violent offenses is dramatic, in that blacks comprise only 15% of the youthful U.S. population (Uniform Crime Reports 1987:183).

Despite an ongoing decline in detention rates, the average length of stay is increasing; many juveniles are remaining in detention longer, and the same young people are being admitted more often than in the past

(Juvenile Justice Bulletin 1989). Overcrowding, which places a strain on all resident, staff, and facility resources, has in many jurisdictions become critical.

These problems continue to be manifested in the detention environment, leading some youth to display disruptive and sometimes violent behavior consistently. This not only affects the ongoing program but also results in personal injury and the destruction of property. Staff members often spend an inordinate amount of time and resources contending with young people who are in detention because some of them don't understand that their abusive actions have consequences. If this highly volatile situation could to some extent be remediated, detention programming would be positively affected (Askeland 1989).

Therefore, when residents act out violently they must be restricted or confined to their rooms until the situation can be resolved. Room restriction is used as a cooling-off time for minor infractions for a time not to exceed one hour. Room confinement is used as a last resort for major infractions "after all other techniques and resources have failed and only when [there is] a danger to self, others, property or to prevent escape...or the inciting of others" (OCJJDC 1989).

One way that a juvenile detention program can be characterized as successful or unsuccessful is by monitoring the process of discipline applied when youth seriously misbehave—room restriction and/or confinement. While some degree of insubordination and conflict is normative in this environment, the focus of this paper reflects our attempt to study what occurs when youth commit serious behavioral infractions and must be disciplined by the use of room confinement.

DESIGN

This study was designed to measure negative behavior incidents that occur within a detention facility for juveniles awaiting disposition and/or placement. Data were collected from the daily incident reports, room confinement records, daily log and resident files over a seven-month period beginning June 1, 1988, and ending December 31, 1988. The following variables were operationalized (turned into numbers): race, gender, age, type of infraction, chargeable offense, time of day infraction occurred, location of incident, disciplinary hearing, injury, disciplinary action taken, length of assigned confinement, actual time in confinement, precautionary warning code (suicidal, violent, etc.), behavioral level, prescore (daily behavioral evaluation before confinement for infraction), postscore (daily behavioral evaluation after confinement for infraction), and number of times held at this detention facility.

The average length of stay at this detention center is eight days. Some juveniles are there for as long as six months, others for a few hours. During the seven months in which the data were collected, 103 residents committed 236 behavioral infractions that were "written up." While there were numerous minor incidents that resulted in a brief room restriction (less than one hour), almost all (191) of the 236 infractions were considered serious enough to receive a one-hour or greater confinement penalty. Those infractions that were "written up" during this seven-month period comprise the data being analyzed in this study.

RESULTS AND CONCLUSIONS

Any conclusions that we draw will be limited by several problems encountered while collecting the data. The Oklahoma County Juvenile

Detention Center is a relatively new facility; the program has only been on line for about three years. Problems, such as the ones listed below, are gradually being worked out. Many have been solved since the data for this study were collected. With the recent addition of a state-of-the-art computer system, future data collection should encounter few, if any, of these problems: (1) some days no incidents were reported, but records showed that several incidents occurred; (2) several incident reports were not documented in the daily restriction log; the incident was written up but there was no record of any time served; (3) dates on the incident reports often did not correspond with the actual date in the restriction log. Sometimes this was because the room confinement occurred the day after the incident, but there was no record keeping that allowed the researcher to ascertain if this was the case; (4) times and dates were sometimes not entered, especially for release from confinement, making it impossible to determine the actual length of time in detention; (5) on several occasions there was more than one incident committed by the same person during a given day, but only one was written up. Since the written up incidents were not coded as such, it was difficult, if not impossible, to compare sentence with actual length of time in confinement; (6) the pre/post comparison was lost in cases where individuals were released from the facility before obtaining a postscore; and finally, (7) the limited access to important information (gender, race, age, length of employment) about those who "write up" residents and impose sanctions restricted our ability to analyze the results fully. If race is a meaningful variable in determining who is most likely to be written up and confined for a particular incident, what role does the racial composition of the staff play in influencing this outcome? Gender? Length of employment?

With these limitations in mind, the following conclusions utilize those variables and variable relationships that best explain negative behavior incidents at this particular detention facility.

Prescore and Postscore

While there are many significant findings in this study, perhaps the most meaningful one tends to confirm the room confinement process itself as workable. Administrators and staff sometimes question the functional viability of this type of behavior modification because of the high standards of fairness and legality they have imposed on themselves by requesting accreditation by the American Correctional Association.

Detention officers score the behavior of each resident at the close of the morning and evening shifts. Training is provided in this behavior rating process and unit supervisors regularly check for reliability and validity. Scores are assigned on a scale of 10 (negative) to 100 (positive). The average prescore (assigned the day prior to incidents for which room confinement was given) was 50.98. The average postscore (assigned the day after room confinement was served) was 73.60. This finding was extremely significant. Under very controlled conditions room confinement is used as negative reinforcement to increase the likelihood of reasonably conforming behavior and the extinction of violent, abusive behavior. In learning theory terms, negative reinforcement involves the application of an aversive stimulus (temporary withdrawal of program privileges and room confinement) contingent upon the occurrence of a desired behavior (the cessation of the problem behavior). The aversive stimulus (room confinement) is terminated if the desirable behavior (obedience to the rules) occurs, thereby increasing the likelihood of this desired behavior continuing. Our data clearly show that the program is at least achieving success in regulating the behavior of certain residents. Due to the limitations of our study we cannot determine to what extent, if any, the program is successful in permanently altering attitudes and behavior patterns.

Dominant Offenders

Another compelling finding would seem to be important for program development. Seventeen percent (17%) of all incidents during this seven-month period were instigated by three male residents. Six male residents instigated twenty-seven percent (27%) of all incidents. To be clear, while 103 residents committed 236 infractions serious enough to earn them room restriction or confinement, only six residents were responsible for 64 infractions. It is difficult to determine how many other incidents were stimulated because of the chronic negative influence of these few offenders.

One implication from this finding is that negative incidents might be reduced by as much as 25 to 50 percent over time by the differential treatment of chronic program disrupters. Perhaps specified juveniles could be "flagged" for special treatment. For example, upon the commission of the second violent or serious offense while in detention, the juvenile could be selected into a special program planned and staffed to address obvious behavioral problems, one that clearly segregates him from others. A special program of this type would be enriched by a much higher staff-to-resident ratio so that staff, to meet the intense needs of residents, could effect more moment-by-moment attention, communication, and feedback. Caution must be used to ensure that in no way would this program be considered or interpreted as punitive. Since the inception of this study, individualized treatments have been implemented for several dominant offenders. While no follow-up study has been done to confirm this, staff members feel that there has been some significant success in the overall reduction of negative behavior.

We take our cue from the adult criminal justice literature on selective incapacitation (Greenwood 1982), which seeks to identify those offenders who are most likely to commit future crimes. Our research showing that a disproportionate amount of serious incidents are committed by a minority of offenders supports the idea that selectively treating those few would result in less program disruption. Not only could a special program be developed to meet the needs of chronic disrupters, but the existing program, using room confinement as necessary, should run more efficiently.

Race

A number of interesting findings emerge when the racial composition of detention (FY 1988) is compared with the number of infractions committed by each group. Black youth comprised 47.3 percent of the population while whites comprised 41.9 percent. But blacks were charged with 58.5 percent of the infractions, while white youth committed 34.3 percent. The discrepancy between their respective numbers in the population and their reported infractions is significant ($p<.01$). This may reflect the extent to which violence is more normative in the black youth subculture than among the white youth. Some might contend that these statistics reflect less toleration by staff when confronted by black youth acting out in the program, but this position would seem to be contradicted by observation and by the fact that many of the detention officers are black.

Recidivism was significantly (p=.0008) related to race, with American Indians, others, and blacks detained at this facility more often than whites. Recent examination of detention practices in the United States noted that black and Hispanic youth constitute well over 50 percent of the youth being confined in detention, and that this proportion has been increasing through the 70's and 80's (Schwartz et al. 1987:219–235). In Oklahoma urban areas, such as metropolitan Oklahoma City, the percentage of blacks detained (47.3) is much higher when compared to whites (41.9). Askeland (1989) reports that juveniles detained from rural Oklahoma counties are predominantly white, while juveniles detained from metro Oklahoma City are predominantly black. Other minorities make up about 11 percent of the population at the Oklahoma County Juvenile Detention facility. It is possible that if we controlled for poverty, a factor differentially permeating the black and Hispanic cultures when compared with white culture, race might diminish as a meaningful variable. Hopefully, any follow-up studies might be able to examine poverty as a possible contributing factor.

Behavioral level and race were significantly (p=.0283) related, with blacks having a lower behavioral level than whites prior to the infraction. The differential acting out activity we have noted among the black and white cohorts in detention appears to correlate quite well with the differential arrest rates of juveniles by racial groups. As indicated by 1986 data (Uniform Crime Reports 1987:183), the probability of young blacks being arrested for crimes of violence is higher than for young whites.

It is not likely that any inherent connection between racial background and delinquent behavior exists. The high incidence of antisocial behavior may be related more to the poor socioeconomic circumstances of inner-city minority groups than to the biology of race (Bynum and Thompson 1989:111).

If blacks are differentially arrested and differentially detained, perhaps they are differentially disciplined while in detention. This disturbing question is raised by a recent study on factors affecting the detention decision. Using a sample of 55,000 cases from one state, Frazier and Bishop (1985) found that neither relevant legal variables (offense severity and prior record) nor sociodemographic characteristics had much impact on detention decisions. One possible conclusion of this line of research is that the entire detention decision "process is idiosyncratic, causing some juveniles to suffer significant deprivations of liberty based on considerations that are irrelevant to the approved purposes of detention" (p. 1151).

The question at least needs to be asked, if data exists to seriously question decisions to arrest and detain by race, is it possible that decisions to discipline within detention are also affected by the racial variable? A follow-up study might address this issue, among others. We have no way of analyzing staff activity in these incidents. Perhaps the age, sex, and race of staff influence the various transactions with residents leading up to decisions to institute sanctions such as room confinement.

Sex

Males comprised 87 percent of the detention population, while females comprised 13 percent (FY 1988). However, males were responsible for 95 percent of the infractions (p<.001), as compared to 4.2 percent for females. Perhaps females present significantly less of a threat to staff and therefore are not "written up" as often, or the infraction does not result in room confinement as often because their behavior can be de-escalated through mediation, whereas male behavior during these incidents tends to escalate and often ends in violent confrontation. This conclusion is somewhat supported by the results of the prescore and sex hypothesis. Females scored significantly (p=.017) higher than males on their daily evaluation prior to an incident. Even if an incident occurs, it is usually not precipitated by an ongoing barrage of negative behavior where females are concerned. Simply speaking, it would appear that dealing with the behavior problems of males, especially those few that seem to be consistently causing disruption, is a much greater concern in the implementation of program guidelines.

DISCUSSION

While there were other significant findings in this study, the ones presented above proved to be the most meaningful for program development and implementation. To summarize, there were two principal findings in this study that relate significantly to program modifications. One had to do with the comparison of prescores and postscores recorded on each resident that received the negative reinforcement of room confinement. The second had to do with the relatively high number of offenses meriting room confinement committed by chronic program disrupters or dominant offenders.

The prescore/postscore finding supports the existing method of dealing with negative behavior incidents within this detention setting. The implication is that the program is successful and should be continued. Some professionals feel that any confinement that exceeds one hour may be counter-productive. Our finding does not support this conclusion. The possibility exists that the post scoring process was biased, that staff rated the behavior of residents higher after room confinement to prove to themselves that the program worked, or because they felt sorry for the resident. Staff report that the opposite reaction is more tenable; it is more likely that residents are monitored closely after release from confinement, and staff have to be especially careful to practice discretion so as not to rate them lower.

We suggest that the room confinement process remain in place as it is for now. Since there are already several meaningful modifications to the existing procedures at this facility, i.e., individualized programming for problem residents, computerized intake and information retrieval, and more could occur after this evaluation is completed, any follow-up study should carefully reevaluate the room confinement process, with special attention given to the prescore/postscore comparison.

Another compelling finding has to do with chronic program disrupters. These dominant offenders committed over one-quarter of all serious offenses in detention, and their negative presence could extend to as many as half of the incidents.

Detained offenders are almost always male. They are more often non-white (usually black at this facility), of low socioeconomic status, have experienced more family disruption and school discipline problems, completed fewer grades in school, and measure lower on intelligence tests. Studies have shown that expressions of violence are part of the norms of the lower socioeconomic classes and are a learned response to pressures of survival. Young males, often black, particularly from female-headed households in socially deprived areas, tend to develop norms of violence or disruption as a means of achieving status among their peers. They are frustrated in their search for self-esteem, lack of success, and desire for material goods. Therefore, their violence may not be rooted in psychological disorder as much as it is normatively prescribed: violence that is goal-oriented behavior, normal for that group.

It is reasonable to assume that chronic program disrupters in detention have characteristics similar to these chronic juvenile offenders. Their control and treatment in the short-term detention setting is a serious challenge. Space limitations usually will not permit the physical isolation and separation of these dominant offenders. We recommend the continued utilization of the individualized programming (maybe one-on-one if possible) that began after this study was initiated. Since dominant offenders tend to come to detention more often and stay longer, it makes sense for staff to continue to develop highly individualized programs for these residents oriented around their special needs. This should be coupled with a group dynamic approach that challenges and confronts these individuals, one that provides them opportunities to examine and re-evaluate their life experiences, handicaps, deficiencies and strengths. The use of group counseling, positive peer culture, reality therapy, role playing sessions, and token self-government programs are all aimed at getting troubled youth to assume the role of responsible people so that they might better understand why they act out their frustrations, and to convince them that ultimately they must assume part of the responsibility for solving their own problems.

Hopefully, this will facilitate some meaningful attitude changes. Realistically, it at least serves to isolate these disruptive influences from the larger group. As we see it, this process contains three potentially positive outcomes: (1) the chronic disrupter is isolated from the major group in a way that reduces his opportunity for negative behavior, (2) this reduces the "ripple" effect from his chronic disruption, and (3) it enhances the probability that both he and all the others in the detention environment can receive the greatest benefits from the rehabilitation effort.

Any program additions and modifications should also consider some of the other findings from this study. The most important of these results primarily centers around race and gender. The residents at this facility are predominantly minority (most often black) males. Since the inception of this study the composition has moved even further in this direction. For the most part this is due to the infiltration of drug-related gangs into the metropolitan area. Greater emphasis is being placed on controlling the negative influence of these gangs on the communities, and consequently, more arrests are occurring from the sector most likely to participate—young, black males. Many bring with them the norms associated with aggression and violence we discussed earlier. Race is highly associated with recidivism and behavioral level, and those returning often and behaving negatively tend to be black males. Any program modifications should consider the changing nature of the detention population and target the rehabilitation of the young black male as a high priority.

If this study is replicated in the near future, and we feel that it should be, most, if not all, of the limitations outlined at the beginning of the design section will have been corrected. The computer system described earlier should significantly reduce the error associated with the data collection process and also help in the measurement of other variables connected to the system of controlling negative behavior incidents, especially those concerning staff input. Also, an individualized instruction program for chronic program disrupters was already set in motion at this facility before the findings from this study were reported.

We believe that this facility represents a model program for dealing with juvenile offenders awaiting trial or placement. The entire organization is oriented toward helping those young people who find themselves in trouble with the system. Many people have written them off as hopeless, but the philosophy at this facility is one of hope through help. Administrators and staff continue to pursue the idea that one positive experience can make a difference, and every youth detained should have a chance to change.

Many of these delinquent youths will go on to become career criminals. Some will spend the majority of their lives behind bars. Those who act out violently in the detention setting, particularly the chronic offenders, will probably continue to act out violently in the community, becoming more and more dangerous with each encounter with a punitive judicial and correction system. To paraphrase the director, if they can somehow become aware of the consequences of their actions and be shown that what they think and feel matters, maybe the experience they have in this environment might help to prevent them, when pointing a gun at someone, from pulling the trigger.

REFERENCES

Askeland, Dean. 1989. Director of Dentention, Oklahoma County Juvenile Justice Center. Interview. August.

Bynum, Jack E. and William E. Thompson. 1989. *Juvenile Delinquency: A Sociological Approach*. Boston, MA: Allyn and Bacon.

Frazier, C. E. and D. M. Bishop. 1985. "The Pretrial Detention of Juveniles and Its Impact on Case Dispositions." *Journal of Criminal Law and Criminology* 76 (Winter): 1132-1152.

Gendreau, P. and R. R. Ross. 1987. "Revivification of Rehabilitation: Evidence from the 1980's." *Justice Quarterly* 4(3):349–407.

Glaser, D. 1969. *The Effectiveness of a Prison and Parole System.* Indianapolis, IN: Bobbs-Merrill.

Greenwood, P.W. 1982. *Selective Incapacitation.* Santa Monica, CA: Rand.

Juvenile Justice Bulletin. 1989. *OJJDP Update on Statistics.* 1(1):1–4.

Krisberg, Barry and Ira Schwartz. 1983. "Rethinking Juvenile Justice." *Crime and Delinquency* 29(July):333–364.

Lipton, Douglas, Robert Martinson and Judith Wilks. 1975. *The Effectiveness of Correctional Treatment.* New York: Praeger.

Martinson, Robert. 1974. "What Works? Questions and Answers about Prison Reform." *The Public Interest.* 35(Spring):22–54.

Norman, Sherwood. 1960. *Detention Practice.* New York: National Probation and Parole Association.

Office of Justice Programs. 1989. *Fact Sheets on Children in Custody.* Washington, DC: U.S. Department of Justice.

Oklahoma County Juvenile Justice Detention Center (OCJJDC). "Rules and Discipline Policy." Section 3 in *Policy and Procedures Manual.* Pp. 2–3.

Rettig, Richard P. 1980. "Considering the Use and Usefulness of Juvenile Detention: Operationalizing Social Theory." *Adolescence* 15(Summer):443–459.

Rubin, H. Ted. 1979. *Juvenile Justice: Policy, Practice and Law.* New York: Random House.

Schwartz, I. M., G. Fishman, R. Rawson, B. Hatfield, A. Krisberg and Z. Eisikovits. 1987. "Juvenile Detention: The Hidden Closets Revisited." *Justice Quarterly* 4(2):219–235.

Uniform Crime Reports. 1987. *Crime in the United States: 1986.* Washington DC: U.S. Government Printing Office. Table 38:183.

Whitehead, John T. and Steven P. Lab. 1990. *Juvenile Justice: An Introduction.* Cincinnati, OH: Anderson.

SUMMARY

In this chapter we have introduced you to the importance of the case study in criminal justice. Completing a case study will help improve your ability to:

- Design and implement a plan to study a specific case.
- Collect and analyze information carefully and objectively.
- Solve problems effectively.
- Present your ideas and recommendations in clear, written form, directed to a specific audience.

Doing a study of this type allows you to discover some of the issues you will face if you become involved in an actual social situation that parallels your case study. This mode of research provides the criminal justice student or professional with a powerful tool to describe a wide variety of topics within the discipline.

CHAPTER *12*

Policy Analysis Papers

BASICS OF POLICY ANALYSIS

In his 1997 State of the Union Address, President Bill Clinton announced that he would make education the highest priority of his second term. His declared goal is to have the first two years of college become "just as universal in America by the 21st century as a high-school diploma." His 10-point plan to reach this goal includes tax credits for college tuition and a "national crusade" to raise standards in secondary education.

President Clinton's proposals were based on policy analysis. Before he made his recommendations, members of his staff and executive departments had conducted studies that reviewed existing education policies, investigated possible alternative policies, and recommended policy changes and initiatives to the president. The president's advisors conducted their studies under the light of public scrutiny and amid the clamor of competing interest groups. Policy analysis is never completely technical; it is conducted within and immediately affected by numerous currents of political influence.

Policy analysis is conducted at local, state, national, and international levels of government. The most publicized reports tend naturally to be the reports of presidential commissions, which are created by presidents to study possible government policies on a certain topic or problem and report their findings and recommendations.

Policy analysis is examining the components (analysis) of a decision to act according to a set principle or rule in a given set of circumstances (a policy).

PRELUDE TO POLICY ANALYSIS: POLICY ANALYSIS RESEARCH PROPOSALS

Introduction to Policy Analysis Research Proposals

This chapter includes directions for two separate paper assignments. The first is a policy analysis research *proposal*, and the second is a policy analysis research *paper*. The proposal is a description of the research that will be conducted during the course of

Policy Analysis in Action: The Challenge of Crime in a Free Society

Throughout the history of the United States there have been numerous presidential commissions, which have studied a wide range of subjects including crime, poverty, and violence. On July 23,1965, recognizing the urgency of the nation's crime problem and the depth of ignorance about it, President Johnson established the Commission on Law Enforcement and Administration of Justice through Executive Order 11236.

In the process of developing the findings and policy recommendations of the report, the commission called three national conferences, conducted five national surveys, held hundreds of meetings, and interviewed tens of thousands of people. In its report, entitled *A Report by the President's Commission on Law Enforcement and Administration of Justice*, published in February 1967 in Washington, DC, by the Government Printing Office, the commission made more than 200 specific recommendations, concrete steps the commission believed could lead to a safer and more just society. These recommendations called for a greatly increased effort to enhance public safety on the part of the federal government, the states, counties, cities, civic organizations, religious institutions, business groups, and individual citizens. The recommendations called for basic changes in the operations of police, schools, prosecutors, employment agencies, defenders, social workers, prisons, housing authorities, and probation and parole officers. The central conclusion of the commission was that a significant reduction in crime, although taking years to achieve, would be possible if the following objectives were vigorously pursued:

1. Society must seek to prevent crime before it happens by assuring all Americans a stake in the benefits and responsibilities of American life, by strengthening law enforcement, and by reducing criminal opportunities.

2. Society's aim of reducing crime would be better served if the system of criminal justice developed a far broader range of techniques with which to deal with individual offenders.

3. The system of criminal justice must eliminate existing injustices if it is to achieve its ideals and win the respect and cooperation of all citizens.

4. The system of criminal justice must attract more people and better people—police, prosecutors, judges, defense attorneys, probation and parole officers, and corrections officials—with more knowledge, expertise, initiative, and integrity,

5. There must be more operational and basic research into the problems of crime and criminal administration by those both within and without the system of criminal justice.

6. The police, courts, and correctional agencies must be given substantially greater amounts of money if they are to improve their ability to control crime.

7. Individual citizens, civic and business organizations, religious institutions, and all levels of government must take responsibility for planning and implementing the changes that must be made in the criminal justice system if crime is to be reduced.

In pursuit of these objectives, the commission compiled over 200 specific policy recommendations. For example, society should undertake the following actions:

- Adopt centralized procedures in each city for handling crime reports from citizens, with controls to make those procedures effective.

- Separate the present Index of Reported Crime into two entirely separate parts, one for crimes of violence and one for crimes against property.

- Formulate police department guidelines for handling juveniles.

- Provide alternatives to adjudication through Youth Services Bureau.

- Divide court hearings for juveniles into adjudicatory and dispositional proceedings.

- Establish community relations units in police departments serving substantial minority populations.

- Clarify the statute authority of police to stop persons for questioning.

- Adopt limiting use of firearms by officers.

- Enact comprehensive state bail reform legislation.

- Revise sentencing provisions of penal codes.

- Improve university research and training in corrections.

- Adopt state drug abuse control legislation.

- Enact laws prohibiting transportation and possession of military-type weapons.
- Require permit for possessing or carrying a handgun.

Well over 100 of the commission's specific policy recommendations, including all the specific recommendations above, have resulted in policy formation at the state and federal levels. Today these stand as accomplished laws, rules, and regulations for which specific policies and procedures have been put into place.

writing the research paper. The proposal assignment is included in this chapter because students who hope to become policy analysts will find that in actual working situations, they will almost always be required to submit a proposal explaining and justifying the research that they expect to do before they are commissioned or funded to conduct the research itself. The proposal exercise that follows, therefore, prepares students for a task that they will face in the course of their careers when working in or consulting with public and private organizations.

The Purpose of Research Proposals

Research proposals are sales jobs. Their purpose is to sell the idea that a research study needs to be done. Before conducting a policy analysis research study for any public or private agency you will need to sell the job. This means that you will need to convince someone that:

- The study needs to be written.
- The study will provide helpful information.
- The study will be properly conducted.
- You are qualified to conduct the study.
- The cost of the study will be reasonable in comparison to the benefit it will provide.

Before a policy analysis study may begin, therefore, the person who will conduct the study must submit a *policy analysis research proposal* to the person who has authority to conduct the research. The purpose of this research proposal is to accomplish the following seven tasks:

1. Convince the people for whom the study is being done that the study is necessary.
2. Describe the objectives of the study.

3. Explain how the study will be done: the methods that will be used to conduct it.

4. Describe the resources—time, people, equipment, facilities—that will be needed to do the job.

5. Construct a project schedule that tells when the project will begin, when it will end, and important dates and times in between.

6. Prepare a project budget which specifies the financial costs and the amount to be billed (if any) to the funding agency.

7. Carefully define what the research project will produce, what kind of study will be conducted, its length, and what it will contain.

The Content of Research Proposals

In form, policy analysis proposals contain the following four parts:

1. Title page
2. Outline page
3. Text
4. Reference page

In substance, policy analysis papers contain the information necessary to complete the tasks listed in the preceding section. An outline of the content of policy analysis proposals appears below.

Outline of the Contents of a Policy Analysis Research Proposal

   I. The *need* for a policy analysis study
     A. An initial description of the current policy problem
       1. A definition of the deficiency in or problem with the current policy
       2. A brief history of the policy problem
       3. The legal framework and institutional setting of the policy problem
       4. The character of the policy problem, size, extent, and importance of the policy problem
     B. Policy analysis imperatives
       1. The probable costs of taking no action
       2. The expected benefits of conducting a policy analysis study
  II. The *objectives* of the proposed policy analysis study
     A. Clarification of the current policy problem
       1. A better problem definition
       2. A better estimate of the quality and quantity of the current problem
       3. A more accurate projection of policy problem development
     B. An accurate evaluation of current relevant public policy
       1. An evaluation of the primary current applicable public policy

           a. A clarification of the primary policy
           b. A clarification of the legal foundation of the primary policy
           c. A clarification of the historical development of the policy
           d. A clarification of the "environment" of the policy
           e. A description of current policy implementation
           f. An evaluation of the effectiveness and efficiency of the policy
      2. An evaluation of secondary applicable public policies
    C. An evaluation of alternatives to present policies
      1. A presentation of possible alternative policies
      2. A comparative evaluation of the expected costs and benefits of the present and alternative policies
III. The *methodology* of the proposed policy analysis
    A. Project management methods to be used during the study
    B. Research methods to be used in conducting the study
    C. Data analysis methods to be used in conducting the study
IV. The *resources* necessary to conduct the study
    A. The material resources
    B. The human resources
    C. A description of financial resources
V. The *schedule* for the policy analysis project
VI. The *budget* for the policy analysis project
VII. The *product* of the policy analysis project

WRITING THE TITLE PAGE FOR A POLICY ANALYSIS PROPOSAL

The title page for a research proposal should follow a standard format. You may follow the format prescribed by your instructor or institution or use the format shown in Chapter 3.

WRITING THE OUTLINE PAGE FOR A POLICY ANALYSIS PROPOSAL

The outline page of the policy analysis proposal is very important and must be done correctly. Directions for preparing an outline and an example of a policy analysis proposal outline are provided in Chapter 3.

WRITING THE TEXT OF RESEARCH PROPOSALS

The text of a policy analysis research proposal contains the following seven elements:

1. An explanation of the *need* for the study
2. A description the *objectives* of the study
3. An explanation of the *methods* that will be used to conduct the study
4. A list of the human, material, and financial *resources* needed to conduct the study

    5. A project *schedule*
    6. A project *budget*
    7. A description of the anticipated *product* of the research project

EXPLANATION OF THE NEED FOR THE STUDY.   Have you ever listened to an automobile salesperson who is trying to sell a car to someone? The first thing that the salesperson will usually ask a customer, after getting the customer's name is, "What kind of a vehicle do you *need*?" Perhaps the salesperson will follow up that question with, "How many people are in your family?" and then say something like, "It seems that you *need* a large vehicle." The good salesperson will not stop this line of questioning until the customer has agreed upon some statement of need. The first objective of a research proposal is to demonstrate that the people for whom it will be written need the information that the policy analysis will contain. They *need* the information because they are faced with one or more problems that their present policies are inadequate to handle.

Start your proposal, therefore, with a clearly written statement of need. Suppose that you believe, for example, that the current policy of the Springfield Board of Education is inadequate as it relates to predelinquent children. Your statement of need might be constructed like this:

> According to reports from school administrators, the Springfield Board of Education's policy on provision of supplemental services for predelinquent children (a policy that provides only for minimal services) leaves some district children without sufficient resources to complete their secondary education; this results in an increase in dropout rates and the possible outcome of serious delinquency.

This statement clearly indicates a need for a review of the district's policy. Your need statement should be comprehensive enough to impress people that a definite need exists. It must be clear enough for people to understand the point immediately.

The policy problem and the policy deficiency.   A *policy problem* is an actual problem that a public policy is supposed to solve. A policy problem is therefore a deficiency in a public policy that is caused by a problem that is independent of that policy. The *policy* of the Springfield Board of Education (minimal services) is deficient because it does not solve a *problem* (some children are assessed as predelinquent). In this case, the policy did not create the problem. The policy is deficient because it does not solve the actual problem. The policy problem in this case, therefore, is that some of the students are in trouble with the law. The policy *deficiency* is the fact that the current policy does not solve the problem of children in trouble, which in turn means that the district's goal of providing a secondary education to all district children cannot be achieved. Statements of need in policy analysis proposals should clearly identify both a specific policy problem and a specific policy deficiency.

Research imperatives.   If a study is "imperative," it must be done. Not every need that an organization has will be called an imperative, because there are always more needs than can be met. Every successful organization, however, meets the needs that are imperative and leaves some that are not imperative unfulfilled, at least temporarily. If your proposal merely states a need, the people to whom you are writing may decide that meeting the need you have identified is not imperative and may choose not to proceed with the study. A good proposal, therefore, includes a statement of research imperatives. This statement will impress people with the necessity of the proposed research.

To continue our example, policy imperatives for the problem of predelinquent children may include the idea that the school district, if it does not change its policy, may:

- Fail to meet its fundamental obligation to the children involved
- Fail to meet the community's need for educated, self-sufficient citizens
- Fail to meet state and federal standards for education

When formulating a statement of policy imperatives, it is vitally important to follow two principles:

1. Make a strong case that the research is imperative.
2. Be completely accurate and honest: do not overstate your case.

DESCRIPTION OF THE OBJECTIVES OF THE STUDY.   Think about the person for whom you are writing your research proposal. The first question this person will ask when presented with a research proposal, as we have already noted, is, "Why do I need this study?" After you have answered this question, that person will ask, "What will this study do for me?" If you were selling this person an automobile, you might say, "It will take you from 0 to 60 in 5.5 seconds!" or " It will take you, your five children, your dog, and your parakeet to Altoona and back in complete comfort." Since you are selling policy analysis instead of automobiles, however, your answer to the question "What will this study do for me?" will be, in general terms, "The proposed policy analysis research study will (1) more clearly define your problem, (2) identify deficiencies in your present policy, (3) examine different ways of overcoming these deficiencies, and (4) recommend the most promising solution."

Problem clarification.   Your policy analysis research *proposal* will include an initial definition and explanation of the problem, but since you have not yet investigated the policy problem in detail, the proposal will not provide a sufficiently clear picture of the character and extent of the problem being studied. Your proposal, therefore, will explain that the policy analysis study to be conducted will further clarify and examine the nature and size of the problem. In our continuing example, our proposal will state something like the following:

The proposed policy analysis research study will clarify and quantify the policy problem: predelinquent children among district school children. The study will (1) determine the exact number of children in the district who experience some form of predelinquent labeling, and (2) determine the form and extent of delinquent behavior that each of these children has manifested.

Your proposal will now briefly explain how these tasks will be carried out. Using the case above, for example, you will want to explain whether the juvenile court will be consulted to determine the degree and extent of delinquent behavior or whether you will rely on school records to determine the status of each child.

Evaluation of current policy.   Your proposal will then tell its readers that you will, if the research study is authorized, provide a thorough examination of current relevant policy. For our Springfield Board of Education, you will write something like:

> The proposed policy analysis research study will evaluate the extent to which the Springfield District's current policy meets and fails to meet the needs of children who have experienced the label of predelinquent.

You must now explain how you will carry out this task. Give the reader of the proposal a brief or general idea of what criteria you will use to evaluate the current policy.

Comparative evaluation of policy alternatives.   Because the current policy is inadequate, the major purpose of a policy research study is to examine different ways of solving the policy problem. If the present policy does not work, what other policies might do a better job? Your proposal will promise to conduct an evaluation of alternative policies. Following our example, you might say something like this:

> The proposed policy analysis research study will identify and evaluate alternatives to the present policy. It will list the comparative advantages and disadvantages of each policy option.

Follow up this statement with a brief description of some of the alternatives that you, in the actual policy analysis study, may evaluate.

Presentation of recommendations.   Your policy analysis study may or may not actually recommend which option to choose. You determine whether or not to include a policy recommendation by asking the person or persons to whom the proposal is being submitted, before you submit it, if they want a recommendation included. Their answer will depend on a number of social, political, or economic considerations specific to their particular circumstances. Many public policy issues are decided not on the basis of the technical merits but upon political or economic considerations. The decision of whether to build a stadium for sporting events or to build an auditorium for theater and ballet, for example, will probably depend more on who supports sports and who supports ballet than on the technical advantages of one facility over the other. Do not assume that you know if a recommendation should be included. Always ask. If the answer is affirmative, you may state something like this:

> Based on an examination of the comparative advantages and disadvantages of each option, the proposed study will recommend the adoption of a specific policy.

EXPLANATION OF THE STUDY'S METHODS.   By this time the person or persons to whom you are submitting your proposal may be impressed with the precision, if not the length, of your answers. However, they will still ask, "How do you propose to do all this?" At this point, back in the showroom, our automobile salesperson has just been asked, "*How* does it take you from 0 to 60 in 5.5 seconds?" The automobile salesperson answers, "It's the fuel-injected V12 engine." Like the automobile salesperson, you will need to answer the question "How do you propose to do all this?" At this point you explain your *methodology*, the steps you will take in conducting your analysis. They will include, as a minimum, collecting and analyzing information and presenting it in a form that people can understand.

Research process and methods.   In your research proposal you describe briefly the steps you will take to find, evaluate, and draw conclusions from the information pertinent to your study. The research process normally proceeds in three steps:

1. *Data (information) collection:* gathering the appropriate information
2. *Data analysis:* organizing the data and determining its meaning or implications
3. *Data evaluation:* determining exactly what conclusions may be drawn from the data

Your research proposal will (1) state that you intend to carry out these three steps, and (2) explain briefly how you intend to do them. Returning to our Springfield Board of Education example, your research proposal will say something like this:

The proposed policy analysis research study will (1) review the records of the district's children who have been labeled or classified as predelinquent; (2) using standards methods in social research, determine from these records how many children experience social and academic impairment and the extent of this impairment; and (3) using treatment perspectives recommended in the literature, determine the programs and equipment necessary to address the problems of each child.

Quality control.   *Quality control* is a formal procedure to ensure that a product meets all relevant standards and is free of defects. Quality control is important in development of any product, including a policy analysis report. In policy analysis it is normally provided by experts, people who have years of experience in dealing with the problem at hand. Your proposal should state (1) that quality control will be provided for the study, and (2) how it will be provided. Following our example, a proposal might say something like this:

Dr. William Enright of Northwest Central University and Dr. Susan Bray of the American Juvenile Justice Association will provide quality control for the proposed study by reviewing the methods and results of the research.

LISTING THE RESOURCES NEEDED TO CONDUCT THE STUDY.   Finally, the person who has commissioned your study will want to know how much money, time, and other resources the project will require. This section is most important in scientific or engineering studies where extensive experimentation or design work is carried out. For most policy analysis studies this section may be brief, although it should in some way address the material and describe the human resources that will be necessary to conduct the study. Following our Springfield example, your proposal may say:

Conducting the proposed study will require the use of a computer with an integrated word-processing data management software program. Paper for report production and reproduction equipment for making copies of the report will also be needed. The principal investigator possesses the necessary computer equipment and will contract for copy services.

Conducting the study will require the following human resources:

- A principal investigator familiar with policy and data analysis techniques
- Two quality control advisers, one of whom is familiar with the standards of the American Juvenile Justice Association and another who is familiar with policy analysis research methods
- A research assistant who is capable of entering data from juvenile court records and school forms into the computer

PROJECT SCHEDULE.   You should include a *research schedule* in the proposal which states:

- When the project will begin
- When the major phases of the project will begin and end
- When any preliminary, interim, or final reports will be issued
- When any special or particular events in the research or analysis process will occur
- When the project will end

PROJECT BUDGET.   A project budget is the next section to be included in a research proposal. The budget will normally contain the following categories:

- Materials (paper, computer discs, supplies, etc.)
- Facilities (conference rooms or places with special capabilities)
- Equipment (laboratory equipment, copy machines, computers)
- Travel and other expenses
- Personnel

For each category, list the item needed and its cost. The personnel section should list each person or position separately, the rate of pay, and the total amount per person.

DESCRIPTION OF THE ANTICIPATED PRODUCT OF THE RESEARCH PROJECT.
The final section of the proposal will describe the anticipated product of your study. In other words, you tell the person or persons to whom you are writing the proposal exactly what they will receive when the project is done. If you are writing this paper for a class in social or criminal justice policy analysis, you will probably write something like the following:

> The final product will be a policy analysis research study from 25 to 30 pages in length, which will provide an analysis of the policy problem and an evaluation of alternative new policies that may solve the problem.

CRIMINAL JUSTICE POLICY ANALYSIS PAPERS

Definition and Purpose of Criminal Justice Policy Analysis Papers

DEFINITION OF A POLICY ANALYSIS PAPER

A policy analysis paper evaluates a decision. It reviews current and potential social policies. It is a document written to help decision makers select the best policy to solve a particular problem. In writing a policy analysis paper, the author

- Selects and clearly defines a specific policy
- Carefully defines the social, governmental, economic or other problem the policy is designed to solve
- Describes the economic, social, and political environments in which the problem arose and the existing policy was developed
- Evaluates the effectiveness of the current policy or lack of policy in dealing with the problem
- Identifies alternative policies that could be adopted to solve the selected problem, and *estimates* the economic, social, environmental, and political *cost and benefits* of each alternative policy
- Provides a summary comparison of all policies examined

Policy analysis papers are written at all levels of government every day. Public officials are constantly challenged to initiate new policies or change old ones. If they have a formal policy at all, they want to know how effective their current policy is. They then want to know what options are available to them, what changes they might make to improve current policy, and what the consequences of those changes will be. Policies are reviewed under a number of circumstances. Policy analyses are sometimes conducted as part of the normal agency budgeting processes. They help decision makers decide what policies should be continued or discontinued. They may be very narrow in scope, such as deciding the hours of shift change at a juvenile detention center. Or they may be very broad in scope, such as deciding how the state will provide treatment of delinquents or protection for its citizens.

PURPOSE OF POLICY ANALYSIS PAPERS

Successful policy analysis papers all share the same general purpose and the same general objective. The objective of a policy analysis paper is to inform policymakers about how public policy in a specific area of concern may be improved.

Public officials are employed full time in the business of making public policy. Program directors at the state and national levels employ professional staff people and consultants who continually investigate bureaucratic policy issues and seek ways to improve standing policy. At the national level, the *Congressional Research Service* continually finds information for representatives and senators. Each committee of Congress employs staff members who help it review current laws and define options for making new ones. State legislatures also employ their own research agencies and committee staff. Legislators and other policymakers are also given policy information by hundreds of public-interest groups and research organizations.

A policy analysis paper is a *practical* exercise. Its focus is neither theoretical nor general in nature. The object of the exercise is to identify and evaluate the policy options that are available on a selected specific topic of interest.

Contents of a Criminal Justice Policy Analysis Paper

SUMMARY OF THE CONTENTS

Criminal justice policy analysis papers contain six basic elements:

1. A title page
2. An executive summary
3. A table of contents, including a list of tables and illustrations
4. The text, or body, of the paper
5. References to sources of information
6. Appendixes

PARAMETERS OF THE TEXT

Ask your instructor for the number of pages required for the policy analysis paper for the course you are taking. Policy analysis papers for undergraduate courses in social policy analysis often range from 20 to 50 pages (double spaced, typed) in length.

Two general rules govern the amount of information presented in the body of the paper. First, content must be adequate to make a good policy evaluation. All the facts necessary for understanding the significant strengths and weaknesses of a policy and its alternatives must be included in the paper. If your paper omits a fact that is critical to the decision, that decision will probably be a poor one.

Never omit important facts merely because they tend to support a perspective other than your own. It is your responsibility to present the facts as clearly as possible so as not to bias the evaluation in a particular direction.

The second guideline for determining the length of a policy analysis paper is to omit extraneous material. Include only the information that is helpful in making the particular decision at hand.

Format of a Policy Analysis Paper

TITLE PAGE

The title page for a policy analysis paper should follow the format provided in Chapter 3.

EXECUTIVE SUMMARY

A one- to two-page executive summary immediately follows the title page. (The summary may be longer if the policy analysis paper requires it.) The executive summary for a policy analysis paper should follow the format provided in Chapter 3.

An executive summary is composed of carefully written sentences expressing the central concepts that are more fully explained in the text of the paper. The purpose of the summary is to allow the decision maker to understand, in as little time as possible, the major considerations to be discussed in the paper. Each statement in the summary must be clearly defined and carefully prepared so that the decision maker should be able to get a thorough and clear overview of the entire policy problem and the value and costs of available policy options by reading nothing but the summary.

The content of the executive summary follows the content of the text of the paper. A sample executive summary for a hypothetical policy analysis paper is presented below. A good way to structure the executive summary is to use the most important topic statements of the text as the sentences in the summary.

Provision of Supplemental Services for the Predelinquent

Executive Summary

The Springfield School District serves 18,000 students who attend three high schools, seven middle schools, and 12 elementary schools. Two hundred and twenty-three elementary students have been assessed as having significant predelinquent behavior requiring additional instructional resources. The current policy of the school district is to provide only minimal resources in response to this need. These resources include the part-time services of one special education teacher, who has had special training in suitable instructional techniques. A budget for counseling, library, and other instructional resources has increased from $250 per year in 1985 to $725 in 1993. This amount meets about 20 percent of present need, which includes reading materials, cassette tapes, and moral enhancement literature for teachers and counselors.

In recent years national disabilities assistance programs have raised social awareness, and teachers, administrators, and students are becoming more sensitive to the needs of students in trouble with the law. Budget cutbacks in the school system, however, have made it difficult even to approach needed materials and special teaching assistance. When the Air Force closed the Springfield Base last fall the county unemployment rate rose to 11 percent, and real estate values dropped 14 percent. During the last election two conservative members were elected to the Board of Education, who pledged to fight to reduce school operating expenses.

These troubled children are receiving only 15 percent of the total services needed. Special reading materials and skilled professionals are in short supply, limiting the opportunities for the children to learn. Children labeled predelinquent average about 2.7 years below reading ability and comprehension for their age. Three alternatives to the present policy of minimal assistance could be initiated to alleviate these problems. First, the school district could provide new additional funding for current activities by redirecting funds from other academic programs. The second alternative is to redirect funds from athletic programs to the special needs of the predelinquent. The third option is to redirect the current student volunteer activities program to raising revenue and direct tutoring services to designated students. The third alternative is more acceptable politically than the first two but would have less direct benefit.

TABLE OF CONTENTS

The table of contents of a policy analysis paper must follow the organization of the paper's text. A table of contents for a policy analysis paper should follow the format shown in Chapter 3.

TEXT OF A POLICY ANALYSIS PAPER

The text, or body, of the paper should contain five kinds of information:

1. A description of the policy to be analyzed
2. A description of the social, physical, economic, and political (including legal and institutional) environments in which the policy has been or will be developed
3. An evaluation of the effectiveness and efficiency of the applicable current policy
4. An evaluation of alternatives to the current policy
5. A summary comparison of policy options

A policy analysis paper should follow the outline shown below. Study this summary carefully.

Outline of the Contents of the Text of a Policy Analysis Paper

    I. Policy description
- A. A clear, concise statement of the policy selected
- B. A brief history of the policy
- C. A description of the problem the policy was aimed at resolving, including an estimate of the extent and importance of the problem

   II. Policy environment
- A. A description of the social and physical environmental factors affecting origin, development, and implementation of the policy
- B. A description of the economic factors affecting origin, development, and implementation of the policy
- C. A description of the political factors affecting origin, development, and implementation of the policy

 III. Effectiveness and efficiency of the current policy
- A. Effectiveness: How well does the existing policy do what it was designed to do?
- B. Efficiency: How well does the policy perform in relation to the effort and resources committed to it?

  IV. Policy alternatives
- A. Possible alterations of the present policy, with estimated costs and benefits of each alteration
- B. Alternatives to the present policy with estimated costs and benefits of each alternative

   V. Summary comparison of policy options

POLICY DESCRIPTION.   The first task of a policy paper is to describe the policy that currently exists. The purpose is to allow the reader to understand the present situation and how this situation developed. Policy descriptions contain three basic elements. The first is a clear and concise statement of the policy selected. You may find that there is no written policy on the subject under consideration. If this is the case, you should first inform your readers of the lack of a written policy that addresses the subject, and then list and describe any policies that may indirectly affect the problem you are addressing. For example, a school district may have no policy that explicitly addresses destructive gang activities, but it may have policies on acceptable attire in school, rules of order in the classroom, and so on.

Where written formal policies exist, quote them directly from the documents that state the policies and provide the source of the quotation. If the policy is established under the authority of more general legislation, quote and cite the legislation also. For example, the laws of Indiana may include a law that says, in part, "School districts may establish appropriate rules of behavior and guidelines for suspension or expulsion for violations of these rules." The public schools of the city of Indianapolis, then, may have a regulation that says, "Students shall not wear clothing that unduly distracts or offends other students." Further, a particular school principal may have a policy that states, "shirts without sleeves shall not be worn in class during school hours except when participating in athletic activities." In these three examples we find three levels of public policy, all leading to a specific guideline applied in a specific school. Preparing a complete description of the policy at hand is very important if analysis of the problem is to be accurate and beneficial.

The second part of this section of your policy analysis paper should include a brief history of the policy. Several basic questions should be answered here. When was the existing policy first initiated? How did it come about? In response to what problem or need did it come about? What effects did the policy have? Remember that the purpose of this narrative in the paper is to help the reader understand what the present policy is and how it came about.

The third part of this section is a description of the problem the policy was aimed at resolving, including an estimation of the extent and importance of the problem. Carefully define the original problem that gave rise to the present policy. Estimate the size and extent of this problem. If the policy being examined is a school's dress code, estimate the number of students who have violated the code and the seriousness of the violation. These estimates are crucial for proper policy formulation. For example, suppose that a school district has 18,000 students. If six students at one high school are wearing fluorescent shorts, a relatively minor problem exists. If 200 students come to school wearing gang insignia, a vastly more difficult problem has arisen. You need to provide the reader with an accurate assessment of the extent of the problem.

POLICY ENVIRONMENT.   No policy exists in a vacuum. Wardens, police chiefs, and program directors do not sit in ivory towers cut off from the real world, and if they act as if they do, they are likely to pay a heavy political cost. Policies almost always arise from genuine needs, but they often reflect the needs of certain part of the population more than others. Policy is formulated within a number of environments. The most important of these are:

1. The *social environment:* the cultural, ethnic, and religious habits, practices, expectations, and patterns of relating to one another that every society establishes

2. The *physical environment:* the climate, architecture, topography, natural resources, and other physical features that shape the patterns of life in a society

3. The *economic environment:* the content and vitality of economic life, including the type of industry and commerce, the relative wealth or poverty of the area affected by the policy, the unemployment rate, and the rate of economic growth

4. The *political environment:* the government structures, the applicable laws, the political parties, the prevalent ideologies of the people, and the salient issues of the day

The policy paper should describe each of these environments, giving more emphasis to those that have greater effects on the policy under consideration. A juvenile detention center's dress code policy, for example, may be much more responsive to the social and economic environments than to the physical or political environments in a community. In each case, describe the environmental factors that affect the policy. A dress code will probably be influenced by the socioeconomic class or homogeneity of the neighborhood the facility is in. The policy paper should include separate discussions of the social, physical, economic, and political environments affecting policy development, giving different amounts of attention to each one according to what is important to the particular policy being discussed.

POLICY EFFECTIVENESS AND EFFICIENCY

Policy effectiveness. An evaluation of policy effectiveness should tell the reader how well a specific policy does what it is intended to do. There are many methods for evaluating effectiveness and many factors that could be used in the analysis. We do not explain these methods where, but descriptions are available in many basic texts on policy analysis. Instead of explaining the wide array of policy evaluation methods, we describe the basic steps that must be taken to complete any evaluation. *Ask the course instructor for specific directions or methods for policy evaluation.* The general explanation provided here may or may not be sufficient for the analysis paper that you are assigned.

Evaluation of policy effectiveness proceeds in three steps:

1. Constructing an evaluation framework
2. Applying the framework to the policy being examined
3. Drawing conclusions from your application

The first step in policy evaluation is to establish an evaluation framework. An evaluation framework starts with a clearly defined policy to be evaluated. It then adds to the policy definition (1) a list of the general goals the policy is designed to meet, (2) a list of specific objectives that lead to the goals, (3) a list of criteria for judging the extent to which the objectives are met, and (4) a list of specific measurements for quantifying the fulfillment of the criteria.

To construct an evaluation framework:

1. Define the *general goals* the policy is intended to meet. Goals are general statements of the ends for which policy is made. The goal of a policy limiting the number of continuous hours that may be worked by a correctional officer, for example, is to maintain security for inmates, staff, and citizens in the community. Sometimes goals have been defined by the policymaking body that issues the policy. If not, attempt through interviews or researched documents to determine the goals for which the policy was made.

2. Define *specific objectives* that indicate partial accomplishment of the goals. Objectives are specific steps toward reaching goals. If the goal of the National Association of Police Chiefs is to make citizens feel more secure, for example, an objective might be to improve community policing programs in urban areas.

3. Define specific *criteria* for determining the extent to which the objectives are met. Criteria help you know the extent to which objectives are met. If the objective of a policy is to improve community policing programs, criteria for determining the quantity and quality of services related to neighborhood foot patrol and answering calls for help need to be determined. One criterion might be the increase in personal contacts with citizens. Another criterion might be reduction in criminal and delinquent activity. Still another might be the effectiveness and visibility of 24-hour neighborhood foot patrols. Establishing the proper evaluation criteria is one of the most difficult and important tasks in writing a policy analysis paper.

4. Define specific *measurements* for applying the criteria to the objectives. Measurements determine quantities. If a criterion for good community policing programs is the quantity and quality of neighborhood foot patrols, valid measurements of productive contacts might include (1) the number of contacts per hour, (2) the number of problems or incidents handled, or (3) the reduction of criminal or delinquent acts in the neighborhood.

After establishing your framework, use the measurements you have designed. Try to make as many quantitative measurements as the study will allow. You may also need to make qualitative evaluations of variables that are not easily quantifiable (e.g., citizens' feelings about the officers that patrol their neighborhood).

Your final step may now be taken: drawing conclusions from your measurements. A good general practice is to be conservative in your evaluations. This means that you should interpret the data to indicate only what the data clearly demonstrate—not tendencies or implications that still need more proof.

Efficiency.   Efficiency goes a step beyond effectiveness. Efficiency relates cost to accomplishment. Efficiency concerns not only how well a job is done, but also the amount of resources committed to getting the job done. In other words, when one inquires about the efficiency of a policy, one is asking the question, "How well did the policy perform in relation to effort and resources committed to it?" Fuel efficiency in an automobile is determined by dividing the number of miles traveled by the number of gallons of gasoline consumed. An automobile that travels 50 miles for every gallon of gas is considered highly efficient. A program to reduce the number of neighborhood crimes across the city may require the expenditure of $2 million. If it reduces the number of criminal or delinquent acts by 1000, the efficiency of the program may be expressed in terms of the cost/crime prevention ratio, or $2000 per crime reduced.

Evaluating efficiency is often more difficult than it appears. The most important factor in producing a valid efficiency evaluation is selecting the proper factors to place in the ratio. For example, to evaluate the efficiency of a prison arts program, one may divide the number of dollars in the annual budget for this program (perhaps $25,000) by the number of inmates who complete the requirements of the program (perhaps 250). The resultant figure would be $200 per inmate. This figure does not, however, provide any information about the quality of education that the inmates received or the effectiveness of the program in combating recidivism. It is, therefore, a limited measure of efficiency. When writing your policy analysis paper, try to construct an efficiency ratio for the measurements you have made. Be very careful, however, to point out the limitations of the ratio you construct.

POLICY ALTERNATIVES.   As author of a policy analysis paper, you want to be effective in clearly analyzing a policy and in assisting a public official to improve it. Having defined the deficiencies in the present policy, the next question you will ask is, "What can I do about it?" One of the most common mistakes of students who write policy analysis papers is their failure to answer this question correctly. To define options does *not* mean to describe several different measures that are all combined in one approach, but instead, to describe *different approaches* to solving the problem. *Options* in policy analysis papers are different, mutually exclusive approaches to a problem. If one alternative is selected, the others are rejected. Sometimes students mistake the steps necessary to complete one course of action for distinct, separate approaches to the problem. If student Jan Smith is studying prison overcrowding policy, she may list as alternative approaches:

- *Option A.* Demonstrate present prison overcrowding.
- *Option B.* Draw up plans for a new state prison.
- *Option C.* Generate funds and state legislative support for the facility.
- *Option D.* Construct the prison in three phases over a two-year period.

Do you see a problem here? All four "options" are actually only four steps in carrying out *one* option: to build a prison.

Again, *steps toward a single solution are not options.* An actual set of options for solving the problem of prison overcrowding might be:

- *Option A.* Continue present policy of encouraging prerelease work centers.
- *Option B.* Plan and construct a new prison.
- *Option C.* Expand alternatives to incarceration.
- *Option D.* Broaden parole and probation services.

Conducting a simplified benefit/cost analysis.   For each available option the student should describe first the benefits and then the costs. *Benefits* are the positive outcomes expected. *Costs* include time, money, and resources expected, and also probable or possible negative outcomes (known as *disbenefits*). Both benefits and costs may include economic, social, political, and environmental factors. Benefits of improving the public penal system, for example, may include:

1. Less prison overcrowding
2. Safety of staff, inmates, and citizens in the community
3. Decreased criminal activity
4. Increased economic development
5. Increased community security

Costs of improving the prison system may include:

1. Construction costs of many millions of dollars
2. Fewer resources for other community projects, such as common education
3. Political opposition from areas in the community that do not benefit directly

As mentioned previously, all reasonable costs and benefits should be included in the paper. The student should never exclude possible costs or benefits of any one option in order to make another option appear more or less attractive. The policy analysis paper will be submitted to someone else who is responsible for making the proper decision. If an option other than the one recommended is selected and full information has been provided, the writer of the position paper has acted appropriately. Elected and appointed officials may legitimately choose options that are technically not the most cost-effective. But if a policymaker selects the wrong option, making a decision based on incomplete information in the policy analysis paper, the writer of the position paper is clearly responsible.

Lengthy books have been written on how to conduct benefit-cost analyses. Only a simplified (but very helpful) process will be outlined here. To analyze benefits and costs *for each option*, always proceed with the same set of steps. The first step is to list the benefits and then the costs of that option. The second step is to assign a monetary value to each cost and benefit. Value estimates should be made according to the advice of experts, who usually include government officials, engineers, or consultants, or members of private organizations with expertise in the area. Price estimates for construction costs may be obtained from engineers in local, state, or national government agencies. Personnel cost estimates may be determined by multiplying the number of person-hours or days by the cost per hour for the services desired.

Some costs are more difficult to estimate. Intangible items such as "political discontent" are not easily quantified, yet an attempt may reasonably be made to do so. Public policy analysts call such estimates *compensating variations*.

A compensating variation allows analysts, for comparison purposes, to place a dollar value on intangible factors. The dollar value of an intangible cost is the amount that the average person would normally accept as fair compensation for having paid a particular cost or endured a particular disbenefit.

For example, suppose that Mrs. Williamson lives in a quiet residential neighborhood. A community treatment center is planned at the end of her street that will increase traffic, noise, and personal risk near her home. Mrs. Williamson is unhappy about the treatment center. If asked if she would prefer that it not be built, she would answer yes. Suppose, however, that Mrs. Williamson was offered this choice: either (1) no center will be built; or (2) the center will be built and Mrs. Williamson will be paid $100. Mrs. Williamson may still prefer alternative 1. Suppose that the offer was increased to $1000. Mrs. Williamson might then choose to have the money and the treatment center rather than neither the money nor the center. The compensating variation in this case would be the amount that Mrs. Williamson would be willing to accept as fair compensation for the treatment center. The social cost of building the treatment center may then be calculated as the sum of the compensating variations of the residents to be affected adversely by the facility.

Remember that all such estimates can be held to the judgment of the people who will read the paper. Estimates need be neither exact nor perfect. It is important to realize that someone must make a decision about whether or not to make the corrections system improvements and that a reasonable estimate is more helpful than no estimate at all.

Economists and urban planners have long known that attitudes affect development potential. Beliefs about the strength of the economy, for example, have a direct daily effect on stock exchanges. Popular discontent makes it less likely that people will find a particular neighborhood a desirable place to live. In order to estimate discontent as a compensating variation, a brief survey of community attitudes would be necessary. Telephone calls to the 15 homes closest to the planned treatment center would yield several interviews with homeowners. Asking a few simple open-ended questions would make it possible to estimate the strength of sentiment about the corrections facility in the neighborhood. It makes a major difference to the study whether one or two people are mildly concerned or whether 15 families are planning to move immediately if the facility is built. Mild discontent might be assigned no economic value ($0), whereas widespread strong feelings may make the neighborhood so undesirable that property values decline by 25 percent (a total loss in property value of $328,125). Both extremes are unlikely in this case, but one can see that it is possible to put a ballpark estimate on popular discontent.

The second part of benefit/cost analysis in the paper is entered in the first section of Part III of your paper: Recommendation. Here a summary of benefit/cost analyses for all alternatives is presented in table form, followed by a paragraph or two of explanatory comparisons. The table for student Jan Smith's paper might look like this:

Benefit/Cost Analysis Summary Table

Alternative	Benefit	Dollar Value	Cost	Dollar Value
A. Prerelease center	Reduces prison population, moderate economic development	1.5M	Maintenance, increase in public anxiety	4K per inmate/ per year
B. New prison	Containment, high economic development	14M	Maintenance, large outlay of taxpayers' money	Construction plus 25K per inmate/per year
C. Broader parole and probation programs	Quick to install, low disruption, no new construction	2M	Maintenance, more ex-cons on the street	2M per year

Presentation of Policy Analysis Papers

All sources of information in a policy analysis must be properly cited. Follow the directions in Chapter 4.

Appendices can be helpful to the reader of policy analysis papers. They provide information that supplements the important facts contained in the text. For many local development and public works projects, a map and a diagram are often very helpful. The student should attach the appendices to the end of the paper after the reference page. The student should not append entire government reports, journal articles, or other publications, but selected charts, graphs, or other pages may be appended. The source of the information should always be evident on the pages appended.

CHAPTER 13

Legal Case Briefs

AMICUS CURIAE BRIEFS FOR THE U.S. SUPREME COURT

When people are parties to disputes before the U.S. Supreme Court, the attorneys representing each side prepare written documents called *briefs on the merit*, which explain the nature of the dispute and present an argument for the side the attorney represents. The justices read the briefs, hear oral arguments, hold conferences to discuss the case, and then write opinions to announce both the Court's decision and the views of justices who disagree in whole or in part with that decision. Cases that come before the Supreme Court are usually important to many people who are not actually parties to the specific case being presented, because the Court's decisions contain principles and guidelines that all lower courts must follow in deciding similar cases. *Reno v. ACLU*, for example, did not become famous because it allowed one person to publish his material on the Internet but because it set forth the principle that Congress may not unduly restrict freedom of the press in order to curb pornography.

Because Supreme Court cases are important to people other than those directly involved in the case, sometimes groups and individuals outside the proceedings of a specific case want their views on cases to be heard by the Court before it makes a decision. It is not proper, however, to go to the justices directly and try to influence them to decide a case in a particular way. Influencing government officials directly through visits, phone calls, or letters is called *lobbying*. When people want to influence the way Congress handles a law, they lobby their representatives by writing letters or talking to them personally. The lobbying of Supreme Court justices, however, is considered improper because the Court is supposed to make decisions based on the content of the Constitution and not upon the political preferences of one or more groups in society.

There is a way, however, for outsiders to submit their views to the Supreme Court. The Court invites interested parties, most often organizations, to submit *amicus curiae* briefs. (*Amicus curiae* means "friend of the Court.") A party that submits an amicus curiae brief becomes a friend of the Court by giving it information that it may find helpful in making a decision. As the Court explains, "an amicus curiae brief which brings relevant matter to the attention of the Court that has not already been brought to its attention by the parties is of considerable help to the Court. An amicus brief which does not serve this purpose simply burdens the staff and facilities of the Court and its filing is not favored" (*Rules of the Supreme Court* 1990:45).

The case of *Reno, Attorney General of the United States, et al. v. American Civil Liberties Union et al.* was argued in the Supreme Court on March 19 and decided on June 26, 1997. The case concerned two provisions of the Communications Decency Act of 1996 (CDA), which sought to protect minors from harmful material on the Internet. The first provision mandated criminal penalties for knowingly transmitting "obscene or indecent" messages to any recipient under 18 years of age. The second provision prohibited knowingly "sending or displaying to a person under 18" any message "that, in context, depicts or describes, in terms patently offensive as measured by contemporary community standards, sexual or excretory activities or organs."

The American Civil Liberties Union (ACLU) and other parties filed suit in U.S. district court against Janet Reno, who as U.S. Attorney General is the nation's chief law enforcement officer, to keep her from enforcing these two provisions of the CDA. The district court enjoined Reno from enforcing the two controversial sections of the CDA. Reno appealed to the Supreme Court. The Supreme Court agreed with the ACLU that the CDA's provisions were so vague and broad that they violated the protections of freedom of speech and press contained in the first amendment to the Constitution. An interest group called Feminists for Free Expression filed an amicus curiae brief in this case, which said, in part:

> Feminists for Free Expression (FFE) is a national organization of women and men who share a commitment to both gender equality and freedom of expression. FFE was founded on the tenet that the right of free speech is a prerequisite to attaining gender equality and cannot be disregarded for fashionable causes without inevitably harming women's rights. FFE is thus dedicated to opposing censorship that, however well-intended, is ultimately counterproductive to the goal of equality for women.

As many of FFE's writer and artist members can attest, feminist expression is inherently controversial and often blamed for social problems ranging from divorce to teenage pregnancy, just as some erotic speech is made the scapegoat for other social ills. Indeed, any written or visual work that deals frankly with women's lives and sexuality is at risk of censorship. In recent years, many feminist artists and writers have learned from firsthand experience that the urge to censor "offensive" material is prevalent in our society, and feminist work is particularly vulnerable to such censorship.

Because the freedom to put forth controversial feminist ideas and to combat ignorance regarding sexuality, reproduction, and abuse is critical to women's rights and well-being, FFE believes that it is particularly incumbent upon women to oppose censorship in all forms. Few forms of censorship, however, are as threatening to women's interests as the Communications Decency Act's restrictions on "indecent" and "offensive" speech on the Internet. The Internet offers unprecedented opportunities for individuals to exchange information and debate ideas, making it the front line in free speech. Indeed, it is the first forum in the "marketplace of ideas" that is so accessible to all as to make Justice Brandeis' answer to false speech—more speech—truly work. Ignorance is countered by information, controversies are debated on their merits, and the truth wins out—as long as it is not censored.

FFE views the Internet as key to achieving gender equality, a goal that will be greatly harmed by the Congress's attempted restrictions on Internet communications. FFE therefore has a strong interest in ensuring that the Internet remains free from censorship that is inconsistent with the fundamental free-speech rights that are so crucial to women.

SCOPE AND PURPOSE OF AN AMICUS CURIAE BRIEF

Your task in this chapter is to write an amicus curiae brief for a case that is being considered by the U.S. Supreme Court. You will write your own brief, making your own argument about how the case should be decided. Of course, you do not have to be entirely original. You will examine the arguments used in others' briefs, add new arguments of your own, and write the entire brief in your own carefully chosen words. In completing this assignment you will also be meeting five more personal learning objectives:

1. You will become familiar with the source, form, and content of legal documents.
2. You will become acquainted with the procedures of brief preparation.
3. You will become familiar with the details of a selected case currently before the Court. As you follow the news reports on this case, you will eventually learn the Court's decision.
4. You will come to understand a Supreme Court case in sufficient depth to be able to integrate the arguments of actual amicus curiae briefs into your own argument.
5. You will learn how to write a clear, logical, effective, persuasive argument.

Remember that your goal is to persuade the Supreme Court to make a certain decision. Before you begin, reread the first part of this book, especially the sections on how to write clearly and persuasively.

GENERAL CONSIDERATIONS AND FORMAT OF AN AMICUS CURIAE BRIEF

Briefs provide the Court with the facts in a particular case and make arguments about how the case should be decided. The *Rules* of the Court state that "a brief must be compact, logically arranged with proper headings, concise, and free from burdensome, irrelevant, immaterial and scandalous matter. A brief not complying with this paragraph may be disregarded and stricken by the Court" (*Rules.* 28). The Court also requires those who submit an amicus curiae brief to provide a statement of permission, which may be either (1) evidence that permission to submit the amicus curiae brief has been granted by both parties to the dispute; or if the permission of both parties has not been granted, (2) the reason for the denial and the reason that the Court should consider the amicus brief despite the absence of permission of the parties.

Of course, as a student writing an amicus brief for a class in criminal justice, you will not actually submit your brief to the Supreme Court, so you will not need to write a statement of permission. Information on such statements is provided here so that you will understand their purpose when you encounter them in your research.

Ask your instructor about the page limit for your assignment. The Supreme Court's limit for the actual text of amicus curiae briefs (exclusive of questions presented page, subject index, table of authorities, and appendix) is 30 pages, single spaced. Your brief will, however, be double spaced for the convenience of your instructor, and have as few as 15 pages, depending on your instructor's requirements. Your brief will be shorter because a central purpose of this assignment is for you to understand the arguments to be made in the case, whereas actual amicus briefs submitted to the Court require much more detail than you will need to know. As you read actual amicus briefs, use your own judgment to select the material that you believe is most important for the Court to understand and include this information, in your own words, in your brief.

The proper presentation of briefs is essential. Briefs to the Supreme Court are normally professionally printed, and the *Rules* include directions for this process. The Court does, however, also accept typed briefs, and your amicus curiae brief will conform to the Court's instructions for typed briefs in most respects, with modifications to allow your instructor sufficient space to write comments. You must therefore prepare your amicus curiae brief according to the following specifications:

- Black type on white paper, 8 by 11 inches, double spaced, printed on one side only
- Text and footnotes in 12-point type
- A typeface as close as possible to that used in actual briefs
- Margins of 1½″ on the left and 1″ on all other sides
- A binding that meets the requirements of your instructor

You will submit one copy of your brief to your instructor. It is always wise, when submitting any paper, to retain a copy for yourself in case the original is lost. (The Supreme Court requires that 60 copies of a brief be submitted for a case coming to it directly under its original jurisdiction, and 40 copies for cases coming to it under appellate jurisdiction from lower courts.)

RESOURCES FOR WRITING AN AMICUS CURIAE BRIEF

You will find resources for amicus curiae briefs in the library and on the Internet. When you conduct your research, you will need access to two periodicals that may be found in some college libraries and in most if not all law school libraries:

1. *Preview of United States Supreme Court Cases*, a publication of the American Bar Association's Public Education Division
2. *The United States Law Week*, published by the Bureau of National Affairs, Inc.

If they are not available in your college library, you may request copies through interlibrary loan or ask your instructor to request that the department or library order them.

Preview of United States Supreme Court Cases contains a summary of the following information about cases that have been filed with, but not yet been decided by, the Court:

- Title
- Docket number
- Date of oral argument (when lawyers present their arguments before the justices in the courtroom)
- Issue discussed
- Facts
- Background and significance
- Arguments for each side
- Counsels of record for each side
- Names of groups submitting amicus curiae briefs in support of each side

The United States Law Week lists the following information relevant to cases at all stages of development before the Court:

- Oral arguments, with names of presenters and dates
- Name
- Docket number
- Subject summary
- Internet resources for writing an amicus curiae brief

Chapter 7 provides an introduction to the Internet, and if you are not familiar with the Internet or with criminal justice resources on the Internet, you may want to read its directions before proceeding. The Internet provides a wealth of material related to constitutional and international law.

To find cases on the Internet that are currently before the Supreme Court but not yet decided, the best place to start is at the U.S. government's page entitled "U.S. Judicial Branch Resources" (http://lcweb.loc.gov/global/judiciary.html). Upon reaching this site you will be informed that "This page contains links to U.S. Judicial Branch Resources as well as other Web sites specializing in legal information." Here you will find links to a wealth of information about statutes, regulations, and judicial opinions. Under the title "Judicial Opinions" on this page you will find this statement: "The following are Judicial Opinions available on the Internet. The Internet should not be considered a comprehensive source for caselaw." This announcement is followed by a list of links to the many types of information, including the following:

Federal Courts

- U.S. Federal Courts Home Page
- Supreme Court of the United States
  - Supreme Court Opinions (via Cornell Law School)
  - Supreme Court Order Lists and Per Curiam Opinions (via Cornell Law School)
  - Current Supreme Court Term
  - Search Historic Supreme Court Opinions
  - Supreme Court Opinions, 1937–1975:
    - By case name (via FedWorld)
    - By keyword (via FedWorld)
    - By U.S. Reports volume number (via Villanova Law School)
  - Leading Supreme Court Opinions, 1793–1966 (via USSC+)
  - Comprehensive Supreme Court Opinions, 1966–1996 (via USSC+)
- Circuit Courts of Appeal
  - Search All Circuit Court Opinions Available on the Internet (via Cornell Law School)
  - District of Columbia Circuit (via Georgetown University Law Center) February 1995 to Current
  - First Circuit (via Emory Law School) November 1995 to Current
  - Second Circuit (via Pace University Law School) September 1995 to Current
  - Third Circuit (via Villanova Law School) January 1994 to Current
  - Fourth Circuit (via Emory Law School) January 1995 to Current
  - Fifth Circuit (via Fifth Circuit) January 1992 to Current
  - Sixth Circuit (via Emory Law School) January 1995 to Current
  - Seventh Circuit (via Emory Law School) August 1995 to Current
  - Eighth Circuit (via Washington University Law School) October 30, 1995 to Current
  - Ninth Circuit (via Villanova Law School) January 1995 to Current
  - Tenth Circuit (via Emory Law School) August 1995 to Current
  - Eleventh Circuit (via Emory Law School) November 1994 to Current
  - Federal Circuit (via Emory Law School) August 1995 to Current
  - Map of the United States displaying and linking to each Circuit (via Georgetown University Law School)
  - The Federal Court Locator (via Villanova Law School)

If you click on the link entitled "Supreme Court Opinions (via Cornell Law School)" you will find a page maintained by Cornell University Law School (http://supct.law.cornell.edu/supct/) which is entitled "The LII and Hermes." This site contains links to many Court decisions available on the Internet plus a link entitled

"Schedule of Oral Arguments." If you click on this link you will come to a page that lists the current cases for which oral arguments are scheduled (http://supct.law.cornell.edu/supct/argcal97.html). Some of the case names on the list are links to briefs that have been written either for the Supreme Court or for lower courts. If you find a reference in one of these links to a circuit or district court, you can return to the U.S. Judicial Branch Resources page, which provides links to briefs prepared for those courts. By following these links you will find much of the material you need (for the most important cases currently before the courts).

STEPS IN WRITING AN AMICUS CURIAE BRIEF

Select a Case and a Side

Using the most recent issues of *Preview of United States Supreme Court Cases*, *The United States Law Week*, or the appropriate Internet sites, select a case and decide which side of the argument you support. The case you choose must fulfill the following two requirements:

1. It must be of personal interest to you.
2. It must be a case that has not yet been decided by the Court.

Obtain Copies of the Amicus Briefs

Your next step is to obtain copies of the briefs on the merits of the appellant and the respondent and any available amicus briefs on the side of the case that you support and the one amicus brief on the opposing side. There are three ways to obtain amicus briefs. You may obtain them by going in person to the Office of the Clerk of the United States Supreme Court at the following address, where you will be allowed to photocopy the briefs (the clerk will not send copies of the briefs in the mail):

Office of the Clerk

Supreme Court of the United States

1 First Street, N.E.

Washington, DC 20543

Telephone: (202) 479-3000

The second way to obtain the briefs is to request them from the attorneys of record for the organizations that are filing the briefs; *Preview of United States Supreme Court Cases* lists their names, addresses, and telephone numbers. The *United States Law Week* provides this information for some cases and not for others. If this information is not given in either of these publications, you may request it by mail or telephone from the Clerk of the Supreme Court at the address above. Be sure to provide the name and the docket number of the case in which you are interested.

When you contact the attorneys of record, tell them:

- Your name and address
- The college or university you attend
- The nature of your assignment
- The name and docket number of the case in which you are interested
- Your interest in obtaining a copy of their amicus brief
- Your appreciation of their assistance

The third way to obtain the briefs is to print or download them from the appropriate sources on the Internet.

Write an Argument Outline

Read the arguments in the briefs you have collected, and then construct an outline of an argument that makes the points you believe are most important. Your outline should normally have from two to six main points. Follow the directions for constructing outlines provided in Chapter 1. *Submit this outline to your instructor for advice before continuing.*

Write the Argument

Following the outline you have constructed, write your argument. Your writing needs to be clear and sharply focused. Follow the directions for writing in the first part of this manual. The first sentence of each paragraph should state its main point.

The Rules of the Court state that the argument of a brief must exhibit "clearly the points of fact and of law being presented and citing the authorities and statutes relied upon" (*Rules*. 27). The Court also wants to read briefs that are "as short as possible" (*Rules*. 27). In addition to conforming to page limitations set by your instructor, the length of your argument should be guided by two considerations. First, content must be of adequate length to help the Court make a good decision. All the arguments necessary to making a decision must be present. Write this paper as if you are an officer of the Court. Under no circumstances should you make a false or misleading statement. Be persuasive, but be truthful. You do not need to make the opponents' argument for them, but the facts that you present must be accurate to the best of your knowledge.

The second guideline for determining the length of your argument is to omit extraneous material. Include only the information that is helpful to the Court in making the particular decision at hand. The Rules of the Court require that an amicus brief includes a "conclusion, specifying with particularity the relief which the party seeks." Read the conclusions of the briefs you collect, and then write your own, retaining the same format but combining the arguments for the groups you are representing, and limiting your conclusion to two pages.

Write the Argument Summary

After you have written the argument itself, write the summary, which should be a clearly written series of paragraphs that includes all the main points. It should be brief (not more than three double-spaced typed pages).

According to the *Rules* of the Court, briefs should contain a "summary of the argument, suitably paragraphed, which should be a succinct, but accurate and clear, condensation of the argument actually made in the body of the brief. A mere repetition of the headings under which the argument is arranged is not sufficient" (*Rules*. 27).

The summary of your argument may easily be assembled by taking the topic sentences from each paragraph and forming them into new paragraphs. The topic sentences contain more information than your subject headings. As complete sentences arranged in logical order, they provide an excellent synopsis of the contents of your brief. Your argument summary should not exceed two pages, double-spaced.

HOW TO READ A UNITED STATES COURT DECISION

When courts in the United States decide a particular case that is brought before them, they state the reasons for whatever they decide in a document known as a *decision*. They publish their decisions in bound volumes known as *reporters*. The decisions of the U.S. Supreme Court, for example, are published in the *Supreme Court Reporter*. Printed in the text are the first and last pages of a sample decision. The opposite numbers in the sample pages refer to the numbers at the beginning of each of the following paragraphs.

(1) The name of the case comprises the name of the party who initiates the action, followed by "v." (meaning "versus"), followed by the name of the party against which the action is brought.

(2) West publishing provides the reader the correct citation for the case: "Cite as 117 S.Ct. 1573 (1997)." This citation means that this case appears in Volume 117 of the *Supreme Court Reporter* on page 1573, published in 1997.

(3) Jon E. Edmond is a *Petitioner*. This means that Edmond has petitioned the Court, asking the justices to review his case. You may also see in this space the word *Plaintiff*, meaning the party that seeks a redress of a grievance, or *Appellant*, the party who appeals the case from a lower court.

(4) UNITED STATES, meaning the government of the United States, is the party against whom the action is being brought. In some cases, such as *ACLU v. Reno*, the government official who represents the United States is named instead of the government itself. This party may also be called *Defendant*, *Appellee*, or *Respondent*.

(5) The number 96-262 represents the Court's docket or calendar number. This number means that this was the 262nd case listed on the Court's docket in 1996.

(6) The date the case was orally presented before the Court by attorneys representing each side is listed, followed by the date the Court announced its decision. Other dates may be listed in this space, such as the date the case was granted appeal.

(7) This paragraph summarizes the actions taken in the case.

(8) The judgment of the Court, with respect to the lower Court's judgment, is listed. In this case, *Affirmed* means that the decision of the Court of Appeals for the Armed Forces (that the Secretary of Transportation and not the Judge Advocate General has authority to appoint judges to military courts of appeal) was upheld by the Supreme Court.

(9) The Supreme Court's decision is based on an agreement of a majority of the

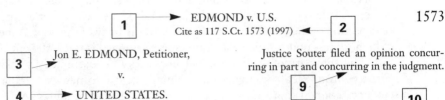

EDMOND v. U.S.   1573
Cite as 117 S.Ct. 1573 (1997)

Jon E. EDMOND, Petitioner,

v.

UNITED STATES.

Jake A. LAZENBY, Petitioner,

v.

UNITED STATES.

Michael B. LEAVER, Petitioner,

v.

UNITED STATES.

James A. LEONARD, Petitioner,

v.

UNITED STATES.

Robert J. NICHOLS, Petitioner,

v.

UNITED STATES.

Donald H. VENABLE, Petitioner,

v.

UNITED STATES.
No. 96-262.
Argued Feb. 24, 1997.
Decided May 19, 1997.

Coast Guard members who were convicted by court-martial and whose convictions were affirmed, in whole or in part, by Coast Guard Court of Criminal Appeals, appealed their convictions. The Court of Appeals for the Armed Forces affirmed, 45 M.19, and Coast Guard members sought review in consolidated petition for writ of certiorari. After writ was granted, the Supreme Court, Justice Scalia, held that: (1) appointment of judges of Coast Guard Court of Criminal Appeals is vested by statute in Secretary of Transportation, and (2) judge of Court of Criminal Appeals is "inferior officer" for purposes of appointments clause, so that grant of authority to appoint to Secretary of Transportation does not violate appointments clause.

Affirmed.

Justice Souter filed an opinion concurring in part and concurring in the judgment.

1. Armed Services ⇨ **43**
Uniform Code of Military Jusrice (UCMJ) does not give Judge Advocates General authority to appoint judges to military Courts of Criminal Appeals, and instead, such authroity is vested by statute in Secretary of Transportation. UCMJ, Art. 66(a), 10 U.S.C.A. § 866(a); Interstate Commerce Act, § 223(a), as amended, 49 US.C.App. (1982 Ed.) § 323(a).

2. Statutes ⇨ **223.4**
Odinarily, where specific statutory provision conflicts with general one, the specific governs.

3. Constitutional Law ⇨ **48(1)**
Court must avoid interpreting statute in manner tht would render it clearly unconstitutional if there is another reasonable interpretation available.

4. Constitutional Law ⇨ **46(1)**
Constitutional question confronted in order to preserve, if possible, congressional enactment is not constitutional question confronted unnecessarily.

5. United States ⇨ **35**
Appointments clause of Article II is more than matter of etiquette or protocol, but rather is among significant structural safeguards of constitutional scheme, and by vesting President with exclusive power to select principle, or noninferior, officers of the United States, appointments clause prevents congressional encroachment upon Executive and Judicial Branches. U.S.C.A. Const. Art. 2, § 2, cl. 2.

6. United States ⇨ **35**
Grant of authority to select principal officers of the United States to the President under appointments clause was designed to assure higher quality of appointments, as framers anticipated that President would be less vulnerable to interest-group pressure and personal favoritism than would collective body. U.S.C.A. Const. Art. 2, § 2, cl. 2.

16

117 SUPREME COURT REPORTER

22

45 M.J. 19 (first judgment), 44 M.J. 273 (second, third, fifth, and sixth judgments), and 44 M.J. 272 (fourth judgment), affirmed.

SCALIA, J., delivered the opinion of the Court, in which REHNQUIST, C.J., and STEVENS, O'CONNOR, KENNEDY, THOMAS, GINSBURG, and BREYER, J.J., joined, and in which SOUTER, J., joined as to Parts I and II. SOUTER, J., filed an opinion concurring in part and concurring in the judgment.

17

Alan B. Morrison, Washington, DC, for petitioners.

Malcolm L. Stewart, Washington, DC, for respondent.

18

For U.S. Supreme Court briefs, see:
1996 WL 739245 (Pet. Brief).
1997 WL 33018 (Resp. Brief).
1997 WL 63403 (Reply.Brief).

19

Justice SCALIA delivered the opinion of the Court.

We must determine in this case whether Congress has authorized the Secretary of Transportation to appoint civilian members of the Coast Guard Court of Criminal Appeals, and if so, whether this authorization is constitutional under the Appointments Clause of Article II.

20

21

I

The Coast Guard Court of Criminal Appeals (formerly known as the Coast Guard Court of Military Reviwe) is an intermediate court within the military justice system. It is one of four military Courts of Criminal Appeals; others exist for the Army, the Air Force, and the Navy–Marine Corps. The Coast Guard Court of Criminal Appeals hears appeals from the decisions of courts-martial, and its decisions are subject to review by the United States Court of Appeals for the Armed Forces (formerly known as the United States Court of Military Appeals).[1]

Appellate military judges who are assigned to a Court of Criminal Appeals must be members of the bar, but may be commissioned officers or civilians. Art. 66(a). Uniform Code of Military Justice (UCMJ), 10 U.S.C. § 866(a). During the times relevant to this case, the Coast Guard Court of Criminal Appeals has had two civilian members, Chief Judge Joseph H. Baum and Associate Judge Alfred F. Bridgman, Jr. These judges were originally assigned to serve on the court by the General Counsel of the Department of Transportation, who is, ex officio, the Judge Advocate General of the Coast Guard, Art. 1(1), UCMJ, 10 U.S.C. § 801(1). Subsequent events, however, called into question the validity of these assignments.

In *Weiss v. United States*, 510 U.S. 163, 114 S.Ct. 752, 127 L.Ed.2d 1 (1994), we considered whether the assignment of commissioned military officers to serve as military judges without reappointment under the Appointments Clause was constitutional. We held that military trial and appellate judges are officers of the United States and must be appointed pursuant to the Appointments Clause. *Id.*, at 170, 114 S.Ct., at 757. We upheld the judicial assignments at issue in *Weiss* because each of the military judges had been previously appointed by the President as a commissioned military officer, and was serving on active duty under that commission at the time he was assigned to a military court. We noted, however, that "allowing civilians to be assigned to Courts of Military Review, without being appointed pursuant to the Appointments Clause, obviously presents a quite different question. *Id.*, at 170, n. 4, 114 S.Ct., at 757, n. 4.

In anticipation of our decision in *Weiss*, Chief Judge Baum sent a memorandum to the Chief Counsel of the Coast Guard requesting that the Secretary, in his capacity as a department head, reappoint the judges so the court would be constitutionally valid beyond any doubt. See *United States v. Senior*, 36 M.J. 1016, 1018 (C.G.C.M.R.1993). On January 15, 1993, the Secretary of Transportation issued a memorandum "adopting"

1. The names of the Courts of Military Review and the United States Court of Military Appeals were changed, effective October 5, 1994, by Pub.L. 103–337, § 924, 108 Stat. 2831.

nine justices. Justices who disagree with the decision may file a *dissent*, which explains their reason for disagreeing. Justices who agree with a decision, but who have a different basis for reaching that decision, may state their reasons in a *concurring opinion*.

(10) Next appear constitutional provisions and laws relevant to the case.

(11) The West Publishing Company inserts a topic (in this case *Armed Services*) *followed by a* key symbol (⟳). The key symbol is an indexing tool. It means that in this or other volumes that West publishes, information relevant to this topic may be found under the heading *Armed Services*.

(12) The information listed here includes general principles of law that would normally be applicable to the case.

(13, 14, and 15) There is a hierarchy of constitutional law. This means that the Constitution is the supreme law of the land, followed by treaties, acts of Congress and federal regulations, followed next by state and then local law. Any provision of a lower level, such as local ordinances, that conflict with higher level laws (such as state statutes) are invalid with respect to the inconsistency between them.

(16) The Supreme Court frequently refers to statutes and judgments of lower courts. A court may make several judgments about several different issues in a single case. This citation means that the Supreme Court is referring to the second, third, fifth, and sixth judgments in military justice (MJ) cases cited as *45 M.J. 19 and 44 M.J. 273*.

(17) In Supreme Court cases, one justice is selected to write the opinion, although she or he may ask the advice of the others. Justice Scalia wrote this unanimously approved decision, and Justice Souter filed a concurring opinion.

(18 and 19) The attorneys representing each side in the case are listed next, along with the city in which their law practice is based. The numbers assigned by the Court to the briefs (written arguments) submitted to the Court by the attorneys on each side are listed.

(20 and 21) Justice Scalia begins his decision by referring to the constitutional principle at issue in the case, and then proceeds to describe the circumstances under which the case arose.

(22) The justice who writes the decision normally reviews the major factors in deciding the case, including relevant sections of the constitution, the facts of the dispute, the strengths and weaknesses of arguments on both sides, and the reasons for which the Court has come to a particular decision. In stating its reasons, the Court will cite its previous decisions, writings of the authors of the Constitution, current social conditions, and many other factors.

Glossary

accountability   The obligation to perform responsibly and exercise authority in terms of established performance standards.

accreditation   The status achieved by a correctional program, police agency, court, or other facility when it is recognized as having met certain national standards following an on-site audit by the relevant commission on accreditation.

accusation   A formal charge against a person inferring that he or she may be guilty of a punishable offense.

accusatory instrument   As usually defined, an indictment, information, simplified traffic information, prosecutor's information, misdemeanor complaint, or felony complaint. Every accusatory instrument, regardless of the person designated therein as the accuser, constitutes an accusation on behalf of the state as plaintiff and must be entitled "the people of the state of..." against a designated person, known as the *defendant*.

accusatory stage   In police practice, the investigation that occurs after suspicion has focused on one or more particular individuals as having guilty knowledge of the offense. Distinguished from the investigatory stage, during which the offense is the subject of general investigation before suspicion has focused on a particular accused. Also use to mean the stages in a criminal prosecution from arrest to conviction or acquittal.

accused   The generic name for the defendant in a criminal case.

acquittal   A legal and formal certification of the innocence of a person charged.

act of God   An act occasioned exclusively by violence of nature without the interference of any human agency; an act, event, happening, or occurrence due to natural causes.

actus reus   The criminal act; the act of a person committing a crime.

adaptative behaviors   Various responses through which inmates adjust to the institutional setting, including such psychological defense mechanisms as rejecting authority, projecting blame, or rationalization.

addict   Someone who has a physical and psychological dependence on one or more drug(s), who has built up a physical tolerance that results in taking increasingly larger doses, and who has an overpowering desire to continue taking the drug(s). One can become addicted to illegal as well as legal drugs (such as alcohol).

adjudicate   To determine finally; to adjudge.

adjudication   Giving or pronouncing a judgment or decree in a cause; also, the judgment given. The equivalent of "determination"; the formal finding of guilt or innocence by a court of law. The stage that would be considered "trial" in the criminal justice system, which in juvenile court refers to a hearing to establish the facts of the case.

administration   The act of administering, or the state of being administered. Management of direction of affairs; the total activity of a manager.

administrative remedies   Formal administrative mechanisms used within correctional institutions to proactively reduce litigation, such as the implementation of grievance procedures to identify and address complaints.

administrative segregation   Separate confinement for inmates who, for any of a number of reasons, need closer attention or supervision than is available in the general population.

administrative sentencing model   A sentencing plan in which legislatures and judges prescribe boundaries but administrative agencies determine the actual length of sentence.

adversary   An opponent; the opposite party in a writ or action.

adversary proceeding   One having opposing parties, as distinguished from an ex-parte proceeding.

adversary process   The view of criminal justice as a contest between the government and the individual.

adversary system   The practice of conducting a legal proceeding as a battle between opposing parties under the judge as an impartial umpire with the outcome determined by the pleading and evidence introduced into courts; in Anglo-American jurisprudence includes the presumption of innocence of the accused. To be distinguished from the accusatory system used in continental law, where the accusation is taken as evidence of guilt that must be disproved by the accused.

advocate   One who assists, defends, or pleads for another.

affidavit   A written or printed declaration or statement of facts, taken before an officer having authority to administer oaths.

affirmative action   Programs instituted by government to increase the number of minority employees in the public and private sectors.

aftercare   Follow-up services and supervision provided upon release from a juvenile correctional institution, similar to parole or supervised mandatory release in the adult system.

aggravated assault   Assault with intent to kill or for the purpose of inflicting severe bodily injury; assault with the use of a deadly weapon.

aggregate crime rates   The number of crimes per 100,000 of the general population.

aggregate data   Data on large numbers of subjects showing a common characteristic.

aggressive field investigation   An investigatory model in which police consistently check out suspicious circumstances, places, and persons.

alcoholism   The disease associated with abuse of legally available drugs (such as beer, wine, and/or liquor). Tendencies toward alcoholism may be inherited genetically, as well as precipitated by social and psychological factors.

alias   Otherwise, in another manner; a fictitious name.

alienist   One who specializes in the study of mental disease.

allocution   The court's inquiry of a prisoner as to whether he or she has any legal cause why judgment should not be pronounced against him or her upon conviction.

alternative dispute resolution   A type of formal diversion in which a neutral third party attempts to reach an agreeable compromise between the victim and the offender to resolve the case outside the criminal justice system.

amicus curiae   A friend of the court. Also, a person who has no right to appear in a suit but is allowed to introduce argument, authority, or evidence to protect his interest.

anomie   The weakening of social norms, which has been linked with crime and delinquency.

anonymity   The assurance that research subjects' identities will not be disclosed.

anthropology   A discipline focusing on the nature of human culture, in which field research is the primary method of study.

appeal   The removal of a case from a court of inferior jurisdiction to one of superior jurisdiction for the purpose of obtaining a review and retrial.

appearance   The coming into court as party to a suit.

appearance ticket   A written notice issued by a public servant, requiring a person to appear before a local criminal court in connection with an accusatory instrument to be filed against him therein.

appellant   The party who takes an appeal from one court of justice to another. In criminal law, usually the defendant in the lower court.

appellant jurisdiction   The right of a court to review the decision of a lower court; the power to hear cases appealed from a lower court.

appellee   The party in a cause against whom an appeal is taken; in criminal law, usually the state or the United States.

applied research   Research for which one of the primary purposes is that the study may have some practical use.

archival research   A method of studying organizations or societies based on the collected records they have produced.

argot   The unique vocabulary used in communication between inmates and street criminals.

arraign   To bring a prisoner before the court to answer an indictment or information. In practice, used to refer to any appearance of the accused before a magistrate or before a trial court to enter a plea. *See also* arraignment.

arraignment   The proceeding for arraignment of the accused at which he enters a plea to the charge.

arrest   The taking of a person into custody to answer to a criminal charge. A detention of a suspect subject to investigation and prosecution.

arson   The intentional and unlawful burning of property. At common law, the malicious burning of the dwelling or outhouse of another.

asportation   The removal of things from one place to another, such as required in the offense of larceny in some states.

assault   The intentional unlawful use of force by one person upon another. If severe bodily harm is inflicted or a weapon is used, the offense is *aggravated assault*. The lesser degree of the crime is called assault or *simple assault*.

assault and battery   A battery is an unlawful touching of the person of another. *See also* assault.

assessment   A screening procedure in which a candidate's strengths and weaknesses are evaluated by a team of trained assessors on the basis of performance.

assessment center   The place where screening procedure or assessment is implemented.

atavistic   Having the characteristics of savages, as in early forms of human evolution.

attrition   The loss of members of a sample, usually as a result of their refusal to respond or the researcher's inability to contact them.

attrition of cases   Cases dropped at various stages in the criminal process.

Auburn system   The approach that focused on congregate work and harsh discipline, as practiced at the correctional facility in Auburn, New York.

authority   The sum of the powers and rights assigned to a position, such as a chief of police or a warden.

auto theft   Stealing or driving away and abandoning a motor vehicle. May exclude taking for temporary use, or the taking for temporary use may carry a smaller penalty.

back-door strategy   Reducing a prison population by the early release of prisoners.

background forces   Psychological, biological, and sociological causes of crime.

bail   To procure the release of a person from legal custody by instructing that he or she must appear at the time and place designated and submit himself or herself to the jurisdiction and judgment of the court.

bail bond   A bond executed by a defendant who has been arrested, together with other persons as sureties, naming the sheriff, constable, or marshal as obligee, to receive a court-specified sum on condition that the defendant must appear to answer the legal process.

bailee   One to whom goods are delivered under a contract or agreement of bailment.

bailor   One who delivers goods under a contract or agreement of bailment.

bailment A delivery of goods or personal property by one person to another to carry out a special purpose and redeliver the goods to the bailor.

banishment and exile (also called *transportation*) Forms of punishment in which offenders were transported from Europe to distant lands (such as the Americas and Australia).

bar graph A graph on which the categories of a variable are presented on the horizontal axis and their frequencies on the vertical axis. The height of each bar represents the frequency of each attribute of a variable. The bars have gaps between them on the scale.

basic research Research whose primary purpose is to contribute to systematic knowledge in a discipline.

behavior modification Changing behavior through the conditioning power of such reinforcements as rewards and punishments.

bench warrant A process issued by the court itself, or "from the bench," for the attachment or arrest of a person; either in case of contempt, or whether an indictment has been found, or to bring in a witness who does not obey a subpoena. So called to distinguish it from a warrant issued by a justice of the peace or magistrate.

beyond a reasonable doubt Proof to a moral certainty, satisfying the judgment and consciences of the jury, as reasonable men and women, that the crime charged has been committed by the defendant. Moral certainty is not a requirement in some states.

bivariate table A two-variable table.

bond Money or property required to obtain release from jail for a criminal charge in order to assure appearance at trial.

booking Creating an administrative record of an arrest. The clerical process involving the entry on the police "blotter" or arrest book of the suspect's name, the time of the arrest, the offense charged, and the name of the arresting officer. Used in practice to refer to the police-station-house procedures that take place from arrest to the initial appearance of the accused before the magistrate.

brainstorming The exploration, discovery, and development of details to be used in a research study.

breach of the peace A violation or disturbance of the public tranquility and order.

breaking and entering Any unlawful entry even if no force was used to gain entrance.

building-tender system Where prisoners assist officers in managing cell blocks.

burglary Breaking and entering with intent to commit a felony or theft, or in some states, with intent to commit any offense.

capability The range, variety, and depth of skills that a person holds in a certain job or position in the organization. It is also the sum total of the structure, process, and systems that make up the organization itself.

capacity The outside limits of a person or organization or population that determines the amount of accomplishment or production that can done. Capacity, for example, can be increased by adding resources, restructuring the application of resources, or increasing the capability of resources within the organization. In criminal justice, population capacity is usually a matter of law.

career criminals   Criminals who devote the greater part of their lives to crime.

career-criminal units   Prosecutors who specialize in the prosecution of repeat offenders.

carnal knowledge   Sexual intercourse; the slightest penetration of the sexual organ of the female by the sexual organ of the male.

carrying concealed weapons   All violations of regulations or status controlling the carrying, using, possessing, furnishing, and manufacturing of deadly weapons.

case   A general term for an action, cause, suit, or controversy in law or equity; a question contested before a court of justice.

case studies   Observational studies of a single environment (a detention center, a police precinct, a public place). Field research is often based on a single case study.

caseload   The workload of a probation (or parole) officer, usually measured by the number of cases being supervised and/or investigated.

caseload classification (also called *case management*)   Separating cases according to the intensity of supervision needed by the client.

causation   One or more variables produces a result. *See also* independent variable.

cell   In a cross-classification table, the position where two categories meet. In a 2×3 bivariate table, there will be six cells. Also, an inmate's living quarters.

cell searches (also called *shakedowns*)   A thorough examination of the structure and contents of a cell to detect and remove any contraband items. Searches may be conducted routinely, randomly, or based on suspicion, but not for harassment.

central intake (often called a *diagnostic* or *reception center*)   The place where new inmates are received, processed, tested, and assigned to housing.

certification   Using a legal process to treat juveniles as adults for criminal prosecution.

certiorari   To be informed of, to be made certain in regard to. The name of a writ of review or inquiry; a writ directed by a superior court to an inferior court asking that the record of a case be sent up for review; a method of obtaining a review of a case by the U.S. Supreme Court.

change of venue   The removal of a action begun in one county or district to another county or district for trial.

charge   To initiate formal criminal court proceedings; to impose a burden, duty, or obligation; to claim, demand, or accuse; to instruct a jury on matters of law.

charge bargaining   Plea negotiations over the charge the government will file.

chronic stress   The stress associated with the long-term effect of experiencing continual pressures and problems in the work environment.

circumstances   The attendant facts. Any fact may be a circumstance with reference to another fact.

circumstantial evidence   All evidence of an indirect nature. The existence of a principal fact is inferred from circumstances.

citation   An order to appear in court; or, in writing, the citation of a documentable source.

citizen   One who under the constitution and laws of the United States or of a particular state is a member of the political community.

civil liability   Being held accountable in a civil court of law, where nominal, compensatory, and/or punitive damages can be awarded against those held liable for actions or in actions that resulted in harm, injury, or death.

civilian review boards   Commissions set up outside the police or corrections department to hear and review citizen complaints against the police or the correctional system.

classification   The separation of inmates at all levels into groups according to characteristics that they share in common.

client   Someone who is under the care, custody, or control of a correctional agency.

closed-ended question   Questions in a questionnaire that force the respondent to select from a list of possible responses (also called *forced-choice questions*).

co-correctional institutions (also known as coed prisons)   Correctional facilities where both men and women are housed within one compound. Although they do not share living quarters in the United States, males and females interact socially and have access to the same institutional programs.

coercion   Compulsion, constraint, or compelling by force.

cognitive dissonance   A perceived discrepancy between what is stated to be reality and what is reality in fact.

colloquy   The formal discussion between judge and defendant to determine if defendants have pleaded knowingly and voluntarily.

commercial bail   The private business of bail bonding.

common law   A custom translated into law over time and social circumstances.

communication and feedback systems   The kind and amount of information flow among people, within an organization, and between an organization and people.

community policing   Citizen participation in setting police priorities and police operations.

community residential centers   Minimum-security community-based residential facilities that typically provide such programs as work release, drug treatment, and educational opportunity.

community service internships   Field experiences offering officers or students opportunities to gain broad perspectives on crime and criminal law enforcement.

community-based supervision   Services, programs, or facilities provided within the community to offenders who are not incarcerated in high-security confinement.

complaint   In criminal law, a charge preferred before a magistrate having jurisdiction that a person named has committed a specific offense. Usually, the first document filed with a court charging the offense. In some states, the term *complaint* is interchangeable with information; it is also sometimes used interchangeably with *affidavit. See also* information.

concept   A general idea in management stated in a formalized manner so that it can be communicated in a standardized fashion.

concurrent sentences   Sentences run at the same time and each day served by the prisoner is credited on each of the concurrent sentences.

conditional release   The release of an offender from incarceration under certain conditions, violation of which allows for reactivation of the unserved portion of the sentence.

conditioning   The expectation that a certain reaction will follow a certain stimulus, which is reinforced by repetition of the stimulus/response pattern.

conflict perspective   Conflict, not agreement, is the normal state of society. Crime is the product of the power structure.

conglomerate   A complex organization composed of numerous diverse functions.

conjugal visits   The authorization of visits that involve sexual intimacy.

consecutive sentences   Sentences that are served one after the other. Inmates refer to such sentences as *stacked* or as *boxcars*.

consensus perspective   General agreement on values in society.

consensus prison management   A balance of control and responsibility management.

consent decree   A response to a lawsuit whereby the court agrees to delay direct intervention in exchange for voluntary compliance with certain stipulated conditions.

consent search   A search conducted with knowing and voluntary consent.

consistent supervisory style   An approach to inmate management in which the correctional officer responds in a uniform manner whenever similar situations are encountered.

conspiracy   The agreement between or among parties to commit a crime.

constructive intent   The conscious or unconscious creation of risk of harm.

contact visits   The authorization of physical contact (within specified limits) during visits in jails and correctional centers.

contempt   A willful disregard or disobedience of a public authority.

contempt of court   Any act that is calculated to embarrass, hinder, or obstruct the court in the administration of justice, or which is calculated to lessen its authority or dignity. Directed contempts (also called *criminal contempts*) are those committed in the immediate view of the court (such as insulting language or acts of violence) and are punishable summarily. Constructive (or indirect) contempts are those which arise from matters not occurring in or near the presence of the court but with reference to the failure or refusal of a party to obey a lawful or decree of court.

contempt powers   The power of a court to punish for contempt. A court of record has this power.

contingency contracting   An agreement between parties (e.g., an inmate and the correctional administration) whereby one agrees to take specified action if the other meets certain conditions stipulated in the contract.

contraband   Any item that people are not authorized to possess, or an authorized item that is altered from its original state.

contract labor   The practice of using prisoners to work under contract to private industry.

control model of management   Prison management emphasizing obedience, work, and education of prisoners.

controlled movement   Restricting freedom of movement to better ensure institutional security.

controlling   Making certain that plans succeed by measuring and correcting activities of employees. Controlling is closely related to the organizational planning system.

conventional goals   Socially established goals (such as money, status, and prestige) that are recognized as desirable throughout society.

conviction   In a general sense, the result of a criminal trial that ends in a judgment or sentence that the person is guilty as charged.

corpus delicti   The body of the crime; the essential elements of the crime; the substantial fact that a crime has been committed; the actual commission by someone of the offense charged.

correctional boot camps   Shock incarceration for youthful first-time nonviolent offenders.

correlation   An association, but not necessarily causal.

count   The plaintiff's statement of his or her cause of action. Also used to specify the several parts of an indictment or information, each charging a distinct offense. Often used synonymously with the word *charge*.

counts   Periodic verifications of the total number of inmates in custody.

court above, court below   In appellate practice, the court above is the one to which a cause is removed for review, whether by appeal, writ of error, or certiorari; while the court below is the one from which the case is removed.

court of appeal   An appellate tribunal; the name given to the court of last resort in several states; the court of last resort of a particular type of case; or in some states, an intermediate appellate court below the supreme court.

court of common pleas   In English law, one of the four superior courts at Westminster. In U.S. law, the name given to a court of original and general jurisdiction for the trial of issues and law. The superior court of the District of Columbia is called the Court of Common Pleas.

court of competent jurisdiction   One having power and authority of law at the time of acting to do the particular act.

court of errors and appeals   The court of last resort in the state of New Jersey. Formerly, the same title was given to the highest court of appeal in New York.

court of general sessions   The name given in some states to a court of general original jurisdiction in criminal cases.

court of record   A court in which appeals are heard on the record. A court whose judicial acts and proceedings are recorded which has the power to fine or imprison for contempt.

court of special sessions   A court of inferior criminal jurisdiction in Oklahoma. Jurisdiction roughly equivalent to that of a justice of the peace.

court of star chamber   An English court of very ancient origin. Originally, its jurisdiction extended legally over riots, perjury, misbehavior of sheriffs, and other misdemeanors contrary to the laws of the land; afterward, stretched to the asserting of all orders of state; becoming both a court of law to determine civil rights and a court of revenue to enrich the treasury. It was finally abolished "to the general satisfaction of the whole nation."

court martial   A military court convened under the authority of the government and the Uniform Code of Military Justice for trying and punishing offenses committed by members of the armed forces.

courts of appeals   A system of courts of the U.S. (one in each circuit) created by act of Congress, composed of three or more judges (provision also being made for allotment of the justices of the Supreme Court among the circuits) and having appellate jurisdiction as defined by statute. Called the U.S. Courts of Appeals; formerly called the Circuit Courts of Appeals or U.S. Circuit Courts of Appeals.

courts of the United States   Comprise the Senate of the United States as a Court of Impeachment, the U.S. Supreme Court, the courts of appeals, the district courts, the court of claims, the court of customs and patent appeals, the customs court, the tax court, the provisional courts, and courts of territories and outlying possessions.

crime   An act in violation of penal law. An offense against the state.

crime control   The value or goal of reducing crime, emphasizing informal discretionary decision making.

crime control model   Values discretion to quickly sort out factually innocent from factually guilty.

crimes cleared by arrest   Crimes known to the police but removed from active police records.

criminal   One who has committed a criminal offense. One who has been legally convicted of a crime. One adjudged guilty of a crime.

criminal action   The whole or any part of the procedure that law provides for bringing offenders to justice.

criminal charge   An accusation of crime in a written complaint, information, or indictment.

criminal court   A court charged with the administration of the criminal laws and empowered to sentence the guilty person to fine or imprisonment. In New York, the criminal courts are comprised of the superior and local criminal courts. *Superior court* means the supreme court or a county court. *Local criminal court* means a district court, or the New York City criminal court, or a city court, or a town court, or a village court, or a supreme court justice sitting as a local criminal court or a county judge sitting as a local criminal court.

criminal event   The commission of a specific crime.

criminal history   A record of prior offenses.

criminal homicide   All willful felonious homicides as distinguished from deaths caused by negligence.

criminal information   A formal accusation of crime, differing from an indictment only in that it is preferred by a prosecuting officer instead of a grand jury.

criminal intent   An intent to commit a crime; malice, as evidenced by a criminal act; an intent to deprive or defraud the true owner of his property.

criminal justice process   The sequence of steps taken from the initial contact of an offender with the law until he or she is released back into a free society.

criminal justice system   A loose confederation of agencies, including police, courts, and corrections.

criminal law   That branch or division of law that deals with crime and punishment.

criminal negligence   The unconscious creation of a high risk of harm.

criminal procedure   The law prescribing how the government enforces criminal law. A method for the apprehension, trial, prosecution, and fixing the punishment of persons who have broken the law.

criminal proceeding   One instituted and conducted for the purpose of preventing the commission of crime, of fixing guilt for a crime already committed, and of punishing the offender.

criminal prosecution   An action or proceeding instituted in a proper court on behalf of the public for the purpose of securing the conviction and punishment of one accused of crime.

criminal recklessness   The conscious creation of a high risk of harm.

criminogenic forces   The causes of crime in the society, such numerous variables as poverty, socioeconomic status, or physical or mental impairment, among many others.

cross examination   The examination of a witness in a trial or hearing by the party opposed to the one who produced him, on the evidence given; to test its truth, to further develop it, or for other relevant purposes.

crowded prisoners   Prisoners who must live in less than 60 square feet of floor space.

curfew offenses   Offenses relating to violation of local curfew or loitering ordinances which provide regulations as to when a person (usually a juvenile) may lawfully be on the streets.

curtilage   The enclosed space of ground and buildings immediately surrounding the dwelling house.

custodial institution   A secure physical structure where offenders are confined with strict limitations on their access to free society.

cycle of violence   The hypothesis that childhood abuse creates a predisposition to later violent behavior.

D.A.R.E. (Drug Abuse Resistance Education)   Specially trained police officers are assigned to schools to teach drug prevention.

day in court   The opportunity to present one's claim before a competent tribunal.

daylight   That portion of time after sunrise and before sunset. Nighttime is the period between sunset and sunrise. Often important as to assessment of the degree of criminal culpability.

dealer   In the popular sense, one who buys to sell—not one who buys to keep.

decision-making process   Consists of who decides what is going to be done with the plan, how they decide, when and how fast they decide, and how their decisions will be put into action. Decision making also means who is going to solve problems and in what ways these problems are going to be solved.

decree   The judgment of the court; a declaration of the court announcing the legal consequences of the facts found.

decriminalization   Removing status offenses from juvenile jurisdiction.

defendant   The person defending or denying; the party against whom relief or recovery is sought in an action or suit. In criminal law, the party charged with a crime.

defense   In a criminal action, the answer made by the defendant to the state's case.

defense attorney   The attorney representing the accused in a criminal action.

defenses of excuse   To admit to the wrongfulness of crime but deny responsibility.

defenses of justification   To admit to the crime but assert that it was morally or ethically right to do it.

deferred release decisions   The setting of release after the determination that a prisoner has reformed and/or completed a task or judicial assignment.

deinstitutionalization   Community-based noninstitutional treatment as an alternative to incarceration.

delegation   The work a manager performs to entrust responsibility and authority to others and to create accountability for results. For example, a state director of corrections delegates authority and responsibility to a warden or area superintendent.

deliberate   As applied to a jury, the weighing of the evidence and the law for the purpose of determining the guilt or innocence of a defendant. In the case of jury sentencing, the deliberation may be for the purpose of fixing the sentence.

delinquency   Behavior that would be criminal if committed by adults.

delinquent juvenile   A person of no more than a specific age who has violated any law or ordinance or is incorrigible; a person who has been adjudicated a delinquent child by a juvenile court while of juvenile court age.

density   The number of square feet of floor space per prisoner.

deprivation model   An explanation of the prisonization process which maintains that it is a function of adapting to an abnormal environment that is characterized by numerous deprivations.

descriptive guidelines   Sentencing ranges based on actual past sentence practices.

detainer   A kind of "hold order" filed against an incarcerated man by another state or jurisdiction, which seeks to take the person into custody to answer to another criminal charge or conviction whenever he is released from the current imprisonment.

detention centers   Secure, temporary holding facilities, usually designated for juvenile offenders. A municipal jail.

diagnostic reception center   A central intake location where newly arriving inmates are interviewed, tested, examined, and evaluated for classification purposes.

differential association   Criminal behavior depends on association.

differential response   Police response to routine calls differs from that to emergency calls.

diminished capacity   Mental impairment less disabling than insanity.

direct evidence   That means of proof which tends to show the existence of a fact in question without the intervention of the proof of any other fact. Is distinguished from circumstantial evidence, which is often called *indirect*.

direct examination   In practice, the first interrogation or examination of a witness, on the merits, by the party on whose behalf he is called.

direct information   Facts known by direct knowledge.

direct supervision   Officers are in constant direct contact with the prisoners they supervise.

directing   Guiding, overseeing, coaching, and leading people toward goals and objectives while staying within the policies, procedures, and standards of the organization. Directing, more than any other management function, involves functional personal relationships.

discharge   The removal of a client from supervision, generally as a result of satisfactory completion of the conditions of probation or parole.

discretion   Decision making without formal recourse to laws and other written rules.

disorderly conduct   Conduct against public order. Sometimes used synonymously with *breach of peace*, although not all disorderly conduct is a breach of peace.

disposition hearing   To determine what treatment and custody should follow finding of delinquency.

district attorney   In many states, a district attorney or an assistant district attorney, and where appropriate, the attorney general or an assistant attorney general.

diversion   Removal from juvenile justice system to alternative programs, or transferring defendants into some alternative to criminal prosecution.

doubt   Uncertainty of mind; the absence of a settled opinion or conviction; the state of the case which, after the entire comparison and consideration of the evidence, leaves the minds of the jurors in such a condition that they cannot say with a moral certainty, of the truth of the charge. If upon proof there is a reasonable doubt remaining, the accused is entitled to the benefit of an acquittal.

dual system of justice   Separate systems for adults and juveniles.

duces tecum   From the Latin "bring with you." A subpoena *duces tecum* requires a party to appear in court and bring with him certain documents, pieces of evidence, or other matters to be inspected by the court.

due process   The value of formal rules and procedures to limit the power of government and protect the rights of individuals.

due process clause   The guarantee of fair procedures and protection of life, liberty, and property.

due process model   Emphasizes formal legal adversary process at the heart of the criminal process.

due process of law   The fundamental rights of the accused to a fair trial; the prescribed forms of conducting a criminal prosecution; the safeguards and protection of the law given to one accused of a crime. In substantive criminal law, the right to have crimes and punishments clearly defined in the law. Government can act only according to rules.

due process revolution   The expansion by the Supreme Court during the 1960s of the rights of criminal defendants and the application of the rights to state proceedings.

duress   To commit a crime under coercion.

d. w. i. (driving while intoxicated)   Driving or operating any motor vehicle while drunk or under the influence of liquor or narcotics.

effectiveness   The measurement of a program, plan, or effort in terms of its result or impact and not in terms of its resource cost. A program could, therefore, be highly effective (in terms of client service) but not efficient in terms of dollars, time, or other costs. Usually, programs are best measured in terms of both effectiveness and efficiency in order to attain a favorable benefit-cost ratio. However, this is not always possible in matters of custody or treatment.

efficiency   Planning in an organization and its work so that objectives can be attained with the lowest possible costs, which may mean money costs, human costs, or other resource costs.

embezzlement   The misappropriation or misapplication of money or property entrusted into one's care, custody, or control.

empiricism   The idea that all knowledge results from sense experience; a scientific method that relies on direct observation and the analysis of data.

equal protection of the law   Prevents unreasonable classifications.

et al.   And elsewhere; and others.

ethnographic study   Research by intensive field observation and interviews.

ethnography   The observational description of a people or some other social unit.

evaluation, impact   Showing whether the program, after implementation, has helped or not helped the group of people for whom the program was intended. Sometimes referred to as *product evaluation*.

evaluation, process   Assessment of a plan during the time it is being implemented. Process evaluation should be done at least weekly, and some critical parts of the plan should be assessed daily. This allows the planner to stay "on top" of the plan as it is being put into action.

evaluation research   Research to measure the effectiveness of a social program or institution.

evidence   Any species of proof, presented at the trial for the purpose of inducing belief in the minds of the court or jury.

ex parte   On one side only; by or for one party; done for; in behalf of, or on the application, of one party only.

ex post facto   After the fact.

ex post facto design   An after-only evaluation research design where pretesting is not possible.

ex post facto law   A law passed after the occurrence of a fact or commission of an act that retrospectively changes the legal consequences or relations of such fact or deed. A retroactive laws. Forbidden to both the states and the federal government by the U.S. Constitution.

ex rel   By or on the information of. Used in case title to designate the person at whose instance the government or public official is acting.

exception, management by   A feature of delegation where routine and frequently recurring matters should be handled by subordinates, allowing the manager to concentrate time and energies on exceptional and very important matters.

exclusionary rule   The rule that excludes from the trial of an accused, evidence illegally seized or obtained; prohibiting the use of illegally obtained evidence to prove guilt.

exclusive jurisdiction   The sole authority to hear and decide cases.

executive clemency or pardon   The authority of presidents and governors to eliminate a sentence.

existing statistics   Created statistical data that are available to researchers for analysis.

experiment   A research method that seeks to isolate the effects of an independent variable on a dependent variable under strictly controlled conditions.

experimental group   The group in an experiment that is exposed to the experimental treatment.

experimental mortality   Loss of subjects in an experiment over time. This is a potential cause of internal validity problems.

expert evidence   The testimony given in relation to some scientific, technical, or professional matter by experts (i.e. persons qualified to speak authoritatively by reason of their special training, skill, or familiarity with the subject).

expert witness   One who gives the results of a process of reasoning that can be mastered only by special scientists; one who has skilled experience or extensive knowledge in his calling or in any branch of learning; person competent to give expert testimony.

express bargaining A direct meeting to decide concessions.

external validity The generalizability of an experiment to other settings, other treatments, other subjects.

face validity A form of content validity; a careful consideration and examination of the measurement instrument is made to determine whether the instrument is measuring what it purports to measure.

face-to-face interview A method of administering a survey in which an interviewer questions an interviewee using a structured set of questions. *See also* interview schedule.

factorial design The design of an experiment in which more than one independent variable is being measured.

factual guilt Defendant has actually committed a crime, or has knowledge of guilt but not necessarily provable in court.

family crime Crimes against people known to the offender.

federal question A case that contains a major issue involving the U.S. Constitution or statutes. The jurisdiction of the federal courts is governed, in part, by the existence of a federal question.

federalism The division of power between federal and state governments.

felonies Serious crimes punishable by one year or more in prison. Crimes of a graver or more atrocious nature than those designated as a misdemeanor.

felony complaint A verified written accusation by a person, filed with a local criminal court, which charges one or more defendants with the commission of one or more felonies and which serves to begin a criminal action but not as a basis for prosecution thereof.

field experiment An experiment taking place in a real-world environment, where it is more difficult to impose controls.

field research A research method based on careful observation of behavior in a natural social environment.

focus group A small group of individuals drawn together to express views on a specific set of questions in a group environment. This method may serve a number of functions in social research; as a starting point for developing a survey, to recognize potential problems in a research design, or to interpret evidence.

follow-up research procedures The methods of following up nonrespondents to mail questionnaires to increase response rate. Methods include sending postcard reminders, sending second questionnaires and request, and telephoning to solicit cooperation or to get the responses over the telephone.

forcible rape Rape by force, or against the consent of the victim.

forecasting The work a manager performs to estimate the future.

forgery Making, altering, uttering (passing), or possessing anything false that is made to appear true, with intent to defraud.

formal criminal justice   The law and other written rules that determine the outer boundaries of action in criminal justice.

formalization   Replacing discretion with rules.

formative evaluation   An evaluation of a program in process, information from which will be used to reform or improve the program. *See* summative evaluation.

frequency distribution   The distribution of cases across the categories of a variable, presented in numbers and percentages.

frisk search   The physical pat-down of a clothed subject to determine whether weapons or other contraband items are concealed externally within clothes, shoes, hair, mouth, and so on.

fruits of a crime   Material objects acquired by means of and in consequence of the commission of a crime, and sometimes constituting the subject matter of the crime.

function   The total of positions encompassing one kind of work grouped to form an administrative unit. A group or family of related kinds of management work, made up of activities that are closely related to one another and have characteristics in common derived from the essential nature of the work done.

functional unit management   A decentralized approach wherein a unit manager, case manager, and counselor, along with supportive custodial, clerical, and treatment personnel, maintain full responsibility for providing services, making decisions, and addressing the needs of inmates assigned to a living unit.

fundamental fairness doctrine   A due process definition focusing on substantive due process.

funnel effect   The result of sorting decisions that lead to fewer individuals remaining at successive stages in the criminal justice process.

furlough   The privilege granted of temporary release from confinement, with the understanding that an inmate will return to the institution at a given time.

gambling   Promoting, permitting, or engaging in gambling.

general deterrence   To prevent crime in general population by threatening punishment.

general intent   The intent to commit the actus reus.

general jurisdiction   The authority to hear and decide all criminal cases.

general population inmate   Prisoner without special problems.

general principles of criminal law   The broad general rules that provide the basis for other rules.

goal   The broadest, most long-range statement, in management terms, of the purpose or mission of an organization or unit within the organization. *See also* objective.

goal maintenance   The process of working toward an established goal according to a plan, the application and guidance of resources toward the goal, and assessment of the degree and rate of progress toward attainment of the goal. It is appropriate within this process to redefine or redevelop goals as necessary.

goal setting   The identification of individual or organizational purposes and intent; their specification as to time, resources needed, planning, and how to measure and report results.

good time   Days deducted from prison terms based on good behavior of prisoners.

good-time laws   The reduction of sentence length by one third or one half based on behavior in prison.

grand jury   A jury of inquiry authorized to return indictments. Citizens who test the government's case and agree or disagree on prosecutable indictments.

grand larceny   Larceny of the grade of felony, generally expressed in dollar value of amount stolen.

gross misdemeanors   Crimes punishable by jail terms of 30 days to a year.

group home   A relatively open, community-based facility.

guided discretion statutes   Laws requiring juries to use guidelines on mitigating and aggravating circumstances.

habeas corpus (literally, "you have the body")   *See* writ of habeas corpus.

halfway house   Institutions in the community for parolees and probationers.

hands-off doctrine   Prison management left to discretion of prison administrators.

Hawthorne principle   The finding that creation of a new and closely watched project produces temporary positive results.

hearing   In a broad sense, whatever takes place before a court or a magistrate clothed with judicial function and sitting without a jury. A trial is a hearing, but not all hearings require the formalities of a trial.

hearsay   Information acquired through a third person; evidence offered by someone who does not know its truth firsthand.

home confinement   A sentence to detention at home except for work, study, service, or treatment.

homicide   The killing of one human being by another.

homogeneous groups   In sampling, strata formed by sets of individuals who share certain characteristics (gender, race, age, etc.).

hung jury   A jury so irreconcilably divided in opinion that it cannot agree upon any verdict.

hypothesis   A conditional statement relating the expected effect of one variable on another, subject to testing.

impeachment   A criminal procedure against a public officer to remove him or her from office. In the law of evidence, the adducing of proof that a witness is unworthy of belief.

importation hypothesis   The theory that prison society has its roots in the criminal and conventional societies outside the prison.

in re   In the affair; in the matter of; concerning. This is the usual method of entitling a judicial proceeding in which there are no adversary parties. For this reason, used in the title of cases in a juvenile court.

incapacitation   To prevent crime by incarceration, mutilation, or capital punishment.

incident report   A patrol or a correctional officer's description of a crime or broken regulation, usually detailing witnesses and suspects.

incident-based reporting   Reporting of each offense separately, whether part of the same event or not.

incident-driven strategies   Isolated event determines response by officers.

incorporation doctrine   Due process focusing on procedural regularity.

independent variable   The variable, in an experiment or survey, that exercises an effect on a dependent variable. The *cause* in a cause-and-effect model.

indeterminate sentence   An open-ended penalty tailored to the needs of individual offenders.

index   A composite measure developed to represent different components of a concept.

index crimes   The crimes used by the Federal Bureau of Investigation in reporting the incidence of crime in the U.S. in the Uniform Crime Reports. The statistics on the Index Crimes are taken as an index of the incidence of crime in the U.S.

indicators   Observable phenomena that can be used to measure dimensions of a concept.

indictment   The formal accusation of a crime by a grand jury.

indigenous theory   The belief that conditions inside a prison shape prison society.

indigent defendants   Defendants too poor to afford a lawyer.

inducement test   Entrapment focusing on government actions.

infamous crime   A crime that reflects infamy on the one who has committed it; crimes punishable by imprisonment in the state prison or penitentiary. At common law, all felonies were considered to be infamous crimes.

inferences   An accurate guess or conclusion based on evidence gathered on a relatively small probability sample, extrapolated to a much larger population.

inferential statistics   Statistics that allow a researcher to draw conclusions regarding the general population from the findings of a representative sample drawn from that population; statistics that utilize probability in decision making; hypothesis-testing statistics.

informa pauperis   In the form of a pauper; as a poor person or indigent. Permission to bring legal action without the payment of required fees for counsel, writs, transcripts and the like.

information   An accusation exhibited against a person for some criminal offense, without an indictment. An accusation in the nature of an indictment, from which it differs only in being presented by a competent public officer on his or her oath of office, instead of a grand jury on their oath. Formal accusation of a crime by a prosecutor.

informed consent   This is achieved when subjects in a research study comprehend its objectives, understand their level of confidentiality, and agree to cooperate.

informer   A person who informs or prefers an accusation against another whom he or she suspects of a violation of some penal statute.

infraction   The name given to minor offenses (chiefly traffic offenses) in the California Infractions Code.

initial case screening   Prosecutors reviewing whether to charge, divert, or dismiss a case.

injunction   A writ prohibiting an individual or organization from performing some specified action.

insanity   The legal term excusing criminal liability; not synonymous with mental illness.

institutional review board   Committees in institutions where scientific research is being carried out who review the research methods to be sure that the rights of human (or animal) subjects are being protected.

institutional support   Prisoners who work in maintaining the jail to pay part of the expenses of incarceration.

instrumentalities of a crime   The tools or implements used to commit a crime.

intake   The initial juvenile court process following a serious infraction of the law, unless preceded by diversion.

intensity structure   The patterns that make best sense of the multiple items in a scale, and their interrelation.

intensive probation supervision   Closely supervised probation, stressing retribution, incapacitation, and economy.

interaction effect   The tendency for a third variable to interact with the independent variable, thereby altering the relationship of the independent variable to the dependent variable. This means that the relationship between the independent and dependent variables will vary under different conditions of the third variable.

intermediate appellate courts   Courts that hear initial appeals.

intermediate punishment   Sanctions somewhere between the extremes of incarceration and straight probation.

intermittent incarceration   Incarceration at night and on weekends with release for school, work, treatment, or community service.

internal affairs unit   Units created to investigate, report, and recommend with respect to civilian complaints against police officers.

internal grievance mechanisms   Procedures inside prisons for dealing with grievances.

internal validity   The extent to which an experiment actually has caused what it appeared to cause.

interrogation   The process used in questioning suspects, usually after arrest and prior to filing charges.

intersubjectivity   The shared perceptions of individual observers. The greater the intersubjectivity, the greater the validity and reliability of the observations.

intervening variable   A third variable in a trivariate study that logically falls in a time sequence between the independent and dependent variables.

interview schedule   A set of questions with guided instructions for an interviewer to use in carrying out an interview.

invasion of privacy   A possible abuse in social research, in which rights of privacy have been ignored. Must be weighed in relation to the public's right to know. *See also* informed consent.

investigatory stage   In police practice the stage of investigation during which the offense is the subject of general inquiry before suspicion has focused on a particular person or persons. Distinguished from the *accusatory stage*, which covers the investigation that occurs after suspicion has focused on one or more particular individuals as being guilty of the offense.

issue   A single, certain, and material point, deduced from the pleadings of the parties, which is affirmed by one side and denied on the other; a fact put in controversy by the pleadings; in criminal law a fact that must be proved to convict the accused, or which is in controversy.

item analysis   A test for validity of an index in which a cross tabulation of total index scores to separate items making up the index is examined.

jail time   The credit allowed on a sentence for the time spent in jail awaiting trial or mandate on appeal.

judge   An officer so named in his commission, who presides in some court.

judgment   In general, the official and authentic decision of a court of justice upon the respective rights and claims of the parties to the action or suit therein litigated and submitted to its determination.

judicial process   The sequence of steps taken by the courts in deciding cases or disposing of legal controversies.

jurisdiction   The power conferred on a court to hear certain cases; the power of the police or judicial officer to act. The extent of the power of a public official to act by virtue of his or her authority.

jury panel   A list of jurors returned by a sheriff, to service at a particular court or for the trial of a particular case. The word may be used to denote either the entire body of the persons summoned as jurors for a particular term of court, or those selected by the clerk by lot.

justice model   Justice demands punishment for the crime committed. Focus on rights and rules in corrections.

juvenile delinquent   A youth who has committed either a status or a delinquency offense.

labeling theory   Society's response to crime defines some people as criminals.

laboratory experiment   An experiment taking place in a laboratory setting, where it is possible to maintain a large number of controls.

larceny   The taking of property from the possession of another with intent of the taker to convert it to his or her own use. Depending on the value of the property taken, the offensive is a felony or a misdemeanor.

law   Law is the formal means of social control that involves the use of rules that are interpreted, and are enforceable, by the courts of a political community. Law is the effort of society to protect persons, in their rights and relations, to guard them in their property, enforce their contracts, hold them to liabilities for their torts, and punish their crimes by means of sanctions administered by government.

leader   A person who enables other people to work together to attain identified ends.

leadership   The guidance and direction of the efforts of others. In management, the work of planning, organizing, directing, staffing, and controlling performed by a person in a leadership position to enable people to work most effectively together to attain identified ends.

leadership evolution   The systematic and continuing adaptation of a leader to the needs of the person, group, or organization.

leading questions   Questions that steer witnesses to a desired answer.

legal   Conforming to the law; according to a law; required or permitted by law; not forbidden or discountenanced by law; good and effectual law.

legal duty   That which the law requires to be done or forborne.

legal ethics   Usages and customs among the legal profession, involving their moral and professional duties toward one another, toward clients, and toward the courts.

legal guilt   Proof beyond a reasonable doubt by admissible evidence.

legal provocation   Provocation sufficient in law to be a defense to the act. Example: justifiable homicide.

legalistic style   Emphasis on criminal law enforcement and formal rules.

legislation   Rules of general application, enacted by a law-making body in a politically organized society. Included in legislation are constitutions, treaties, statutes, ordinances, administrative regulations, and court rules. Distinguished from case law, common law, and "judge-made law."

legislative sentencing model   Legislatures set penalties for offenses.

lesser included offense   A crime committed in the process of committing a crime of more serious degree or grade.

lesser offense   Sometimes used synonymously with a *less serious offense*, or *minor offense*.

levels of measurement   The four commonly defined levels for measuring variables: nominal, for distinct categories with no order; ordinal, for ordered categories; interval, for numerical scales with mathematically defined intervals between points on the scale but no true zero point; and ratio, for numerical scales with mathematically defined intervals and a true zero point.

limitation of actions   The time at the end of which no action at law can be maintained; in criminal law, the time after the commission of the offense within which the indictment must be presented or the information filed.

limited jurisdiction   Courts limited to hearing and deciding minor offenses and preliminary proceedings in felonies.

linear relationship   Shows that an increase (or decrease) in one variable is related to an increase (or decrease) in the other indicated by a diagonal best-fit line in a scattergram.

line-up (also called a *show up*)   A police identification procedure during which the person of a suspect is exhibited, along with others, to witnesses to the crime to determine whether or not they can connect him with the offense.

literature review   In a research project, the task of canvassing publications, usually professional journals, in order to find information about a specific topic.

local criminal courts   *See* criminal court.

local legal culture   The attitudes, values, and expectations toward law and legal practice in specific communities.

lockdown   The suspension of all activities, with prisoners confined to their cells.

longitudinal data   Data gathered over time.

longitudinal designs   Studies based on longitudinal data include trend studies, in which data are compared across time points on different subjects; cohort studies, in which data on subjects from the same age cohort are compared at different points in time; and panel studies, in which the same subjects are compared across time points.

mail survey   A survey consisting of a self-administered questionnaire, instructions, and a request for participation sent out through the mail to a selected sample.

mala in se   Acts or crimes immoral or wrong in and of themselves.

mala prohibita   Crimes wrong because a statute defines them as wrong, although no moral turpitude may be attached, and constituting crimes only because they are prohibited.

management development   The work a manager performs to help managers and candidates for management positions to improve their knowledge, attitudes, and skills.

manager   The person in the organization who may be responsible for any or all of the following: (1) the outcome of her job, (2) the outcomes of some other people's jobs (subordinates), (3) some of the outcomes of other people's jobs (peers, staff, and other managers), and (4) outcomes of activities of some persons outside the organization. A *professional manager* is one who specializes in the work of planning, organizing, directing, staffing, and controlling the efforts of others and does so through systematic use of classified knowledge, and a common vocabulary and principles, and who subscribes to the standards of practice and code of ethics established by a recognized body.

mandatory minimum sentence legislation   The requirement that judges must sentence offenders to a minimum time in prison.

mandatory parole release statutes   Laws requiring the release of prisoners at specified times.

mandatory release   Release based on good behavior and other sentence-reducing devices.

manslaughter   The lowest degree of culpable homicide death caused by culpable recklessness or negligence.

matching   An experimental procedure in which subjects to be placed in the experimental group are matched with subjects possessing similar characteristics in the control group.

material allegation   An allegation essential to the claim of defense, which could not be stricken from the pleading without leaving it insufficient.

material fact   A fact that is essential to a case, defense, or application, without which it could not be supported.

matrix questions   Sets of questions in a questionnaire that use the same set of response categories.

maximum-security prisons   Prisons that focus on preventing prisoners from escaping or hurting themselves or others.

measured capacity One prisoner per cell.

measurement   A process in which numbers are assigned according to rules of correspondence between definitions and observations.

measurement error   Error unavoidably introduced into measurement in the process of observing a phenomenon. An observed measure (or score) is therefore based on the true score plus or minus the error. In social research this error may necessarily be great because of the crudity of the instruments used in measuring social phenomena.

medical model   Views crimes as a disease that requires treatment to cure.

medium-security prisons   Prisons that focus less on security and allow prisoners greater freedom of movement.

mens rea   A guilty mind; a guilty or wrongful purpose; a criminal intent. Guilty knowledge and willfulness.

merit system   The selection of judges by a governor from a list drawn up by a commission of citizens, lawyers, and judges.

middle-range offenders   Those not requiring imprisonment but demanding more than ordinary probation.

minimum-security prisons   Prisons containing prisoners who do not pose security problems and can therefore emphasize trust and a normal life-style.

minor   A person or infant who is under the age of legal competence; one under 21.

Miranda warning   The warning that must be given to a suspect whenever suspicion focuses on him. The officer must warn the suspect (1) that he or she has the right to remain silent; (2) that if the suspect talks, anything that he or she says may be used against him or her; (3) that he or she has the right to be represented by counsel and the right to have counsel present at all questioning; and (4) that if he or she is too poor to afford counsel, counsel will be provided at state expense.

misdemeanor   Any offense that is not a felony, punishable by one year or less in jail.

misdemeanor complaint   As defined in several states, a verified written accusation by a person, filed with a local criminal court, which charges one or more defendants with the commission of one or more offenses, at least one of which is a misdemeanor and none of which is a felony, and which serves to begin a criminal action but which may not, except upon the defendant's consent, serve as a basis for prosecution of the offenses charged therein.

mistake of fact   Ignorance or error concerning facts.

mistake of law   Ignorance or mistake concerning the law.

moot   A subject for argument; unsettled; undecided. A moot point is one not settled by judicial decision.

moot case   A case that seeks to get a judgment on a pretended controversy, or a decision in advance about a right before it has actually been asserted and contested, or a judgment on some matter which, when rendered, for any reason, cannot have any practical legal effect on a then-existing controversy.

moot court   A court held for the arguing of moot (or pretended) cases or questions such as by students in law school.

moral turpitude   An act of baseness, vileness, or depravity in the private and social duties that man owes to his fellow man, or to society in general, contrary to the accepted and customary rule of right and duty between man and man.

motivating   The work a manager performs to inspire, encourage, and impel people to take desired action.

murder   The highest degree of culpable homicide.

narcotic offenses   Offenses relating to narcotic drugs, such as unlawful possession, sale or use. Also used to describe any substance abuse offense.

narcotics   Drugs, such as morphine or heroin, that in medicinal doses relieve pain and induce sleep, and in toxic doses cause convulsions, coma, or death.

National Crime Victim Survey (NCVS)   A national sample of victims surveyed about their victimization.

National Institute of Justice   The research arm of the U.S. Department of Justice.

natural experiment   An experiment that has not been brought about by the efforts of the experimenter but has occurred naturally in the real world and is being selected out for study by the experimenter.

negative evidence   In a field study, the nonoccurrence of expected events, an occurrence that is not reacted to, or one that is distorted in its interpretation or withheld from analysis.

negative (inverse) relationship   A type of relationship between two variables in which cases that are low on one variable are high on the other. *See also* positive (direct) relationships.

negotiated plea   A plea of guilt in exchange for a concession by the government.

negotiation   A give-and-take activity that allows individuals or groups to agree in common to a set of objectives, tasks, and shared use of resources.

net widening   Expanding jurisdiction, such as when sentencing borderline cases to intermediate punishments instead of straight probation.

new-generation jail   A jail that combines architecture, management, and training to provide safe, humane confinement.

new-generation prisons   A prison that combines management and architecture to provide safe, secure confinement for maximum security prisoners.

nonequilvalent control group   A control group that was not selected on the basis of random assignment. Usually created as a rough comparison group to participants in a social intervention program under evaluation. *See also* ex post facto design.

null hypothesis   A logical assumption that there is no relationship between the two variables being studied in the population. This assumption can be tested with inferential statistics.

objective   A specific, time-framed, behavioral expression of some end result or end product that is reasonably attainable, yet sufficiently challenging. Objectives can be long range (several years) or very short range (a day or less).

occupancy   The number of prisoners for each unit of confinement as set by federal and state statutes.

occupational crime   Crimes committed in the course of employment.

operating work   The work a manager performs other than the planning, organizing, directing, staffing, and controlling work that logically belongs to that position.

opportunity theory   The belief that criminal behavior depends on the available criminal opportunities; noncriminal behavior, on noncriminal opportunity structure.

order or recognizance or bail   A securing order releasing a principal on his or her own recognizance or fixing of bail.

organization   Any group of people formally associated to plan, implement, or evaluate a program or idea. The "organization" can be a group of people in need of a program, an agency or office to meet a need, or any other group formed to help meet a need.

organization chart   A schematic representation of organization structure, authority, and relationships.

organization crime   Crimes committed to benefit organizations illegally.

organization structure   The pattern work assumes as it is identified and grouped to be performed by people.

organizing   Establishing a system for performance toward stated goals and objectives. Putting the organization into desired structure and order.

original jurisdiction   The authority to initiate proceedings. Jurisdiction in the first instance; jurisdiction to take cognizance of a case at its inception, impanel a jury, try the case, and pass judgment on the law and facts. Distinguished from *appellate jurisdiction*.

pardon   An act of grace, proceeding from the power entrusted with the execution of the laws, which exempts the person on whom it is bestowed from the punishment the law inflicts for the crime committed.

parens patriae (literally, "father of his country")   The doctrine that the juvenile court treats the child as "a kind of loving father." Government acts as parent.

parole   A conditional release from prison. The release of a prisoner from imprisonment but not from legal custody of the state, for rehabilitation outside prison walls under such conditions and provisions for disciplinary supervision as the parole board or its agents may determine. Parole is an administrative act and follows incarceration.

parole board   A panel of civilians and experts that determines the release from prison to parole.

particularity   The detailed description in a warrant of the object of a search.

pendulum swing   The alternating emphasis on crime control and due process in the history of criminal justice.

per curiam   By the court. An opinion of the court that is authored by the justices collectively.

per se   By himself or itself; taken alone.

performance appraisal   A formal program comparing employees' actual performance with expected performance.

persons arrested   A wide variety of serious and minor offenses reported in raw numbers.

petit jury   A trial jury as distinguished from a grand jury; an ordinary jury of 12 men (or fewer) for the trial of a civil or criminal action.

petit larceny   Larceny of the grade of misdemeanor.

petty misdemeanors   Crimes punishable by fine or up to 30 days in jail.

plain view search   Object of seizure discovered inadvertently where an officer has a right to be.

plan   In management, a predetermined course of action.

planning   Selecting from alternative courses of future action. Determination of goals to be accomplished and how and when they are to be achieved.

plea of guilty   A confession of guilt in open court.

plea of nolo contendere (literally, "no contest")   A plea of neither guilty nor not guilty of a charge in criminal court. One that has the same effect in a criminal action as a plea of guilty but does not bind the defendant in a civil suit for the same wrong.

plea of not guilty   A plea denying the guilt of the accused for the offense charged and putting the state to the proof of all the material elements of the offense.

podular design   Allows greater security and opportunity for surveillance of fewer numbers of prisoners.

police academy   A training school where police socialization begins.

police corruption A form of occupational crime in which officers use their authority for private gain.

police defensiveness The distrust of outsiders, who may not understand the law enforcement policies and procedures.

police depersonalization Treating violence and other unpleasant experiences as matter of fact.

police misconduct A range of illegal behavior, including brutality, constitutional violations, corruption, and unfair treatment of citizens.

police stress The negative pressures associated with police work.

police working personality The character traits of police officers revealed in their work as usually identified by sociologists and psychologists.

police–prosecutor teams Police officers and prosecutors working together from investigation to conviction.

policy A standing decision made to apply to repetitive questions and problems of significance to an organization as a whole.

political community A political community involves forcible maintenance of orderly dominion over a territory and its inhabitants.

population The collection of all elements (either known or unknown) from which a sample is draw. In a probability sample, the population consists of the elements in the sampling frame.

position Work grouped for performance by one person.

positive (direct) relationship A type of relationship between two variables in which cases that are high on one variable tend to be high on the other, and cases that are low on one variable tend to be low on the other. *See also* negative (inverse) relationship.

positivist A person who strives to accumulate facts as the sole means of establishing explanations.

posttraumatic stress syndrome Mental impairment caused by stress during battle or some traumatic event.

precedent An adjudged case or decision of a court of justice considered as furnishing an example of authority for an identical or similar case afterward arising on a similar question of law. *See also* stare decisis.

precoded questionnaire Coding information that is included on the questionnaire instrument itself. This facilitates transferring the data to a computer.

preemptory challenge Self-determined, arbitrary, requiring no cause to be shown. As applied to selection of jurors, challenges allowed by law to both the state and defense to remove a prospective juror without cause from the panel jurors.

preliminary hearing The examination of a person charged with a crime before a magistrate.

preliminary jurisdiction A criminal court has "preliminary jurisdiction" of an offense when regardless of whether it has trial jurisdiction thereof, a criminal action for such an offense may be begun therein, and when such court may conduct proceedings with respect thereto which lead or may lead to prosecution and final disposition of the action in a court having trial jurisdiction thereof.

preponderance of the evidence   Greater weight of evidence. The preponderance of the evidence rests with the evidence that produces the stronger impression and is more convincing as to its truth when weighed against the evidence in opposition.

prescriptive guidelines   Sentencing ranges prescribing new practices.

presentment   The initial appearance by the accused before the magistrate after arrest. Also, a written notice taken by a grand jury of any offense, from their own knowledge or observation, without any bill of indictment laid before them at the suit of the government. *See also* indictment.

presumption of fact   An inference affirmative or disaffirmative of the truth or falsehood of any proposition or fact. Presumptions of fact are not the subject of fixed rules but are merely natural presumptions such as appear from common experience to arise from the particular circumstances.

presumption of innocence   To treat all individuals as innocent until proven guilty according to legally correct proceedings.

presumption of law   A rule of law that courts and judges shall draw a particular inference from a particular fact, or from particular evidence, unless and until the truth of such inference is disproved; and inference that the court will draw from the proof, which no evidence, however strong, will be permitted to overcome. Presumptions of law are reduced to fixed rules and from a part of the system of jurisprudence to which they belong. Presumptions are evidence, or have the effect of evidence.

preventive detention   The detention of defendants prior to trial to protect public safety.

preventive patrol   Moving through the streets to intercept and prevent crime.

prima facie case   A case developed with evidence such as will suffice until contradicted and overcome by other evidence.

prima facie evidence   Evidence good and sufficient on its face; such evidence as, in the judgment of the law, is sufficient to establish a given fact, or the group or chain of facts constituting the party's claim or defense, and which if not rebutted or contradicted will remain sufficient.

principle   A fundamental truth that will tend to apply in new situations in much the same way as it has applied in situations already observed.

principle of least eligibility   Prisoners should earn less than free citizens doing the same work, and should be less eligible than schoolchildren and welfare clients when competing for the same tax dollars.

prisoners' rights   Constitutional rights that survive incarceration.

privatization   The private management of correctional facilities.

pro bono assistance   The representation of criminal defendants without a fee.

pro se filings   Court proceedings in which prisoners file their own papers.

proactive police operations   Operations initiated by police.

probable cause   Reasonable cause; having more evidence for than against. An apparent state of facts that would induce a reasonably intelligent and prudent person to believe, in a criminal case, that the accused person had committed the crime charged. More than suspicion, less than certainty. The quantum of proof required to search or arrest.

probation   The release of a convicted defendant by a court under conditions imposed by the court for a specified period during which the imposition of sentence is suspended. Probation is in lieu of incarceration and is a judicial act.

problem solving   The process of identifying and removing barriers to the setting and attainment of goals.

procedural due process   Limits on criminal procedure.

procedural law   The machinery for carrying on a suit or action.

procedure   A standardized method of performing specified work. The mode of proceeding by which a legal right is enforced as distinguished from the law, which gives or defines the right; the machinery, as distinguished from its product. A form, manner, and order of conducting prosecutions.

proof beyond a reasonable doubt   Enough facts to convict a criminal defendant.

prosecutor   One who prosecutes another for a crime in the name of the government.

prosecutor's information   As defined in New York, a written accusation by a district attorney filed with a local court, which charges one or more defendants with the commission of one or more offenses, none of which is felony, and which serves as a basis for prosecution thereof.

prostitution   Sex offenses of a commercialized nature.

protective custody units   Units devoted to the protection of prisoners with special problems.

provocation   The act of inciting another to do a particular deed; that which arouses moves, calls forth, causes, or occasions.

proximate cause   That which, in a natural and continuous sequence, is unbroken by any efficient intervening cause, produces the injury, and without which the result would not have occurred.

public defender   An attorney designated by law or appointed by the court to represent indigent defendants in criminal proceedings. A public defender is paid by the state or by private agency, or serves without fee.

public order offenses   Minor crimes of public annoyance.

public works crew   Prisoners who work in groups performing public services.

quality arrests   Arrests resulting in conviction.

quantification   Determining or measuring quantity or amount.

quantum of proof   The amount of evidence that justifies government action.

quasi-judicial proceedings   Proceedings that mix formal rules and discretionary judgments.

quasi-military lines   A form of bureaucracy with a hierarchical authority structure.

random sample   A sample in which any person or item in the population has an equal chance of being chosen on each selection.

rape   The unlawful carnal knowledge of a woman by a man forcibly and against her will.

rational decision making   Decisions based on defined goals, alternatives, and information.

real evidence   Evidence furnished by things themselves on view or inspection, as distinguished from a description of them given by a witness.

reasonable suspicion   The quantum of proof required for a stop-and-frisk procedure.

rebuttable presumption   A presumption that may be rebutted by evidence; a species of legal presumption that holds good until disproved.

rebuttal   The introduction of rebutting evidence; showing that a statement of witnesses as to what occurred is not true; the stage of a trial at which such evidence may be introduced; also the rebutting evidence itself.

rebutting evidence   Evidence given to explain, repel, counteract, or disprove facts given in evidence by the adverse party.

receiving stolen property   Buying, receiving, and possessing stolen property with knowledge that it is stolen or under circumstances requiring inquiry as to its origins.

recidivist   A repeat offender.

record   A written account of an act, transaction, or instrument, a written memorial of all the acts and proceedings in an action or suit, in a court of record; the official and authentic history of the cause, consisting in entries in each successive step in the proceedings. At common law, a roll or parchment on which the proceedings and transactions of a court are entered.

rehabilitation   To prevent crime by changing the behavior of individual offenders.

relative deprivation   Feelings of deprivation when compared to persons who are doing better.

release on (own) recognizance   The release of defendants on their promise to appear.

relevant   Applying to the matter in question. A fact is relevant to another fact when according to a common course of events, the existence of one taken alone or in connection with the other fact renders the existence of the other certain or more probable.

relevant evidence   Evidence that relates to the elements of a crime.

reported capacity   The number of prisoners that a jurisdiction decides is the capacity of a facility.

res gestae   Things done. The whole of the transaction under investigation and every part of it. *Res gestae* is considered an exception to the hearsay rule and is extended to include not only declarations by the parties to the suit but also statements made by bystanders and strangers under certain circumstances.

respondent   The defendant on appeal; the party who contends against an appeal.

response time   The time it takes for the police to respond to citizen calls.

responsibility   The responsibility of a subordinate to a superior for authority received by delegation; it is both absolute and tenuous. It is absolute as long as the subordinate maintains and executes the responsibility and authority appropriately. It is tenuous in that it can be taken back at any time by a higher authority in the organization. In any case, no superior can escape ultimate responsibility for any delegation or any activities of subordinates.

restitution   Repayment by offenders for the injuries their crimes caused.

retribution   Looks back in order to punish for the crime committed.

reus   A person judicially accused of a crime; a person criminally proceeded against.

revocation   The retraction of parole.

right of allocution   The right of the convicted person to speak in his own defense before judgment is pronounced. *See also* allocution.

right–wrong test   An insanity definition focusing on impairment of reason.

robbery   Stealing or taking anything of value from a person by force or violence or by putting in fear.

role   The specific relationship you have to other people or to an organization. Any given person can have many roles, depending on how many relationships they have or how many "hats" they wear in the organization. Role also has to be defined as a "two-way street"; half the role is how you see yourself in the relationship, and the other half comes from how the other person (or organization) sees you in the relationship.

role management   The continuous examination and assessment of roles. This could be one's own role, or it could be the roles of others as they affect your own role. The purpose is to modify or adjust your own role, or help others adjust their role, to maintain common interpersonal and organizational objectives.

rule of law   The principle that rules, rather than discretion, govern decisions in criminal law and procedure.

runaway   A juvenile offense; also an offender who has run away from home without his parents' permission.

safety-valve policy   Reducing the minimum sentence of prisoners when prisons exceed capacity.

sample   A small group that, ideally, is representative of a larger group.

sampling frame   That specific part of a population from which a sample is drawn for a survey.

scienter   Knowingly; with guilty knowledge.

Scottsboro case   The case that established the fundamental fairness doctrine.

search   Examining person or property to discover evidence, weapon, or contraband.

search incident to arrest   A search without a warrant conducted at the time of arrest.

Section 1983 actions   Legal actions brought under the Ku Klux Klan Act, permitting citizens to sue government officials for the violation of civil rights.

securing order   In New York, an order of a court committing a principal to the custody of the sheriff, or fixing bail, or releasing the person on his or her own recognizance.

selective hypothesis fallacy   Choosing subjects for research that favor a particular outcome.

selective incapacitation   The policy of imprisoning offenders who commit the most crimes.

self-reports   Collecting data by sampling members of the population who have committed crimes.

sentence   The judgment formally pronounced by the court or judge on a defendant after his or her conviction in a criminal prosecution, and stipulating the punishment to be inflicted.

sentence bargaining   Plea negotiations over the sentence a judge will grant.

sentencing discrimination   The determination of sentences by unacceptable criteria, such as race.

sentencing disparity   A difference in the sentences received by persons who committed similar offenses under similar circumstances.

sentencing guidelines   A range within which judges prescribe specific sentences.

separation of powers   The doctrine that permits the three branches of government—legislative, executive, and judiciary—to perform their own functions without interference from the others.

sequester   To keep a jury together and in isolation from other persons under charge of the bailiff while a trial is pending, sometimes called *separation of the jury*. To keep witnesses apart from other witnesses and unable to hear their testimony.

service of process   The service of writs, summonses, rules, and so on, signifies delivering or leaving them with the party to whom or with whom they ought to be delivered or left, and when they are so delivered, they are then said to be served.

sex offenses   Rape, prostitution, commercialized vice, statutory rape, and offenses against chastity, common decency, and morals.

shelters   Temporary, nonsecure, community-based holding facilities.

show cause   An order to appear as directed and to present to the court reasons and considerations as to why certain circumstances should be continued, permitted, or prohibited, as the case may be.

simple assault   Assault that is not of an aggravated nature. *See also* assault.

simplified traffic information   A written accusation by a police officer filed with a local criminal court which charges a person with a traffic violation or misdemeanors relating to traffic, and which may serve both to begin a criminal action for such offense and as a basis for prosecution thereof.

skill   A person's mental, emotional, and motor capacity to perform a certain function or task, which could range from the physical skill of operating an office machine to the emotional skills of working with people to the mental skill of computing a complex budget.

social control   The process by which subgroups and persons are influenced to conduct themselves in conformity to group expectations.

social control perspective   The view that obedience to rules depends on institutions to keep the desire to break the rules in check.

social structure of the case   Extralegal or sociological influences on decisions.

solicitation   Asking another person to commit a crime.

solvability factors   Information that leads to the solution of crimes.

special management inmates   Prisoners in need of special care.

specialization   The attempt to confine the work of each person to a single related set of functions, with sets of similar functions grouped together under one department or unit.

specific intent   The intent to do something in addition to the criminal act.

split sentence   Part of a sentence served in jail, the remainder served on probation.

split-sentence probation   A sentence to a specified term of incarceration followed by a specified time on probation.

staffing   Putting people into the proper jobs; the idea of having the right person in the right job at the right time. Staffing includes the selection, placement, development, and appraisal of people for organizational activities.

standing   The qualifications needed to bring legal action.

stare decisis   To abide by, or adhere to, decided cases; doctrine that when a court has once laid down a principle, it be applied to all future cases where facts are substantially the same, regardless of whether the person and the property are the same.

state   The supreme political community; also a state of the United States.

statistics   Figures that summarize and represent factual data.

status offenses   Behavior that only juveniles commit.

statutory law   All laws enacted by federal, state, or local legislatures.

statutory rape   Carnal knowledge of a female child below the age fixed by statute. Neither force nor lack of content are necessary elements of this offense.

stop and frisk   Less intrusive seizures and searches protected by the Fourth Amendment.

straight plea   A plea of guilty without plea negotiations.

strain theory   A belief that pressures in the social structure cause crime.

street crimes   One-on-one crimes against strangers.

strict liability   Criminal liability without criminal intent.

subculture of competition   The concept that success is more important than the means by which it is achieved.

subculture of violence   A subculture that condones violence.

subpoena   A process issued by a court to cause a witness to appear and give testimony for the party named.

substantial capacity test   An insanity definition focusing on impairments of either or both reason and will.

substantive due process   Constitutional limits on criminal law.

summons   A notification of proceedings against defendants and requirements of their appearance in court.

superior courts   Used generally to denote courts of general trial jurisdiction. The name given to felony courts in California and Illinois.

supervision   The day-to-day direct management of personnel and activities within a program. Each person and each activity should have an immediate supervisor who is responsible for the proper application of that person's skills and the proper direction of that activity.

supreme court   The highest court of the United States, created by the Constitution; the name given in most states to the highest court of appeals, the court of last resort.

suspect   To have a slight or even vague idea concerning; not necessarily involving knowledge of belief of likelihood; sometimes used in place of the word *believe*. Also, a person who is suspected of having committed an offense or who is believed to have committed an offense.

systems paradigm   The decision-making perspective that treats the criminal justice agencies as an integrated whole.

tasks   The specific items of activity for which each person in an organization is held accountable.

testimony   Evidence given by a competent witness, under oath or affirmation; as distinguished from evidence derived from writings and other sources. Testimony is one species of evidence, but the words *testimony* and *evidence* are often used interchangeably.

the great writ   A name given to the writ of habeas corpus.

theft   A popular name for larceny.

theory X   A management theory that employees can be motivated only by fear (of job loss, for example).

theory Y   A management theory that employees can be motivated by better challenges, personal growth, and improved work performance and productivity.

theory Z   A management theory that employees should be involved, should participate, and should be treated like family.

tort   A noncriminal legal wrong. A private or civil wrong or injury; a legal wrong committed upon a person or property independent of contract which is redressed in a civil court. A *personal tort* involves or consists of an injury to the person or to the reputation of feelings as distinguished from an injury or damage to real or personal property, called a *property tort*.

tort reasor   One who commits a tort.

training   The provision of a variety of ongoing opportunities for staff development, including coaching, workshops, seminars, and classes in higher education.

training schools   Secure detention facilities.

transcript of record   The printed record as made up in case for review by a higher court; also a copy of any kind. In referring to the written documents on appeal, the words *transcript*, *record*, and *record on appeal* are used interchangeably.

transferred intent   The concept that the intent to cause one harm results in causing harm to another.

trial jurisdiction   Jurisdiction by a criminal court of an offense when an indictment or an information charging such offense may properly be filed with such court, and when such court has authority to accept a plea to, try, or otherwise finally dispose of such as accusatory instrument. *See also* original jurisdiction.

typology   A classification of phenomena according to differing characteristics.

Uniform Crime Reports   A summary of information provided by local police agencies to the FBI.

unity of command   The principle that the more complete a reporting relationship a person has to a single superior, the less the problem of conflict in instructions and evaluation and the greater the feeling of personal responsibility for results.

unity of objectives   The concept that if persons in each position fulfill clearly defined objectives logically related to each other, the goal of the entire organization will be met.

utilitarian punishment   Looks forward to preventing crime in the future.

validity   The characteristic that a measuring instrument such as a survey has when it actually measures what it purports to measure.

values   The beliefs, attitudes, and expressed behavior that a person holds in terms of what they will accept, reject, or feel neutral toward. The body of history, policies, goals, leadership, and so on, that determine what an organization will produce as goods or services and how it will go about achieving that production.

vandalism   Willful or malicious destruction, injury, disfigurement, or defacement of property without consent of the owner or person having custody or control.

variables   The elements of an equation, experiment, or formula that are under study and subject to change in accordance with changes in the environment; anything that varies.

vehicle search   The search of vehicles without a warrant but not without probable cause.

venire (from the Latin for "to come," "to appear")   The name given to the writ for summoning a jury, and also the body of jury summoned.

venireman   A member of a jury; a juror summoned by the writ of venire facias.

venue   A neighborhood, place, or county in which an injury is declared to have been done or a fact declared to have happened. *Jurisdiction* of the court is the inherent power to decide a case, whereas *venue* designates the particular county or city in which a court with jurisdiction may hear and determine the case.

verdict   A formal and unanimous decision or finding made by a jury, impaneled and sworn for trial of a cause, and reported to the court upon the matters or questions duly summitted to them upon the trial. From the Latin *verdictum*, a "true declaration."

victimless crimes   Crimes without complaining victims.

violation   An incident punishable by a small fine that does not carry with it a criminal record.

violence   Physical force.

violent predators   Career criminals who commit a range of street crimes.

void for vagueness   Statutes must define crimes precisely.

voir dire (literally, "to speak the truth")   The preliminary examination of a witness or juror as to his competency, interest, and so on.

waive   To abandon or throw away; in modern law, to abandon, throw away, renounce, repudiate, or surrender a claim, privilege, or right, or the opportunity to take advantage of some defect irregularity or wrong.

warrant   A document issued by a magistrate that the Constitution requires for a search or arrest.

warrant of arrest   A written order issued and signed by a magistrate, directed to a peace officer or some other person specially named, commanding him or her to arrest the body of a person named in it, who is accused of an offense.

watchman style of policing   Focus on order maintenance and discretionary decision making.

work release   A program allowing prisoners to leave confinement to work.

writ of habeas corpus   A writ directed to a person detaining another and commanding him or her to produce the body of the prisoner or person detained.

zero-based budgeting   A method of budgeting that starts with no base from the preceding budget period. Most criminal justice vendors are subject to this method.

References

Abel, E. L. 1984. *A Dictionary of Drug Abuse Terms and Terminology*. Westport, CT: Greenwood.

Abstracts in Social Gerontology. 1990 to present. Thousand Oaks, CA: Sage.

Aby, S. H. 1987. *Sociology: A Guide to Reference and Information Sources*. Littleton, CO: Libraries Unlimited.

Aday, R. H. 1988. *Crime and the Elderly: An Annotated Bibliography*. Westport, CT: Greenwood.

Addictionary: A Primer of Recovery Terms and Concepts, from Abstinence to Withdrawal. 1992. New York: Fireside/Parkside, a division of Simon & Schuster.

Adler, L. L., ed. 1993. *International Handbook on Gender Roles*. Westport, CT: Greenwood.

Allen, Harry E. and Clifford Simonsen. 1998. *Corrections in America*, 8th ed. Upper Saddle River, NJ: Prentice Hall.

American Journal of Sociology. 1895. Chicago, IL: University of Chicago Press.

American Sociological Association. 1996. *ASA Style Guide*. Washington, DC: American Sociological Association.

American Sociological Review. 1936 to present. Washington, DC: American Sociological Association.

American Statistics Index. 1973 to present. Washington, DC: Congressional Information Service.

Annual Review of Criminal Justice. Annually. Palo Alto, CA: Annual Reviews.

Annual Review of Sociology. Annually. Palo Alto, CA: Annual Reviews.

Baker, T. O. 1992. *Operator's Manual for a Witness Chair*. Kansas City, MO: Baker and Sterchi.

Bart, P. and L. Frankel. 1986. *The Student Sociologist's Handbook*. 4th ed. New York: Random House.

Becker, Howard S., Blanche Geer, Everett C. Hughes and Anselm L. Strauss. 1961. *Boys in White: Student Culture in Medical School*. Chicago, IL: University of Chicago Press.

Becker, Ronald F. 1997. *Specific Evidence and Expert Testimony Handbook: A Guide for Lawyers, Criminal Investigators and Forensic Specialists*. Springfield, IL: Charles C Thomas.

Bellenir, Karen. 1996. *Substance Abuse Sourcebook*. Detroit, MI: Omnigraphics.

_____ and Peter D. Dresser, eds. 1995. *AIDS Sourcebook*. Detroit, MI: Omnigraphics.

Bentley, William K. and James M. Corbett. 1992. *Prison Slang: Words and Expressions Depicting Life behind Bars*. Jefferson, NC: McFarland.

Berndt, J. 1986. *Rural Sociology: A Bibliography of Bibliographies*. Metuchen, NJ: Scarecrow.

Bernes, William J., ed. 1989. *Personal Computer Programming Encyclopedia*. New York: McGraw-Hill.

Bibliographic Index.1937 to present. New York: H.W. Wilson.

Binstock, R. H. and L. K. George, eds. 1990. *Handbook of Aging and the Social Sciences*. San Diego, CA: Academic Press.

Bintliff, Russell. 1990. *Training Manual for Law Enforcement Officers*. Upper Saddle River, NJ: Prentice Hall.

Bird, F. F. 1988. *Management Guide to Loss Control*. Loganville, LA: International Loss Control Institute.

Black, Henry Campbell. 1990. *Black's Law Dictionary*. 6th ed. St. Paul, MN: West Publishing.

Borgatta, E. F. and M. L. Borgatta, eds. 1992. *Encyclopedia of Sociology*. New York: Macmillan.

Bouma, Gary D. and G. B. J. Atkinson. 1995. *A Handbook of Social Science Research: A Comprehensive and Practical Guide for Students*. 2d ed. New York: Oxford University Press.

Bray, R., ed. 1996. *Guide to Reference Books*. Chicago, IL: American Library Association.

Bruhn, J. G., B. U. Philips and P. L. Levine. 1985. *Medical Sociology: An Annotated Bibliography*. New York: Garland.

Butts, Jeffery A. 1995. *Juvenile Justice and Delinquency Prevention Bulletin* (December). Washington, DC: Office of Juvenile Justice and Delinquency Prevention, U.S. Department of Justice.

_____, Howard N. Snyder, Terrence A. Finnegan, Anne L. Aughenbaugh and Rowen S. Poole. 1996. *Juvenile Court Statistics 1994*. Washington, DC: Office of Juvenile Justice and Delinquency Prevention, U.S. Department of Justice.

Chicago Manual of Style, The. 1993. 14th ed. Chicago, IL: University of Chicago Press.

Child Development Abstracts and Bibliography. 1928 to present. Chicago, IL: University of Chicago Press.

Clark, R. E. and J. F. Clark, eds. 1989. *The Encyclopedia of Child Abuse*. New York: Facts on File.

Commager, Henry S., ed. 1963. *Documents of American History*. 7th ed. New York: Appleton-Century-Crofts.

Contemporary Sociology: A Journal of Reviews. 1971 to present. Washington, DC: American Sociological Association.

Creating Safe and Drug Free Schools: An Action Guide. 1996. Washington, DC: U.S. Department of Education.

Criminal Justice Abstracts. 1968 to present. Hackensack, NJ: National Council on Crime and Delinquency.

Cumulative Subject Index to the Monthly Catalog of United States Government Publications, 1900–1971. 1973. Washington, DC: Carrollton Press.

Dabney, M. L. 1984. *Incest: An Annotated Bibliography*. Jefferson, NC: McFarland.

Darnay, A. J., ed. 1994. *Statistical Record of Older Americans*. Detroit, MI: Gale Research.

Demographic Yearbook. 1994 to present. New York: United Nations Statistical Office.

DeSala, Ralph. 1980. *Crime Dictionary*. New York: Facts on File.

Desktop Guide to Good Juvenile Detention Practice. 1996. Rockville, MD: Juvenile Justice Clearinghouse.

De Young, Mary. 1987. *Child Molestation: An Annotated Bibliography*. Jefferson, NC: McFarland.

DiCanio, M. 1993. *The Encyclopedia of Violence: Origins, Attitudes, Consequences*. New York: Facts on File.

Drucker, Peter. 1993. *The Effective Executive*. New York: HarperCollins.

Duffee, David. 1986. *Correctional Management: Change and Control in Correctional Organizations*. Prospect Heights, IL: Waveland Press.

Ellmore, R. T. 1991. NTC's *Mass Media Dictionary*. Lincolnwood, IL: National Textbook.

Encyclopedia Dictionary of American Government. 1986. Guilford, CT: Dushkin Publishing Group.

Engeldinger, E. A. 1986. *Spouse Abuse: An Annotated Bibliography of Violence Between Mates*. Metuchen, NJ: Scarecrow.

Evans, G., R. O'Brien and S. Cohen, eds. 1991. *The Encyclopedia of Drug Abuse*. New York: Facts on File.

Factbook on Intelligence. 1992. Washington, DC: Central Intelligence Agency.

Family Life, Delinquency, and Crime: A Policymaker's Guide. 1994. Rockville, MD: Juvenile Justice Clearinghouse.

Fay, J. J., ed., 1988. *The Alcohol/Drug Abuse Dictionary and Encyclopedia*. Springfield, IL: Charles C Thomas.

_____, ed., 1989. *Butterworth's Security Dictionary*. Newton, MA: Butterworth-Heinemann.

_____, ed., 1993. *Encyclopedia of Security Management*. Newton, MA: Butterworth-Heinemann.

F.B.I. Facts and History. 1992. Washington, DC: Federal Bureau of Investigation, U.S. Department of Justice.

Fennelly, L. J. 1992. *Handbook of Loss Prevention and Crime Prevention*. Newton, MA: Butterworth-Heinemann.

Ficke, R. C. 1992. *Digest of Data on Persons with Disabilities*. Washington, DC: National Institute on Disability and Rehabilitation Research.

Friedman, Lawrence, Nicholes F. Fleming, David H. Roberts and Steven E. Hyman, eds. 1996. *Sourcebook of Substance Abuse and Addiction*. Baltimore, MD: Williams & Wilkins.

Gall, S. B. and T. L. Gall, eds. 1993. *Statistical Record of Asian Americans*. Detroit, MI: Gale Research.

Gall, Timothy L. and Daniel M. Lucus, eds. 1996. *Statistics on Alcohol, Drug, and Tobacco Use*. Detroit, MI: Gale Research.

Ghorayshi, P. 1990. *The Sociology of Work: A Critical Annotated Bibliography*. New York: Garland.

Gilliard, Darrel K. and Allen J. Beck. 1996. *Bureau of Justice Statistics Bulletin* (August). Washington, DC: Office of Justice Programs, U.S. Department of Justice.

Gould, J. and W. L. Kolb. 1964. *A Dictionary of the Social Sciences*. New York: Free Press.

Guide for Implementing the Comprehensive Strategy for Serious, Violent, and Chronic Juvenile Offenders. 1995. Rockville, MD: Juvenile Justice Clearinghouse.

Hagedorn, John M. 1996. [review of Mark S. Fleisher's *Beggars and Thieves: Lives of Urban Street Criminals*] *American Journal of Sociology* 102(2).

Handbook of Forensic Evidence. 1984. Washington, DC: Federal Bureau of Investigation, U.S. Department of Justice.

Handbook of Forensic Sciences. 1990. Washington, DC: Federal Bureau of Investigation, U.S. Department of Justice.

Harris, D. K. 1988. *Dictionary of Gerontology*. Westport, CT: Greenwood.

Hartwell, Patrick. 1985. "Grammar, Grammars, and the Teaching of Grammar." *College English* 47:111.

Helping Victims and Witnesses in the Juvenile Justice System: A Program Handbook. 1991. Rockville, MD: Juvenile Justice Clearinghouse.

Heydel, C., ed. 1982. *The Encyclopedia of Management*. 3d ed. New York: Van Nostrand Reinhold.

Historical Statistics of the United States: Colonial Times to 1970. 1971. Washington, DC: Government Printing Office.

Hoover, Kenneth and Todd Donovan. 1995. *The Elements of Social Science Thinking*. 6th ed. New York: St. Martin's Press.

Horton, C. P. and J. C. Smith, eds. 1990. *Statistical Record of Black America*. Detroit, MI: Gale.

Huizinga, D.H., S. Menard and D. Elliott. 1989. "Delinquency and Drug Use: Temporal and Developmental Patterns." *Justice Quarterly*. 6:419–455.

Hunter, David E. and Phillip Whitten, eds. 1976. *Encyclopedia of Anthropology*. New York: Harper & Row.

Hurdle, Angela and Andrea Yurasits, eds. 1996. *Demographics USA: County Addition*. New York: Bill Communications.

Hurrelmann, K. ed. 1994. *International Handbook of Adolescence*. Westport, CT: Greenwood.

Inciardi, J. A. 1981. *The Drugs-Crime Connection*. Beverly Hills, CA: Sage Publications.

International Bibliography of Sociology. 1955 to present. London: Tavistock.

Inventory of Marriage and Family Literature. 1973. St. Paul, MN: National Council on Family Relations.

Isaac, Stephen and William B. Michael. 1981. *Handbook in Research and Evaluation*. 2d ed. San Diego, CA: EdITS Publishers.

Jacob, Herbert. 1987. "The Criminal Justice System." Pp. 111–127, in *Encyclopedia of the American Judicial System*, vol. 2, edited by R. B. Janosik. New York: Charles Scribner & Sons.

Johnson, Allan G. 1995. *The Blackwell Dictionary of Sociology*. Cambridge, MA: Blackwell.

Johnson, William A. and Richard P. Rettig. 1990. "An Analysis of Negative Behavior Incidents and Their Impact on Program Implementation at the Oklahoma County Juvenile Detention Center." *Journal for Juvenile Justice and Detention Services* 5(2):13–20.

Kadish, Sanford H., ed. 1983. *The Encyclopedia of Crime and Justice*. 3 vols. New York: Free Press.

Kaiser Index to Black Resources: 1948–1986. 1992. Brooklyn, NY: Carlson.

Katz, W. 1978. *Magazines for Libraries*. 3d ed. New York: Bowker.

Kinl, G. C.1987. *Social Stratification: An Annotated Bibliography*. New York: Garland.

Kuhn, Thomas. 1970. *The Structure of Scientific Revolutions*. 2d ed. Chicago, IL: University of Chicago Press.

Lerner, R., A. C. Petersen and J. Brooks-Gunn, eds. 1991. *Encyclopedia of Adolescence*. 2 vols. New York: Garland.

Levin, Jack and James Alan Fox. 1997. *Elementary Statistics in Social Research*. 7th ed. Reading, MA: Addison-Wesley Longman.

_____, Arnold Arluke and Amita Mody-Desbareau. 1986. "The Gossip Tabloid as an Agent of Social Control." Presented at the annual meeting of the American Sociological Association.

Lindsey, M. P. 1989. *Dictionary of Mental Handicap*. New York: Routledge.

Lu, J. K. *U.S. Government Publications Relating to the Social Sciences*. Thousand Oaks, CA: Sage.

Lunsford, Andrea and Robert Connors. 1992. *The St. Martin's Handbook*. 2d ed. (annotated instructor's ed.). New York: St. Martin's.

Maddox, G. L., ed. 1987. *The Encyclopedia of Aging*. New York: Springer.

Maguire, Kathleen and Ann L. Pastore, eds. 1995. *Sourcebook of Criminal Justice Statistics*. Washington, DC: Bureau of Justice Statistics, Office of Justice Programs.

Manstead, Anthony S. R. and Miles Hewstone. 1995. *The Blackwell Encyclopedia of Social Psychology*. 2 vols. Cambridge, MA: Blackwell.

McShane, M. D. and F. P. Williams III. 1996. *Encyclopedia of American Prisons*. New York: Garland Reference Library.

Miller, Eleanor M. 1996. [review of Mark S. Fleisher's *Beggars and Thieves: Lives of Urban Street Criminals*] *Contemporary Sociology* 25(4):531–533.

Mills, J. 1992. *Womanwords: A Dictionary of Words about Women*. New York: Free Press.

Morgan, Kathleen O'Leary, ed. 1995. *State Rankings: A Statistical View of the 50 United States*. 6th ed. Lawrence, KS: Morgan Quinto Corporation.

_____, Scott Morgan and Neal Quinto, eds. 1995 *City Crime Rankings: Crime in Metropolitan America*. Lawrence, KS: Morgan Quinto Corporation.

Mullins, Waymon C. 1996. *A Sourcebook on Domestic and International Terrorism*. 2d ed. Springfield, IL: Charles C Thomas.

Nash, Jay Robert. 1989. *Encyclopedia of World Crime: Criminal Justice, Criminology, and Law Enforcement*. 7 vols. Wilamette, IL: Crime Books.

_____, ed., 1992. *World Encyclopedia of Organized Crime*. New York: Paragon House.

_____. 1992. *World Encyclopedia of 20th Century Murder*. New York: Paragon House.

National Data Book, The. 1992. 116th ed. Washington, DC: Statistical Abstract of the United States, U.S. Department of Commerce.

Newman, R. 1981. *Black Index: Afro-Americana in Selected Periodicals, 1907–1949*. New York: Garland.

NewsBank. 1975 to present. Greenwich, CT: Urban Affairs Library.

New York Public Library Desk Reference, The. 1993. New York: Stonesong Press.

New York Times Index. 1913 to present. New York: New York Times.

Nordquest, J. 1988. *The Homeless in America: A Bibliography*. Santa Cruz, CA: Reference and Research Services.

_____. 1988. *Substance Abuse I: Drug Abuse: A Bibliography*. Santa Cruz, CA: Reference and Research Services.

_____. 1990. *Substance Abuse II: Alcohol Abuse: A Bibliography*. Santa Cruz, CA: Reference and Research Services.

_____. 1991. *The Elderly in America: A Bibliography*. Santa Cruz, CA: Reference and Research Services

O'Brien, R. and M. Chafetz, eds. 1991. *The Encyclopedia of Alcoholism*. New York: Facts on File.

Oklahoma Department of Commerce. 1991. *1989 Demographic State of the State*. Oklahoma City, OK: Publications Clearinghouse of the Oklahoma Department of Libraries.

Pearce, Catherine Owens, ed. 1958. *A Scientist of Two Worlds: Louis Agassiz*. Philadelphia, PA: Lippincott.

Philliber, Susan G., Mary R. Schwab and G. Sam Sloss. 1980. *Social Reasearch*. Itasca, IL: F.E. Peacock.

Popper, Karl. 1959. *The Logic of Scientific Discovery*. New York: Basic Books.

Population Index. 1935 to present. Princeton, NJ: Office of Population Research, Princeton University and Population Association of America.

Questions and Answers on the Defense Industrial Security Program. 1991. Washington, DC: Defense Investigative Service, U.S. Department of Defense.

Reddy, M. A., ed. 1993. *Statistical Record of Hispanic Americans*. Detroit, MI: Gale Research.

_____, ed. 1993.*Statistical Record of Native North Americans*. Detroit, MI: Gale Research.

Report by the President's Commission on Law Enforcement and Administration of Justice. 1967 (February). Washington, DC: Government Printing Office.

Resource Manual for Juvenile Detention and Corrections: Effective and Innovative Programs. 1995. Rockville, MD: Juvenile Justice Clearinghouse.

Richter, A. 1993. *Dictionary of Sexual Slang*. New York: Wiley.

Roth, Martin. 1990. *The Writer's Complete Crime Reference Book*. Writer's Digest Books. Cincinnati, OH: F.W. Publications.

Roy, F. H. and C. Russell, eds. 1992. *The Encyclopedia of Aging and the Elderly*. New York: Facts on File.

Rush, George E. 1986. *The Dictionary of Criminal Justice*. 2d ed. Guilford, CT: Dushkin Publishing Group.

Sage Family Studies Abstracts. 1979 to present. Thousand Oaks, CA: Sage.

Sage Race Relations Abstracts. 1975 to present. Thousand Oaks, CA: Sage.

Schick, F. L. and R. Schick, eds. 1994. *Statistical Handbook on Aging Americans*. Phoenix, AZ: Oryx.

Sells, David A. 1979. *International Encyclopedia of the Social Sciences*. New York: Macmillan.

Selth, J. P. 1985. *Alternative Lifestyles: A Guide to Research Collections on Intentional Communities, Nudism, and Sexual Freedom*. Westport, CT: Greenwood.

Sheehy, E. P., ed. 1986. *Guide to Reference Books*. 10th ed. Chicago, IL: American Library Association.

Simon Market Research Bureau. 1992. *The New American Family: Significant and Diversified Lifestyles*. New York: SMRB.

Smelser, N. J., ed. 1988. *Handbook of Sociology*. Thousand Oaks, CA: Sage.

Social Forces. 1922. Chapel Hill, NC: University of North Carolina Press.

Social Sciences Citation Index. 1972 to present. Philadelphia, PA: Institute for Scientific Information.

Social Sciences Index. 1974/75 to present. New York: HW Wilson.

Society. 1967 to present. New Brunswick, NJ: Rutgers University Press.

Sociological Abstracts. 1952 to present. New York: Sociological Abstracts.

Soliday, G. L. et al., eds. 1980. *History of the Family and Kinship: A Select International Bibliography*. Millwood, NY: Kraus International.

Stanley, H. W. and R. G. Niemi, eds. 1993. *Vital Statistics on American Politics*. 5th ed. Washington, DC: Congressional Quarterly.

Statistical Reference Index Annual Abstracts. Annually. Bethesda, MD: Congressional Information Service.

Statistical Yearbook. Annually. New York: United Nations Statistical Office.

Statistical Yearbook. Annually. Paris: UNESCO.

Stuart, Henry. 1994. *Inside Jobs: A Realistic Guide to Criminal Justice Careers for College Students*. Salem, WI: Sheffield.

Theodorson, G. A. and A. G. Theodorson. 1969. *A Modern Dictionary of Sociology*. New York: Barnes & Noble.

Tierney, H., ed. 1989–1991. *Women's Studies Encyclopedia: Views from the Inside*. Westport, CT: Greenwood.

Turecki, Given, ed. 1996. *Cyberhound's Guide to Internet Libraries*. Detroit, MI: Gale Research.

Uniform Crime Reports. 1995. Washington, DC: Federal Bureau Investigation, U.S. Department of Justice.

U.S. Bureau of the Census. 1790 to present. *Bureau of the Census Catalog*. Washington, DC: Government Printing Office.

U.S. Bureau of the Census. 1949 to present. *County and City Data Book*. Washington, DC: Government Printing Office.

U.S. Federal Bureau of Investigation. Annually. *Uniform Crime Reports for the United States*. Washington, DC: Government Printing Office.

U.S. Library of Congress. 1950 to present. *Subject Catalog: A Cumulative List of Works Represented by Library of Congress Printed Cards*. Washington, DC: Library of Congress.

U.S. Superintendent of Documents. 1885 to present. *Monthly Catalog of United States Government Publications*. Washington, DC: Government Printing Office.

Vital Statistics of the United States. Annually. 2 vols. Hyattsville, MD: U.S. Department of Health and Human Services.

Walker, Monica A., ed. 1995. *Interpreting Crime Statistics*. New York: Oxford University Press.

Wasserman, Sterss, Jacqueline Wasserman-O'Brian and Bosnia Shaw Pfaff, eds. 1991. *Law and Legal Information Directory*. Detroit, MI: Gale Research.

White, C. 1973. *Sources of Information in the Social Sciences*. 2d ed. Chicago, IL: American Library Association.

Whitehead, Kenneth D. *Federal Personnel Guide*. Washington, DC: Key Communications Group.

Women's Studies Abstracts. 1972 to present. New York: Rush.

Women's Studies Index. 1991. Boston, MA: G.K. Hall Citation Indexes.

Woods, G. 1993. *Drug Abuse in Society: A Reference Handbook*. Santa Barbara, CA: ABC-CLIO.

Yearbook of Labour Statistics. Annually. Geneva: International Labour Office.

Zophy, A. H. and F. M. Karenik, eds. 1990. *Handbook of American Women's History*. New York: Garland.

Index

335